Hungary,
the Great Powers,
and the Danubian Crisis

Hungary, the Great Powers, and the Danubian Crisis 1936–1939

Thomas L. Sakmyster

The University of Georgia Press

Athens

Copyright © 1980 by the University of Georgia Press
Athens 30602

Set in 11 on 13 point Caledonia type
Printed in the United States of America

Library of Congress Cataloging in Publication Data

Sakmyster, Thomas L
  Hungary, the Great Powers, and the Danubian crisis,
1936–1939.
  Bibliography.
  Includes index.
  1. Hungary—Foreign relations—1918–1945. 2. Dan-
ube Valley—Politics and government. 3. Munich four-
power agreement, 1938. 4. World politics—1933–1945.
I. Title.
DB955.S24   327.439   78-23678
            ISBN 0-8203-0469-7

For Diane

Contents

Preface

It is a paradox of interwar European history that when Hitler's bold move to remilitarize the Rhineland proved successful in March 1936, the shock waves were felt most intensely not in nearby France and England, but along the banks of the Danube river in the eastern regions of Europe. Frenchmen could still take some comfort in the security the Maginot Line seemed to offer. Across the Channel the British could maintain equanimity and rationalize the situation by pointing out that the Germans were merely taking control of their own backyard. But in the countries of Danubian Europe,* the repercussions of Hitler's coup seemed more far-reaching and profound. For if Hitler could move with such impunity to disrupt the status quo in Western Europe, what would prevent him from turning to Germany's eastern flank for future territorial expansion?

In time it became clear that Hitler's remilitarization of the Rhineland was merely the overture to a period of turmoil and European armed conflict, the opening phase of which might be called the Danubian crisis. In the three years from March 1936 to March 1939, the political fate of two key countries of the Danubian area became the central concern of the European great powers. In March 1938 Austria was absorbed into the German Reich. During the remaining months of that year, the position of Czechoslovakia was steadily undermined, until finally the great powers sanctioned a partial dismemberment. Even this arrangement proved short-lived: Hitler's determination to achieve what he regarded as a "strategic border" in Bohemia led, in March of the following year, to complete destruction of the Czechoslovak state. In these critical events a third Danubian country, Hungary, played a role of considerable importance. The only country that

---

*In this study the term "Danubian Europe" refers to Austria, Czechoslovakia, Hungary, Yugoslavia, Romania, and Bulgaria. The broader terms "East Central Europe" and "East Europe" are used interchangeably to denote the area bounded on the west by Germany and on the east by Russia.

was contiguous to both of Germany's victims, Hungary, though small and weak, was in a position to facilitate or temporarily thwart Hitler's policies in East Central Europe. The manner in which the leadership in Budapest met the challenge of these events and shaped a foreign policy that would be compatible with certain domestic goals is the subject of this study.

Most of Hungary's leaders in this period, notably Kálmán Kánya, Pál Teleki, István Bethlen, Béla Imrédy, and Miklós Horthy, were conservatives whose social and political attitudes had been formed in the decades before World War I. In the late 1930s they were confronted with a range of foreign and domestic problems that they were, by temperament and experience, ill prepared to solve. By definition, political conservatives work best when they have the luxury of a status quo they regard as desirable and worth preserving. When required to fashion a policy that aims to disrupt the established order, they tend to manifest a sense of unease and marked ambivalence. This was true of Hungary's conservative establishment, which regarded the peace treaty imposed on the Magyars in 1919–20 as patently unwise and unjust, and which was fervently committed to a policy of territorial revisionism. However, most Hungarian statesmen hesitated to resort to the kind of dynamic and bellicose policies that, in the opinion of the Hungarian General Staff and, in the late 1930s, of Adolf Hitler, were most likely to bring rapid results. An active and aggressive irredentist policy during the Danubian crisis would have entailed risks that people like Kánya and Teleki were loath to take. Such a policy of military adventure might provoke severe retaliation from Hungary's militarily superior neighbors and extinguish any sympathy for Hungary in the Western democracies. Moreover, as the Great War had amply demonstrated, a military conflict could serve as a catalyst for the rapid destruction of traditional values and political systems. It was quite clear to Hungary's conservative leadership in the 1930s that a new war would unleash passions that could not easily be controlled and that quite likely would undermine their position of traditional authority.

Ambiguity, caution, and patience were the essence of the foreign policy constructed by Hungary's adroit foreign minister, Kálmán Kánya, as the Danubian crisis unfolded after 1936. Earlier in the interwar period Hungarian conservatives, feeling a special affinity for an authoritarian, nationalist Germany, had not been averse to the idea of promoting Germany's eastward expansion in exchange for Berlin's support in the destruction of the peace settlement in East Central Europe. But their willingness to link Hungary's fortunes with that of Germany sharply diminished when it became apparent that Hitler was in no sense a reincarnated Bismarck. The desire of the Hungarians to harness the power of National Socialist Germany in the cause of Hungary's revisionist campaign was soon tempered by the fear that alliance with such an aggressive and totalitarian state could have disastrous consequences for the country's domestic life and its position in Europe. In an effort to maintain Hungary's freedom of maneuver in European affairs, Budapest turned to Italy and Great Britain for assistance. But the policies of these two powers were flawed by vacillation, cynicism, and a reluctance to incur the wrath of a rearmed and powerful Germany. In the dramatic events of late 1938 and early 1939, the Hungarians were thus left largely on their own to find an appropriate solution to their "revisionist dilemma."

A study of this kind could not have been completed without the assistance of numerous individuals both in the United States and abroad. Above all I wish to thank the directors and staffs of the libraries and archives in which I worked. I am especially grateful to György Ránki, the Acting Director of the Institute of History in Budapest, who greatly facilitated my work in Hungary; and to C. A. Macartney, who gave his kind permission to examine documentary material he has placed on deposit in the library of St. Antony's College, Oxford. I have benefited from the suggestions and advice of a number of people who have read earlier drafts of this work, especially Denis Sinor, Barbara Jelavich, Charles Jelavich and Istvan Deak. Two colleagues, Leslie Tihany and Arnold Schrier, have read the manuscript carefully and have made most helpful suggestions. I am indebted to Juanita Decker for her invaluable advice in matters of style and syntax, and to Alvena Stanfield for her splendid typing of the manuscript.

The research for this study could not have been conducted without the generous support of the Foreign Area Fellowship Program of the Social Sciences Research Council of the American Council of Learned Societies, the University Research Council of the University of Cincinnati, and the Charles Phelps Taft Memorial Fund.

Abbreviations

AD	Austrian Documents
CSH	*Csak szolgálati használatra!*
DBFP	*Documents on British Foreign Policy*
DIA	*Documents on International Affairs*
DIMK	*Diplomáciai iratok Magyarország külpolitikájához, 1936–1945*
FRUS	*Foreign Relations of the United States*
GFM	German Foreign Ministry
IET	*Iratok az ellenforradalmi történetéhez*
KN	*Az országgyűlés képviselőházának naplója*
MMV	*Magyarország és a második világháború*
NPA	Neues Politisches Archiv
PRO	Public Record Office
USSD	United States State Department

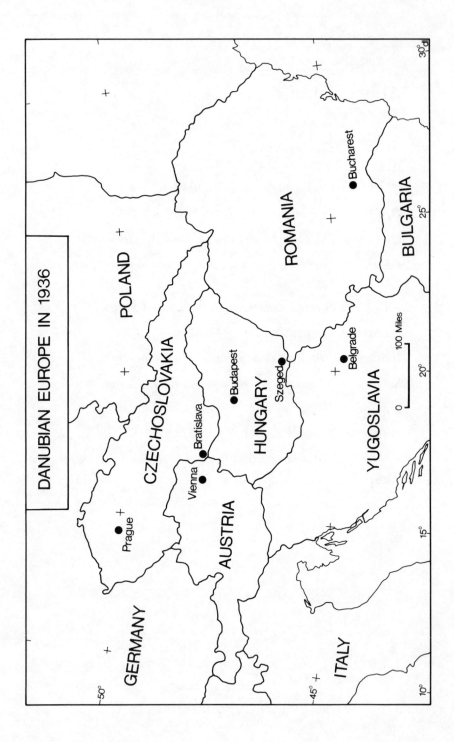

DANUBIAN EUROPE IN 1936

GERMANY

POLAND

CZECHOSLOVAKIA

Prague

AUSTRIA

Vienna

Bratislava

HUNGARY

Budapest

Szeged

ROMANIA

Bucharest

YUGOSLAVIA

Belgrade

BULGARIA

ITALY

100 Miles

0

50°

45°

30°

25°

20°

15°

10°

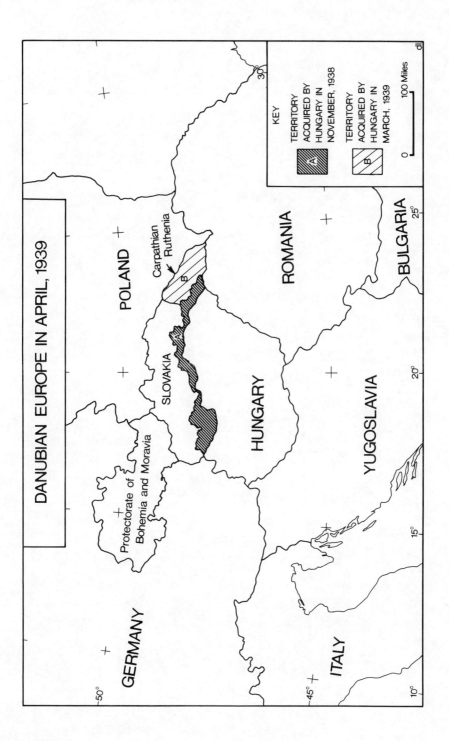

DANUBIAN EUROPE IN APRIL, 1939

GERMANY

POLAND

Protectorate of
Bohemia and Moravia

SLOVAKIA

Carpathian
Ruthenia

A

B

HUNGARY

ROMANIA

ITALY

YUGOSLAVIA

BULGARIA

KEY

TERRITORY
ACQUIRED BY
HUNGARY IN
NOVEMBER, 1938

A

TERRITORY
ACQUIRED BY
HUNGARY IN
MARCH, 1939

B

0   100 Miles

30°

50°

25°

45°

20°

15°

10°

Hungary,
the Great Powers,
and the Danubian Crisis

Chapter 1

Hungary in Turmoil, 1918–1921: The Roots of Interwar Foreign Policy

In the autumn of 1918, as the long and enervating war neared its end in Central Europe, two voices of despair and foreboding commanded attention in Hungary. On 17 October Count István Tisza, the "symbol and paragon of the old order,"[1] rose in Parliament to concede that his rivals on the left were correct: "we have lost the war."[2] At about the same time Endre Ady, a powerful poet and the spiritual and political protagonist of Tisza, sensed that Hungary was on the threshold of a time of terrible misfortune and humiliation. In moving terms he implored the victors not to "ride roughshod over our poor and beautiful heart."[3]

Despite the disparity in their political and social views, Tisza and Ady were united in apprehension of their country's fate. Their fears were to prove justified. In the coming three years Hungary was to undergo a series of convulsions that severely jolted national life and did immense damage to the economic, social, and political fabric of society. The signing of an armistice in November 1918 technically brought an end to the war, but in fact it marked only the beginning of new struggles for Hungary. Quite quickly a kind of civil war erupted, with Hungary's former subject nationalities taking advantage of Austria-Hungary's defeat to withdraw from the Kingdom of Hungary and to join with their ethnic brothers in forming new national states.

Meanwhile, political life took on a kaleidoscopic quality. Over a period of three years, from 31 October 1918, when a democratic government under Mihály Károlyi assumed power in Budapest, to 23 October 1921, when the second of former King Karl's efforts to claim the Hungarian throne was thwarted, Hungary experienced almost continual crises. Károlyi's government soon succumbed to the Soviet Republic under Béla Kun, which survived only 133 days, and in the subsequent chaos Budapest was subjected to a humiliating occupation by Romanian troops. The departure of the Romanians brought in its wake a triumph of the counterrevolutionaries under Admiral Miklós Horthy, but domestic turmoil continued virtually unabated. The earlier flagrant violence of the Red Terror was matched by the excesses of the White Terror against Jews and leftists. Social instability was aggravated by the influx of desperate refugees from the occupied territories of Hungary. The task of political reconstruction was hampered also by the drastic peace terms the victorious powers were attempting to impose. In short, Hungary in these early postwar years received a brief but concentrated taste of many of the economic and social dislocations and of the outbursts of racial and nationalistic intolerance that were to plague interwar Europe and lead to renewed war in 1939.

As a number of historians have rightly emphasized,[4] the frenetic three years following the end of hostilities in 1918 were bound to leave a lasting imprint on the foreign and domestic politics of the Hungarian state. Indeed, an understanding of Hungary's role in the grave crisis that enveloped Europe in the late 1930s is greatly enhanced by an examination of the assumptions, attitudes, and plans that came to the surface in this period. Much of what was to occur in Hungary between 1936 and 1939, as described in later chapters, will be seen to echo events from the immediate postwar Hungarian scene.

The Hungary that emerged in the early 1920s from the "time of troubles" was, in its political and social framework, largely a continuation of the old order that Tisza had symbolized. Tisza himself, it is true, was no longer on the scene, having been assassinated by irate soldiers not long after his painful admission of defeat. But his spiritual successors, notably Counts István Bethlen and Pál Teleki, proved quite adept at restoring in its broad outlines the prewar system. Yet the appearance of continuity was somewhat deceptive. Many leading figures of Hungary's political establishment had been "radicalized" by the events after the war's end, particularly the drastic peace terms and the brief supremacy of a communist regime. Moreover, Hungarian policy-makers found themselves confronted by problems and tasks unique to postwar Hungary; methods and solutions employed before 1914 were in many cases no longer appropriate or efficacious.

Probably the most striking change brought on by the war and its aftermath was the severe territorial losses imposed on Hungary. Rarely in history has a country the size of Hungary, whose statesmen had played a vital role in the political life of a European great power, been reduced so suddenly to small-power status. Count Mihály Károlyi, president of the fledgling Hungarian republic established in November 1918, had hoped that his program of political democratization, conciliation of the minorities, pacifism, and full cooperation with the Allies would win the confidence of the victors and Hungary's non-Magyar nationalities, thereby making possible the maintenance of Hungary's territorial integrity in a federative structure. But the Allies and Hungary's neighbors showed little patience or good will toward the Hungarian Republic. Indeed, various compacts and understandings arrived at during the war made it almost certain that extensive territorial changes would occur in the Danubian Basin upon the ending of hostilities.[5] In fact, Károlyi's approach hastened the dismemberment of Hungary. With the signing of the armistice, Hungarian troops were ordered to give up their arms and return to inner Hungary; most soldiers, weary from the years of futile fighting, had begun even earlier to trudge homeward. But the Czechs, Serbs, and Romanians, exhilarated by the favorable turn of events and eager to satisfy what quickly became inordinate territorial ambitions, were not about to hold back, leaving vital frontier questions to some future peace conference. Basing their actions on decisions made by hastily assembled National Councils in Slovakia, Transylvania, and the Bánát, the Czech, Serb, and Romanian governments sent in their troops to seize the territories they claimed. Károlyi, still reluctant to incur the displeasure of the Allies, refused to offer serious military resistance, and, even before the Paris Peace Conference deliberations, the partition of Hungary had been accomplished by a series of *faits accomplis*.[6]

Since the question of frontier revision loomed so large in interwar Hungarian policy, it is important at this point to examine the map of Danubian Europe that was sanctioned by the peacemakers in 1919 and 1920. According to the terms of the Treaty of Trianon, the "thousand year kingdom" of Hungary, once one of the great powers of Europe, was reduced to one third of its former area, shorn of Croatia, Slovakia, Transylvania, Ruthenia (the Carpatho-Ukraine or Sub-Carpathian Russia[7]), Burgenland (West

Hungary), and other smaller areas. Of the ten million Magyars who had formed only a bare majority in old Hungary, more than three million were transferred to the new, multinational states of Czechoslovakia, Romania, and Yugoslavia, while rump Hungary was to form an almost homogenous national state. Cities like Kolozsvár (Cluj), Pozsony (Bratislava), Kassa (Košice), and Temesvár (Timişoara), cherished by the Hungarians for historical, traditional, and economic reasons, were assigned to the Successor States. Many of these transfers were found to be inevitable because of the patchwork ethnic map. Thus the large bloc of Magyars, known as Székelys, in the southeastern edge of Transylvania, separated from the central mass of their countrymen by millions of Romanians, could not easily have remained in Hungary. On the other hand, most of the Magyar-inhabited areas ceded to Czechoslovakia, and a large part of that to Romania, were contiguous with Trianon Hungary's borders. In all, about 1.5 million of the 3 million Magyars to be transferred lived in areas directly touching the central mass of Magyars.[8]

The decision of the Peace Conference was greeted in Hungary with a mixture of bewilderment, indignation, and profound humiliation. That such an obvious "injustice" could be condoned by supposedly enlightened and well-meaning statesmen was simply incomprehensible to virtually all politically conscious Magyars. The national consensus that spontaneously developed spanned the entire political spectrum: from Béla Kun on the left to Miklós Horthy on the right, all prominent political spokesmen opposed the peace terms and branded them unjust, unwise, and ultimately untenable. The decision was accordingly challenged immediately and vociferously. The incorrigible nationalists wondered why the peacemakers had even dared to tamper with what they regarded as the economically and geographically perfect unit that Hungary had represented, almost as if divinely ordained, for one thousand years. But even the more reasonable Hungarians, who conceded that they had indeed been on the losing side in a devastating war and would have to pay some price, raised disturbing questions. If changes were to be made on the basis of the right of self-determination, they argued, why was it necessary to transfer so many Magyars to the new states? No one had consulted them, nor for that matter the Germans, Ruthenes, or Slovaks in Hungary, about which country they wished to join. Why could not plebiscites be conducted in disputed areas, as were planned on the German-Polish borders? No official replies to these queries were to come from the Peace Conference, for by the time the Hungarian delegation arrived in Paris in early 1920, the matter was for all purposes already past history. The Successor States, acting on a Peace Conference pronouncement of June 1919, had already commenced the formal incorporation of the new territory. Only superior force could have dislodged them. The Hungarians were allowed to present their case briefly to the Council of Ambassadors, but no meaningful discussion was allowed.[9]

Certain legal mechanisms, provided in the League of Nations charter and other less formal documents, did seem to offer the possibility for obtaining redress of Hungarian grievances in a peaceful manner at some future date. However, these offered little solace to the Magyars. Prospects of such peaceful revision seemed quite remote, and the rigid attitude of Hungary's new neighbors, who by 1921 had banded together in a "Little Entente" to protect themselves against Hungarian territorial revisionism, gave substance to the belief of the statesmen of the Successor States that the frontiers in that region should now be considered permanent, even "eternal." For their part, Hungary's frustrated and indignant leaders, convinced that justice and history were on their side, bitterly denounced Trianon as the "scandal of civilization"[10] and declared treaty revision to be the one overriding goal to which all national energies should be devoted. Moreover, so convinced were the Hungarians that they had been unconscionably deceived and unfairly treated that many were willing to condone a variety of political and military initiatives that in prewar days might have been deemed either illegal, immoral, or simply too undignified for a proper Magyar gentleman. The psychological jolt of the sudden demotion and humiliation of their country apparently now predisposed them to tolerate, if not actively promote, forgery, violent subversion of foreign governments, and bellicose military operations. Such activities came to fall under the euphemistic rubric of "patriotic enthusiasm" (hazafias felbuzdulás). This willingness to employ unsavory means to right what was perceived as a terrible wrong done Hungary in 1919 and 1920 was to be a lingering phenomenon in Hungary's foreign policy through the entire interwar period.

A second characteristic of the immediate postwar period that was to leave a lasting imprint on Hungarian political life was the swing to the left that began with Károlyi and ended with the 133-day Soviet Republic of Béla Kun. The appearance of these leftist regimes had a shattering impact on the conservative Hungarian political establishment, which recoiled in fear, horror, and disgust. At first the conservatives fled in disarray to havens outside or on the fringes of the country. But as conditions continued to deteriorate within Hungary in 1919, the conservatives were gradually emboldened to begin mobilizing their resources for a campaign to rid the country of all traces of Bolshevism and other leftist influences. In fact, the actual task of dealing the final military blow to the Soviet Republic fell to the Romanian army, but the rightist forces, under the command of one of Hungary's few genuine war heroes, Admiral Miklós Horthy, were on hand in late 1919 to fill the political void once Kun's government had collapsed.

Hungarian society in later years was afflicted by bitter memories of Károlyi and Kun, two names that became intertwined in the political nightmares of Hungarian rightists. Among politically articulate Hungarians revulsion against the pacifism of Károlyi and the anticlericalism and violence of Kun's "Lenin Boys"[11] was genuine and pervasive. Even among less sophisticated Hungarians the experience with leftist politics had proved painful. It was not difficult for the factory worker or soldier out of work, the peasant disillusioned by unkept promises, or the destitute refugees from Slovakia or Transylvania to blame their current troubles on the most recent "scoundrels" in office, Károlyi and Kun, but István Tisza, by then almost forgotten, escaped recrimination.

This "popular counterrevolution"[12] was a decidedly favorable turn of events for the spokesmen of the restored Hungarian government. Many Hungarian politicians were learned in constitutional history and theory, and they no doubt were familiar with Jean Bodin's venerable political axiom that the best way to preserve order and prevent sedition within a state is to find an enemy against which all citizens can make common cause. The Trianon Treaty seemed perfectly designed for this purpose, but the egregious blunders and general ineffectiveness of both Kun and Károlyi made it possible to focus public resentment and frustrations on them as well. In the process, of course, Count Tisza and his successors in postwar Hungary managed to escape the opprobrium that in normal circumstances would have been their due.

The tactic of directing national anger against convenient scapegoats was really an adjunct to a more general strategy developed by the ideologues of Hungary's political establishment. In his provocative study of the dynamics of counterrevolution in Europe, Arno Mayer has pointed out that in times of acute crisis conservatives are challenged to articulate and reaffirm the social and institutional values that, in normal times, they take for granted.[13] This was the task confronting Hungarian conservatives after 1918, and it is symptomatic that in large part their response consisted of resurrecting a set of traditional political myths the roots of which threaded back through the centuries. These collective beliefs, which in most (though not all) cases were based only loosely on reality, were appropriately embellished to meet the peculiar needs of postwar conditions.

Of course, the use of myths was not unique to Hungary's political establishment. East Europe in general has provided extraordinarily fertile ground for political mythmakers among all national groups. But the Magyars historically have proved to be the most prolific and adroit in this practice, their myths having often served as models for their neighbors to emulate.[14] When properly employed, these ideological conceptions have been of great value to ruling elites: they have served to bolster the self-esteem of the nation, solidify the political and social system, and promote various foreign policy goals. In the case of Hungary after 1918, the political myths that were developed or redefined were embraced by the great majority of politically minded Hungarians, and they came to form a neatly constructed mosaic that sustained the interwar leadership, served as the underpinning for the revisionist campaign, and kept alive the dream of the return of Magyar hegemony in the Danubian world.

The most prominent myth devised in this period served quite effectively to obscure the responsibility of Hungary's prewar leadership for the coming of World War I and for the consequences of defeat. The myth was composed of three related elements. On the one hand, it was argued that far from promoting war in 1914, István Tisza had strongly urged caution and restraint. A score of Hungarian historians and scholars from other disciplines, often working in such patriotic-scholarly organizations as the *Magyar Külügyi Társaság* (Hungarian Society of Foreign Affairs), diligently collated the evidence that seemed to demonstrate that Tisza could not be counted among the warmongers in 1914.[15] Critics suggested that the real guilt of the Hungarian prewar government lay not so much in its actions in the weeks leading up to the war as in the policy of intolerance towards internal nationalities, practiced over the course of decades. The Hungarian reply, in its most succinct form, was simply a denial that Hungary's minorities had been mistreated. The notion that Hungary had not been an aggressive country, that her prime minister had worked to preserve the peace, and that Hungary therefore did not deserve the punishment meted out in 1919, took firm hold in Hungarian society. Though foreigners on the whole seemed unimpressed, such leading figures as Miklós Horthy, Hungary's regent, repeatedly used this argument to buttress their pleas for revision throughout the interwar period.

Another element of this fundamental myth was an attempt to place the blame for the terrible misfortunes befalling Hungary in 1919 and 1920 directly on the shoulders of the true "gravediggers of Hungary," Károlyi and Kun. It was not the consequences of a lost war but their inept, destructive, and traitorous policies that had led to Hungary's dismemberment and social and economic chaos. Károlyi, it was claimed, had bargained away the country to further his own political ambitions. His pacifism, combined with a lack of diplomatic skill, had promoted the breakup of Hungary. Moreover, as right-thinking Magyars had quickly realized, Károlyi was a "disguised Bolshevik" and his democratic government proved to be merely a "stalking horse" for Communism and the complete ruin of the country.[16] As for Kun, his "internationalist" orientation and close ties with revolutionary Russia had obviously hardened the attitude of the peacemakers and insured that no sympathy would be shown to Hungary.

In some Hungarian political circles, particularly among the radicalized right wing, the Jews represented another scapegoat that could conveniently be linked with Kun and Károlyi as agents of destruction in Hungary. Political anti-Semitism had been a relatively insignificant phenomenon in prewar Hungarian society, but the shattering events of the war and its aftermath seemed to spur the growth of new, more virulent attacks on the Jews. Gyula Gömbös, a junior officer in the Habsburg general staff who was later to become the leader of the Hungarian radical right, sounded the opening call. Already in the fall of 1918, before the establishment of the Soviet Republic, he published a pamphlet, *Die Juden in Ungarn*, in which the Jews were depicted as a destructive, malicious force. Later Gömbös was to become the chief propagandist of a Hungarian version of the "stab in the back" theory. Pointing out that Hungarian troops in October 1918, stood everywhere on foreign soil, Gömbös asserted that Hungary had not really been on the brink of defeat. It was only the impotence of Hungarian statesmen and the baneful influence of pacifists, internationalists, and Bolsheviks, most of them Jews, that brought on a breakdown of morale among the soldiers and the collapse of the front.[17]

The growth of anti-Semitism was facilitated by the undeniable and all too evident fact that Jews, with Béla Kun himself the most prominent, had dominated the leftist movement in Hungary and the government of the Soviet Republic. In the popular mind, Jews thus came to be indiscriminately linked together with socialists and Communists as traitors, and in the chaos and destitution of 1919 and 1920 a campaign to rid the country of Bolsheviks degenerated in many cases into violence and terror against Jews, many of whom had had no connection whatsoever with the governments of Kun or Károlyi. Though these excesses were eventually tempered, anti-Semitism was to remain a persistent theme in right-wing propaganda, and the myth that Jews, socialists, and Communists were somehow responsible for all of Hungary's misfortunes was to remain a fundamental tenet of many prominent members of Hungary's political establishment.

A second major myth that pervaded the political creed of the interwar Hungarian governing elite amounted to a kind of cultural chauvinism bordering on racism. Even before the war, many Hungarians had shown a proclivity for emphasizing what they considered to be the unique talents of the Magyar in government and statesmanship. In the humiliating circumstances of the interwar period, greater stress was placed on this supposed capacity for "statebuilding," the ability to establish and preserve an orderly government and society. Hungarian historians, including the two most influential after 1918, Gyula Szekfű and Balint Hóman, gave their imprimatur to this interpretation of the Magyar character. In history books Hungarians were now portrayed as the only national group that, because of its superior qualities, had been able to overcome tremendous odds and establish a viable and effective state in the Danubian Basin. Moreover, for over a thousand years this political unit, the Kingdom of Hungary, had fulfilled a vital dual

mission for the rest of Christian Europe. In the first place, it had
served as a bulwark against repeated invasions of Europe by bar-
barians and infidels from the East. Hungary, it was argued, had
valiantly borne the brunt of attacks by Mongols, Turks, and, in
recent times, Bolsheviks, thereby sparing Western Europe the
ravages of these incursions.[18]

Nor was this all: at the same time the Magyars had for centuries
carried out a "cultural mission" on the eastern fringes of European
civilization. Under their benevolent guidance the less advanced
peoples of Danubian Europe, the Slovaks, Romanians, and South
Slavs, had begun the slow journey from "semi-oriental" conditions
to a more civilized way of life. This conception permeated the pre-
sentations made by the Hungarians at the Paris Peace Conference
in 1920 and later revisionist tracts. Count Albert Apponyi, the eloquent spokesman for the Hungarian delegation, tried to persuade
the Allied leaders that the Hungarians were uniquely qualified to
serve as the propagator of Western culture in Eastern Europe.
His argument, then and in later writings, was that the political
aptitude of the Magyars and "that peculiar combination of original-
ity and receptive capacity which characterizes her national genius"
had enabled Hungary successfully to undertake "the defence and
the peaceful extension of the higher standards of Western life."[19]
Given these realities of history, was it not both foolish and unwise,
Apponyi asked the peacemakers in 1920, to impose on Hungary
the severe territorial changes stipulated in the Trianon Treaty?
Such a mutilation of the historic Kingdom of Hungary, he asserted, amounted to "the transference of national hegemony to an
inferior grade of civilization" and this "could not be a matter of
indifference to the great interests of humanity."[20]

In later years Hungarian spokesmen further buttressed their plea
for treaty revision by pointing out that the partition of their country rendered it impossible for the Magyars to continue their thou-
sand-year-old mission of defense of the West against enemies
from the East. The precondition of the continued success of that
mission, Apponyi later argued, was restoration of the historic frontiers of Hungary.[21] The latest threat to Western civilization, Soviet
Russia, could be contained only if Christian Europe came to its
senses and recognized the great debt it owed the Hungarian nation. The Magyars, as always, stood ready to mount guard on the
Carpathian mountains: all they needed was the proper territorial

framework. From 1920 to the last years of World War II, this line
of reasoning was to form a common thread in the foreign policies
of successive Hungarian governments.

In political terminology the attitudes and assumptions described
in the preceding pages were conveniently summarized by one succinct phrase: a "Christian national" policy (*keresztény nemzeti*).
Almost all politically active Hungarians professed their dedication
to and support of this concept. The "Christian" element consisted
of a commonly shared desire to curtail what was considered undue
Jewish influence in society and enhance the prestige of the churches after the official atheism of the Kun regime. The strengthening
of the Christian churches was considered desirable from the standpoint of restoring order and discipline to a society that had had a
dangerous if brief experience with democratic and socialist ideas.
But affirmation of the role of Christianity in Hungarian history
and society had even broader implications for interwar Hungarian
foreign policy. Historic Hungary was often referred to as the Kingdom of St. Stephen, and the crown of that famous king was regarded as a symbol of the inviolability of Hungary's traditional
frontiers. In Hungarian Catholic circles this concept tended to lend
a religious sanction to the campaign to regain Hungary's lost territories. Such novel concepts as national self-determination and ethnic rights could thus be more easily denigrated, and Hungary's
Christian churches, both Catholic and Protestant, could rationalize
their support for the campaign to restore Hungarian hegemony
over millions of non-Magyars.[22]

The "national" implications of the "Christian national" formula
involved a rejection of the international and cosmopolitan flavor
of left-wing movements, particularly Communism, and a commitment to accepted national goals, above all, to treaty revision. It
of course connoted a deep, passionate nationalism and a firm commitment to the restoration of a Greater Hungary. Rarely has a
society been so thoroughly and fanatically dedicated to one single
national goal, namely, revision of the Trianon Treaty. The struggle
against Trianon became imbedded in the national routine, a regular, relentless activity that absorbed the energies and talents of a
great number of Hungarians. In 1920 Hungarian flags were low-
ered to half mast as a sign of national mourning; they were not to
be raised again for almost two decades. "Nem, nem, soha!" (No,
no, never!), the national shout of defiance to the Paris peacemak-

ers, reverberated throughout the land. Postcards and placards carried maps of Hungary "before and after," the grandeur of the prewar state contrasted with "mutilated" Hungary.

To a certain extent this national frenzy may have been consciously fomented by the rightist government to divert attention from pressing social and economic problems. But the dynamism of the revisionist movement must in large part be attributed to the genuine conviction among educated Hungarians of all political persuasions that their cause was a just one. In the mid-1920s, Hungary's prime minister, István Bethlen, observed that the success of the revisionist campaign depended on participation of individuals "on all levels . . . in science and literature, in the press, in connection with Church conferences; indeed every member of Hungarian society must do his duty."[23] In fact, Bethlen's call had already been heeded; from the start Hungarians had responded to the challenge with enthusiasm and determination.

Every Hungarian institution seemed to play a role in the irredentist campaign. The churches, as has been seen, lent their moral support. Hungary's scholarly community seemed to feel no compunction about offering its services. Such organizations as the Sociological Institute and the Cartographic Institute placed their facilities in the service of the revisionist movement, the latter going so far as to forge foreign currency.[24] Geographers proved particularly active, largely because of the influence of Count Pál Teleki, whose prewar contributions to geographical studies had won him accolades throughout the world. It was largely through the efforts of Teleki, who effectively mobilized the resources of his discipline in Hungary, that the Hungarian delegation at Paris was able to submit a splendid array of maps and statistical material, albeit to no avail. His most lasting tangible contribution came in 1919, when he published an ingenious ethnographic map of prewar Hungary that was to accompany virtually every book of Hungarian propaganda produced in the interwar period. In later years, except for his tenure as prime minister in 1920 and 1921, Teleki was regarded as a kind of titular leader of the revisionist movement. He was particularly active in Western Europe and the United States, where he enjoyed a reputation as a moderate in politics and a humane scholar.

Hungarian historians, too, joined in the great national crusade, though the dean of the historical community, Gyula Szekfű, was later to chide his colleagues for failing to mount an effort comparable to that of historians in Germany, France, Yugoslavia, and elsewhere.[25] Nonetheless, historians frequently lent their names to various propagandistic publications, including the volume entitled *Justice for Hungary*, which appeared in 1928 in various Western languages and was distributed free to many libraries abroad, influential individuals in England and the United States, and Western tourists in Hungary. This book, of course, was but a trickle in the tremendous flood of Hungarian revisionist literature from the 1920s, most of it intended to persuade the educated elite in Germany, Italy, France, and the Anglo-Saxon countries.

To ensure that the next generation of Hungarians would not be lax in its commitment to revisionism, the schools and various youth organizations were also enlisted in the struggle. Not surprisingly, the inflamed nationalism that characterized society as a whole came to be expressed in the classroom. Nor was Hungary alone in this: throughout Eastern Europe instruction was, in the words of Peter Sugar, "narrowly nationalistic, filled with self-praise and hero worship."[26] At a very young age the Hungarian student learned a chant that was to be a part of the daily regimen in the years ahead: "Mutilated Hungary is not a country, Greater Hungary is heaven." School textbooks at all levels tended to reflect the political myths that were basic to Hungary's interwar political ideology.[27] Thus, no student, indeed no Hungarian, could escape the barrage of reminders that his nation had been gravely humiliated at Paris and that three million (Hungarian sources typically placed this figure much higher) of his countrymen were "languishing" in neighboring countries, awaiting their liberation.

Those Hungarians who fervently embraced a "Christian national" ideology and the concomitant political mythology described above can clearly be placed at the rightist end of the political spectrum. Indeed, in the interwar era Hungary was in almost all respects a rightist country. The forces of the left had been badly routed in the early postwar period, when everything supposedly tainted with the socialist, liberal, or cosmopolitan spirit, be it Bolshevism, social democracy, or freemasonry, was suspect. An effective campaign of armed-band terrorism and political coercion and harassment in 1919 and 1920 drove most of the leaders of the moderate or extreme left into the underground, exile, or prison. With most of its most capable or popular leaders in exile, the Social Democratic Party that continued to exist in Hungary was forced to make unpalatable compromises with the conservative governments. No Communist party was officially tolerated, and that which survived in clandestine form had little influence on political developments.

Most debates in interwar Hungarian political life thus transpired in a very restricted quarter of the political spectrum, among a relatively small number of politically active individuals who comprised a kind of "exclusive club."[28] Yet this apparent conformity of political views did tend to obscure the existence of some fundamental differences among the Hungarian rightists. Students of modern Hungary have traditionally identified two distinct poles of rightist thought after 1918: the conservatives and the radical right-wingers. However, no political parties bearing precisely these names ever appeared on the scene, and the alignment was not in any case completely rigid. Not every Hungarian political figure can be readily assigned to one or the other group. In the vicissitudes of interwar political life, individuals from time to time shuffled from one camp to the other, or attempted to combine elements of both programs to form a new synthesis. Some Hungarians found it difficult to decide which ideology best suited their interests and temperament. This was particularly true of Regent Miklós Horthy, in whom the impulses of right radicalism and conservatism waged a visible, increasing struggle through the whole period. To understand the nature and cause of the vacillations of Horthy and some of his colleagues, it is necessary to examine closely the composition and ideology of the two rightist camps. Only by focussing on their differences can the vagaries of interwar Hungarian politics and foreign policy be properly comprehended.

In 1918 the foremost spokesmen for the conservative movement in Hungary bore surnames that over the centuries had been a birthright to high government office. Such aristocratic families as the Bethlens and Telekis had again and again provided the sons who would assume leading roles in the nation's political life. In the political turmoil of 1918 and 1919, however, many of these magnates were forced to flee to the more familiar and secure surroundings of Vienna. There they were joined by men of lesser social stature but similar political beliefs, such as Kálmán Kánya and Gusztáv Gratz, and even a number of Hungary's most prominent Jewish capitalists, with whom the conservatives had maintained a kind of tacit alliance in prewar political life. These individuals, under the leadership of such aristocrats as Count István Bethlen, Count Pál Teleki, and Count Anton Sigray, began the painstaking task of laying the foundation for a true counterrevolution in Hungary. Their guiding principles were those of traditional nineteenth-century European conservatism: they were deeply suspicious of social experimentation, political democratization, and demagoguery, while extolling the virtues of social order, religion, and national unity. A tendency toward authoritarianism, however, was tempered by an ingrained respect for parliamentarianism that had been shaped by centuries of struggle against absolutist Habsburg rule and by certain liberal influences in Hungary after 1867.

In foreign affairs the Hungarian conservatives, many of whom had served in the Austro-Hungarian diplomatic service, were likewise wedded to nineteenth-century concepts. Faced with the bewildering array of problems confronting Hungary in 1919 and 1920, their instinct was to search for or devise diplomatic solutions. It is true that some conservatives, enraged by the indignities to which their native land was being subjected, for a time showed a willingness to accept more violent and nontraditional methods. Whenever possible, however, they tried to fit the "Hungarian problem" into a European framework, so that the great powers, in the grand traditions of the Concert of Europe, could be persuaded to contribute to the return of a stable, conservative government in Budapest. Towards this end the Vienna conservatives in 1919 organized the Anti-Bolshevik Committee, the members of which worked assiduously to convince representatives of the victorious powers, particularly the British, to equip and support an expeditionary force that would topple the Soviet Republic and prevent a dismemberment of Hungary by her neighbors.[29]

Once the counterrevolution gained the upper hand again in late 1919, Hungary's conservatives returned from exile, confident of their ability again to assume the task of directing the affairs of the nation. Though small in number and hampered by a temporarily more liberal franchise, the conservatives possessed the unique leadership experience and diplomatic skills that ensured they would play a leading role in the reconstruction of social and political values. In 1919, however, they encountered a new, vigorous political force that loomed as both a valuable ally and a possible rival. While Bethlen and his fellow aristocrats had been assembling in Vienna, another core of counterrevolutionary activity had been forming in the southern Hungarian city of Szeged, which since the armistice had been occupied by French troops. Some conservatives, most prominently Count Gyula Károlyi and, in the later period, Count Pál Teleki, were to be found in Szeged, but the driving force behind what was to be called the "Szeged movement" were men of lower social standing and considerably more modest financial means.

In the revolutionary period Szeged proved a powerful magnet for the malcontent and dislocated lower gentry and middle class of Hungary. Forced to flee by the hostile attitude and policies of the Romanians in Transylvania and the Czech authorities in Slovakia, as well as the revolutionary edicts of the Kun regime in Hungary proper, these former civil servants, teachers, and army officers were undergoing what one historian has aptly termed the "radicalizing effects of the refugee experience."[30] Most of these destitute, uprooted individuals had lost their jobs, suffered deep humiliation at the hands of former subject nationalities and social inferiors, and fallen with their families into a state of previously unimagined penury. Unlike Hungary's aristocrats and affluent businessmen, they lacked the financial resources and historic sense of self-importance to preserve equanimity in a time of such travail. In their utter despondency they were thus open to radical and violent solutions, to a venting of their inner rage against those seemingly responsible for their personal plight and for the dismemberment of their country. In the Szeged camp the fury of these men acted as a catalyst in the fusing into a powerful political force of a fierce anti-Semitism, antisocialism, militarism, and irredentism.

Though the "Szeged idea," as the vaguely articulated ideology of the movement came to be called, was a new phenomenon in Hungarian political life, it in many ways paralleled the programs of early fascist or national socialist groups that were emerging at the same time in Central and Eastern Europe. In Hungary, as has been noted, the radical rightists[31] shared with the conservatives a broad set of basic political assumptions. But the men of Szeged were distinctly more militant in their rhetoric and methods. Their nationalism was more intense and intolerant, their anti-Semitism more invidious and vulgar, their political approach more open to demagoguery and the techniques of modern mass politics. Above all they showed a propensity for violence and terror as a political tactic that for the most part was alien to the conservative mentality.

The effort to promote the radical expression of national and social grievances was greatly facilitated by the fact that the major military organization of the counterrevolution was developed by the Szeged radicals. Under the direction of Admiral Miklós Horthy, an able military commander, the small but effective National Army was organized in 1919. Into its ranks were drawn many of the dispossessed and despondent who had flocked to Szeged. The bulk of them were reserve officers, whose war experiences had inured them to violence, and refugees, who were eager to "punish" those, particularly the Jews and Communists, who, they believed, were the cause of their misfortunes.

The numerous "primitive warriors"[32] in the ranks of the National Army and certain paramilitary "special detachments" were the driving force behind the conflagration known as the White Terror, an outpouring of violence that spread across Hungary as Horthy's troops marched toward Budapest. Moreover, it was the National Army that "liberated" Budapest as the Romanians withdrew in the autumn of 1919. The radical rightists were thus able to pose as the champions of national independence and the best guarantee against a resurgence of the pacifism of a Mihály Károlyi or the social radicalism of a Béla Kun. In Budapest the most radical factions of the Szeged group were reluctant to abandon their violent ways, despite increasing protests from conservative spokesmen.[33] The latter had remained largely silent as the White Terror had engulfed the countryside in the summer of 1919. A brief and concentrated application of terror, some of them reasoned, was a distasteful but necessary step in the process of reconstruction. But the continued anti-Semitic excesses and wanton shedding of blood even after the recapture of Budapest made the conservatives uneasy. Their aim was the creation of a stable civilian government that would not have to rely explicitly on the National Army for its legitimacy. Towards this end the "special detachments" would have to be tamed and the inordinate power that had been assumed by the army general staff in 1919 would have to be returned to the appropriate civilian government organs.

In the political struggle that developed by 1920 the radical rightists were hindered by the dearth of leadership experience in their ranks. It was characteristic that the leading spokesman for the

Szeged movement, Gyula Gömbös, was a mere captain and, by traditional Hungarian standards, could hardly present suitable credentials for government service. Others prominent in the National Army were noncommissioned officers who by education and social position were unqualified to participate in the delicate task of restoring an efficient government and administration. It is perhaps not surprising that as the radical rightists came to realize the weakness of their position vis à vis the conservatives, there was increased talk in their ranks of the necessity for a coup d'état and establishment of a military dictatorship. But the appearance of Allied military representatives militated against this possibility, leaving only one alternative for the Szeged camp. Their greatest asset in the struggle for political influence was the close identification of Admiral Miklós Horthy with the "Szeged idea." When the consensus developed that Hungary needed a regent to serve temporarily as head of state, the radical right vigorously promoted the candidacy of their hero. On this point many conservatives, conscious of the need to appease the Szeged group and to recognize in some way their important contribution to the counterrevolutionary effort, were willing to relent.[34] Moreover, Horthy had the tacit support of many of the Allied representatives in Hungary, notably the British minister. On 1 March 1920 Miklós Horthy was thus elected regent by the National Assembly. It was a major victory for the radical rightists, an apparent guarantee that the "Szeged idea" would be a dominant influence in future policymaking.

The confidence of the radical right in Horthy stemmed in large part from the active support and inspiration he gave to their program for overcoming the isolation and humiliation into which Hungary had fallen by 1920. Unversed in the subtleties of diplomacy and accustomed to the employment of stealth and stark military force to achieve desired goals, the Szeged camp in 1919 began to lay the groundwork for a foreign policy that in its assumptions and strategy, though not in its ultimate goal, contrasted sharply with that of the Anti-Bolshevik Committee in Vienna. The inclination of Horthy, Gömbös, and their colleagues was to seek bold, military solutions to Hungary's problems. It would be national suicide, they argued, if Hungary were meekly to accept the imposed peace terms. The situation in 1919 and 1920 seemed conducive to a policy of obstruction: the Danubian world remained in flux and the full complement of the Allied Military Commission, which could have guarded against military escapades of the Hungarian General Staff, had not yet arrived. Horthy and his advisors were thus prompted to devise plans whereby at least some of the territory that had been seized by the Successor States could be regained through a series of brilliant military strokes. The radical rightists were confident that, with the help of ideologically compatible groups in Austria, Germany, Bohemia, and Poland, the sparks of democracy and socialism could be extinguished in Central Europe and Hungary could be reestablished in its historic frontiers.

The program of the radical right received its first concrete expression in a memorandum drawn up under Horthy's name in the fall of 1919.[35] It called for an "armed settling of accounts" with Romania, restoration of a "common border" with Poland through the reannexation of Slovakia, and a campaign to exploit ethnic diversity in the new South Slav State. Over the next two years specific military plans to achieve these goals were drafted by officers of the Army General Staff, often working independently of the civilian government. Attention was focussed on two areas, Slovakia and Burgenland, where the chances for success seemed greatest. With Horthy's approval, specific schemes were developed for undermining Czech rule in Slovakia and promoting an uprising of the Magyars and pro-Hungarian Slovaks. In the resulting civil war Hungarian, and perhaps Polish, military units would be introduced to "restore order."[36] In 1920 and 1921 parallel plans for the overthrow of the socialist regime in Austria and the securing of Burgenland were discussed and drafted in the General Staff. For a time even the idea of a joint Hungarian-Bavarian invasion of Austria was given serious consideration.[37]

While the radical right occupied itself with the details of these ambitious, clandestine plans, official Hungarian foreign policy as articulated by the Foreign Ministry and its representatives seemed to be proceeding along quite different lines. If the General Staff was the bastion of the radical right, the Foreign Ministry might be thought of as serving a similar function for the conservatives. The prominent figures in the Foreign Ministry, notably Pál Teleki, Gusztáv Gratz, and Kálmán Kánya, shared an ambivalent attitude toward the plans emanating from the General Staff and the circle around Horthy. On the one hand, an opportunism born of despair over Hungary's future and disdain for Hungary's new neighbors prompted them to approve, either actively or more often tacitly, some of the least objectionable of the plans put forward by the officers and the Szeged radicals. Certain unsavory activities, such as sabotage and blatant interference in the internal politics of other states, which violated the rules of diplomacy that had supposedly governed the relations of European states in the nineteenth century, were condoned by the Hungarian Foreign Ministry. Substantial funds were made available to help finance irredentist projects in Slovakia and the effort to hasten the downfall of the socialist government in Austria and its replacement by a regime of the right.[38]

There is no doubt, however, that Teleki and others in the Foreign Ministry, as well as the most influential political figure outside the government, István Bethlen, harbored a fundamental distrust of the schemes of the radical rightists and deeply resented the intrusion of the General Staff into the realm of foreign policy-making. It seemed to them that if the soldiers had their way, Hungary, by her bellicose and provocative policies, would plunge Danubian Europe into renewed warfare. The outcome of a new conflagration could hardly redound to Hungary's favor, given the disorganized state of the National Army and the superior forces with which it would have to contend. A renewed flare-up of Bolshevism and an even more severe dismemberment of Hungary might be the price exacted for a foolish policy of military adventurism.[39] Yet until 1921 the conservatives in the Foreign Ministry and the Cabinet simply were not in the position to exercise a veto. The unstable conditions that persisted in Central Europe so long after the armistice allowed the General Staff and paramilitary groups to continue to operate as if the war were still being waged. Moreover, any direct attack on the radicals in the General Staff would have been tantamount to a challenge to their patron, Regent Horthy. The conservatives wished to avoid such a risky confrontation until the turbulence subsided in Danubian Europe and the danger of a military coup d'état became more remote.

Despite their limited acquiescence in the program of the radical rightists, the conservatives in the Cabinet and Foreign Ministry, most notably Teleki, continued to strive to fashion a foreign policy that would promote Hungary's national goals through diplomatic channels. They were convinced that the only realistic course for Hungary in the long run was to accept the main features of the

Trianon treaty, restore political, economic, and social stability, and work patiently for a program of treaty revision that could be sanctioned by several great powers. To Teleki, Bethlen, Kánya, and others of similar persuasion, it seemed self-evident that Hungary on her own would never be able to redraw the map of Danubian Europe. Since an unfavorable European diplomatic constellation had been the ruin of Hungary from 1918 to 1920, only a more favorable one in the future could sweep away Trianon and restore the country to her former grandeur.

Central to Count Teleki's vision of an efficacious foreign policy was the conviction that the strengthening of Hungary was the necessary precondition for a successful European confrontation with Soviet Russia.[40] For a time, events in 1920 seemed to suggest the validity of this approach. When Poland attacked Russia in the spring, the Hungarian government quickly offered to join in what could well have developed into an anti-Bolshevik crusade. Portraying Czechoslovakia as the weak link and Hungary as a reliable ally in a struggle against the Soviet Union, Hungarian spokesmen in Paris and London pleaded for a sympathetic review of the harsh peace terms Budapest was being pressured to sign.[41] Though most Hungarians regarded England as the great power most likely to understand and support Hungary's case,[42] it was only from France that the Hungarian initiative gained a favorable response. During the spring and summer of 1920, intensive secret negotiations were conducted and the outlines of a major political and economic pact between France and Hungary were sketched. In exchange for a broad ethnic revision in Hungary's favor (that is, return of those territories contiguous to rump Hungary that contained Magyar majorities), Teleki was prepared to make substantial economic concessions to France and participate actively in a French sponsored anti-Bolshevik operation.[43] Though in June Hungary signed the Trianon treaty as a gesture of good faith, the proposed pact proved stillborn. By autumn a Russian advance into Poland was stymied and Paris rapidly lost interest in Hungary as a possible pillar of her policy in Danubian Europe.

Though badly disillusioned by what some regarded as French duplicity, the Hungarian conservatives remained committed to a revisionist policy set in a European framework and anchored in diplomatic procedures. Though it was a painful decision for all concerned, Teleki was able to persuade the Hungarian National

Assembly to ratify the peace treaty in November 1920. In the previous months, Teleki had argued that Hungary had "lost the war and lost it against a powerful world coalition," and that the price for such a defeat had to be paid. Before the ratification, however, the members of the National Assembly approved a declaration that formed a touchstone for interwar Hungary's foreign policy. Declaring that they were bowing to "irresistible pressure," the delegates expressed the hope that "the return of normal conditions, after the passions now reigning have disappeared, will open the road to a rectification of the great injustice inflicted upon us under the guise of a peace treaty."[44]

It is characteristic of the political scene in Hungary that the radical right, whose instinct was for a bolder policy of obstruction, strongly reproached Teleki and his colleagues for their acceptance of the dictated peace. Unruly bands surrounded the National Assembly building on ratification day, angrily abusing those delegates who had voted to accept the treaty. Yet the influence of the Szeged movement would soon be on the wane. By 1921 the appearance of the Allied military overseers on the scene had led to a gradual disbanding of the paramilitary bands and the dissolution of the General Staff. Several surreptitious military plans were still being toyed with by Horthy and his conspiratorial friends, but the conservatives, now more securely at the helm of the civilian government, were in the position to respond more vigorously. In the spring of 1921, Prime Minister Teleki had decided to seek a rapprochement with Czechoslovakia that might lead to territorial concessions on the part of Prague. When it was suggested to him that the earlier scheme for Polish-Hungarian military cooperation aimed at wresting Slovakia from Czech rule would better serve Hungary's interest, Teleki's response was a succinct expression of the sentiments of those Hungarians who over the past several years had been forced to conceal their doubts about such plans. A military solution, Teleki asserted, was unwise and impractical, for "to play *va banque*, to risk the whole country in the interests of a plan for the realisation of which, according to my conviction, there is very little hope, would be a policy with which I could not identify myself."[45]

The naming of Count István Bethlen as prime minister in April 1921, marked the symbolic end of Hungary's "time of troubles" and the establishment of a stable civilian government. Bethlen, a consummate politician, very cleverly arranged for the political neutralization of the radical right. The explosive potential of the numerous discontented and restless army officers was defused by their gradual absorption into an increasingly bloated civil service and various governmental ministries. Many of the radicalized refugees from Hungary's lost provinces were given a place in the political process as delegates to the National Assembly in Bethlen's "Party of Unity." Through these methods Bethlen was able to forge a unified front among the rightists. By stressing a common dedication to "Christian national" principles and the need to present a unified front in the revisionist struggle, Bethlen was able to contain the centrifugal forces that had caused serious strains in the immediate postwar period.

Yet the gulf that had formed between the two Hungarian rightist camps in vital questions of foreign policy could not easily be bridged. The "Szeged spirit" might be temporarily tamed, but its zealous adherents, many of them occupying positions of influence in industry, government, and the military, were not about to abandon the cause that had fired their imagination in 1919. Moreover, the disproportionate representation in the Parliament during the 1920s of refugees from the lost provinces ensured that a most virulent form of treaty revisionism would remain at the focus of Hungary's interwar foreign policy.[46]

Chapter 2

Hungarian Policy and the Policymakers, 1921–1936

For the small nations of Eastern Europe, wedged between such powerful and often expansionist countries as Germany and Russia, the primary foreign policy goal in modern times has been the eviction of foreign rulers and the establishment of an independent state. At the end of World War I, however, a unique era began to unfold for the people on the eastern fringes of the continent. The simultaneous discomfiture of both Germany and Russia, a startling and completely unexpected event, made possible the carving out of numerous new nation states from the remains of the Austrian, German, and Russian empires. In the first years of independence, a mood of exhilaration and optimism prevailed, but keen observers of the European scene even then sensed the fragility of the new system. Despite the fact that Germany had had imposed on her what many considered a punitive peace, and that Russia had been weakened by a long and enervating civil war, the elements of national power that had enabled the two peoples to exert a dominant political influence in the territory separating them had remained largely unimpaired.[1] It seemed inevitable that at some future point Germany and Russia would reemerge as major powers; when this happened, the frontiers drawn in 1919 might well face a vigorous challenge. Thus the major task of the statesmen of the numerous new states was to preserve a status quo in which the national independence of their countries was guaranteed. It was, as events would demonstrate, an assignment beyond the capabilities of even the most talented Czechoslovak, Polish, or Yugoslav diplomats.

Compared to the Hungarians, however, the statesmen of the Successor States were relatively well off. Possessing what they considered satisfactory borders, the latter could give unstinting support to all agencies and endeavors, such as the League of Nations, that served to preserve the peace and the status quo. The Hungarians enjoyed no such luxury; seized by a passionate desire to right the "wrongs" of the peace settlement, they saw no long-range alternative to an active, revisionist policy. Yet a small, weak country that wishes to disrupt the status quo is usually confronted with a dilemma: to succeed, it must enlist the support of stronger powers, but in doing so it must almost inevitably sacrifice a degree of national independence. The greatest risk, of course, is a complete loss of independence to the very power whose assistance had been solicited.

The task of Hungarian policymakers was thus to devise a policy that would lead to a revision of the Trianon Treaty but would not at the same time jeopardize national independence. Prospects for success were hardly auspicious. The international position of Hungary as she emerged from the turmoil of the early postwar period verged on the hopeless. Without a sponsor among the great powers, consigned to isolation by hostile neighbors who had banded together in the Little Entente, and weakened by the devastating impact of the war and the harsh economic terms of the peace treaty, Hungary was in no position to conduct an active policy of any sort. Many European statesmen at the time urged the Magyars to resign themselves to their fate, and there is no doubt that the stability of Danubian Europe would have been enhanced had they accepted the new frontiers and a greatly reduced role in European affairs. In the past, some nations, most notably the Swedes, had been able to acquiesce gracefully in their demotion from the ranks of the major powers. Not so the Hungarians. It soon became evident that fervid nationalism had so tenacious a grip on Hungarian public opinion that no government that attempted to abandon the revisionist cause could expect to survive.

The need to revise the Treaty of Trianon was the unspoken assumption of all foreign policy discussions in interwar Hungary. Though various groups or political parties might differ fundamentally on questions of internal policy, all joined in condemning Trianon. In the few forums where foreign policy problems could be discussed more or less openly, such as the Parliament or the columns of the numerous newspapers published in Budapest, no one ever tried to argue that Hungary would do best to forget about territorial revision and concentrate on other problems. The pattern was established quite early: in 1921 the Social Democrats, the only major party of the left tolerated by the Horthy regime, agreed to a political compromise that included, among other features, a pledge on their part to adopt a "rigorously Hungarian viewpoint in all disputed foreign policy questions touching on the national community."[2]

Even the two *bêtes noires* of the Hungarian rightists, the Jews and Communists, joined their countrymen in a rejection of the peace settlement. The outlawed Hungarian Communist Party, following the lead of the Third International, regularly condemned Trianon as "a treaty of plunder" that had violated the principle of national self-determination. On the basis of both pragmatic and genuinely patriotic motives, Hungary's Jewish community also chose to espouse the revisionist cause. In the mid 1920s Hungary's Jewish leadership rejected the opportunity to appeal to the League of Nations for protection against the *numerus clausus* law, which was construed by many at the time to be a violation of a clause in the Trianon Treaty protecting religious minorities. The reasoning of the Jewish representatives is revealing: "We are Hungarians. We feel ourselves part of the Hungarian nation. Consequently, the Treaty of Trianon, which is an affliction to our nation, can never be a source of justice for us."[3]

This national consensus greatly facilitated the work of Hungary's foreign policy makers. It was tacitly agreed by those who participated in the governmental process, most importantly members of Parliament, that it would be unpatriotic to belabor the foreign minister with constant criticisms or requests for clarification of this or that diplomatic move. In other words, anything that would likely weaken the united national front in the revisionist question was to be avoided. This did not imply, however, that the government would be immune from all criticism in foreign policy matters. The basic goals of Hungarian foreign policy could not be questioned, but the precise tactics and strategy to be employed could be and often were the subject of intense debate, especially after 1932. The key question was not Should we seek to undo Trianon?, but How much revision, and how could it best be accomplished? Thus everyone came to agree that the assistance of powerful friends was essential in the revisionist campaign, but the choice of this or that great power usually reflected the ideological predilections of various groups or political parties. The radical right opted for Fascist Italy or, in the later period, Nazi Germany; the Social Democrats looked to France or England; the Communists most naturally to the Soviet Union and Europe's working classes.

How much revision? was an equally divisive question. Most politicians of the right yearned for integral revision, the restoration of the kingdom of St. Stephen within its historic frontiers. Of course, this desire was rarely expressed in public, since it would have been injudicious to alienate potential friends among the great powers, none of which at any point felt it to be in its own interests to support the more extravagant of Hungary's claims. Within Hungary the program of *"mindent vissza!"* (get everything back!) was decried by a small number of articulate representatives of the intelligentsia and political groups of the left and center. These moderate men of humanitarian, if somewhat utopian, impulse, such as Pál Auer and Pál Ignotus, believed that Hungary's future could be secured only when harmony and good will were established among the peoples of the Danubian Basin. Hungary's leaders would have to recognize the community of interests that united Czechs, Magyars, Romanians, and the others. Only then could they rise above the petty antipathies and cultural chauvinism of the past and extend the hand of friendship to their neighbors. The latter, for their part, would have to agree to a rectification of the most blatant territorial inequities of the peace settlement.[4]

This call for "ethnic revision," the return of those territories with Magyar majorities that were contiguous to Trianon Hungary, gained few open adherents in Hungary and even fewer in Czechoslovakia, Yugoslavia, and Romania. Hungary's interwar leaders tended to shun diplomatic contacts with the statesmen of the Successor States, believing, no doubt correctly, that the prospects for revision through direct negotiation were negligible. In any case, Regent Horthy and his ministers suspected that any acquiescence on their part in an agreement for limited revision would be interpreted as a willingness to forgo their more extensive claims. Of course, these calculations were purely academic, since only one prominent statesman in the Successor States—Thomas Masaryk, the president of Czechoslovakia—ever showed even the slightest sympathy for Hungary's plight. But Masaryk's occasional hints in the 1920s and early 1930s that Prague might be willing to make certain territorial concessions always evaporated quickly in the hostile atmosphere of mutual recriminations in Danubian Europe.[5]

The Hungarian foreign policy making process in the "Horthy

era" was clearly elitist in nature. For the bulk of the nation, the
millions of peasants and impoverished agricultural workers in the
countryside, politics remained "the affairs of the gentry,"[6] a remote, mysterious activity about which they knew and cared little.
Even the small number of journalists, intellectuals, businessmen,
officers, and government officials in Budapest who constituted the
politically aware segment of Hungarian society rarely could exert
direct influence on the shaping of foreign policy. This remained
the prerogative of a handful of individuals at the highest levels
of government. For this reason, an analysis of the attitudes and
programs of the most influential Hungarian statesmen will provide helpful insights into Hungary's role in the years of the Danubian crisis in the late 1930s.

The central figure, of course, was Miklós Horthy. During his
twenty-four-year tenure (1920–44) as regent, he presided over political developments in the absence of the king who, after two futile
attempts at a restoration in 1921, was never to return. A fervent
nationalist and intransigent revisionist, Horthy was a leader who
truly reflected the frustrations and ambitions of counterrevolutionary Hungary. However, his direct role in the formulation of
foreign policy was usually limited. This task he preferred to entrust
to his prime ministers and foreign ministers, and for the period in
question three men played the dominant role: István Bethlen,
Gyula Gömbös, and Kálmán Kánya. The development of Hungary's foreign policy up to 1936 is thus most conveniently seen in
terms of the personalities, ideas, and programs of these four
leaders.

The career of Miklós Horthy is one of the most remarkable in
recent East European history.[7] Born of a Calvinist gentry family
in Central Hungary one year after the *Ausgleich* of 1867, Horthy
chose to pursue what for a Magyar youth was an unlikely career:
that of an officer in the Austro-Hungarian navy. His training in
Vienna and at the naval academy in Fiume seems to have been
quite narrow in scope, infusing him primarily with an excellent
knack for naval tactics, a fluent knowledge of German and sundry
other languages (to the detriment of his Hungarian, which many
years after assuming the regency he had still not completely mas-
tered), and a Mahanist conviction that the greatness of nations

was directly related to the naval power they possessed. As an officer in the Habsburg navy Horthy progressed steadily in the ranks, gaining distinction for his general competence, dutifulness, and personal charm. During the war he fought bravely in adverse conditions, and near the end he had the good fortune to be appointed commander-in-chief of the fleet by the new Austrian emperor and king of Hungary, Karl.

Horthy had had the opportunity first hand to observe political life in *fin de siècle* Vienna and Budapest, but he had never been particularly moved by political ambition. Yet when the world he knew and loved was collapsing around him in 1918 and 1919, he responded to a call from some military colleagues and left his country estate to assume command of the newly organized National Army, and, in early 1920, to serve as regent. Few Hungarians at the time could have imagined that the "temporary" office of regent would be occupied by the admiral for some two and one-half decades. Indeed, this is one of the great mysteries of interwar Hungarian history: how Horthy, a man of modest intellectual resources, limited political vision, and notoriously poor oratorical skills[8] could have attained such high political office and retained it so long without a serious challenge from any quarter.

It is true that Horthy possessed attractive personal qualities that endeared him to virtually everyone he met: unpretentiousness, affability, courage, incorruptibility. In many ways he was a paragon of the "gentleman" that upperclass Hungarian—indeed European —society had always extolled. Though lacking an incisive intellect, he nonetheless possessed a certain native shrewdness that, if infrequently evident, would sometimes come to the fore in the most unexpected circumstances. In addition, Horthy brought from his years of naval service valuable experience in organization and dealing with subordinates. His ability to win over others through charm and personal example served him in good stead in the political arena. Above all, of course, there was his popularity as Hungary's only important war hero. But these not inconsiderable qualities are rarely enough to ensure such lasting political success, and in Horthy's case they were balanced by other less positive traits. He possessed a remarkable political naiveté; internal power struggles and clashes in the diplomatic arena appeared to him in purely black and white terms. An indiscrete manner and garrulousness made him largely unsuited to the system of personal diplomacy. Moreover,

Horthy had neither the inclination nor keenness of mind to learn much through study or experience. Many of the crude political and social notions to which he subscribed in 1920 continued to be his constant guiding principles up to 1945 and beyond.

Yet with all his personal shortcomings, Horthy did meet several vital requirements of counterrevolutionary Hungary. In the first place, the nature of the office turned out to be such that it was not necessary for the regent to be exceptionally brilliant or politically sophisticated. The day-to-day political tasks fell to the prime minister and his cabinet, leaving the regent, like the Habsburg kings, to devote much of his time to ceremony and protocol. Far more important as qualifications for this post were a political philosophy compatible with the nationalistic goals of postwar Hungary and rapport with the two rightist camps. Horthy was the only individual of stature in Hungary who fit these requirements.

Miklós Horthy occupied a unique position in the swirl of political currents that comprised counterrevolutionary Hungary. In his political sympathies one sees displayed a kind of schizophrenia, in that he felt a strong attraction to both the Szeged group and the conservatives. Consequently, both sides labored to win him over, and he became at once the focal point of rivalry and the "link and the compromise"[9] between them. The year spent in close contact with the radicals in the National Army had won for him impeccable credentials among proponents of the "Szeged idea," and he seems to have been the guiding spirit behind most of the clandestine, militarist schemes that emanated from the general staff of Gömbös and the paramilitary chiefs in 1919 and 1920.

Yet, when Horthy's career is viewed as a whole, this "Szeged phase" represents something of an aberration. By social standing and family ties, Horthy really stood closer to the conservative camp. On domestic issues he firmly shared their disdain for ambitious social and land reform and their acceptance of capitalist big business as the necessary framework for a sound economy. Once the turbulence of the immediate postwar period had subsided, and Horthy's personal contacts with his Szeged friends became less direct and more infrequent, the tug of more traditional forces exerted a greater influence on him. The admiral was notorious for his malleability: Hungarian policymakers quickly realized that his point of view on many questions reflected that of the last person who had explained the matter to him. Count Bethlen, prime minister in the 1920s, cleverly exploited the regent's weakness to guide him along conservative lines; in time Bethlen supplanted Gömbös as the power behind the throne.[10]

Horthy's reconversion to conservative politics was not complete, for even after 1921 there remained within him an atavistic impulse that was never fully eradicated. Horthy openly admitted, even to foreign diplomats, that there was a little of the "Awakening Magyar" (one of the radical rightist organizations) in him as in all Hungarians.[11] Through most of his twenty-four years in office one can see struggling within him the caution of the conservative *grand seigneur* and the impulsiveness of the Szeged veteran. The regent valued the friendships he had formed in the National Army: to have shared the camaraderie and exhilaration of the Szeged days was to have slept on Mount Parnassus. Thus, in the period between the wars the door to the regent's office was open to former colleagues, to whom Horthy would always lend a sympathetic ear. It became known in right radical circles, particularly in the General Staff of the 1930s, that talk of rapid territorial revision or grandiose anti-Bolshevik crusades would fire Horthy's imagination and tempt him to bypass his more cautious advisors and ministers, as he had done on occasion in 1919 and 1920. Moreover, the regent took quite seriously his constitutional responsibilities as "Supreme War Lord" of the armed forces, which included a general authority over all military questions. Ambitious army officers from time to time attempted to capitalize on this by presenting to Horthy, rather than to the civilian leadership, assorted plans for secret rearmament or sinister military plots against Hungary's neighbors. In the 1936–39 period this friction between two contending camps and Horthy's ambivalent attitudes combined to create a deep tension in the Hungarian government that had its inevitable impact on foreign policy.

Theoretically, Horthy as regent was the final arbiter of all matters affecting Hungarian foreign policy, since he could dismiss any prime minister whose program did not meet his approval. In practice, though he was naturally consulted on all major questions, Horthy did not often interfere with the everyday conduct of foreign policy. Only on rare occasions did he veto a policy supported by both the prime minister and foreign minister. In general, Horthy made no great effort to study the intricacies of diplomatic relations in twentieth-century Europe. He had learned early in life certain "truths" about Danubian and European affairs and these opinions were virtually unaltered by the passage of time. Foreign visitors noticed this, and more than one went away agreeing with Ciano, the Italian foreign minister, that while Horthy seemed to have much influence in internal matters, he was "little informed" about foreign affairs.[12]

The Hungarian Foreign Ministry was aware of Horthy's limitations, and they strove to curtail the number of occasions when he was required to conduct personal diplomacy. No one was allowed an audience without prior consent of the Foreign Ministry. Correspondents were required to submit the copy of any interview so that any sensational utterances could be judiciously deleted.[13] The problem was a simple one: Horthy's almost pathetic sincerity and buoyant nationalism combined with his loquaciousness to produce unfortunate indiscretions. After working himself up in a customary cataloguing of Hungary's woes under the Treaty of Trianon, he was likely, in a further attempt to buttress his case, to give an overly frank exposition of Hungary's irredentist plans and activities or to outline one of his remarkable schemes for solving Europe's problems.

Still, it was inevitable that Horthy, as Hungary's head of state, would meet foreign dignitaries when they visited Budapest or when he travelled abroad. Indeed, Horthy's visits to Germany and conversations with Hitler provide the most dramatic moments in this narrative. The regent's naive bluntness was a useful, if perhaps unconscious, weapon in negotiations with Hitler, who was unaccustomed to being challenged verbally by the statesmen of lesser powers.

Though Horthy was poorly equipped to conduct day-to-day diplomatic affairs and tended not to interfere in the deliberations of Hungarian foreign policy makers, very early in his regency he seized on two fundamental tenets that served as a guideline for him and set the limits within which his foreign ministers were to operate. This rudimentary foreign policy program, which mirrored the views of most politically-minded Hungarians and in its essence remained unchanged during Horthy's twenty-four-year tenure, was predicated on a fanatical devotion to anti-Bolshevism and treaty revisionism. Miklós Horthy was one of Europe's earliest and most persistent opponents of the Soviet Union and world Communism. His fiery hatred for the Bolsheviks, forged at the time of the Béla Kun regime, gave rise to a compulsion to organize a crusade to destroy Soviet Russia. Already in 1920 and 1921 he had participated in the clandestine plans of certain right-wing German groups, led by General Ludendorff, to promote counterrevolutionary regimes in Central Europe and the formation of a "White International" to combat Bolshevism wherever it appeared. The ultimate goal was to have been the toppling of the Communist regime in Russia.[14] These specific plans proved stillborn, but the seed was planted and Horthy carefully nurtured it, with the hope that he could bring it to flower at some more propitious time.

Not surprisingly, Regent Horthy saw no useful purpose in establishing normal diplomatic relations with Soviet Russia. In the mid-1920s, when Count Bethlen and the more pragmatic leaders of Hungary's Foreign Ministry negotiated a political and economic pact with Moscow similar to the Rapallo Treaty, Horthy at the last moment vetoed the agreement. Moved by a combination of a deep ideological commitment and a sense of duty, he declared that he could not imagine any kind of agreement between Moscow and Budapest that would meet his approval.[15]

The second major element in Horthy's foreign policy involved a nemesis that, like Bolshevik Russia, haunted him throughout the interwar period: the Treaty of Trianon. Like virtually all his contemporaries in Hungary, Horthy regarded the peace settlement imposed by the Allies as utterly foolish and unjust. Upon election to the regency, he took upon himself the moral duty of working unstintingly for treaty revision and restoration of the historic kingdom of Hungary. He was fully convinced that the Magyars, being the only "state building" people in the Danubian region, were an indispensable advance guard for Christian Europe. Such groups as the Czechs ("disguised Bolsheviks") or the Romanians ("corrupt bribetakers") lacked the will, discipline, and fighting spirit to stem the recurring invasions of Europe from the East. The creation of Trianon Hungary was thus not merely an injustice but a perverse crime against Western Civilization. How could Hungary play her traditional role as defender of the West, he asked of French and British visitors, if she did not possess her natural borders on the Carpathians and an outlet to the sea?[16]

When it came to the problem of translating his twin goals of destroying Bolshevism and redrawing the frontiers of Danubian Europe into a concrete policy, Horthy realized that his country would need powerful allies. Among the great powers two seemed most suitable: Great Britain and Germany. Horthy had long admired and respected England, which he had had an opportunity to visit as a Habsburg naval officer. He later cherished the image of Great Britain as a land tied to traditional ways and dedicated to justice in international affairs, one, in other words, that would feel sympathy for Hungary's plight. Equally important in Admiral Horthy's thinking was the powerful British fleet. In his naval training Horthy had been steeped in the teachings of Alfred Mahan, and he firmly believed that sea power was the key factor in determining national power. When Britain emerged victorious from World War I, the validity of this concept was seemingly confirmed. Clearly the British would be an essential ally should war again erupt in Europe. Moreover, it struck Horthy that both England and Hungary were essentially conservative states whose common interest in combatting Bolshevism would inevitably draw them together in a coordinated approach to European affairs. Horthy's greatest hope, as the crisis of the late 1930s approached, was that Britain would be drawn into continental affairs and be persuaded to lead a campaign of peaceful revision of the peace treaties and an anti-Bolshevik crusade.

Because of its proximity to Danubian Europe, Germany, the second great power prominent in Regent Horthy's calculations, seemed more likely than England to take an active interest in the fate of the peace settlement in that area. As a naval officer Horthy's direct experiences with Germans before and during the War had not been extensive, and the general opinion he seems to have formed was that many Germans were overbearing and arrogant. Nonetheless, in his communications with Germans in the postwar period he often professed to believe in the existence of a unique German-Hungarian community of fate. This almost mystical bond had been forged by the common shedding of blood by their valiant soldiers in World War I, fighting shoulder to shoulder on the battlefields of Central Europe, and sealed by the scandalous peace treaties imposed on the two countries.[17] Horthy felt a special affinity for the nationalist right wing in Germany, particularly for the military officers prominent in its leadership. At different times in the 1920s he established contacts with Generals Ludendorff and Seeckt and attempted to coordinate a joint revisionist policy aimed above all at Czechoslovakia. Their contempt for the Weimar government was fully shared by the regent, who looked forward to the eventual emergence of an authoritarian right-wing regime, a more compatible partner for Hungary. The resurgence of such a Germany, Horthy declared in 1925, would signify a "better and more beautiful future" for Hungary as well.[18]

The coming to power in 1933 of a National Socialist regime set the stage for a more intimate German-Hungarian relationship. Horthy had certain misgivings about Hitler, whose social origins, vulgarity, and theatrical ways were hardly the marks of a true gentleman, but the Führer's pronounced anti-Communism and the dynamic domestic programs he initiated quickly won the regent's admiration. Moreover, all reports from Hungarians who visited Berlin suggested that for Hitler, as for Horthy and his colleagues, the Czechoslovak state represented a "*Saisonstaat*" (a seasonal or ephemeral state) whose eventual demise would have to be hastened.[19] There was thus the distinct possibility that the support of a powerful Germany dominated by the National Socialist Party might be enlisted to help reverse some or all of the territorial provisions of the Trianon Treaty, a prospect that greatly excited the regent's interest.

It must be noted that at no point in the interwar period did Miklós Horthy ever seriously consider the possibility of solving Hungary's problems through a genuine rapprochement with one or more of her Danubian neighbors. True, from time to time he sensed the tactical advantage of seeking a pact or at least the appearance of friendly relations with one of the Little Entente countries. For example, in the mid-1920s he was persuaded by Bethlen to help set the stage for an amicable settlement of differences with Yugoslavia. Yet, try as he might, Horthy could never completely overcome his ingrained prejudices and chauvinistic assumptions. Though he sincerely liked the Croatians ("fine sailors") and respected the Serbs for their fighting skills, he remained convinced that the two South Slav groups would never be able to live together and that their state was "a purely geographical concept." For the Czechs he had no sympathy: the state that Masaryk and Beneš had fashioned was a "cancerous tumor" that would have to be exterminated.[20] Horthy sensed that major territorial changes in the Danubian area could not easily be effected without war. Yet he also recognized that a "lost war would wipe Hungary off the map."[21] With this in mind, he hoped in the mid-1930s to devise some plan that would provide for a peaceful program of treaty revision under the auspices of those great powers who, in Horthy's estimation, were fundamentally sympathetic to Hungary, namely Germany, England, and Italy. At the same time, there lurked within him the atavistic impulse to employ the kind of drastic, belligerent solutions with which he had toyed in his Szeged days. The events of the approaching European crisis after 1936 were to compel Horthy to choose between these conflicting emotions and to assume a more direct role in the formulation of policy. The manner in which the regent responded profoundly shaped the role Hungary was to play in the unfolding Danubian crisis.

If Horthy was more a product than a molder of counterrevolutionary Hungary, Count István Bethlen was its true creator.[22] A member of one of the great aristocratic families of Transylvania, Bethlen was appointed prime minister by Horthy in April 1921. This post he held for over a decade, more than sufficient time to mold Hungary's destiny along the conservative, undemocratic lines of his political philosophy.

The long-term program envisioned by Bethlen was bold in conception: the establishment of a great and powerful Hungary, with the Magyars once again in their rightful place as the dominant nation in the Danubian Basin. Here he was at one with virtually all politically active Hungarians. But Bethlen, in contrast to the impulsive Horthy and the Szeged radicals, saw the true implications of Hungary's defeat in war. Surrounded by the hostile Little Entente, confronted by a powerful alignment of great powers supporting the status quo, and enormously weakened militarily and economically by the war and revolutions, Hungary, in Bethlen's view, was totally incapable of conducting an active, dynamic foreign policy. This was the blunt message to his countrymen in his maiden speech to the National Assembly in 1921.[23]

Bethlen's scheme for Hungarian recovery involved a patient, long-term effort by a united nation, and it was based on the conviction that the "prerequisite of a correct foreign policy is a correct domestic policy."[24] Unity—this was the concept he extolled above all in the first years of office, and it was the keystone in what he considered a "correct domestic policy." It implied, above all, a drawing together of all the energies of the nation and the rejection of extremist, disruptive movements of any kind, whether emanating from the left or the right. To achieve this Bethlen fashioned a political system of remarkable inconsistency: true liberal practices were tolerated as well as occasional terror and political oppression.[25] Although the political process precluded all but the "government party" from forming a majority, and the authorities were not averse to the sporadic use of telephone surveillance and electoral intimidation, there nonetheless lingered the legacy of a kind of Whig-Liberalism that allowed for the maintenance of a parliamentary system embracing parties of the left as well as the right. With the vital stipulation that the fundamental tenets of the counterrevolutionary regime were not to be called into question, a relatively open expression of political ideas and thought was permitted in the press and literature.[26]

Once order and authority could be reestablished at home, Count Bethlen was prepared to forge a foreign policy predicated on the realities of Hungary's exposed position. The goal, restoration of a large and powerful Hungary, remained constant, but the tactics were made to correspond to the extent of Hungary's recovery and changes in the European balance of power. But as early as 1921 he made it clear that only one approach was conceivable for Hungary: she had to cling tenaciously, if at first unobtrusively, to her demands until a more suitable European diplomatic constellation arose. Underlying this perseverance was the familiar belief, deeply embedded in the thinking of Hungarian statesmen, that the Magyars were predestined by geography to play the leading role in the Danubian region.[27]

This assumption naturally led Bethlen to deduce that conditions in East Central Europe were artificial and transitory. All the new countries, not only Czechoslovakia and Yugoslavia, but truncated Hungary and Austria as well, were incapable of prolonged life. Thus, Bethlen argued, it was senseless to seek a basic rapprochement with Hungary's new neighbors. They would use all the resources at their disposal to defend their new gains, and even in the unlikely event that minor revisions were offered by one or another of the Successor States, this would have to be refused, since it would make it all the more difficult for Hungary to achieve more extensive gains in the future.[28] Accordingly, Bethlen rejected all schemes for a wider collaboration, such as a Danubian Confederation, which, he averred, would merely lead to Hungarian submission to Slav domination.[29]

Yet at the outset Bethlen saw no alternative to a "policy of fulfillment" of the Treaty of Trianon. Hungary simply could not achieve the desired financial stabilization and economic recovery without the support of West Europe and resumption of normal trade with the Successor States. To lure badly needed capital investment into the country, Hungary had to demonstrate to the satisfaction of Western bankers and statesmen her acceptance of the peace settlement. Disruptions, such as anti-Semitic excesses or armed band activity in Burgenland, could no longer be condoned. Blatant violations of the military clauses of Trianon had to be avoided, and Hungary would have to promote her political rehabilitation by gaining admission to the League of Nations. An assiduous effort along these lines by Bethlen produced fairly rapid results. In September 1922, Hungary won admission to the League, after having been rejected in its first bid a year earlier. In early 1924 the support of Great Britain enabled Hungary to secure a badly needed loan and a moratorium on reparation payments.[30]

Bethlen's strategy proved highly effective. Hungary's currency was soon stabilized, Western capital began to flow in quite vigorously, and, buoyed by high world wheat prices, the economy by 1928 was flourishing.[31] Even Hungary's radical right-wingers, who had opposed Bethlen's "policy of fulfillment" as a "sell-out" of Hungarian interests, were silenced by the speedy recovery.

Bethlen's successes were widely admired in Great Britain as well, even though most Britons, if we are to believe a popular jingle of the 1920s, preferred to

> let the hairy Magyar
>   Stew in his horrid juice.[32]

Sentiment in the Foreign Office was quite favorable to Bethlen, who came to enjoy a reputation as "a straightforward, honest, intensely patriotic man . . . with whom it's easy to do business."[33] A measure of his acceptance by the British political establishment was the granting of an audience with the king in 1930, thus making him the first leader of a defeated Central Power to be so honored. Bethlen carefully nurtured this image of a responsible and moderate statesman by frequently affirming his respect and admiration for England[34] and by giving public and private assurances that, though he regarded eventual revision of the Treaty of Trianon as essential, he would employ only peaceful methods to achieve this goal.

The assiduous efforts of Count Bethlen to ingratiate himself with the English political and financial establishment might lead one to conclude that he believed that among the great powers Britain was the most likely and important champion of Hungary's revisionist cause. Yet the evidence would not sustain such a conclusion. It is true that Bethlen, like so many of his contemporaries of similar social and political background in Hungary, was an Anglophile and naturally would have been delighted to accept a British offer of help in redrawing the borders of Danubian Europe. Yet he was a realist who harbored no illusions about the possibility for direct British support for Hungarian revisionism. It was quite clear to him that the pro-Hungarian utterances of such mavericks as David Lloyd George and Lord Rothermere and a small but vigorous contingent in the House of Lords did not count for much in the arena of European international relations. Far more significant was the fact that the British government, wedded as it was to the status quo and the concept of collective security, could not in the foreseeable future openly champion, or even acknowledge the validity of, Hungary's territorial claims. At no point in the 1920s did London ever express even limited approval of Hungary's efforts to undo the Trianon treaty. Lord Curzon, British Foreign Secretary in the immediate postwar period, had enunciated in 1920 a principle that remained at the core of Britain's Danubian policy for most of the interwar period. Hungary's hope for prosperity, he had asserted, could be based only on the "abandonment of such dreams as Hungarian political parties seem freely to indulge in of recovering the position that Hungary formerly held in Central Europe."[35]

That Count Bethlen continued to court the British government in spite of the bleak prospects for any concrete dividends reflected not only his recognition of the key role that Western capital had to play in Hungary's economic recovery, but a political pragmatism that formed part of his Transylvanian heritage. A review of Transylvania's rather successful diplomatic balancing act between the Turks and Habsburgs in the sixteenth and seventeenth centuries may well have suggested to Bethlen that a skillful, realistic foreign policy that left open a multitude of options could bring remarkable rewards for a small and essentially weak East European state. It was this tradition that seems to have enlightened Bethlen's policy toward France and the Anglo-Saxon powers in the 1920s. Though to many Magyars it seemed unlikely, some day in the future, in a diplomatic context that statesmen in the 1920s could hardly envision, one or more of these more remote powers might be persuaded to champion Hungary's revisionist cause, or at least give tacit approval to territorial changes in Danubian Europe. Thus, Bethlen apparently reasoned, nothing should be done unduly or capriciously to alienate the British or French; no opportunity be neglected to erode, however imperceptibly, the commitment to the status quo; no compunction be felt about offering assurances of Hungary's pacific intentions, even though secretly the use of force was far from ruled out. It was commensurate with this thinking that Bethlen's foreign policy retained sufficient flexibility so that there always remained a possibility of a rapprochement even with France, the main buttress of the peace settlement and the patron of the Little Entente.

In the mid-1920s, however, when the Allied military control in Hungary was reduced and the opportunity for Hungary to pursue an "active policy" seemed to be unfolding, Bethlen's search for allies among the great powers led him not to Paris or London, but to Rome and Berlin. The first tasks on the agenda, so Bethlen wrote to Horthy in 1926, were an escape from the diplomatic isolation that had been imposed on Hungary and the splitting of the Little Entente. This would be the prelude to a liquidation of Trianon, a task that, in Bethlen's optimistic estimate, could possibly be achieved "in about four or five years."[36]

Given the assumptions and objectives of Count Bethlen's "active" policy of the late 1920s and the realities of European international relations, it was only logical that he should solicit support from those countries and political groups that were dissatisfied with the Paris peace settlement and might be willing to contribute to its disruption. Like the pragmatists in the German Foreign Ministry, Bethlen's initial thought was to pave the way for Hungary's emergence from isolation by a pact with the pariah of Europe, Soviet Russia. But the stubborn anti-Bolshevism of the regent stymied all efforts in this direction and the less spectacular aim of undermining the Little Entente by wooing away Yugoslavia was undertaken. With Horthy's approval, negotiations began in 1925 and continued through the next year. The unexpected result was a pact concluded in 1927, but with Italy, not Yugoslavia. Hungary's interest in a rapprochement with her southern neighbor had drawn the attention of Mussolini, who at the time was seeking to counter France's position of strength in East Europe by staking out an Italian sphere of influence in the Balkans and along the Danube. The Treaty of Friendship and Cooperation thus admirably served the interests of both parties: Italy gained an East European ally around which an anti-French bloc might be built; Hungary, for her part, succeeded in demonstrating that, though weak and reduced to the status of a pawn, she could still play a role on the diplomatic chessboard. The treaty of 1927, the only agreement Hungary was to make with a great power until her adherence to the Anti-Comintern Pact in 1939, opened an era of intimate state relations with Italy that was to extend to the final years of the next European war.

The treaty with Italy was the major diplomatic triumph of Bethlen's career. It won for Hungary the important, if somewhat boisterous, support of Mussolini for the revisionist campaign. A dutiful patron, the Duce did not fail to make ebullient references to Hungary's cause in his speeches and occasional pronouncements. In concrete terms, the forging of close Hungarian-Italian ties greatly increased Budapest's room for maneuver in such matters as military rearmament and efforts to disrupt the Little Entente. However, there is much evidence to support the argument that though Bethlen valued the support of Italy, he doubted that the treaty of 1927 could alone serve as an adequate framework for a successful Hungarian revisionist policy. Perhaps, like Horthy, he could not completely overcome a fundamental distrust of Italy as an ally, a distrust stemming from what many Hungarians regarded as Italy's perfidious conduct during the World War. More likely, Bethlen simply shared the skepticism of some other prescient European statesmen about Italy's ability in the long run to sustain the role of a great power in Europe.

In any case, Count Bethlen made it clear privately, though never publicly, that the natural and necessary complement to Hungary's treaty with Italy was a similar relationship with Germany.[37] Both Central European powers were desirable allies for Hungary, he argued, since each, albeit for different reasons, was disenchanted with the status quo and inclined in the long run to favor certain revisions in the peace treaties. In fact, it seems most likely that of the two possible partners, Germany loomed as the more important in Bethlen's calculations. As early as 1921 he had justified his temporary "policy of fulfillment" of the peace treaty by explaining that only a rejuvenated Germany could provide the "favorable European constellation" for a successful revision of the Trianon treaty.[38] Once Italy had been won over to the support of Hungary, there thus remained the pressing task of enlisting Germany's assistance as well.

In 1926 Count Bethlen told a confidant that "the axis of my policy is mediation between Italy and Germany."[39] Accordingly, after conclusion of the treaty with Italy the Hungarian leader worked assiduously, though in vain, to facilitate an Italian-German rapprochement that would set the stage for a German-Italian-Hungarian alignment. Though on several occasions in the 1920s Count Bethlen emphasized to German diplomats his belief in a "community of fate" between their two countries and the need for collaboration in a revisionist program,[40] a close political relationship between Berlin and Budapest also proved elusive. The leadership of the Weimar government seemed uninterested in forging close political ties with a country that, after all, carried little weight in European affairs.

Yet Bethlen was not daunted; indeed, it seems that when he spoke of a community of interest between Magyars and Germans, Bethlen was referring not so much to those Germans who had created the Weimar Republic and remained fervently committed to it, but to those individuals, particularly of the National Right, who in spirit were hostile to the political and social reforms enacted in Germany after the Great War. It is characteristic that the German with whom Bethlen maintained the most cordial relations and discussed his most secret plans was not Gustav Stresemann but General Hans Seeckt, Chief of the Army Command until 1926. Moreover, several German political groups antagonistic to the Weimar experiment, most notably the Stahlhelm, were the beneficiaries of fairly substantial subsidies from Budapest during the Bethlen era.[41]

It is from the records of Bethlen's candid conversations with General Seeckt and Mussolini that the outlines of his ambitious long term revisionist program may be discerned. This evidence suggests that he believed that once the proper diplomatic constellation was formed in Central Europe (the nucleus of which would be Germany, Italy, Austria, and Hungary, with Bulgaria, Turkey, or Poland playing supporting roles), an opportunity would arise for the dissolution of the Little Entente and significant territorial changes in Hungary's favor, though not necessarily a complete restoration of the Kingdom of St. Stephen as it existed before the War.

Though Count Bethlen dreamed of regaining for Hungary certain territories in each of the Little Entente countries, the necessity of a confrontation with Czechoslovakia seemed to dominate his thoughts from the start. As he graphically explained to Mussolini in 1927, "so long as the Czechoslovak frontier is thirty kilometers from Budapest, Hungary is not capable of action."[42] Having received the Duce's encouragement and promise of Italian arms to prepare for a possible military conflict in Central Europe, Bethlen proceeded to consult with General Seeckt about the logistical and organizational problems that the Hungarian army would face. Bethlen spoke bluntly, though it seems more in a theoretical than practical sense, of Hungary's firm resolve to attack Czechoslovakia and, if possible, destroy it. The goal, he explained, was the reannexation of Slovakia, where Czech rule had not taken strong roots.[43]

Bethlen's overall program for territorial expansion and the reestablishment of Magyar hegemony in Danubian Europe seems to have been aimed at the eventual recovery of the Bánát, Slovakia, Ruthenia, and a strip of territory in Western Romania, all territories containing large, though not preponderant, Magyar populations. Croatia and Transylvania would, in effect, become Hungarian protectorates.[44] However, aside from his apparently hypothetical remark to Seeckt that Hungary was intent on attacking Czechoslovakia, there are few clues to indicate what means Bethlen proposed to employ to achieve these goals. It has been suggested that Bethlen's "active policy" after 1927 was synonymous with an "aggressive policy."[45] Yet there is no firm evidence, in the form of specific military plans or the like, to sustain this judgment. The only concrete steps undertaken during the Bethlen era, aside from a modest attempt at surreptitious rearming, involved clandestine financial and political support for separatists in Slovakia and Croatia, in the hope that civil order would be disrupted and Hungary could take advantage of the subsequent turmoil.[46] This, of course, represented blatant interference in the domestic affairs of other countries and greatly contributed to the poisoning of the political atmosphere in the Danubian world. Still, it is worth noting that, though future disruptions of the status quo were intrinsic to the foreign policy plans of Bethlen and his colleagues, Hungary concluded no pacts of an aggressive nature in this period.

In any case, sufficient time was not available to Bethlen to act on his ambitious goals. Unable to cope with the growing economic crisis, he was compelled to withdraw from office in 1931. The legacy of the Bethlen era in Hungarian foreign policy was thus an ambiguous one. On the one hand, his rejection of a moderate revisionist policy,[47] his willingness to contemplate the use of offensive military force, and his emphasis on the need for Hungarian cooperation with a fascist Italy and a rightist Germany seemed to set the foundation for an alignment on the side of the Axis powers before and during World War II. On the other hand, Count Bethlen had imparted to Hungarian policy a strain of the pragmatism that permeated his political thinking and strategy. In 1931 Hungary seemed still to have many options open to it; in certain conditions an alignment even with the West European powers was not precluded.

However, this greater flexibility in Hungarian foreign policy in the early 1930s was not to last, for late in 1932 the regent empowered Gyula Gömbös, his comrade from the Szeged period, to form a new government. In background and personality Gömbös was quite a different man from Horthy and Bethlen.[48] He had been born in 1886 into a Swabian (that is, German-Hungarian) family of modest means, and chose a career not atypical to one from such a background: military service in the imperial army. But unlike the Magyar aristocrats who as Habsburg officers were usually imbued with a staunch loyalty for the Habsburg monarchy, Gömbös decided even before the war that Hungary needed a completely independent national army.[49] After having served as a general staff officer in Vienna during World War I, he returned to Hungary in 1918, full of resentment against those whom he regarded as responsible for the military collapse in the autumn of that year. Like Hitler and many Germans, Gömbös refused to accept the reality of his country's defeat and sought instead to place the blame on incompetent statesmen and assorted traitors from within, particularly Jews.[50]

Gömbös for a brief period supported the Károlyi government, even serving as military attaché in the new South Slav State. By the beginning of 1919, however, he became disgusted with Károlyi's pacifism and the increase of Communist agitation in Hungary. Joining the newly formed Hungarian Association of National Defense (known as MOVE), he launched a violent attack on Károlyi, and, as a result of the public attention gained thereby, was elected president of the organization in January. The MOVE was quickly disbanded by the government, and Gömbös moved to Szeged, via Vienna, to contribute to the burgeoning counterrevolutionary movement.

Though many Hungarians in the "Christian national" camp recognized Gömbös's leadership skills, not everyone approved the novel political tactics and methods he espoused. Gömbös reveled in an atmosphere of intrigue and conspiracy: coup d'états, guerrilla actions, and grandiose military campaigns stirred his imagination. Moreover, he seemed to have a knack for establishing contact with right-wing adventurers and secret agents from all over Central and Eastern Europe. Often he would justify his proposals or actions by referring to information he had received from "confidential sources" that he was not always at liberty to identify.[51] This conspiratorial flamboyance, combined with a tendency toward arrogance, an almost mystical nationalism, and a commitment to a very radical brand of right-wing politics, caused uneasiness among Hungary's conservative establishment. He was accepted, but only with a certain reluctance, and it was probably only Miklós Horthy's rapid rise to prominence that enabled Gömbös, his protegé, to play a role in national politics that traditionally was beyond the reach of an army captain.

After the signing of the peace treaty and Bethlen's selection as prime minister, Gömbös's influence began to wane. His penchant for conspiratorial activity and his eagerness to employ force against domestic and foreign enemies were increasingly out of harmony with the orientation of the government. The inevitable break with Bethlen came in the summer of 1923, Gömbös withdrawing from the "Party of Unity" to form his own "Party of Racial Defense." For the next five years he remained active in political affairs as a member of Parliament and the titular head of MOVE and the remnants of the Szeged movement. And in general he advanced his political views in numerous articles contributed on a regular basis to several newspapers, particularly *Szózat*.

In time, however, the role of the leader of a small oppositional party proved too confining to a man who enjoyed being at or near the center of power. In 1927, at the instigation of Horthy, Gömbös was welcomed back into the government party and in 1928 was appointed minister of defense. The assumption was that he would find the "active policy" that Bethlen had initiated in 1927 more congenial, and that he would temper the radicalism of his policies and methods. This new position admirably served Gömbös's political ambitions, for it enabled him to reassert his influence in military circles and to insinuate himself into a variety of enterprises in related fields, such as rearmament and the revisionist movement. In all, the experience gained and friends won by Gömbös as he moved about in the highest political circles made it easier for him to aspire to the prime ministry after Bethlen succumbed to the economic crisis in 1931.

Over the course of the 1920s, Gyula Gömbös had formulated a set of foreign policy ideas that was to serve as the framework for the program he would pursue in later years. Needless to say, all of his speculations about the future of Hungary were based on the premise that the Magyars were destined to resume their leading role in the Danubian area.[52] In certain ways the program Gömbös outlined resembled Bethlen's, but in both methods and strategy Gömbös was much less pragmatic and flexible. Whereas Bethlen sought support from any great power that showed an interest in Hungary's recovery and well-being, Gömbös tended to focus on only those countries that had strongly rightist governments, or the potential for such an orientation. Thus, he was skeptical of the value of relying on the democratic Western powers for assistance in Hungary's reconstruction. From the start Gömbös argued that Britain and France would and should have no say in the settlement of vital territorial issues in Central Europe. He felt a particular bitterness toward France, which, he claimed, "always kicked Hungary around like a ball."[53] Nor was he moved, as so many of his countrymen were, by the sentimental notion that England and Hungary had a community of interests and that England, the champion of justice, would eventually support Hungary in her revisionist wishes.

In Gömbös's view, Germany and Italy would be the ultimate arbiters of Europe. In a remarkable parliamentary speech in 1922, before Mussolini's march on Rome, he predicted that "the axis of European policy will lead from Rome to Berlin."[54] Later in the decade Gömbös suggested that this "axis" would form the core of a powerful political bloc with which Hungary would link up. This powerful grouping of ideologically compatible states would then be in a position to "change the map of Europe."[55]

In 1932 Regent Horthy, searching for a way out of the economic crisis, chose to entrust the reins of government to Gömbös, his old Szeged comrade. Gömbös was to direct Hungary's affairs until his death in 1936, and these four years were sufficient time to undertake bold initiatives in foreign and domestic policy that Hungarian conservatives were to find highly unpalatable. In foreign affairs, however, the impatient Gömbös found that the pieces did not fall into place as neatly as his rather utopian foreign policy blueprint had posited. Germany in 1932 was in disarray and was pursuing an economic policy inimical to Hungarian agrarian interests. Mussolini, on the other hand, was quite willing to continue and expand the close ties with Hungary that Bethlen had forged. Mussolini, like Gömbös, aimed to weaken and disrupt the French system of alliances in Eastern Europe, but the Duce showed no inclination to collaborate with Germany in this project. Indeed, he professed to fear German expansionism to the south and southeast into areas he regarded as within the Italian sphere of influence. For this reason Mussolini strongly opposed the Anschluss and was intent on preserving Austria as an independent state tied closely to Italy. In the circumstances, Gömbös concluded that his primary task would be the cementing of Hungary's relations with Italy; the creation of a grand revisionist bloc would come later, when conditions were more propitious. In talks with Mussolini in late 1934, Gömbös did sketch his plan for a bloc based on a Rome-Berlin axis, but, deferring to the Duce's strong feelings on the subject, he now suggested that Austria could join the projected grouping as a "connecting state" between Hungary, Germany, and Italy.[56]

Events in Germany in the first month of 1933 dramatically transformed the situation in Central Europe and greatly excited Gömbös's interest. A National Socialist Germany headed by Adolf Hitler—here was the proper partner for the Rome-Berlin axis.

Gömbös lost little time in establishing contact with the new German leader and sketching the outlines of his grand diplomatic project. In a letter of 6 February and two others over the course of the next year, Gömbös, suggesting that he and Hitler were "old racial-nationalist comrades holding the same *Weltanschauung*," urged the new German chancellor to consider restoring the "old Bismarckian concept" in Hungarian-German relations. A strong Hungary, "firmly anchored upon its historic territory in the Carpathian Basin," would serve the vital interests of the Reich, since only a powerful Hungary could "successfully keep down the unjust aspirations of the peoples hostile to us." In general, then, Gömbös was asking Hitler to lend his support to Hungary's campaign for territorial revision; more specifically, he hoped the Führer would work for improved economic relations and closer contact and cooperation between German and Magyar minorities in the Successor States.[57]

To demonstrate his eagerness to win Hitler's favor, Gömbös seized an opportunity in June 1933 and journeyed to Germany for a one-day unofficial visit, thus becoming the first foreign statesman so to honor the Führer. The planning for the trip was carried out in an almost furtive manner: officials of the National Socialist Party handled the arrangements and few people in Hungary, not even Kálmán Kánya, the foreign minister, were informed beforehand of the prime minister's intentions. Hitler and General Gömbös (he had recently promoted himself) seemed to have established an immediate rapport, the German leader openly and candidly explaining his views on a whole range of European questions.[58] On the key question of treaty revision, Hitler made it clear that military force would have to be employed, since France would otherwise not permit the frontiers of Central and Eastern Europe to be redrawn. This thought doubtless met with Gömbös's approval; less encouraging, however, was Hitler's unreceptiveness to the notion of restoring Hungary to her former grandeur and thus reviving the "old Bismarckian concept." Hitler's advice to Gömbös, monotonously repeated thereafter, was that Hungary concentrate her efforts on Czechoslovakia and abandon hopes for recovery of territory now belonging to Yugoslavia and Romania. On the delicate issue of Austria, the two leaders likewise found little common ground, Gömbös suggesting that some sort of *modus vivendi* be achieved to assuage Mussolini's fears and Hitler expressing his dislike for Dollfuss and flatly refusing to disinterest himself in the problem.[59]

Though Gömbös returned from Berlin with promises of cooperation in such matters as trade relations and rearmament, any sense of gratification was mingled with and perhaps overwhelmed by keen disappointment. The dream of securing German assistance in the restoration of "Greater Hungary" was dealt a shattering, perhaps fatal, blow when Hitler suggested that the Magyars should be content with recovery of territory in Czechoslovakia. For Gömbös and many of his countrymen the reannexation of Slovakia and Ruthenia would be merely the first step, not the capstone, of a revisionist program. Contributing to the predicament in which Gömbös now found himself was the fact that his trip to Berlin had disconcerted a good many people in Hungary. Those who placed their faith in traditional diplomatic methods and procedures, such as Kálmán Kánya, were appalled by what they regarded as the unconventional, unseemly, and tactless behavior of the prime minister.[60] In certain segments of the press and in Parliament, strong criticism was expressed of what appeared to be the opening of a new and potentially dangerous orientation in Hungarian foreign policy. The most eloquent and outspoken critic was Endre Bajcsy-Zsilinszky, a former colleague of Gömbös from his "race-protecting" days, who since the mid-1920s had been the leading spokesman for those who feared that German imperialism would some day engulf Hungary. In a public session of the Parliament, Bajcsy-Zsilinszky bitterly denounced Gömbös and suggested that he resign, for by his "unfortunate trip" he had "set himself against the vital foreign policy interests of the Hungarian nation."[61]

Scathing criticisms of this kind doubtless made a deep impression on Gömbös, but he was not inclined to abandon altogether his scheme for a powerful bloc based on a Rome-Berlin axis just because of these initial setbacks. However, a slight shift in emphasis did seem to be in order. If German support would be offered only against Czechoslovakia, all was not lost, because Italian assistance seemed assured if and when a confrontation with Yugoslavia occurred. Thus, as Gömbös now began to say privately, Hungary would pursue a policy that "south of the Danube is based on Italy and north of the Danube is based on Germany." Hungary would be left to play the leading role in the "Carpathian region."[62]

During 1933 Mussolini, intent on strengthening Italy's hinterland before Hitler had a chance to interfere forcefully in Danubian affairs, proposed that Italian-Hungarian-Austrian political relations be put on a more concrete basis. For some time Gömbös hesitated, fearing the repercussions such a move would have in Berlin. Finally, however, he journeyed to Rome in March 1934 and signed a tripartite pact with the Duce and Chancellor Dollfuss.[63] This Rome Pact, in the form of a set of protocols, strengthened general economic and political cooperation among the three signatories and implicitly affirmed the necessity of preserving Austrian independence. Yet despite the significant advantages in terms of trade, security, and prestige that the Rome Protocols offered, Gömbös was still uneasy about committing Hungary so firmly to one of the two poles of his proposed Rome-Berlin axis. He told Mussolini that he would have preferred a political and economic pact that included Germany, and managed to get his views on this subject expressed in a secret protocol to the Rome Pact.[64]

By 1936, however, conditions were becoming more propitious for the forging of the diplomatic alignment that Gömbös favored. The signing of a German-Austrian "Gentlemen's Agreement" in July 1936 removed one of the obstacles preventing a German-Italian rapprochement. This temporary settlement of the Austrian problem was but one reflection of the important diplomatic realignments that occurred in Europe beginning in late 1935. Mussolini's decision to embark on a military adventure in Africa had important repercussions in East Central Europe. To Gömbös it was a signal that Berlin would soon be gaining a more dominant influence in Danubian affairs. Thus he was prepared once again to attempt to draw Hungary into closer harmony with Nazi Germany. In the realm of economics and trade, relations between the two countries had in fact been improving dramatically since early 1934 when a secret trade agreement had been signed. Germany's expressed willingness to increase its purchases of Hungarian agricultural products led to a substantial expansion in trade almost overnight: by 1935 grain shipments to Germany had doubled and that country became Hungary's most important trading partner.[65] However, political relations between the two countries had remained quite cool. Prospects for a favorable change in Hitler's attitude toward Hungarian revisionism seemed no brighter; indeed, the Führer's emissary, Marshal Göring, had visited Yugoslavia and Hungary in 1934 and had bluntly informed both sides that Germany would never lift a finger in support of Hungarian revisionism in Yugoslavia or Romania.[66]

Despite this ominous development, Gömbös remained hopeful that something could be worked out, especially if he could have another opportunity to discuss matters personally with Hitler and his colleagues. In September 1935 a second visit to Germany was thus arranged on Gömbös's initiative, once again against the advice of Kálmán Kánya. The Germans apparently gave no indication that they would change their earlier advice that Hungary focus its revisionist campaign on Czechoslovakia, but Gömbös gained the impression that they were no longer avidly interested in a Hungarian-Yugoslav rapprochement, and that, as he told a Hungarian friend, "although Hitler had promised him revision against Czechoslovakia, he was confident that Hungary would end up by getting everything back with Germany's help."[67] Once back in Budapest Gömbös spoke glowingly of the accomplishments of Hitler's regime over the past two years, of the dynamism and vitality of National Socialism. The skillful and imaginative use of propaganda had particularly impressed him. The prominent leaders in the German government and Nazi party, with most of whom he had had the chance to talk at length, Gömbös characterized as "a group of exceptionally gifted, able, and resolute men."[68]

In his exuberance Gömbös concluded two agreements with the Germans that seemed to represent the opening of an era in German-Hungarian relations. After discussions with Göring and Schacht, Gömbös was able to confirm the arrangements for a deal whereby Hungary could obtain certain German armaments in exchange for increased grain shipments.[69] At the same time Gömbös drew up with Göring a secret personal compact so far-reaching that, had they known of it at the time, the regent, Kánya, and most Cabinet members would never have concurred. Apparently convinced that Hitler might more readily assume the role of a champion of Hungarian revisionism if Hungary's political and social institutions were more closely attuned to that of Nazi Germany, Gömbös undertook to introduce within two years a political system based on radical rightist, totalitarian principles. In other points of the agreement, he seems to have vowed to regulate the position of the Catholic Church and to deal with the "Jewish question."[70]

Hungary, in retrospect, may well have been on the threshold

of major internal and external changes as 1935 drew to a close. But the would-be Magyar dictator was not given the opportunity to carry out the provisions of his private agreement with Göring. He fell ill in the spring of 1936, went to a German sanitarium for treatment late in the summer, and died on 6 October. In any case, had Gömbös attempted to establish a dictatorship in Hungary, he would certainly have had to contend with an aroused opposition. Resentment and suspicion had been building up for some time in Hungary, for even though the existence of the Gömbös-Göring agreement was never revealed to the public, there were other unmistakable clues as to what the prime minister had in mind.

Since 1933 Gömbös's foreign policy had been under almost constant attack from a small group of Social Democrats, legitimists, and individual Germanophobes like Bajcsy-Zsiliniszky. By early 1936 this amorphous grouping was unofficially joined by Count Bethlen and other conservatives in the government party. Here was a truly ironic development, for, to all appearances, Gömbös was merely proceeding along a path that Bethlen himself had blazed a decade earlier. It is true that Bethlen, Kánya, and other influential conservatives strongly favored precisely what Gömbös had earlier requested of Hitler: restoration of the "old Bismarckian concept" in German-Hungarian relations. Bismarck, it may be recalled, had subscribed to a "kleindeutsch" policy, leaving affairs in Danubian and Balkan Europe to be presided over by Austria and Hungary. During the Bismarck era there had been no thought of expansion to the southeast, intervention in favor of German minorities in Hungary, or political cooperation with the South Slavs. Bismarck had considered it to be in Germany's (and Europe's) interests that the Magyars exercise hegemony in Danubian Europe. Moreover, the Germany of Bismarck's era had been governed in an authoritarian and conservative, but not totalitarian, manner. This was the Bismarck and this was the Germany for which the Hungarian conservatives had been searching since 1918.

What deeply troubled the conservatives was that Hitler was clearly not carrying on in the tradition of Bismarck, and that Gömbös did not understand this or simply did not care. *Mein Kampf* was not unknown in Hungary, and many Hungarians feared that if and when Hitler embarked on the expansionist program adumbrated in his book, he might not command his troops to halt at the "gates of Sopron," the traditional line demarcating Austrian and Hungarian spheres of influence. On other key points as well Hitler's policies seemed in strong contrast to those of Bismarck. Perhaps most importantly, Hitler was most decidedly not formed from the same ideological mold as Bismarck: his right-wing politics were of a radical, excessively violent, and totalitarian variety. Such an extremist ideology, the Hungarian conservatives believed, was alien to Hungarian society, whether it was based on National Socialist principles or the "Szeged idea."[71] If close ties with Nazi Germany could be achieved only after the introduction of fascist-like institutions in Hungary, the effort was not worth making, for a Hungary of that sort would inevitably become a mere satrapy of its more powerful neighbor.

The decision of Bethlen and the other conservatives to turn decisively against Gömbös was founded on the belief that the prime minister was, in fact, intent on altering Hungary's political and constitutional system to render it more compatible with that of Italy and Germany. By the beginning of 1936 there were unmistakable signs that Gömbös was proceeding along these lines. The important turning point had come in May 1935, when Horthy had permitted Gömbös to organize a new election of Parliament. The result was a dramatic rise in the number of delegates in the government party committed to a radical right ideology. The Parliament was thus given an injection of the Szeged spirit it was never to eliminate from its system.[72] Later that year Gömbös was able to effect a similar changing of the guard in the army officer corps. By placing men of his own political persuasion in many of the important positions, particularly in the General Staff, he was able to refashion the military establishment so that it became the main pillar of radical right-wing ideology in Hungary.[73] A series of other government measures in 1935 edged Hungary closer to a totalitarian society. Press censorship was expanded, secrecy of the mail was violated on a regular basis, and a system of political informants was introduced.[74] Gömbös's mimicry of Mussolini's mannerisms (speeches from balconies, adoption of the appelation *vezér* [Duce], etc.) and his open hints about the need for a "one-party, corporative State," naturally deepened the suspicions of his opponents.[75]

As early as the middle of 1935 a bloc was forming under the direction of Count Bethlen and Tibor Eckhardt[76] in opposition to Gömbös's dictatorial aspirations. This rather loosely joined group was united only in a belief in the desirability of the "defense of the Constitution" and in a fear that the prime minister was leading the country to disaster. Bajcsy-Zsilinszky summed up their sentiments when he wrote in March 1936 that "we cannot place the future of the country in jeopardy . . . just so that Gyula Gömbös, in his immeasurable ignorance, egotistical rashness, and utter blindness, should thoughtlessly play a political game that is unworthy of him."[77] Though Bethlen, Eckhardt, Bajcsy-Zsilinszky, and the others were probably unaware of the agreement that Gömbös had made with Göring, they nonetheless felt the need to keep a careful watch on the prime minister's activities and subject his foreign policy to the closest scrutiny in Parliament.[78] When his illness forced Gömbös to withdraw partially from public duties in 1936, they interceded with the regent to reverse the fascist course Gömbös seemed to be plotting. In fact, Horthy, having for a variety of reasons come to the conclusion that Gömbös was not a true "gentleman," decided in the late summer to dismiss him. Gömbös protested and did manage to cling to the office until his death a few months later.

Miklós Horthy, István Bethlen, and Gyula Gömbös: this was the triumvirate that created the Hungary that found itself in 1936 on the brink of a European crisis. During the unfolding of this Danubian crisis from 1936 to 1939, they naturally continued to wield great influence in the determination of Hungarian foreign policy. Gömbös had passed from the scene, but the men he had installed in the government party, officer corps, and civil service were to carry on in the tradition of their mentor. Regent Horthy developed a greater personal interest in the formulation of policy, and Bethlen, though not a member of the government, managed through articles, speeches, and consultations with the regent and members of the Cabinet to insure himself a voice in most vital decisions. But the true direction of Hungary's foreign policy after the death of Gömbös was in the hands of one man, Kálmán Kánya, who, in the judgment of C. A. Macartney, was "the only Hungarian Foreign Minister of the inter-war period to be the real controller of his country's foreign policy."[79]

In appearance and methods Kánya was the epitome of the nineteenth-century Habsburg diplomat in whom the traditions of the

"Ballplatz" were deeply rooted.[80] His apprenticeship in the Austro-Hungarian diplomatic corps had included valuable service to Count Aehrenthal as chief of press and a lengthy tour of duty as minister to Mexico before and during World War I. After the war his diplomatic experience and bureaucratic skills were put to use in the organization of an independent Hungarian Foreign Ministry. Thereafter he played a prominent role, as protegé and counsellor to Count Bethlen, in the general formulation and implementation of policy. In 1925 he became Hungarian minister in Berlin, where he remained until asked by Gömbös in 1933 to assume direction of the Foreign Ministry.

Kánya's political views, as far as they can be determined, were in harmony with the moderate conservatism of his mentor, István Bethlen. But in a certain sense Kánya was a unique figure in Hungarian political life. For the first three decades of his adult life he had lived abroad: Moscow, Constantinople, Kiev, Salonika, and certainly Vienna had become more familiar to him than Budapest. As a dedicated servant of the Habsburg monarch and a statesman thoroughly schooled in the ways of traditional European diplomacy, Kánya had learned to view things from a broad European rather than narrowly Magyar perspective. The Great War he observed from a distant shore; its passions were tempered once they crossed the Atlantic and reached the Habsburg minister in Mexico City.

Thus, when Kánya returned to Hungary in 1918 to join in the process of creating an independent foreign ministry, he brought to the task the kind of linguistic skills and cosmopolitan experience that few individuals in Hungary possessed. More importantly, he was able to approach the array of problems confronting Hungary with a dispassion and pragmatic spirit that only an "outsider" could offer. The emotional and even mystical nationalism so prevalent in Hungary after the war, particularly in the Szeged movement, struck no responsive chord in Kánya. It was not that he was lacking in patriotism, but that he distrusted any kind of emotional or sentimental excess.[81] This deeply influenced his attitude toward the issue that was so central to interwar Hungarian political life, treaty revisionism.

C. A. Macartney has suggested that Kánya was zealous to his commitment to revisionism and that he was nicknamed "the old tiger" precisely because of his enthusiastic participation in *Felt-*

ámadás (Resurrection), a secret irredentist association.[82] However, the evidence now available does not seem to sustain the portrait of Kánya as a fiery irredentist. Of course, as foreign minister his aim was to strengthen the country as much as possible, and in Hungary's case this meant overturning the peace settlement and regaining at least some of the lost territories. But in this, as in all political matters, Kánya felt constrained to put aside sentimentality and wishful thinking in order to examine Hungary's situation in a completely dispassionate and realistic manner. His aim was to construct a policy commensurate with Hungary's strength and position in Europe, and his guiding principle was borrowed from another Habsburg statesman, Prince Kaunitz: "In politics one should strive not for the desirable, but for the attainable."[83] The evidence seems to suggest that in the period before 1938 Kánya, almost alone among prominent Hungarian political figures, regarded territorial revision as a kind of dream or ideal that could be attained, if at all, only "in some better world of the future."[84] Hungary would have to work patiently toward this goal, but the taste of success might come only to future Hungarian generations.

Having worked for so many years in the diplomatic service of a great power, Kánya was equipped to view the European scene with a worldliness, realism, and cynicism few of his contemporaries possessed. His instincts told him that in the harsh world of international politics no state acted unselfishly, and that Trianon Hungary, a weak and indigent country, could not expect the altruistic support of any European power.[85] Grandiose schemes, according to which other countries would assist Hungary in recovering all her territories, he regarded as mere pipe dreams. Kánya realized, too, that Hungary, surrounded by hostile neighbors and militarily weak to the point of impotence, was in no position to conduct too ambitious or disruptive a foreign policy.

For these reasons Kánya thought the outright linking of Hungary's fate with any one power or bloc the height of folly. His program, more modest in conception though not any less difficult in execution, was elaborated first in his inaugural speech in Parliament in 1933. It called for maintenance of a "free hand" in European politics, whereby Hungary proceeded cautiously through the maze of international relations, making no binding military or political commitment to anyone.[86] If, along the way, this or that great power offered to help Hungary to achieve her goals, he was more than glad to accept, so long as it did not compromise the guiding principle of his policy. But, especially after 1936, he was extremely reluctant to place Hungary irrevocably into either of two camps, the Axis or the West, which seemed headed for a certain future confrontation.

It was difficult for other European statesmen, and even some of Kánya's colleagues in Budapest, to accept at face value Kánya's claim that he wished to keep Hungary free of commitments to any great power. For during his tenure as minister in Berlin during the 1920s he had gained the reputation of being a stalwart Germanophile. But any pro-German sentiments coloring Kánya's political views did not survive the rise to power of Adolf Hitler. Gyula Gömbös might speak enthusiastically of his admiration for the National Socialist leadership, but in Kánya's eyes they were a despicable lot, unfit to manage the foreign affairs of a great power. In private conversations with diplomats of the "old school" he made no attempt to conceal his displeasure at the triumph of the Nazis and his contempt for Hitler ("a common rabblerouser"), Göring ("a brute"), and Goebbels ("a buffoon").[87] Of course, pragmatic and realistic considerations compelled him to seek to avoid any sort of clash with Germany, whatever the nature of its government at any given time. Hungary could certainly maintain its independence better if Germany considered her a friend rather than an enemy.[88] However, the idea of forging an intimate relationship with Germany he regarded as foolish, dangerous, and inconsistent with his "free hand" policy. For this reason Kánya devoted much of his attention between 1933 and 1936 to an effort to harness and restrain the impatient and impetuous Gömbös.

Yet if Kánya managed to purge himself of many of the chauvinistic assumptions that might have restricted his freedom of maneuver in the diplomatic arena, there nonetheless remained in him some of the arrogance of the nineteenth century Habsburg diplomat who found it most difficult to adjust to some of the realities of the postwar period. Above all, he considered it a most distasteful chore to have to deal on an equal basis with statesmen of the Successor States. To him the Slovaks and Romanians remained "subject peoples" unprepared to take on the duties of responsible statesmanship. The Serbs he denigrated as an uncivilized nation given to a barbaric political life. Whenever possible Kánya preferred to deal with representatives of the great powers rather than the leaders of Romania, Czechoslovakia, and Yugoslavia. Still, when in 1937 and 1938 an effort to improve relations with the Little Entente seemed desirable in purely pragmatic terms, Kánya showed no hesitation about embarking on this path, despite the criticism leveled at him by the more zealous revisionists in Hungary.

As foreign minister, Kánya's diplomatic methods and attitudes harkened back to the "Age of Metternich." Foreign policy, he believed, should be conceived and implemented by men who had been specifically trained for a diplomatic career and had acquired the necessary linguistic skills and intimate knowledge of foreign countries. The gradual eclipse of the traditional diplomatic establishment after 1918 and the increasing tendency in certain European countries for foreign affairs to be presided over by soldiers, former revolutionaries, champagne merchants, and the like, he regarded as most unfortunate. He found it difficult to disguise his contempt for amateur diplomats, particularly those, like Gömbös or Colonel Beck in Poland, whose experience had been largely as military officers. Indeed, a fear of the dangerous consequences of permitting military men to meddle in policymaking pervaded much of his thinking in the period of crisis beginning in 1936.

The injection of mass politics into foreign policy formulation likewise made Kánya uneasy. He much preferred that important transactions among European powers be conducted behind the scenes by competent statesmen who, given sufficient time, could usually devise a diplomatic solution to the most intractable problems. Even the question of treaty revision would best be handled in this way: after all, a conference of great powers had drawn the borders of Europe in 1919, and a similar conference could redraw them in the future. This reliance on patient, private diplomacy also implied a rejection of a foreign policy designed for mass approval. Kánya was averse to any form of histrionics in the diplomatic arena: catchy slogans, boisterous rallies, and ostentatious boasting were completely alien to his style and demeanor.[89]

Caution, patience, ambiguity—these were the trademarks of the man who was to dominate Hungarian foreign policy through almost the entire course of the Danubian crisis. He tried at all times to preserve for Hungary a multiplicity of options, a truly "free hand." By simultaneously pursuing several policies that to the untrained or unsophisticated eye might seem incompatible, Kánya aimed always to have some policy on which to fall back, no matter what turn European affairs might take. Needless to say, this habit of keeping several irons in the fire contributed to a certain amount of confusion about Hungarian policy. While Kánya was directing Hungary's affairs, no one (sometimes not even his own diplomats) could be certain what the true goals and principles of Hungarian foreign policy were, and thus no one could be entirely surprised to find Hungary standing at the side of those countries that emerged supreme in the coming European struggle.[90]

Although Kánya conducted his policy with a great amount of skill and dexterity, a propensity for devastating sarcasm and the inherent ambiguity of his approach were bound to evoke some criticism and scorn both at home and abroad. Hitler certainly did not understand or appreciate what Kánya was attempting to do in the summer of 1938, nor, at other times, did Mussolini or Ciano. The British most of the time were merely confounded by Kánya's tactics, and considered the Hungarian foreign minister a devious individual.[91] At home Kánya at first received firm support from all quarters; increasingly, however, the radical rightists clamored for a total commitment on the side of the Axis. This, of course, was precisely the kind of commitment Kánya very much hoped to avoid, but the task of restraining his more zealous countrymen was to prove formidable.

Chapter 3

Hungary and the "Half-Armed Peace," 1936–1937

When on 7 March 1936 German troops began to advance into the previously demilitarized zone of the Rhineland, the eyes of all European statesmen turned to Paris. How would France respond to this blatant violation of an integral provision of the Locarno Pact and the Versailles Treaty, a provision that has been termed the "single most important guarantee of peace in Europe" during the interwar period?[1] As the weeks passed and the realization grew that the German initiative would not be challenged militarily, diplomatic observers in East Central Europe began to ponder the significance of Hitler's triumph. French inaction had enormous implications for the countries in that region. The entire postwar diplomatic settlement in East Central Europe had been predicated on the assumption that Paris would be its guarantor even when Germany regained its power and influence. France's treaty ties with Poland, Czechoslovakia, Yugoslavia, and Romania, combined with vigorous support for the Little Entente, were the framework of this system. The remilitarization of the Rhineland seemed to strike at the very foundations of that structure, for if France had not moved to thwart a major treaty violation by Germany on her very borders, how could Prague, Warsaw, or Belgrade expect French military support against a German advance far from French soil?[2]

In fact, as French military planners were soon to discover, the German occupation of the strategic Rhineland area rendered French military assistance for her East European allies virtually impossible from a purely operational point of view.[3] The conclusion now became inescapable: France's allies were no longer assets but liabilities.[4] If France's ability to influence events in East Central Europe had been severely diminished by the events of March 1936, that of Germany was considerably enhanced. From this point on no state in that part of Europe could afford to make a move in the diplomatic arena without considering the interests and acknowledging the important role of National Socialist Germany.[5] In the next two years each East European country was forced to reexamine its relationship with Germany and, where appropriate, seek an accommodation with this resurgent power. Milan Stojadinović, Prime Minister of Yugoslavia, reflected sentiments common to many political leaders in Eastern Europe when he explained to the French that "we are now obliged to reckon with the German danger, which you have allowed to emerge and spread."[6]

The reassertion of German influence in Eastern Europe was hastened and facilitated by two other factors. One was the growing dislocation of French political life and the turn to the left in June 1936. The Popular Front experiment was unpopular in most of Eastern Europe, where, by contrast, rightist forces were emboldened by Hitler's success and began to put increasing pressure on the existing governments. Some observers, taking note of the confusion to which French political life now seemed prone, undoubtedly began to speculate on whether, in a future crisis in Central or Eastern Europe, France would have a government sufficiently strong and stable to take a firm stand. If she did not, and if Great Britain continued to limit its commitments on the continent to a defense of Belgium and France, the smaller states of Europe would have to fend for themselves.

A second development that proved highly advantageous to Germany was the gradual withdrawal of intense Italian interest in East Central Europe. This was one of the grave consequences of Italy's exhausting military campaigns in Ethiopia and, beginning in July 1936, Spain. As early as January of that year Mussolini expressed a desire for a rapprochement with Germany and settlement of the chief point of friction between them: the Austrian problem. At about the same time the Duce, obviously profoundly disturbed by the treatment accorded him by the Western democracies, informed the Hungarian minister that "for Italy there was no returning to the Stresa Front."[7] The gulf separating Italy from France and Great Britain had thus become a deep and pronounced one, capable of being temporarily papered over but never again completely bridged. After Mussolini sent out diplomatic feelers in early 1936, the forging of the German-Italian rapprochement was ac-

complished in regular stages. By the summer of that year, a satisfactory agreement was reached concerning Austria, by November
the Duce proudly announced the formation of the Berlin-Rome
Axis, and a year later Italy adhered to the Anti-Comintern Pact.

The swiftness and success of Hitler's Rhineland coup and the
passivity of the West made a deep impression in Hungary, as in
all of Danubian Europe. If the German chancellor was bold
enough to risk so much in the West, might he not turn soon to
the East and settle accounts with the Czechs? And if he did shatter
Masaryk's Republic, could not Hungary hope to gain something in
the process? These thoughts no doubt were turned around in the
minds of many politically conscious Hungarians in the aftermath
of the Rhineland operation. But mixed with this cautious opportunism was a lingering anxiety. Hitler's methods were brash and
unconventional, and the Hungarians could never be absolutely
certain what his aims would be once he rearmed fully and turned
his attention eastward. Perhaps, as those of right radical persuasion
were wont to suggest, he would become a friendly patron of Hungary; or perhaps, as Bajcsy-Zsilinszky and others feared, he would
in the end convert the country into another "Gau" in his Reich.

This vital question of Hitler's intentions, of the true nature of
his Danubian policy, was to perplex and bedevil Hungarian policy-
makers at each important juncture of the unfolding crisis after
1936. That contemporary political observers, in Hungary and elsewhere, should have expressed bewilderment as they sought to
fathom Hitler's foreign policy program is quite comprehensible,
since even in retrospect the precise nature of Hitler's goals in East
Central Europe are not always easy to discern. However, the available evidence on Hitler's thinking in the period before 1936 does
seem to indicate that, in the region between Russia and Germany,
he was intent eventually on effecting important political and territorial changes that, concisely stated, would result in the creation
of a kind of National Socialist "Mitteleuropa."[8] A first priority was
to be annexation of those areas contiguous to the Reich that Hitler
considered to be German in character. The Anschluss of Austria,
perhaps preceded by a period in which Austria would survive as a
kind of autonomous province under German tutelage, was considered essential.[9] Equally important was the destruction of
Czechoslovakia and the incorporation into the Reich of Bohemia

and Moravia. In addition, Poland would be forced to cede certain territory on her western frontiers and in the Corridor.

Once Czechoslovakia and Austria had disappeared from the map of Europe, the other countries of the region would be organized into what Hitler variously called "an alliance of vassal states"[10] or "a German military protectorate,"[11] totally subservient in matters relating to international relations and certain domestic policies, particularly treatment of the Jews. Within these strict limits each country would apparently have retained a degree of autonomy, providing, of course, that certain countries, like Yugoslavia, would "come to their senses" and refrain from any anti-German actions. The resulting bloc of states, composed of Poland, Hungary, Romania, Yugoslavia, and Bulgaria, would be organized to serve as a "protective wall against Russian imperialism"[12] and, perhaps, as a staging area for an eventual military confrontation with the Soviet Union.

By 1931 Hitler had come to regard Hungary as a "natural ally" in the creation of such a German-dominated Eastern Europe.[13] It is true that early in his career Hitler had not formed as definite an opinion of the Magyars as he had, for example, of the Czechs. Significantly, the anti-Magyar sentiments of Karl Lueger, the mayor of Vienna during part of Hitler's sojourn in that city, were not assimilated by the future German chancellor. Instead, on the basis of his indirect contacts with Gömbös and other Hungarian radical rightists in the early 1920s, Hitler seems to have formed an essentially favorable image of the Magyars, or at least of their military officers.[14] In his second book, written in 1928 but not published at the time, Hungary is listed, along with Spain, as sharing with Germany, Italy, and England a "community of interests."[15] After his ascent to power, the Führer privately affirmed the community of interest of Germany and Hungary on several key European questions, above all, treaty revision and anti-Communism. In his public statements he echoed the rhetoric of many Hungarian rightists: the two countries had fought "shoulder to shoulder" in World War I and had suffered a "common misfortune." Thus, the past "relation of close friendship and of genuine and warm sympathy" would certainly hold true in the future as well.[16] Though, as has been noted, Hitler and Gömbös disagreed on several critical questions, Hitler nonetheless seems to have admired the Hungarian leader and appreciated the fact that his trip to Germany had broken the almost total diplomatic isolation in which Germany had found itself in early 1933. Moreover, the frequency with which Hitler met with Hungarian visitors in the first four years of his chancellorship seemed to attest to the importance he attached to cultivating friendly ties with the Magyars.[17]

To a certain extent Hitler was justified in assuming that Hungary was a "natural ally" and would cooperate in the implementation of his plans. Her dissatisfaction with the status quo and her well-earned reputation for hostility toward the Soviet Union might well have suggested to an outsider a willingness to cooperate in a reorganization of East Central Europe carried out under the direction of Germany. But Hitler clearly did not anticipate the pertinacity and self-confidence with which the leaders of a small country like Hungary could cling to a highly ambitious program of territorial revision. Before coming to power, Hitler seems to have been quite favorably disposed toward the Hungarian revisionist cause, though he had not grasped all the essential details and nuances. When in 1931 he speculated about future border changes in Danubian Europe, he assigned Transylvania and the Voivodina (a region in northern Yugoslavia) to Hungary, though he suggested that the Slovaks might form an independent state.[18] All but the most zealous of Hungarian irredentists would no doubt have been delighted by the prospect of such territorial changes, especially since the eventual annexation of Slovakia was not precluded.

By the time he became chancellor, however, Hitler had completely reversed his position on this question of vital importance to Hungary. Instead of voicing general support for Hungarian aspirations, we find him privately scoffing at the notion that he might, for sentimental reasons, help Hungary regain her historic borders.[19] His position now, as he bluntly informed Gömbös and other Hungarians with whom he spoke in the ensuing years, was that Hungary would have to be satisfied with whatever gains she might be able to win at the expense of Czechoslovakia. What prompted this abrupt turnabout in Hitler's attitude? Undoubtedly it reflected a decision made by Hitler, perhaps at the urging of Göring and Arthur Rosenberg, to lure Romania and Yugoslavia out of the French orbit and into the anti-Communist bloc he was contemplating. This could be accomplished, however, only by assuring Bucharest and Belgrade that Germany opposed Hungarian irredentism to the south and east.

That the Hungarians did not enthusiastically welcome Germany's advice in this matter, and in fact bitterly resented the diplomatic initiatives of Marshal Göring in Yugoslavia and Romania, apparently surprised and irritated the Führer. After all, if he was willing to renounce all claims to the South Tirol in order to pave the way for a rapprochement with Italy, why couldn't Hungary, a significantly smaller and weaker state, make similar sacrifices vis à vis Romania and Yugoslavia? By 1936 Hitler began to wonder whether the Magyars, in their stubborn arrogance and utopian view of the possibilities for treaty revisionism, might not prove a handicap rather than an asset in the carrying out of his plans.[20] Still, for the time being at least, he could not afford to permit Hungarian-German relations to become too strained. Hungary might be a small and weak country, but up to 1936 she was one of the few European states that could be considered friendly to National Socialist Germany. Moreover, Hungary bordered on two countries, Austria and Czechoslovakia, that were central to Hitler's plans for expansion, and it probably seemed expedient to foster Hungarian goodwill at least until these questions were settled.

Since up to 1936 the Hungarians had received only inconclusive and sometimes contradictory clues to Hitler's intentions in East Central Europe, the situation seemed to call for caution and fence-straddling, attitudes that epitomized Kálmán Kánya's approach. In the two years after Hitler's bold coup in the Rhineland, a period that A. J. P. Taylor has aptly termed the "half-armed peace,"[21] Hungary moved almost imperceptibly to a less committed position. After Gömbös's death in October 1936, Hungary's ties with Germany and Italy seemingly remained as firm as ever, but this fact was not openly flaunted, and the idea that Hungary had to introduce a fascist political system was officially repudiated. Moreover, a concerted effort was initiated to interest Great Britain in a peaceful reorganization of East Central Europe. Many Hungarians hoped that the slogan "peaceful change" could be applied to Europe as a whole, with England, Germany, and Italy collaborating to revise the peace treaties without the horror of war.

The prospect of a war was a particularly unpleasant one for

Hungary in this period. The term "half-armed peace," though very descriptive of the era for Europe in general, simply could not be applied to Hungary. Europe was unmistakably embarking on a period of large scale rearmament. Nazi Germany's secret rearmament was no longer secret, and in the fall of 1936 an ambitious Four Year Plan was launched with the dynamic Field Marshal Hermann Göring at the helm. In March of the preceding year Britain had issued its White Paper on Defense, and the smaller states, apprehensive of Hitler's plans and increasingly unsure of French determination, now began efforts to improve their military forces. Even Austria unilaterally declared its military equality in April 1936. In Europe only Hungary and Bulgaria remained less than "half-armed," still bound by the disarmament clauses of the peace treaties.

In Hungary's case this was in one sense a mere technicality. Since 1927, when responsibility for military control in Hungary was shifted from the Allied Military Commission to the League of Nations, the country had been rearming and modernizing its military forces to the extent its meager finances permitted. The army, limited by the Treaty of Trianon to 35,000 men, had been gradually expanded and a form of conscription introduced. By late 1937 its size had reached 85,000, still an insignificant figure when ranged against the far larger forces at the disposal of Hungary's neighbors.[22] Moreover, in equipment and military hardware Hungary's forces were hardly modern or impressive in contemporary terms. Since the possibility of evading the peace treaty restrictions on manufacture of arms was obviously limited in a small, open country like Hungary, war material had to be obtained abroad. Italy had been shipping various items since the late 1920s, but much of this was of obsolete World War I vintage. Beginning in 1936, however, substantial loans for military development were proffered by Rome, and over the subsequent two year period a total of 513 million lire was advanced, much of which was devoted to the procurement of fighter planes.[23] Germany began to supply arms to Hungary only in 1935, but those that were made available were modern and sophisticated, although the delivery was often irritatingly slow.[24] In addition to the arms-grain deal Gömbös had concluded in late 1935, an agreement in the summer of 1936 called for Hungary to purchase a number of fighter planes.[25]

Yet by 1938 Hungary still lacked sufficient weapons to defend the country, let alone launch a sustained offensive action. Hungary's military chiefs had been pressing for some time for the construction of fortifications on the Tisza and Danube river banks, but the government, perhaps fearful of Little Entente retaliation, had demurred.[26] Hungary's military situation thus remained quite hopeless, since it no longer enjoyed the pre-1914 luxury of strategic borders and was now completely open to swift enemy invasions. The General Staff was forced to conclude in its yearly reports for 1933 and 1935 that Hungary was highly vulnerable to attack in a war, and that the country was not prepared for a conflict even in the most favorable of conditions.[27] A pronounced military weakness is thus the framework against which all the crucial events of 1937 and 1938 in Hungary must be evaluated.

The question of whether to follow Germany's and Austria's example and declare freedom to rearm was a thorny one for the Hungarian government. Even the officers themselves were not of one voice. In general, the older, more cautious group, represented by Minister of Defense Vilmos Röder, was satisfied with the scope of secret rearmament that Hungary was already pursuing. But many officers, particularly those appointed to high positions in 1935, were eager to embark on the "forced military epoch" that Gömbös had promised. Their spokesman, General Jenő Rátz, was appointed chief of staff late in 1936 and soon began to press for rearmament on a scale that could hardly be concealed from public view.[28] Foreign Minister Kánya proceeded with great circumspection in this question. He sounded out various capitals and discovered that if Hungary followed Austria's example, Italy would offer military assistance should Hungary's neighbors mobilize, but Germany could offer only moral support.[29] In October 1936, the British government hinted that it would support Hungary's claim for military equality if it were advanced, not, as was the case with Germany and Austria, as a *fait accompli*, but by diplomatic steps in the League of Nations.[30]

However, the Little Entente states, particularly Czechoslovakia, were threatening drastic reprisals should Hungary take this unilateral step,[31] and Kánya decided to hold off. This decision, to which Kánya was to cling until overruled in early 1938 by the prime minister and regent, reflected his basic distrust of all things military. In his opinion, Hungary could never really defend itself adequately; lacking natural frontiers, it would require an army of astronomical size to hold off an invader. Thus, the best army for Hungary was one just large enough to keep order.[32] There was another reason for Kánya's reluctance to declare Hungary's military equality. The current situation, he explained to Ciano late in 1936, allowed Hungary to rearm at a modest rate without depriving him of a useful domestic weapon. He could continue to blame a variety of internal and external difficulties on the overbearing surveillance of the Little Entente and the harsh restrictions of the peace treaty. In any case, an open declaration would only create new difficulties for Hungarian minorities abroad.[33] Earlier, during the diplomatic bargaining over a Danubian Pact in 1935, Kánya had expressed a willingness to make certain concessions to gain official Little Entente recognition of Hungary's right to rearm. By 1936/37 he still preferred to obtain this recognition through negotiation, but was increasingly reluctant to offer anything in return, arguing that Hungary's right to rearm was a prerequisite to, not a goal of, negotiations.

Hungary's response to Hitler's occupation of the Rhineland and developments in its aftermath, as has already been suggested, was a curious blend of cautious optimism and mild disquietude. Reaction in government circles, as was so often the case in the interwar period, was deeply ambivalent. Kánya continued to evince a sense of uneasiness. He never really accustomed himself to the Nazi manner of conducting affairs, so brash and overbearing, so scornful of traditional diplomatic methods. What, he asked a colleague from Weimar days, had happened to the old "National Germans," who had none of the propensity for "hysteria" and the "universal madness" of present day Germany?[34]

Balancing Kánya's uneasiness was the enthusiasm displayed by those government officials who believed that Hungary could only benefit by Germany's resurgence. Regent Horthy, though denying any special fondness for the Germans, expressed admiration for the way Hitler had torn up the Locarno treaty.[35] Gömbös, not yet seriously ill, could only applaud Hitler's impressive success. The revisionist movement was given a new injection. At the city of Kaposvár on 14 March, only a few days after the march of German troops, Minister of Industry Bornemissza delivered an impassioned speech calling for the reestablishment of Greater Hungary. Czechoslovakia promptly protested,[36] and Kánya was forced to dissociate himself from the minister's action, which violated the

Foreign Ministry's policy of eliminating open references to revisionist demands by Hungarian officials.

There was a remarkable dichotomy in the German-Hungarian relationship in the period from the remilitarization of the Rhineland to an important visit of Hungarian dignitaries to Berlin in November 1937. Two contradictory forces seemed to be at work, one implying a community of interests with respect to the dissolution of Czechoslovakia, the other emphasizing the various points of friction that had been troubling their ties since 1933. Both elements were present in the months after March 1936, but in the autumn of that year diverse problems, some of which had seethed just below the surface for several years, emerged almost simultaneously to create serious difficulties in the German-Hungarian relationship.

Viewed from the vantage point of Budapest, the events of this period could easily have assumed the appearance of a sinister plot hatched in Berlin and carried out on instructions from the highest German authorities. In the summer there had been only the vaguest hints of the trouble to come. When Regent Horthy visited Hitler for the first time in August at Berchtesgaden, the two leaders got on quite well together and expressed satisfaction at the results of their conversations.[37] Horthy was particularly gratified to learn that the Führer shared his belief in the inevitability of a conflict with Bolshevik Russia. Hitler even took note of the regent's suggestion that Germany would do well to keep on good terms with England. But Hitler's advice to the Hungarians remained the same: Hungary could not expect revision at the expense of Romania or Yugoslavia. He added, in terms that could only be alarming to Budapest, that he was not even ruling out the possibility of a nonaggression pact with Czechoslovakia, if Prague were willing to abandon its ties with the Soviet Union.[38]

During the remainder of the summer there were other disquieting developments. Friction over the treatment of the German minority in Hungary had grown by this time to serious proportions, despite Hitler's earlier instructions that the question not be permitted to disturb German-Hungarian relations.[39] The German concern was such that Foreign Minister Neurath warned Kánya in September that, if a solution were not found, a coolness in relations between the two countries would inevitably ensue.[40] The Hungarians were not happy about this admonition. They had only

reluctantly agreed to discuss the problem at all with the Reich,
as Gömbös had always insisted that it was strictly a domestic concern and that, in any case, the "German minorities here already
live in a paradise."[41] Moreover, Budapest felt sufficiently justified
in delivering its own protests. The accusation that Reich Germans,
visiting Hungary ostensibly as tourists or scholars, were agitating
among the Swabians of Hungary and financing radical right elements was not entirely groundless. The Hungarian government
was already nervous about the noticeable stirring in the summer
and fall of groups formerly identified with the Szeged movement.
The new prime minister, Kálman Darányi, unwittingly encouraged
the right-wing extremists both in and outside the government, by
reviving the patriotic societies that had lain dormant since the
twenties.[42] In the period just before and after the death of Gömbös in October, rumors of an imminent rightiest putsch kept the
temperature of Hungarian political life at a fever pitch. Bethlen
and the opposition groups of the left and center were alarmed by
this continued agitation. They saw the hand of the German Reich
behind the domestic turmoil and in many speeches and articles
tried to make it clear to Berlin that such interference would in the
future not be tolerated.

With the death of Gömbös on 6 October, the personal agreement he had made with Göring also died. The new prime minister,
Kálmán Darányi,[43] a congenial though essentially weak individual,
had no intention of honoring the Göring-Gömbös pact, about
which he and Kánya learned only after Gömbös's passing. The direction of foreign affairs he willingly left to Kánya, who now sought
to undo the damage that Gömbös's meddling had caused. His conviction that Hungary would do well to have more than one "iron
in the fire" implied a willingness to loosen ties with Germany and
encourage British interest in Hungary and Danubian Europe. It
has been suggested that it was this shift in Hungarian policy that
prompted Germany to "turn the heat" on Budapest shortly thereafter, but this seems only partly the case.[44] It is true that at Gömbös's funeral Göring spoke eulogistically of the deceased leader
("We liked him so very well") and showed concern that his policies
would not be carried on.[45] But Göring did not stress the point later,
and the German minister confidently reported to Berlin that for
"the continuation of Gömbös's foreign policy we could wish for no
more reliable successor" than Darányi.[46]

In fact, at first Hungary's shift away from Gömbös's one-sided orientation was one more of tone than substance. Greater attention was indeed shown to the Western democracies,[47] and strident declarations of loyalty to the newly formed Axis were avoided, but, save for the abandonment of Gömbös's personal agreement with Göring, no sudden move was made at this time that could have been construed as anti-German in motivation. In fact, Kánya even assented to German advice and declared in September that he was willing to seek an agreement with Yugoslavia and a *modus vivendi* with Romania.[48] But while in Budapest Göring was occupied with other matters. As newly designated director of the Four Year Plan, the Reich Marshal was anxious to obtain increased grain deliveries from Hungary. He therefore proposed a special "compensation agreement" whereby German arms would be bartered for the required foodstuffs. The transaction would have involved Hungarian exports over and above those that had been pledged in earlier agreements.[49] The Hungarians were unenthusiastic. The trade surplus with Germany that they had enjoyed in 1934 had by this time been converted to a deficit of equal size. There was growing awareness among Hungarian economists and officials of the dangers of too close an economic dependence on Germany. The National Bank, under the competent direction of Béla Imrédy, had resolved to prevent injudicious exporting to the Reich.[50] Darányi thus informed Göring that, because of a poor harvest, Hungary could not expand its grain exports.[51] This response prompted a remarkable series of threats and accusations in the following months. Göring, who seemed to regard the question as of supreme importance, vehemently declared that "it is impossible that Hungary leave Germany in the lurch." What he wanted, in fact, was an assurance of future grain deliveries just as was given to Hungary's Rome Protocol partners.[52]

Though Göring's importunacy was singularly ill-received in Budapest, Darányi eventually decided that to prevent more serious consequences a small concession would have to be made. A minor "compensation agreement" was thus concluded later in November, but Hungary would go no farther, and, after a few more weeks of recriminations, Göring apparently gave up the effort. There is no record of his subsequently attempting to pressure the Hungarians for increased food shipments.

The friction over this issue and that concerning the German

minority had set the stage for the main elements in the cooling
off of German-Hungarian relations after Gömbös's death. The one
great nightmare that had always plagued Hungarian leaders was a
"diplomatic revolution" whereby Germany persuaded the countries of the Little Entente to sever their ties with France and
enter the German orbit. This would leave Hungary completely
isolated in East Central Europe, with virtually no hope of ever
regaining any of her lost territory. In late 1936 and early 1937
the nightmare seemed to be taking on the appearance of reality.
The overture came on 15 November when an article entitled
"Unterdrückte Völker und Revision" appeared in the press organ
of the National Socialist Party, the *Völkischer Beobachter*. The
author, Alfred Rosenberg, editor of the paper, severely criticized
the exaggerated revisionist policy that certain quarters (by implication, Hungary) were pursuing. The move was obviously intended
as a trial balloon, to test the possibilities of winning over the current Romanian government, which, like all Romanian governments, regarded Hungarian revisionism as the greatest threat to
stability in East Central Europe. Rosenberg's article caused great
excitement and consternation in Hungary, where the major newspapers gave it prominent coverage. There was a sullen mood in the
Foreign Ministry, where Kánya was convinced that the article
was authorized by Hitler himself after a conversation with Rosenberg,[53] and that it thus represented official German policy. Budapest was perplexed by this development: there seemed no special
reason for such a severe attack on Hungarian revisionism precisely
at a time when Kánya was demonstrating his willingness to come
to terms with Yugoslavia, and possibly even Romania.

More disconcerting information on Germany's wooing of Romania soon came to the attention of the Hungarians. The efficient
Hungarian intelligence service, which throughout the 1930s was
able to read the in- and out-going messages of the Romanian legation in Budapest, learned in December that Göring had made a far
ranging proposal to the Romanian minister in Berlin. According to
the Hungarian information, which other evidence substantiates, if
Romania pledged itself to remain neutral in a possible conflict involving Russia, Czechoslovakia, or Spain, Germany would oppose
any anti-Romanian move; and if Romania joined an anti-Bolshevik
bloc, Germany would supply armaments, credits, and military

instructors.[54] Göring claimed to have an oral agreement along these lines with Yugoslavia.

These German efforts to woo Romania and Yugoslavia were in fact undertaken with the expressed approval of Hitler, who apparently was persuaded by Rosenberg and Göring that it was a propitious time for such an initiative, and that the advantages of winning over Romania and Yugoslavia would completely overshadow any resulting bitterness in German-Hungarian relations.[55] At this time Hitler seemed more than usually concerned about the "Bolshevik danger"; in his private conversations (for example, with Horthy in August) and public statements the emphasis was reportedly on the grave dangers posed by Soviet Russia. The Four Year Plan, announced in September, and the Anti-Comintern Pact, signed in November, were both conceived and described as weapons to combat Communism. The overtures to Bucharest and Belgrade in the autumn of 1936 can be seen as part of this same heightened propaganda campaign against Communism. When, for example, Hitler met with Georges Bratianu, a conservative Romanian politician, shortly after the appearance of Rosenberg's article, he stressed that Germany was interested in forging closer ties with all countries that would cooperate in a defense against Bolshevism. If Yugoslavia and Romania became "barriers against Bolshevism," they would have little to fear from Hungarian revisionism, for no country would be more interested in maintaining such "outposts of European order."[56]

As in the past, the Hungarians complained bitterly in Berlin about this obvious favoritism toward two countries Hungary regarded as enemies. But there was little Budapest could do, especially as Hitler had repeatedly warned that he intended to maintain friendly relations with Romania and Yugoslavia. It would be a different matter, however, if Germany started to court Czechoslovakia as well, thereby fulfilling the prerequisite conditions for the dreaded "diplomatic revolution." For most of 1936 this had seemed highly unlikely. In fact, Göring, the blunt and usually accurate spokesman for the Führer, had consistently displayed an unfriendly and even threatening attitude toward Prague. Hungary and Germany, he told Sztójay in July, shared a "community of fate and were dependent on each other," since they had a "common goal" in the Czechoslovak question.[57] Later he advised Kánya that

Germany would not "tolerate the bleeding to death under Czech control of the thoroughly German Sudetenland." The impulsive Reich Marshal implied that within two or three years Czechoslovakia would cease to exist.[58] Even during the period of tension after Hungary's coolness to the suggestion of a "compensation agreement," the ubiquitous Göring was interested in drawing Budapest into anti-Czechoslovak activity. In December he established a new organization to carry out intelligence work against Prague, and quickly arranged for the cooperation of the Hungarian and Austrian intelligence agencies.[59]

In the fall of 1936 Hitler gave no hint to visiting Hungarians that his attitude toward Czechoslovakia might be mellowing. In December he told Miklós Kozma, Hungary's minister of the interior, that Czechoslovakia was pursuing a dangerous policy. It wished "to be the airplane mother ship for the Soviet Union, but this ship will then sink."[60] But whatever comfort the words of Hitler and Göring provided Budapest was rudely snatched away only weeks later when in January 1937 Kánya received the disturbing, and as it turned out accurate, news that emissaries of Hitler were in Prague secretly negotiating with Eduard Beneš.[61] Kánya, who harbored an inveterate mistrust of virtually all foreign statesmen, no doubt suspected that Göring's and Hitler's anti-Czech statements in the presence of Hungarians were merely clever camouflage for Germany's efforts in an opposite direction. He immediately complained to the German minister in Budapest that Rosenberg's article and subsequent German activities had created a "critical situation," giving the impression that Hitler's friendship for Hungary "was on a weak footing." If Germany concluded a nonaggression pact with Czechoslovakia, which Hungary itself had just recently refused to do,[62] Hungary would be placed in "an extraordinarily difficult position."[63]

Kánya vented his anger even more forcefully a few days later in a conversation with a reporter from the *Völkischer Beobachter*. It had become fashionable in Germany, he asserted, "to drag out Hungary as a whipping boy, while celebrating the Romanians as heroes and the Yugoslavs as gods." What purpose could Germany serve by reproaching Hungary? In any case, Hungary was perfectly capable of pursuing a new foreign policy, if that proved necessary.[64]

The anxiety of Hungary's conservative leadership was greatly increased in early 1937 by mysterious political disturbances that occurred in March. Since the autumn of the previous year, the resuscitated MOVE and certain other chauvinist organizations had been permitted by Darányi to expand their propaganda activities, apparently on the hope that this would be a relatively harmless outlet for the enthusiasm that had been building up in those circles since Hitler's triumph of the previous year.[65] However, by early 1937 the endeavors of some of the more impetuous radical rightists threatened to get out of hand. Soon ambitious plans were being formulated and implemented for a right radical putsch to be carried out with weapons and money supplied by certain sympathetic organs of the Nazi Party in Germany. But no political secret was ever kept for long in Hungary, least of all planning for a coup d'état, especially when, as in this case, the police had been keeping the "patriotic societies" under constant supervision. By early March a boxcar of German weapons had been intercepted at the border and the detailed plans of the putschists had been uncovered. This information was passed to Minister of Defense Röder, who was appalled to discover that had the putsch been successful, all members of the Cabinet, including himself, would have been arrested. The evidence also suggested that one of the German military attachés had taken part in some of the planning sessions of the conspirators.[66]

Much of this information was passed to Eckhardt and Bethlen, and soon rumors were being spread that a coup was imminent. In this feverish atmosphere during the first two weeks of March, there were in fact scattered outbursts by zealous rightists in several Hungarian cities. Stinkbombs were thrown into Jewish-owned theaters in Budapest, and demonstrations were held in Pécs and elsewhere.[67] But the authorities stepped in quickly to restore order and those responsible for the ambitious plans for a putsch were quietly disciplined. Darányi publicly insisted that there was no cause for alarm, that the rumors of an imminent political upheaval were groundless. Yet the uproar in the Parliament and the press did not subside, and accusations were made that Germany was providing clandestine support to those who would subvert the constitutional system in Hungary. Public suspicion of German compliance was so widespread that Darányi felt constrained to defend the German minister in Budapest in a speech to Parliament.[68]

By the spring of 1937 Germany's popularity in Hungary was thus quite diminished, not only among conservatives but also among politically minded Hungarians of various political persuasions. Even the regent's admiration for Hitler's achievements was now tempered, as he came to realize that the Germans were apparently not above interfering with Hungary's domestic affairs. The bitterness engendered by the events of early 1937 would not easily dissipate, even when it became clear later that year that the feared "diplomatic revolution" would not be consummated and that the pendulum of German policy was again swinging in Hungary's favor.

By April 1937 it was evident to the Germans that the attempt to lure Romania from the French orbit had miscarried. After pondering Göring's offer, King Carol and his advisors decided to hew to the former policy of fealty to traditional alliances and the League of Nations, though they hoped to expand economic relations with Germany. This decision was conveyed to Berlin, and Göring was forced to recognize that Rosenberg's ploy to win over the right wing in Romania had failed.[69] Only Göring's proposal to Belgrade seems to have produced, in the Reich Marshal's own words, "a quite clear agreement," in the form of an oral promise not to join any bloc expressly hostile to the other.[70] Like the approach to Bucharest, the talks with Czechoslovakia had petered out. Whatever his intentions had been earlier,[71] by the spring of 1937 Hitler seems to have come to the firm conclusion that a confrontation with Prague was inevitable.

The difficulties in their relationship with Germany in late 1936 and early 1937 led the Hungarians to strive to cultivate further their ties with Italy and Great Britain. Italy, to all appearances, was still a staunch friend, and the Rome Pact seemed to be a continuing assurance of Italian interest in Central Europe. But, as has already been mentioned, Italy's interest in Danubian Europe was in reality on the wane in 1936 as the military adventures in Ethiopia and Spain began to take their toll. Though Mussolini continued to promote the Hungarian revisionist cause,[72] his new foreign minister, Count Galeazzo Ciano, rather disliked the Magyars and, if not wishing to abandon them altogether, hoped to win over Romania and Yugoslavia with assurances that they had nothing to fear from Hungarian revisionism. Ciano's efforts were rewarded in March 1937 when he concluded a treaty of friendship with Milan Stojadinović, the Yugoslav prime minister. Feelers were then extended to Bucharest as well, but Mussolini, more sentimental about Italy's traditional ties with Hungary, insisted that a pact with Romania would be signed only if Hungary approved beforehand.[73] Ciano, it is true, explained to the Hungarians that his agreement with Yugoslavia was the cornerstone of a Rome-Belgrade-Budapest bloc that could serve, if it proved necessary, as an anti-German instrument. Kánya was prepared to accept this proposition in principle, but strongly resisted Ciano's advice to seek a rapprochement with Romania, pointing out that the Hungarian minority in that country was treated most intolerantly and that their lot was deteriorating with time.[74]

Hungary's annoyance over Ciano's vigorous courting of Romania was increased later in the year when Rome, feeling the economic strain of her efforts in Africa and Spain, informed Vienna and Budapest that the system of preferential tariffs formerly applied to trade among the three Rome Pact members would have to be abandoned. Kánya voiced keen disappointment at this decision, which, he asserted, many observers would see as another step in the progressive weakening of the Rome Protocols.[75] Indeed, after the Austro-German Gentlemen's Agreement the importance of the Rome Protocols rapidly diminished. Rome tacitly acknowledged a German sphere of influence in Austria and Czechoslovakia, and Italian interests became more and more focused on other areas. After November 1936, the signatories of the Rome Pact did not meet again until January 1938, and by then the fate of Austria had already been sealed.

Chapter 4

Great Britain and "Peaceful Change"

With Germany representing an increasingly powerful but (from the Hungarian point of view) unreliable factor in the Danubian Basin, and Italy a basically friendly but weakened and erratic one, Hungary's leadership in late 1937 sought to erect a third pillar on which to base its foreign policy: Great Britain. Relations with England had been cordial but not particularly important in recent years, since Gömbös had been too busy courting Italy and Germany to pay much attention to the West. But Kánya, Horthy, and other Hungarian leaders felt that such a powerful, if aloof, country could not safely be excluded from any diplomatic formula for curing the ills of Europe. In 1936 there had been some signs that Britain was emerging from its isolation and taking a more lively interest in continental affairs. In certain circles of British society there was talk of the necessity for "peaceful change" in Europe, for redress of the inequities of the peace settlement. One spokesman for this point of view was Arnold Toynbee, Director of Studies at the Royal Institute of International Affairs, who visited Budapest in May 1937 and delivered an address in which he declared that unless the satisfied countries met the just demands of the unsatisfied ones by peaceful change, alterations would come sooner or later by force or violence.[1] This call for peaceful revisionism merely echoed that of a number of other prominent individuals who had expressed sympathy for Hungary, notably David Lloyd George and Winston Churchill. Another reflection of an underlying interest in the Hungarian revisionist cause was the frequency with which the subject percolated to the surface in the letters-to-the-editor section of the London *Times*, though one suspects that for the most part these letters were dismissed by many readers as merely typical of the eccentric and esoteric missives commonly printed there. Yet among those interested in continental affairs the "Hungarian question" could evoke passionate concern. A speech by Count Bethlen at the Royal Institute of International Affairs in 1933 set off perhaps the most vigorous debate of any conducted in that institution during the interwar period.[2]

The most conspicuous form in which the case for Hungarian revisionism was aired was Lord Rothermere's *Daily Mail*, but the heart of pro-Magyar sentiment in Great Britain was the House of Lords. Perhaps the members of that august body felt a special obligation to stand up for one of the few countries where the aristocracy still counted for something; perhaps because the House of Lords no longer exercised much political power they felt able to champion causes that seemed worthy in principle but hopelessly unrealistic in terms of practical politics. Whatever the reason, sympathy for Hungary was expressed in the House of Lords as soon as the major provisions of the Trianon Treaty were known in 1920 and continued into the 1930s. The most important manifestation of this support came in 1933, when a resolution sponsored by Sir Robert Gower and sixteen other members of Parliament was introduced into the House of Commons. It called for the revision of the territorial provisions of the Trianon Treaty so as to conform more closely to the ethnic frontiers of East Central Europe. His Majesty's Government was urged to bring the matter before the League of Nations at the earliest opportunity, "in the interest of the pacific settlement of Europe as well as to perform an act of justice to the Hungarian nation." By November of that year, some 161 members of Parliament had signed their names to this motion, a remarkable expression of concern for a relatively remote and insignificant country.

Unfortunately for the Hungarians, the British Foreign Office and the government in general always took great pains to dissociate themselves from such manifestations of support for the Magyars. The central principles of British policy in Eastern Europe were to promote economic stability, avoid disruptions of the existing order, and work to reconcile and reduce local tensions and difficulties.[3] None of these principles would be served by a policy that aimed to alter the frontiers of Danubian Europe, since this would almost certainly precipitate a dangerous crisis and possible war. Thus, even though a few British diplomats felt that Hungary had some legitimate grievances, no one in the Foreign Office believed it was practical or desirable for London to take any initiative in the matter. Moreover, the "Hungarian question" was inextricably bound up with the "German question." If somehow a way could be found to revise the Trianon treaty in a peaceful way, what would the British attitude be to the inevitable demands from Germany for equal treatment, demands that, unlike those of Hungary, might well touch directly on Britain's vital interests? After all, as one British pundit put it, what's "sauce for the Transylvania goose will before long become sauce for the Tanganyika gander."[4]

Kálmán Kánya was sufficiently realistic to know that the prospects for an active intervention by London on behalf of Hungary's revisionist program were exceedingly remote. He recognized, too, that for the time being at least British commitments in Europe were limited to a defense of Belgium and France. Beyond that, as Knox told him shortly after the Rhineland crisis, Britain subscribed only to the principle of collective security as a member of the League of Nations.[5] Yet he sensed that much could be gained for Hungary if ties between the two countries could be strengthened. For if the time did come for an undoing of the peace settlement, Britain would surely have a powerful voice in shaping the contours of a new East Central Europe. And if, on the other hand, Europe should slip once again into war, it would be well for Hungary to remain in the good graces of the Western powers, who likely would emerge victorious. Thus, when German or Italian statesmen talked in 1936 about forming blocs of like-minded states, Kánya always made it a point to suggest that England be included. Horthy, too, urged Hitler not to underestimate either the value of Britain as an ally or its naval prowess.[6] And one of Kánya's chief concerns in 1937 was, with the modest means at his disposal as the foreign minister of a small but interested state, to promote an Anglo-Italian rapprochement.

A great stimulus to Hungary's interest in Britain was provided by the visit to Budapest in April 1936 of Austen Chamberlain, the former foreign secretary. Chamberlain, brother of the later prime minister, had at the time no official connection with the government, but he was the most prominent Englishman to visit Hungary in many years, and his views were given due deference. In his wide-ranging conversations with Horthy, Kánya, Bethlen, Gömbös, and others, Chamberlain tried to stiffen Hungarian resistance to German pressure. British opinion, he told Kánya, was not stirred to the same extent as French, but he was quite sure that if Germany invaded Austria, Britain would march whole-heartedly with France.[7] The distinguished Englishman urged moderation and patience in the revision question. Of great importance was the impression Horthy gained that Chamberlain understood Hungary's claims to be just in principle, and that Hungary should wait for "the right moment" to come, at which time England would step forward and offer her support.[8]

The visit of Austen Chamberlain and the talk of major changes in the European peace-keeping system prompted Regent Horthy to take a more active personal interest in Hungary's foreign affairs. Since 1932, when he had contemplated launching a vast anti-Bolshevik crusade, Horthy had not often intervened in the activities of Kánya and Gömbös, save for the attempt to mediate Austro-German differences. Now the regent decided the time had come to bring his country's case to the attention of the British. On 16 May, avowedly with the approval of Kánya, he dispatched a rambling six-page letter to King Edward VIII.[9] The regent's purpose, so he wrote, was to transmit through unofficial channels "our views on the possible solutions" for the "crisis of the League of Nations." Horthy then proceeded to draw the familiar picture of the injustices that Hungary had suffered at the Paris Peace Conference and at Geneva. The peace treaties, he asserted, "by their economic, military, and territorial decisions had led Europe to the edge of the abyss. Unless a *just peace* is created in Europe, it is useless to dream of an effective League of Nations, much less world peace." Hungary was striving for revision "always and exclusively by peaceful means." What was needed was a new European Congress that would revise the peace treaties, eliminate the distinction between the "satisfied" and the "desperate" states, and clear the way for the most dangerous task: the liquidation of Bolshevism. The continuing danger of Communism was not to be underestimated, the regent warned. The "evil continued to devour"; in its eternal quest for ice-free ports, Russia had its eyes on northern Finland, Sweden, and Norway, from which it would establish itself on the Atlantic coast and "destroy the world." Russia was *"too big."* Those states that at the twelfth hour had freed themselves from the Bolshevik yoke, like Hungary, Poland, Germany, Italy, and Austria, should, with the help of Japan and under the leadership of England, join together "to free the world of this plague and break Russia into its constituent parts." Everyone,

Horthy ended, trusted in England's leadership, and the Hungarians did so unconditionally.[10]

The Foreign Office was unsure exactly how to deal with Horthy's communication, which, in Robert Vansittart's opinion, was "a very wild production." The regent's proposals were obviously naive and unrealistic, but he was, after all, head of state of an important, if small, European country, and could not easily be ignored or offended. Eventually a return letter from King Edward was composed; it was polite, but brief and noncommittal. Horthy did not follow up on the matter, and the whole episode was conveniently forgotten. But the regent's initiative is nonetheless important as an indication of the trend of his thinking in this critical period. The affirmation of his faith in England is significant, and the bloc of states he projected and the idea of a European conference to revise the peace treaties were consistent with Kánya's thinking. Nor was his appeal to the anti-Bolshevik sentiment of the king and his countrymen an outlandish one. There were many people in British society who regarded Soviet Russia a greater menace to peace than Nazi Germany,[11] and perhaps even a few who, in certain circumstances, would have supported an anti-Russian campaign of the kind Horthy outlined. The regent's mistake was in thinking that this might be the attitude of the British government and the Foreign Office, and that as a prelude to an anti-Bolshevik move, Britain would take the lead in a major remaking of the map of Europe to Hungary's advantage. Finally, Horthy's letter did not explain how the almost certain resistance of the Little Entente and France was to be overcome, while still relying exclusively on peaceful methods. Would these countries calmly stand aside while the Successor States were dismantled and historic Hungary was restored? It was certain that any attempt to effect such drastic changes would bring on inevitable war, a war that no one, especially not Britain's leaders, desired.

Though no one in the British Foreign Office took Horthy's communication very seriously, not all Englishmen in official positions were oblivious to Hungary's difficulties. The sympathy for Hungary that had animated financial circles in the immediate postwar period had not diminished with the years. In November 1936 F. Ashton-Gwatkin, Joint Secretary of the Interdepartmental Economic and Financial Committee, urged that the United Kingdom, as the most important free market for the Danubian countries, make an effort to facilitate trade with Hungary. This, he argued, would serve a threefold purpose: Budapest would be better able to pay off her debts, Britain could maintain a share in the Hungarian market, and Hungary would be helped to retain her economic independence of Italy and Germany.[12] No action was taken on Ashton-Gwatkin's suggestion; indeed, it was the inclination of Anthony Eden, the foreign secretary, not to arouse German suspicions by openly thwarting her economic expansion into Danubian Europe. England's minister in Budapest, Geoffrey Knox, was warned in 1937 to temper his anti-German activities, since His Majesty's Government had "no wish to interfere with German trade relations with the Danubian countries."[13] Neville Chamberlain, who became prime minister in May 1937, was equally wary of offending German sensibilities in this question. He, along with a great many of his countrymen, was unconvinced that the extension of German economic influence in East Central Europe could or should be checked.

When Kánya visited London in the spring of 1937 for the coronation of the new king, he detected a certain nervousness about the situation in Central and Eastern Europe. No one castigated Hungary for her relations with Italy and Germany, but Anthony Eden did suggest that Hungary might do well to "form a breakwater against German pressure along with Austria and Czechoslovakia."[14] Kánya was told that the British government was anxious that Danubian Europe not become, like the Balkans before World War I, "a theater of rivalries between the Great Powers." Vansittart tried to convince him that London was very much interested in Danubian affairs, her chief goal being the preservation of the independence of the small states in that part of Europe.[15]

On the surface Kánya's visit to London broke no new ground. Everyone had been intent on affirming England's new interest in East Central Europe, but without concomitant political or military commitments this interest had by necessity to be, in the words of Eden, "platonic."[16] Eden and Vansittart had shown some understanding for Hungary's difficult position,[17] but, beyond the advice that Budapest should seek a rapprochement with Prague, they offered no specific nostrums. Yet Kánya returned to Budapest deeply moved by his experiences. Perhaps he had read too much into Vansittart's words; perhaps his private conversations with other officials had been more outspoken. Whatever the explanation, Kánya's later conviction that England would stand by France if the latter became involved in a major conflict seems to have been given its initial impulse at this time. When he met Ciano a few days later in Budapest, he repeated "several times" his reflections on England's power and the democratic alliances that would come to her assistance in an emergency.[18] Moreover, he seems to have warned Ciano, who was now hinting that Italian support for Austrian independence was weakening, that if the position of Austria were to be undermined because of Italy's ties with Germany, "Hungary would have to search for new alternatives in her foreign policy."[19]

The budget debate in late May, traditionally the time when foreign affairs were intensively discussed in the Hungarian Parliament, afforded an opportunity for Kánya to make a small gesture to England. In listing Hungary's friends, he made it a point to include Great Britain alongside the Axis, Poland, and Austria. England, he declared, was showing "increasing sympathy for one of the most important Hungarian problems, the minorities question," and this development was welcomed by Hungary. Other speakers made friendly references to England. The words of Gyula Lakatos, the budget director of the Foreign Ministry, attracted particular attention, because he was known to be a confidant of Kánya and often was used by the foreign minister to comment on delicate issues that he himself was wary of touching on publicly.[20] In retrospect, Lakatos's speech was a fairly accurate sketch of Kánya's thinking, that is, to the extent that the complex and tortuous workings of his mind can be understood today.

Lakatos spoke more explicitly of Hungary's respect for England.[21] After emphasizing the need for close relations with Italy, he passed over Germany and proceeded to an interesting analysis of Britain's role in European affairs. That country, he noted, had shown an interest in developments on the continent. That London would place its sword on the proper side of the scale, once its rearmament was completed, was of the utmost importance. The Hungarian nation, he continued, felt a certain instinctive sympathy with the English nation. They shared a common constitutional development, the ideal of the gentleman, and a belief in the necessity of fair play. Britons had been the first to cite the unfairness of the peace treaties. Hungarians hoped now that London would work for "peaceful change," for this corresponded precisely to the Hungarian viewpoint.

Lakatos then proceeded to outline the policy that Hungary would do best to follow. His prescription clearly bore Kánya's trademark. Hungary, he explained, was a small country that had to side with others who were interested in reversing the peace treaties and showed sympathy for Hungary's "minimal demands." The primary concern was that Hungarian minorities receive better treatment. For the moment territorial revision was not demanded, but the present situation was obviously untenable. Eventually the Hungarian question, along with other European questions, would have to be settled in a spirit of understanding and equality. It was for this reason that the concept of "peaceful change" so well suited Hungarian interests. Hungary's weapons were "persuasion" and a "correct propaganda," as employed by the Hungarian Foreign Office. The chief goal of Hungarian foreign policy was to "remain apart from the clash of interests of foreign powers, and, if a conflict broke out, to stay out of it if possible." Hungary's geographical position was difficult, wedged as she was between two expansionist powers, the Germans and the Slavs. Throughout history it had always been to the country's advantage to avoid too close an association with either side, for Hungary did not wish to serve foreign interests. She would, in fact, do best to imitate Belgium, which since the end of 1936 had adopted a neutral stance in Europe.

Lakatos's words were a fairly accurate guide to the policy Kánya hoped to pursue.[22] With Germany's attitude unsure, and Italian support for Austria crumbling, it was clearly even more desirable than ever that Hungary follow a circumspect course. Kánya merely desired to hew to the "free hand" policy that he had enunciated in his maiden speech to Parliament in 1933. The idea of following the example of Belgium appealed to him; he used it himself a number of times later in the year. And he later told Gusztáv Gratz that he was still absolutely determined to preserve his "freedom for maneuver," and had therefore refrained from concluding any military agreements with any side. He wanted to wait to see which group emerged strongest at the end of the period of rearmament, and then determine in which direction Hungary should be oriented.[23] His policy was thus highly opportunistic and fraught with danger. But Hungary's position was such that wherever she turned certain dangers lurked. Those who urged Kánya to draw closer to Nazi Germany gravely underestimated the attendant risks and failed to see that Hungary might be drawn into a devastating war. Yet those both in and outside of Hungary who in the period 1936–38 suggested that the Hungarians simply make an abrupt about-face and make peace with her neighbors equally failed to understand the possible consequences of their policy. It is hard to imagine any Hungarian government in this period that could have convinced the country that the battle for revision had to be abandoned. Even the attempt to initiate such a policy might have prompted the radical officers to stage a coup d'état.

Many Hungarians shared Kánya's beliefs. In the second half of 1937, a number of spokesmen from the opposition parties alluded to the dangers of Hungary's position between Nazi Germany and Soviet Russia and the need for a cautious, uncommitted policy. Individuals of widely disparate political views—such as Count Aladár Zichy, a prominent monarchist, László Németh, an influential poet, and Dezső Szabó, a writer who propagated a mystical kind of Hungarian nationalism that glorified the peasant—all found themselves searching for some sort of "third road" that would enable Hungary to resist the expansion of both Germany and Russia.[24]

However, as the purges continued in Russia during 1937, it was Germany that seemed to represent the most immediate danger. Throughout Hungary during the summer of that year suspicion and fear of Germany among all but the most ardent Germanophiles and right-wing extremists were quite pronounced. The events of March had left a deep mark. Bajcsy-Zsilinszky contributed his part by producing yet another scathing attack on German influence in Hungary, A német világ Magyarországon [The German world in Hungary]. It was symptomatic that when Prime Minister Darányi tried to find someone to take on the post of president of a German-Hungarian society, he was forced to evoke "the national interest" to persuade a friend to accept the post.[25] Morever, the evident uneasiness in Hungarian Catholic circles over developments in Germany was deepened by the appearance in the spring of 1937 of a papal encyclical in which the persecution of the Church in Germany was condemned. A summary of the encyclical was published in an easy-to-read pamphlet that was distributed widely in

Catholic parishes in Hungary.[26] This incipient spiritual resistance to Nazism in Hungary received symbolic leadership from Pál Teleki, the country's most prominent lay Catholic, who several times in 1937 rose in parliament to deplore anticlericalism and "neopaganism" in National Socialist Germany.[27]

Yet even those Hungarian leaders who most feared German expansionism believed that it would be best to avoid any diplomatic actions that might arouse Germany's wrath, for who was to come to Hungary's aid if the Reich absorbed Austria and cast its menacing shadow over the Pannonian plain? And if Germany was someday to dominate Danubian Europe, whether with or without the cooperation of England, it was certainly most prudent to remain in her good graces and reap whatever territorial benefits might come Hungary's way.

One very influential Hungarian advocated a policy along these lines. In an important article published on 20 August, István Bethlen suggested a policy that, in its general outline, was embraced by many Hungarian conservatives.[28] Bethlen emphasized that Hungary, if she was to prosper, had to cling to her tradition of "Christian National Democracy." A "Führer-led" dictatorship was simply not possible in Hungary, and the Axis powers had to realize this elementary fact. With this principle recognized, the interested parties could turn to a new arrangement in the Danubian Basin that would provide a geographical, economic, and cultural unity. It would be based on the pattern of St. Stephen's realm a thousand years earlier. Admittedly, that kingdom was Hungarian, but it was federative in structure and no attempt had been made to Magyarize the minorities. The independence of all nations had been safeguarded, and the resulting unity allowed the Danubian people to defend themselves against their powerful neighbors. Was this possible in the twentieth century? The answer, Bethlen declared, depended on England, which, "as the *arbiter mundi*, held in its hands the key to a new European settlement." The suggestion in some quarters that the status quo in Central Europe had to be maintained so that Germany would not grow too powerful was fallacious. It was in England's interest to come to a friendly agreement with Germany, even if this involved a significant accretion of the latter's strength. Present conditions in East Central Europe were highly unstable: the area was like a "bed of coals from which a spark could set Europe into flames." England could not be disinterested; she had to assist in the establishment of a more just and stable system.

Bethlen's article was in effect a call for the restoration of prewar Hungary, with the cruder aspects of Magyar rule eliminated and a federation, rather than a unitary state, as the political form. At least one of the Successor States, Czechoslovakia, would have to disappear, and indeed this is what Bethlen implied when he proposed that Britain make concessions to Germany. Berlin presumably would be allowed to absorb Austria and Bohemia, Slovakia would be returned to Hungary, and a common border with Poland would be a reality. This program, however utopian its suppositions, had great appeal to Hungarians of Bethlen's social position and background, including Minister of Defense Röder and other conservatives in the Army.

Kálmán Kánya was too realistic to base his policy solely on the possibility that England might play the role envisioned by Bethlen, although he would gladly have welcomed Hungarian revision in the north if such a combination did arise. But there were once again perplexing unanswered questions. Even if Great Britain allowed Germany a "free hand" in Central Europe, might not this result too in Hungary's coming into the German sphere of influence? And who could guarantee that Hitler would continue to tolerate parliamentary practices in a small country directly on its borders?

Hungary's right radicals were equally skeptical. If Hungary was to benefit from Germany's resurgence, they argued, it was necessary to identify Hungary's complete policy, both domestic and foreign, more closely with the Third Reich. Radical right-wing discontent in 1937 came increasingly to focus on two groups: the radical army officers in the general staff college, the Ludovika Academy; and the rightist political groups, including the extremist faction of the government party. The extra-parliamentary activity of the rightists received a great impetus and cohesion when in August the party of the most dynamic and popular of the radical rightists, Ferenc Szálasi, was fused with its most important rival. Soon other splinter parties connected themselves with the new unified party, and in October a vigorous "United Hungarian National Socialist Movement" (also called the Arrowcross party) was proclaimed.[29]

The stirring of right-wing sentiment among the officers of the

Hungarian army, or Honvéd, was one of the most important developments in the period after Hitler's Rhineland coup. As was the case in other organs of Hungarian society, there was a certain cleavage in the Hungarian armed forces between conservatives and those who leaned more toward the "Szeged idea." Many of the older soldiers, products of Habsburg days, though by definition eager for the Honvéd to play a vital role in Hungary's recovery, were averse to soldiers taking an active part in the political life of the country. Like their civilian counterparts, they retained a healthy respect for Britain's naval prowess and were wary of too close a cooperation with Nazi Germany. By contrast, many of the younger officers were becoming imbued with the notion that the army had a positive political role to assume in Hungarian society. Led by General Jenő Rátz, this militant-minded group began pressing in late 1936 and 1937 for a more vigorous rearmament program and closer consultation with Germany. Several factors were working in their favor. Rátz had the ear of the regent, who sympathized with his military, though not political, efforts. Rátz was also a close friend of Ferenc Szálasi, and was thus able to keep abreast of the activities of the right-wing political parties. And the officers had a trusted comrade in Döme Sztójay, a former General Staff officer, who in his position as Hungarian minister in Berlin was able to serve as a liaison between the Honvéd and the more militant of the German leaders. The cautious Kánya was often bypassed, which was understandable, since he would not have countenanced much of the activity that was conducted behind his back by his minister to the Wilhelmstrasse.

The Hungarian General Staff was convinced that if war broke out in Central or Eastern Europe, Hungary would inevitably be drawn in, whether or not the government wished to remain neutral. The General Staff believed that the Little Entente would automatically invade Hungary at the outset of any conflict and unless the Hungarians were to bow passively to superior force, a bloody struggle would ensue.[30] In any case, if Hungary wished "to render secure the independent national existence" of the Magyars, it would be necessary to regain a strategic border on the Carpathians. This political goal, however, could never be achieved by peaceful revision. The restoration of Hungary's territorial integrity could be possible only after a war from which Hungary emerged victorious. The army leadership was skeptical of the military capability of Italy; it was to Germany that the officers, especially the younger ones, looked for guidance and cooperation. In the General Staff annual report of 1935, it was estimated that in four or five years Germany would have the greatest potential for war of any European power. It was to be assumed that Berlin would then try to obtain its political goals by force or threat of force. A recognition and appraisal of Germany's plans was therefore imperative.[31]

Despite the conviction that Hungary could secure its future happiness only through armed conflict, the General Staff was forced right up to 1938 to concede in its yearly reports that Hungary was not prepared militarily for a conflict with the Little Entente.[32] In 1937 the right radical officers thus became bolder in expressing their dissatisfaction with the country's slow pace of rearmament. Charges were made that Jewish and socialist elements were hindering progress. Chief of Staff Rátz was particularly disturbed by the pacifist attitude that some Hungarian publications were displaying.[33] Even Cabinet members were not immune from criticism. In the summer of that year both Kánya and Röder were accused of negligence for allowing the army to remain outmoded and impotent.[34] Developments in Germany gave further impetus to the restless officers. The German General Staff had never made a secret of the common interest that they believed the Reichswehr and the Honvéd had in a future campaign against Czechoslovakia.[35] In February 1937 Sztójay, doubtless without instructions from Kánya, approached German Minister of Defense Blomberg with a suggestion for General Staff talks to discuss joint study of possible future campaigns and "to set goals and establish harmony." Sztójay was thinking in terms of a "simultaneous advance," so that the mobilization and initial deployment of the enemy would be thwarted.[36] Blomberg agreed, and although no progress seems to have been made when Röder visited Berlin in April, Rátz decided the time for action had come.

During the spring and summer of 1937, General Rátz submitted to Darányi and the regent a series of memoranda in which he urged government approval of a massive program of military rearmament and modernization. This was necessary, Rátz argued, because in 1940 the Axis powers would enjoy a two-year advantage over France and England and would seek an "armed solution" of their problems. Hungary, by virtue of her geographical position and revisionist goals, would inevitably become involved. Significantly, Rátz went on to suggest that Hungary was in need also of political and moral rearmament. He thus proposed such measures as a "healthy land reform," reduction of Jewish influence, and a more just division of the national wealth.[37]

The immediate reaction to Rátz's proposals was negative. Quite apart from the military recommendations, conservative government leaders were dismayed to find him dealing with political matters completely beyond the sphere of responsibility of the chief of staff, especially since his political proposals paralleled quite closely those being advocated by Ferenc Szálasi. For already familiar reasons Kánya was opposed to the kind of large-scale rearmament Rátz was suggesting. He likewise feared the dangers of a one-sided orientation toward Germany that the memoranda implied. Moreover, experts in the Finance Ministry found the suggested expenditure an impossibility in terms of the limited resources at Hungary's disposal.

With the rejection of Rátz's initial proposals, there developed an intense debate of which few details have survived. Tension between Kánya and the more radical military men remained high, the former insisting that military equality should be achieved through negotiations with the Little Entente, though Hungary would offer no substantial concessions to obtain this recognition. For a time Röder managed to persuade the disgruntled officers to continue to trust in the foreign minister's policy. But the militant officers made it clear that they were tired of the "constant prevarication" and longed for the freedom to train openly and display their weapons.[38] This impetuosity was highly significant in Hungary later, when, as Europe inched closer to crisis, Rátz's ideas found influential supporters in the government.

The spirited debate in Hungary about which great power or powers Hungary would do best to court could not obscure the fact that relations with the Successor States remained a central concern in Hungary's foreign policy. This relationship had undergone a minor but not unimportant change after Gömbös lost control of the government in 1936. It was during the period of German-Hungarian tension in early 1937 that Kánya first began to talk openly of a "normalization" of relations with Hungary's neighbors. The government did not pursue the idea with any great zeal. Judging from the memorandum that Regent Horthy composed in the summer of

1936 for his talks with Hitler, his hostility toward the Successor States continued undiminished. Czechoslovakia he depicted as a "cancerous tumor" that in a future war would have to be exterminated by a joint German-Hungarian action. Nor did Horthy consider Romania or Yugoslavia suitable friends. Instead, like István Tisza before the Great War, he advocated a policy of cooperation with Turkey and Bulgaria.[39]

Kánya was more realistic. Though unwilling to abandon hopes for territorial revision in the long run, and skeptical that a friendly relationship could ever be achieved with Czechoslovakia, Yugoslavia, or Romania, he reasoned that certain distinct advantages could be obtained through friendly talks, or the appearance of friendly talks, with the countries of the Little Entente. Uppermost in his mind was the desire to improve the lot of the Hungarian minorities scattered throughout the Danube Basin. His policy of "defense of the minorities" (kisebbségvédelem) was motivated in part by the fear, which the Successor States' census figures of 1930 had kindled, that in time the Magyar minorities would be whittled away, just as the Slovak nation had been in danger of disappearing before World War I.[40] Kánya also preferred to achieve Hungary's freedom to rearm through the safest method, by negotiation. Besides, parties on all sides had been urging Hungary to come to an understanding with one or another of her neighbors. The British had been giving such advice for years, and Prime Minister Darányi was particularly eager to make some gesture to London to demonstrate his departure from Gömbös's whole-hearted orientation toward the totalitarian powers.

Responding to these counsels, Kánya, with Darányi's support, in late 1936 began to voice a willingness to examine favorably any proposal Hungary's neighbors might make. He insisted only that Hungary be treated as an equal (that is, no longer bound by the military clauses of Trianon) and that the condition of Hungarian minorities in the Successor States be a topic for discussion.[41] At first Kánya hoped to revive Count Bethlen's old plan of reaching a bilateral pact with Yugoslavia and thus driving a wedge between that country and her Little Entente partners. In early spring he was almost able to bring this off; a tentative agreement was reached with Stojadinović in March, but the news of the signing of a Yugoslav-Italian pact of friendship so alarmed Romania and

Czechoslovakia that they imposed a veto on a similar accommodation between Belgrade and Budapest.[42]

At this point Kánya might well have decided, as Gömbös would doubtless have done were he still on the scene, to abandon the idea of an improvement in relations with Hungary's neighbors. But the domestic political events of the winter and spring, and the unpredictability of Hitler's foreign policy, apparently led Kánya to conclude that, distasteful though it would be, the best course for his country in the short run was the initiation of negotiations for some sort of political agreement between Hungary and her hostile neighbors. The whole procedure would be "bristling with difficulties," he admitted to the British minister in Budapest, but perhaps by "modest beginnings" something might be done to bring a happy dénouement in the distant future.[43]

Though Kánya was thus prepared to enter into talks with the Little Entente as a whole, he showed little inclination to accept Eden's advice to join with Austria and Czechoslovakia in a common defense against German expansionism. Though superficially it might have seemed logical for these three exposed countries of Danubian Europe, nations whose cultural, political, and economic history had been closely intertwined, to cooperate to ward off a common danger, the idea had little appeal for Hungarian political leaders and diplomats. In fact, a rabid Czechophobia permeated the Hungarian political establishment: many of Hungary's woes, it was thought, could be attributed directly or indirectly to the machinations of Eduard Beneš and his colleagues in the Hradčany.[44]

It is true that a number of Hungarians, most notably Gusztáv Gratz, Endre Bajcsy-Zsilinszky, Tibor Eckhardt,[45] and most of the monarchists, stepped forward in strong advocacy of this Danubian "Triangle," but all of them regarded some territorial concessions by Prague as the essential catalyst in the formation of such a bloc. Gusztáv Gratz, who was in Paris in March 1937 to sound out opinions in the Quai d'Orsay, warned the French that the Hungarian public could not be expected to accept a frontier with Czechoslovakia that even the highest officials in Prague (including Masaryk and Beneš) had acknowledged to be less than perfect.[46] However, though the Czechoslovaks from time to time showed an interest in a rapprochement with Hungary,[47] they were adamant in their refusal to consider the cession of any territory.

Not unexpectedly, the strongest opposition to territorial concessions to Hungary seems to have come from Slovaks in the Prague
leadership, notably Milan Hodža, who served as prime minister
for several years in the mid-1930s and briefly as foreign minister
in late 1935 and early 1936. A Slovak who before the Great War
had been a member of the Hungarian Parliament, Hodža hoped in
1936 to form a bloc of Danubian countries that would represent
a defensive wall against German expansion. He regarded it as
essential that Austria and, if possible, Hungary join such a bloc,
but he made it clear that there could be no talk of territorial revision in Hungary's favor. As Hodža explained to the Austrians,
Prague believed that the Magyars were being unreasonable and
that perhaps only a future generation would, after certain disillu-
sionments, be willing to come to an understanding with their
neighbors. They had to realize that neither Hitler nor Mussolini
would support their claims, and that no English lord would "fight
on the battlefield for Hungarian revision."[48] On another occasion
he told Schuschnigg that once a "sensible" government appeared
in Budapest, Prague would present it with a whole "bag full of
concessions," albeit not of a territorial nature.[49]

The somewhat chimerical idea of forming a Danubian "Triangle"
thus made little progress in the spring of 1937, though the idea
would not die and, as shall be seen, was revived in the critical
months before the Anschluss. However, conditions in East Central
Europe during the summer proved to be propitious for what Kánya
had termed the "modest beginnings" in an easing of tension between Hungary and the Little Entente. Although at the Little
Entente conference in April Czechoslovakia and Romania had prevented Yugoslavia from signing a separate pact with Hungary,
it had been decided that some sort of agreement with Budapest
was desirable in principle. The Successor States were coming to
realize that really nothing could be done at that late date to prevent
Hungary from achieving the right to rearm. Military reprisals were
by this time out of the question, for if a conflict were sparked in
Danubian Europe, Germany and Italy might intervene on Hungary's side. However, the Little Entente did hope to drive some
sort of bargain, gaining some statement from Hungary emphasizing the "pacific" nature of her rearmament.[50]

In June 1937 the Hungarian minister in Bucharest, László Bárdossy, was informed by the Romanian prime minister that the

Little Entente countries "had agreed on a fair, pliant, and correct proposal that the Hungarian government would not be able to decline."[51] Negotiations thus began that ultimately were to lead to the so-called Bled Agreement of August 1938. During the bargaining over the summer and early fall of 1937, Kánya insisted that an amelioration of the difficult position of the Magyar minorities in the Successor States would have to be the "heart of any agreement." In return, he was willing to offer a pledge of nonaggression to each of the three Little Entente members. In the autumn both Czechoslovakia and Yugoslavia were prepared to accept these conditions, which were a modification of the original proposal submitted by the Little Entente. But Victor Antonescu, the Romanian foreign minister, insisted that his country, unlike Czechoslovakia and Yugoslavia, could not make any concessions as a "gesture" to the Magyar minority in Romania. Any appearance that Bucharest was acting on behest of Budapest to undo the "few wrongs" that had been done would bring an "extraordinarily difficult situation" for the Romanian government, which faced elections at the end of the year. Kánya reiterated that there was no prospect for any agreement that merely recognized Hungarian military equality and that required a nonaggression pledge from Budapest. He "would like to come to an agreement, but not at any price." In any case, he was "in no hurry."[52]

Thus, no agreement could be reached in the autumn of 1937, and the negotiations were postponed until the Romanian elections, which were scheduled for December. The delay was not necessarily deplored by Kánya, who found it advantageous to be conducting negotiations without having to incur any immediate obligations. In particular, it enabled him to keep all interested parties guessing what Hungary really intended to do. His freedom of maneuver remained unimpaired, and, without unduly alarming the Axis powers, the impression was created in the West that Hungary was making a contribution to peace and stability in Eastern Europe. Kánya heightened the ambiguity by providing contradictory explanations for his activities. Hungary's Axis friends were advised that there were no illusions in Budapest about creating friendly, intimate relations with Czechoslovakia, and that the "final goal" of Hungarian policy was always kept in mind; until the decisive point, however, Hungary had to form its policy to meet the present circumstances.[53] Kánya even hinted to Ciano that his real purpose in negotiating with all three Little Entente members was to reach three bilateral pacts, the least desirable of which—that with Prague—would be allowed in time to perish.[54]

When Germany and Italy nonetheless complained that Hungary really did not have to deal with Czechoslovakia, Kánya calmly pointed out that it was their own fault. The Axis wanted Hungary to take a stand against Prague, but they had done practically nothing to make the task easier. Their support of Romania and Yugoslavia had made them more rigid in their talks with Budapest. It had to be kept in mind that if, "contrary to expectations, she were ever abandoned by Germany and Italy, then Hungary would reach a very much more comprehensive agreement with the Little Entente than was perhaps held to be possible today."[55]

It was the latter possibility that Kánya stressed to diplomatic representatives of the West. He told Montgomery, the American minister, that any agreement he might achieve with the Little Entente "would be only a stepping stone toward what he hoped to accomplish."[56] And in his talks with his counterparts in the Little Entente countries, Kánya represented an agreement as a valuable contribution to stability in the Danubian Basin.

In the fall of 1937 the Little Entente had a good opportunity to test Kánya's sincerity. The terms suggested by Hungary were not onerous or unyielding, and they proved acceptable to all concerned in August 1938. But the tide of nationalism in Romania was too strong, and, despite a belated intervention by France in favor of an agreement, the negotiations were suspended until after the Romanian elections, by which time Germany was to be poised for its first major thrust into Danubian Europe.

In addition to the myriad of other problems confronting Hungary in 1937, one in particular came to assume great importance as the year progressed. The fate of Austria, Hungary's neighbor and treaty partner, was of primary concern to Budapest, and the progressive deterioration of Vienna's position was both alarming and frustrating. Hungary could do little to affect the situation. The Rome Protocols called for general political and economic cooperation, but there was no mutual assistance obligation, and Hungary, one of the weakest European countries, could not be expected to intervene militarily if Austrian independence were endangered. This was the responsibility of the great powers who had created Austria, particularly the three (Great Britain, France, and Italy) who in the Stresa Front Declaration of 1935 had reaffirmed the necessity of preserving Austria's sovereignty.

Developments early in the period seemed encouraging. On 11 July 1936, Austria and Germany had come to a Gentlemen's Agreement, which, in Mussolini's opinion, brought "to an end the unhappy situation of Austria as a football of foreign interests."[57] The Gentlemen's Agreement was a landmark in East European history in the interwar period. But instead of securing Austria's position, it gravely endangered it. With this "last and only mortgage"[58] on German-Italian relations removed, the conditions for the formation of the Axis were finally met, and that development was to have the most deleterious impact on Austria. The essential catalyst in the formation of the Rome Pact in 1934 had been Mussolini's desire to maintain an Italian sphere of influence in East Central Europe. In practice this meant a commitment to preserve Austrian independence from the German Reich's encroachments. Despite the fundamental doubts about the feasibility of this endeavor, which both Bethlen and the Duce expressed in 1927, Italy had moved troops to the Austrian border when Austrian Nazis assassinated Dollfuss and attempted a coup d'état in the summer of 1934. But Mussolini was not a statesman remarkable for his political acumen or constancy, and Italian policy often mirrored the tortuous and imprecise nature of his personality. In the years after 1934, momentary moods of pessimism often led to dramatic, but fleeting, shifts in his Austrian policy. At times, when he became angered by "Ballhausplatz inefficiency" or manifestations of Austrian ingratitude, he resolved to abandon Austria completely to Germany. Yet just as rapidly his mood could change, and once again he would speak earnestly of Italy's "Watch on the Brenner." But after the formation of the Axis in November 1936, with the Germans whispering into Italian ears guarantees of hegemony in the Mediterranean, the "Watch on the Brenner" became an anachronistic slogan at the Palazzo Chigi, and Austria was consigned to its agonizing course toward eventual Anschluss to Germany.

Hungarian leaders quickly learned of the fragile foundation on which Austrian independence was placed. Already in November 1936, Ciano conveyed to Kánya his impression that Austrian youth was Nazi in spirit, a condition that sooner or later would have far-reaching consequences.[59] Perhaps of greater influence on thinking in Hungary were the indications that Berlin, despite Hitler's avowed intention of observing the terms of the Gentlemen's Agreement, was set on an eventual annexation of Austria. During their first meeting in the fall of 1936, Göring bluntly told Kánya that "this thoroughly German state [Austria] must in some way sooner or later be annexed to the Reich."[60]

The unflattering truth, however, was that many prominent Hungarian political figures had by this time already abandoned the hope of preserving an independent Austria, and were therefore only too glad to accommodate Germany, especially if Hungary could gain something in the bargain. As has already been noted, the chief architects of interwar Hungary, Horthy, Bethlen, and Gömbös, all discounted the possibility of precluding the Anschluss in the long run. During his brief visit to the Obersalzberg, Regent Horthy had advised Hitler to be patient with regard to Austria. Developments would, in his opinion, "lead eventually to Anschluss" as soon as the older generation died out. In the younger generation he had observed "an almost unanimous will for Anschluss with Germany."[61] The regent's views were shared by Bethlen and the garrulous chef de cabinet of the Foreign Ministry, Count István Csáky, who in early 1938, without Kánya's authorization, advised the Germans of Hungarian indifference to Austria's fate.[62] The Hungarian minister in Vienna from 1936 to 1937, Lajos Rudnay, likewise adopted a cynical attitude. After a conversation with von Papen, his German counterpart, in May 1937, in which the latter alluded to a possible German move against Austria sometime in the future, Rudnay recommended in a report to Budapest that Hungary prepare for such an eventuality. With proper planning it could be made not simply a German annexation, but a joint partition between Hungary and Germany, in which Hungary would seize the Burgenland and Southern Carinthia, exchanging the latter territory with Yugoslavia for the Bácska.[63]

The pessimistic and opportunistic attitude of Horthy, Bethlen, Csáky, and Rudnay was balanced, however, by the more cautious and temperate views of Darányi and Kánya. Prime Minister Darányi did not involve himself too closely in foreign affairs, but Schuschnigg regarded him as a great friend of Austria whose "conciliatory and friendly attitude" was much appreciated.[64] Kánya's policy in the Austrian question was, not unexpectedly, very circumspect. Far more perceptive than Horthy and the others who glibly welcomed the Anschluss, Kánya realized that the appearance of a "German Reich of 70 millions" on Hungary's western borders could be a serious menace to his country's position. Yet Hungary had little room for maneuver in this question, and realizing that the men of Berlin had strong views on the inevitability of the Anschluss, Kánya was wary of alienating the Reich. Thus, although he never even hinted to the Germans that Hungary's interest in Austrian independence might be weakening, he nonetheless did not make a special effort to emphasize publicly Hungary's devotion to her western neighbor, nor to correct the impression that Horthy and Csáky had given that Budapest welcomed the Anschluss. Kánya chose rather to let events take their course, helping Austria whenever it was within Hungary's power to do so, and stiffening Mussolini's resolve, but never giving Germany cause for alarm.

Many governmental leaders below the front rank shared Kánya's views on the Austrian question. Most members of the Cabinet, which from 1936 to 1938 was on the whole a moderate, Western-oriented group, regarded Austria's struggle for independence with sympathy. In this camp could be counted Minister of Finance Fabinyi and Minister of Justice Lazár. In the Foreign Ministry, Baron Apor, the permanent secretary, had lifelong ties with Austria and could be expected to support Kánya's policy. Moreover, General Röder, though perhaps not the majority of his fellow officers, also favored close political and military relations with Austria, and he made a special effort to foster friendly ties with his Viennese counterparts.

Hungarian society, like its leadership, was not of one voice on the Austrian question, although if public opinion could have been tested in those days, a large majority of the population would doubtless have expressed itself in favor of an independent Austria. For a great many Hungarians the problem became submerged in the larger one of Hungary's relationship to Nazi Germany itself, and attitudes were usually formed with this larger consideration in mind. Thus, the amorphous opposition (Social Democrats, monarchists, Smallholders, and other splinter groups) on the whole took a stand for the preservation of Austrian independence. Political ideology played only a small role here; the monarchists did indeed hope to pave the way for the re-establishment of a dual monarchy under Archduke Otto, but the Social Democrats could not be particularly sympathetic to the current Austrian government, which had earlier dealt so severely with its socialist parties. They were merely concerned that Germany's swallowing up of Austria would mean the realization of the nightmare of an expansionist Nazi Germany poised on Hungary's frontier.

The most vociferous opposition to the Anschluss was often voiced by those most removed from power: the Jews, the far left, and the political mavericks. The Social Democrat *Népszava* and the illegal *Dolgozók Lapja* of the Communist Party contained many articles in 1936 and 1937 warning of the perils of German expansion. Very active as well were the Germanophobes like Dezső Szabó and Bajcsy-Zsilinszky. The latter used the political platform that membership in Parliament afforded to launch violent attacks on Germany. In his *A német világ Magyarországon* he argued that while Hungary could not interfere in the domestic affairs of Germany, it could not be considered a domestic concern of the Reich when it "undermined and threatened to sweep away the independence of Austria, which was a friend of Hungary."[65]

In contrast to the attitude of many conservatives and those of the left, Hungary's right radicals tended to view the possibility of Austria's annexation to the Reich with equanimity. Their ideological sympathy with Hitler's regime seems to have diminished any fears that an enlarged Germany might be a threat and not a boon to Hungary.[66] Ferenc Szálasi's views were typical: he had only scorn for Schuschnigg's government, which was engaged in a struggle against the Austrian National Socialists, and he felt that Hungary had sufficient moral and physical strength to hold its own even if Germany proved an obstreperous neighbor.[67] A further motive in favoring the Anschluss was the belief that Hungary might be able to participate in the action. András Mecsér, a right-wing politician and former crony of Gömbös, believed that Hitler had promised Gömbös the Burgenland when Germany moved to annex Austria. As shall be seen, during the hectic days of March 1938 Mecsér was to step forward to try to make good this claim.

Meanwhile, the Hungarian government, though maintaining close economic and military ties with Vienna in 1936 and 1937, clung to a policy that saw Austria's best chance for survival as dependent on a strict compliance with the Gentlemen's Agreement. Indeed, one of Hungary's main diplomatic preoccupations in 1937 was an effort to persuade Vienna to adhere closely to that formula. When in the early months of 1937 Schuschnigg seemed to be laying the groundwork for a possible restoration of the Habsburg monarchy, Budapest quickly stepped in to dissuade him. Kánya, sensing that a restoration in Austria could provoke a violent response from the Reich, even suggested to the Germans that a joint German-Hungarian démarche be delivered to Austria.[68]

Developments in Austria during 1937 proved increasingly discouraging to the Hungarian government. Schuschnigg seemed bent on taking some action to prop up his country, but his ideas often seemed dangerous to the cautious Hungarians. Moreover, month by month Italy's determination to prevent the Anschluss grew perceptibly weaker. In May Kánya could still confidently tell the British that a "cold Anschluss" was out of the question, but Ciano shook this confidence later that same month when he told Kánya that the Anschluss would come "sooner or later," and that Italy would in the future not take up arms to prevent it. When Kánya observed that it seemed that Italy had already abandoned Austria, Ciano hardly protested.[69]

It must be conceded, however, that even while the great powers were leaving Austria to its unpleasant fate, the attitude of the Hungarian government (as opposed to the private utterances of Horthy, Csáky, and Sztójay) was friendly and correct, especially in military and economic affairs.[70] In their speeches Kánya and Darányi right up to the end continued to acknowledge Austria as a good friend of Hungary, and when Italy abruptly abrogated the system of preferential tariffs between Rome Pact members, Kánya agreed to the Austrian suggestion that it be continued between Hungary and Austria.[71] When Schuschnigg periodically embarked on his schemes for Danubian blocs, Kánya, though demonstrably skeptical, was at least willing to consider his proposals. Military ties were also friendly, with frequent exchanges of officers, mutual support in rearmament, and, as shall be seen, even frank discussions of possible military campaigns. But the Hungarians, ever wary of offending Berlin, were reluctant to consider closer ties with Austria, such as a defensive pact. Thus, in the prelude to the Austrian crisis, the Vienna leadership realized that Hungary was their best friend but that in an "emergency" even she would probably find it impossible to give support.[72]

Chapter 5

To the Anschluss

In the first days of 1938, Kálmán Kánya privately expressed the opinion that there was nowhere in Europe a "will to war" and that, barring accidents, peace seemed assured for at least a year.[1] In a technical sense Kánya's prediction was born out by events, but he clearly did not foresee the upheavals that were soon to shatter the status quo in Danubian Europe. Yet, like most of his counterparts in other European capitals, Kánya had sensed that the pace of international events had begun to quicken in the last months of 1937. In October violent incidents in the Bohemian city of Teplitz reminded Europeans of the smoldering minorities problem in the Czechoslovak Republic. In November yet another stage in the German-Italian rapprochement was reached as Rome adhered to the Anti-Comintern Pact. Later in the month Lord Halifax, acting as an emissary of Neville Chamberlain, paid an important visit to Germany.

However, the major development in this period, of which few people outside the narrow coterie around Hitler were aware, was the new determination in Berlin to seize a favorable opportunity in the near future to fulfill German territorial ambitions in Austria and Czechoslovakia. Hitler and his more militant colleagues were becoming increasingly confident that conditions in Europe would soon become suitable for the use of coercion or direct military force to effect the political and territorial changes they desired in Danubian Europe.[2] In a military directive drawn up by the German minister of defense, General Blomberg, in June 1937, the suggestion was made that Germany needed to enhance its readiness for war not only to protect against an enemy's attack but also to be able to exploit any favorable political opportunities.[3] Moreover, when Hitler spoke to his assembled military and political chiefs in early November at the so-called Hossbach meeting, he voiced the opinion that the Western powers, Germany's two "hate-inspired" opponents, had probably written off Austria and Czechoslovakia. In certain circumstances he would make his move against

Vienna and Prague as early as 1938, moving with "lightning speed."[4]

It may be that Hitler's willingness to embark so quickly on his long-range program reflected a growing concern that, like Gyula Gömbös, his life would be cut short by a fatal illness before his program was completed.[5] Yet even apart from this consideration, Hitler's political acumen led him to conclude in 1937 that the other great powers lacked the will and ability to construct a political grouping to thwart German expansion into the Danubian area. Almost by intuition Hitler sensed what historians would later confirm in the documents. The French, despite a brave public posture, were increasingly despondent. In May Yvon Delbos, the French foreign minister, privately remarked that though the problem occupied him "night and day," he could devise no policy to insure peace and prevent Central Europe from falling into German hands. France, he concluded, was "no longer strong enough to maintain the status quo in Central Europe against an opposition composed of Germany and Italy."[6]

A similar pessimism seemed to grip many of Britain's leadership as well. Having started late in the rush to rearm, the British were haunted by fears of military inferiority. The chiefs of staff warned that, though its naval supremacy was secured for many years, Great Britain would not have any ground troops to send to the continent if war broke out. In May the Cabinet did approve an extensive program for the modernization of the army, but this was due for completion only in 1940.[7]

In this period some West European statesmen hoped that the weight of the New World, of the United States, might be thrown into the balance to help thwart possible German expansion. But during the Danubian crisis these hopes proved to be illusory. It is true that since the 1920s the United States had had important economic and financial interests in Europe, including the countries of East Central Europe. True also that certain American diplomats, notably William Bullitt in Paris and Anthony Biddle in Warsaw, were able and often perspicacious observers of European affairs who favored a more active American foreign policy. But on the whole the American public and most of its representatives in Washington were ignorant of the problems of Europe and did not believe that vital American interests could be at stake there, least of all in such seemingly remote places as Czechoslovakia and Hungary.[8] Despite occasional references to the European scene in speeches by President Roosevelt, isolationist sentiments thus continued to dictate American foreign policy as the European crisis unfolded.

In any case, seemingly irreconcilable differences hampered the efforts of England, France, the Soviet Union, and Italy to band together to balance German power. The Soviet Union preached the necessity of combatting Nazism, but was treated as an untrustworthy pariah by most of the others, who were revolted by the inhuman excesses of the purges. Cooperation between Paris and Rome was rendered impossible by the violent clash of ideological and national interests. In many ways England was the key: on good terms with France, and at least superficially interested in cooperation with Italy and Russia, London's policy toward Germany would help determine the position of the other states of Europe, both small and large. But the British were torn by conflicting emotions. Many, perhaps a majority, of politically conscious Britons felt that Germany had justifiable grievances. The problem was whether to satisfy these grievances while National Socialists were in power, or, conversely, whether to respond militarily to prevent Germany from attempting to right the alleged wrongs on its own. Neville Chamberlain, who became prime minister in May 1937, felt that an attempt should be made to reach a comprehensive diplomatic settlement with Hitler's Germany. In exchange for certain "satisfactory assurances" that force would not be used in dealing with Austria and Czechoslovakia, he was prepared to give Berlin what amounted to a free hand in that part of Europe.[9] This was essentially the message that Lord Halifax carried with him to Germany in November. In the Danzig, Austrian, and Czechoslovak problems, he told his hosts, London was "not necessarily concerned to stand for the status quo as to-day," but he did wish to "avoid such treatment of them as would be likely to cause trouble." Halifax made it clear that what England was envisioning was a process of "peaceful change," by which Germany could come to amicable agreements with its neighbors.[10]

Halifax's visit, which came shortly after the Hossbach meeting, could only have strengthened Hitler in his conviction that England was unlikely to intervene in Central Europe, indeed, that London had virtually abandoned the continent and the stability of the European system. But it is unlikely that Hitler shared the rather naive notion that important changes in the East European status quo could be affected by peaceful means. As Hitler had made clear to Gömbös in 1933, force or the threat of force would have to be employed. He probably hoped that the changes could be made with the minimum military risk for Germany; for this reason he welcomed British statements of disinterest and encouraged similar sentiments in France. But, as Hitler told the British ambassador early in 1938, Germany would not allow third parties to interfere in the settlement of problems involving large groups of German nationals. If they persisted, the moment would come when Germany, as a great power, would have to fight.[11]

A few days after Halifax's departure from Germany, a Hungarian delegation led by Darányi and Kánya journeyed to Berlin for a set of talks that were to have a significant impact on Hungary's policy in the unfolding Danubian crisis. Before this visit few in Hungary suspected the far-reaching changes that were in the air. This was true despite the fact that the Hungarian leadership probably was better informed about Hitler's long-term program than that of any other country. As early as the summer of 1936, the Hungarian General Staff had concluded, on the basis of information proffered by friends in the German military establishment, that Hitler's military plans called first for a strengthening of the western fortifications. Once the fortifications were sufficiently strong, Germany would solicit Polish and Hungarian assistance for a military campaign against Czechoslovakia, Germany seizing Bohemia and Moravia, and Poland and Hungary dividing up the remainder.[12]

In 1937 there were renewed hints from Germany that Austria and Czechoslovakia were Hitler's immediate targets. In May the Hungarian representative in Vienna reported a conversation with his German counterpart, Franz von Papen, who had just returned in a militant mood from consultations with Hitler. Papen bluntly cited the dismemberment of Czechoslovakia as a goal of the Reich: "Czechoslovakia can not continue to exist, and I believe that in a favorable international situation a firm decision would also have to be made with regard to Austria."[13] Papen volunteered no timetable, but, on the basis of the information they had garnered, the Hungarian officers projected 1940–41 as the most likely time for renewed war in Europe.[14] When the Hungarian Chief of Staff attended the annual German maneuvers in September, General Ludwig Beck suggested that in two or three years, around 1940, the German army would be ready and the "Czech question" would be ripe for settlement. For the time being what was needed was detailed planning, and Beck, asserting that he hoped to "undo the harm that the politicians on both sides had done," urged that Austria be drawn into the consultations.[15]

If these reports, and earlier belligerent utterances by Göring, could be taken at face value, the Hungarian government could assume that the Germans were in fact planning offensive action to seize Czechoslovakia, and perhaps Austria, some time around 1940. Whether this information represented merely the wishful thinking of the German generals and idle boasting of Göring, or Hitler's true intentions, was difficult for the Hungarians to determine. The trip in November for the talks planned with Hitler thus took on added importance, for it would provide the opportunity to obtain more authoritative information on the Führer's plans. Until then, however, Hungary's main concern in its relationship with Germany continued to focus on those German actions that in the past year had greatly alarmed many Magyars: the proliferation of pan-German and *völkisch* propaganda in Hungary, visits by German agitators posing as tourists or scholars, and unfriendly articles in the German press. Several times in the summer and fall, Kánya and Darányi complained bitterly to the Germans about these activities. The German press was also closely perused for any signs of anti-Hungarian sentiment, and Sztójay was instructed on several occasions to protest against offending articles.

A distinct nervousness about Germany's intentions likewise continued to pervade certain segments of Hungarian society. The speeches of many parliamentary delegates in the early autumn were strewn with warnings about Germanic expansion, and in October a unique attempt was made to bridge the political differences of a number of the oppositional parties. The one thing that united such disparate groups as the monarchists, Social Democrats, Liberals, and Independent Smallholders was the firm conviction that Hungary's independence and parliamentary system had to be protected from Nazi German encroachments. Accordingly, on 10 October representatives from most of these parties and groups held a rally at Körmend in western Hungary and declared that the best course for troubled Hungary was a return of a king to the throne. The leaders of the Smallholder and Liberal parties, Tibor Eckhardt and Károly Rassay, announced their support for and confidence in Otto of Habsburg, the heir to the throne. The Social Democrats, though not present at Körmend, later welcomed the cooperation of all anti-Nazi groups and hinted that in an emergency they would support the reinstitution of monarchy.[16] Few of the speakers at Körmend could actually have believed that a restoration was possible in Hungary in the foreseeable future. The rally had mainly symbolic importance: it demonstrated, to foreigners and Magyars alike, that a significant segment of Hungarian society was alarmed about recent developments and realized the dangers of a close association with Nazi Germany.[17]

This was the political atmosphere in Hungary when Darányi and Kánya departed for Germany on 20 November. That a thorough review of the whole spectrum of common concerns was to be conducted explains the presence in the Hungarian party of officials responsible for problems of minorities, agriculture, and trade. During the course of the five day stay, there was little of the pomp and extravagance that had been lavished on the Duce two months earlier or that would be accorded Milan Stojadinović in early 1938. It was to be truly a straightforward and businesslike affair, with the Hungarians intent on gaining a clearer idea of Hitler's plans for Danubian Europe.

Hitler was prepared to comply. Having determined that he would make his move against Czechoslovakia and Austria as early as 1938 if conditions permitted, Hitler had to reshape his policy toward the countries of East Central Europe. The earlier idea of building a vast anti-Bolshevik bloc in Eastern Europe no longer seemed to have any value, whether propagandistic or utilitarian. Instead, the Führer, intent on paving the way for his campaign against Austria and Czechoslovakia, shrewdly calculated that any misgivings in Hungary, Poland, and Yugoslavia would have to be overcome by appropriate assurances from Germany. Thus, on the very day of the Hossbach meeting, Warsaw was given comforting words on Germany's respect for Polish rights in Danzig.[18] Yugoslavia had for years been advised that Germany had no designs of any sort on her territory, and that no support would be given to Hungary if she advanced any such claims. When Stojadinović visited Germany in January 1938, he was treated to a magnificent reception and laudatory press items on the "New Yugoslavia."

In a sense, Hungary posed a special problem for Hitler, since she bordered on both of his future victims and, if hostile, could cause some embarrassment. The strategy he conceived in 1937 seems clear in retrospect: he would assure Budapest's neutrality in the Anschluss question by allaying fears about German interference in Hungarian domestic affairs and, more importantly, by offering the opportunity for territorial aggrandizement in Czechoslovakia. From his past contacts with the Hungarians, the Führer was convinced that their eagerness for revision would make them willing accomplices. His Hungarian visitors since 1933 had made little effort to conceal their hostility toward Czechoslovakia, and some, like the regent, probably voiced the frank determination to help excise the "cancerous tumor."[19] Thus, when in his military directive of June 1937 General Blomberg discussed the possibility of war in East Central Europe, he suggested that Hungary would "sooner or later join in the action against Czechoslovakia."[20] It is important to reemphasize at this point that Hitler's policy was shaped not by a concern for ameliorating the plight of the Sudeten Germans but by a desire to achieve a strategic border on the Carpathians. For this reason he wanted to annex Bohemia and Moravia, leaving Slovakia and Ruthenia to Hungary if she wanted them. Of the Slovaks he knew little: there is no reason to question his later assertion that until September 1938 he had not realized the strength of the national feeling of that people.[21] With the general direction of his course thus established, Hitler felt sufficiently confident to allow the Hungarians a brief glimpse of the rewards they might expect, so that when the time came Budapest would act as a trusted ally.

Upon their arrival in Berlin, the Hungarians immediately sensed a new mood of friendliness. The German press, which had been carefully instructed beforehand, was filled with articles favorable to Hungary and flattering to Kánya and Darányi.[22] Two important conversations had been planned, the most important of which was that with Hitler on the 25th. Earlier, however, the Hungarians had a *pourparler* with Göring, who had been in a militant mood since the Hossbach meeting.[23] Referring to reports "from a good source," the Reich Marshal began by enumerating what he believed were the misdeeds of Schuschnigg and his "Czech friends," including an attempt to unite Hungary, Czechoslovakia, and Austria in a restored monarchy. Moreover, according to his information the Hungarians were not entirely innocent, but had concluded an agreement with Vienna to give support if Germany and Austria became involved in an armed conflict. "Germany has become a world power again," he declared, "and its power to attract Germans abroad, naturally including the Austrians, has therefore grown tremendously." He thus regarded the union of Austria to the motherland as "a natural and unavoidable development."

Darányi and Kánya succeeded in calming the aroused Göring with assurances that although relations with Austria were "very good," Hungary had no military pact of the kind mentioned, nor had Austria ever proposed such an agreement. Having made his point, Göring then turned to another matter that had always concerned him: the need for a Hungarian-Yugoslav rapprochement. Reiterating what must by this time have sounded like a worn record to the Hungarians, the German leader emphasized that Germany saw only one immediate area ripe for Hungarian revisionism, namely Czechoslovakia. Though he realized the difficulties involved, he thought a reconciliation with Belgrade was imperative. Stojadinović did not trust the Hungarians, and therefore Budapest would have to renounce forever its aspirations to revision in that direction. This would then be guaranteed by the Axis. With regard to his advice that Hungary seek a *modus vivendi* with Romania, Göring suggested that Budapest could, "through a clever policy, and without recognizing the present borders as final, prevent Romania's support of Czechoslovakia in the case of conflict."

In response Kánya complained of "Serbian duplicity" and asserted that it was unlikely that Belgrade would agree to a bilateral pact with Hungary, since the Little Entente countries had decided earlier that year to proceed jointly in negotiations with Hungary. He was prepared, however, to accept Göring's mediation in this question, and was willing to offer to recognize Yugoslavia's borders in exchange for a commitment on Belgrade's part to declare its *désintéressement* should a conflict occur between Hungary and one of its neighbors. This, apparently, was precisely what Göring had had in mind, for he greeted Kánya's statement with much enthusiasm and offered to intercede privately with Belgrade.

After a detailed exposition of his policy toward the Little Entente,[24] Kánya presented some of the grievances that he had resolved to bring once again to the attention of the German leadership. His main argument was that the natural pro-German sentiments of the Hungarian people were being undermined by visiting German agitators and the anti-Hungarian outbursts of the German press. As a result, pressures had been put on him to resist the "Pan-German danger." Moreover, his position was made particularly difficult by the fact that Romania and Yugoslavia, two enemies of Hungary, were given generous treatment in the German press, while Hungary was constantly chastised for its revisionism and supposed maltreatment of minorities. Could not, Kánya asked, correct relations be established between Hungary and the National Socialist Party, just as excellent relations existed with the political and military leadership of Germany?

In response, Göring made a determined effort to mollify the Hungarians. In regard to the question of the German minority, he stressed that Germany was interested primarily in the fulfillment of cultural demands. "It's a crazy idea," he asserted, "to believe that Hitler is thinking also of annexing Hungary." If Germans were agitating in Hungary, stringent measures would be taken, so long as Budapest could identify them by name.[25] In a similar vein, Göring vowed to see to it that the German press was less hostile. Commenting on Rosenberg's article a year earlier, Göring explained that it had been aimed at winning over the right in Romania. But that was in the past, and the Hungarians should realize that though for the present Hitler did not approve of aggressive action against Romania, he did not oppose Hungarian territorial aspirations toward Romania in general. The realization of these goals simply had to be postponed until a later date.

Despite Göring's ranting at the outset, the conversation thus ended in a conciliatory tone highly pleasing to the Hungarians. The accusations about a suspected Hungarian-Austrian military agreement were not repeated, and it is probable that Marshal Göring staged the whole scene in order to intimidate his guests and warn them not to intensify relations with Vienna or Prague.[26] Most gratifying to Darányi and Kánya was Göring's frank reference to Hungarian revision in Czechoslovakia and the hint that something might ultimately be obtained in Romania as well. Hungary was apparently gaining an important place in German policy, and, in the context of Göring's advice, it could mean only that the Czechoslovak question would before long come to the fore. Here, to be sure, Göring had made a crucial stipulation: although the dismemberment of Czechoslovakia was surely necessary, an attack could occur only in the course of a larger war.

Ideas expressed at this initial conversation with Göring appeared again when Hitler spoke with his guests. The only surviving record of this second conversation is the German Foreign Ministry memorandum prepared at the time.[27] However, later references in Hungarian documents make it certain that the German record is not a complete account of Hitler's words. It describes Hitler as opening the talk, like Göring, with an outburst against Schuschnigg and Hodža. But the Führer did not dwell on the subject of Austria. Instead, he repeated the advice that Hungary avoid a "diffusion of her policies in various directions" and instead concentrate on Czechoslovakia. According to the German record, Kánya replied that this was Hungary's opinion too, and that revisionist speeches and articles appearing in Hungary were not to be taken seriously, for the "government knew what it wanted."

It is certain, however, that Hitler was far blunter in his discussion of Czechoslovakia than the German account indicates. A collation of later evidence shows that Hitler on his own initiative mentioned rumors that Germany aspired to certain parts of Slovakia in the event that Czechoslovakia were dismembered. The German leader denied that he laid claim to Bratislava (Pressburg, Pozsony) or any other part of Slovakia.[28] He wanted a "strong Hungary" and a common German-Hungarian border along the Carpathians, especially since this would free some of his army divisions for duty elsewhere.[29]

The Hungarians apparently took note of this with satisfaction, and Darányi was subsequently to remark that the Hungarian government's attitude toward the fate of Czechoslovakia "was completely in accord with the Führer's."[30] By this Darányi meant, however, only that Hungary agreed that if Czechoslovakia were to be parcelled out, all parties, including Germany, should recognize Hungarian claims to Slovakia. Hitler seems not to have given any more information on when or how the dismemberment was to take place, nor for that matter did he specify any actions that he wished Hungary to take. Of course, Kánya much preferred it this way. At the conclusion of their conversation, the Hungarian foreign minister called Hitler's attention to the fact that, contrary to certain rumors, "Hungary had no intention whatever of achieving her revisionist aims by force of arms and thereby unleashing a European war." Hitler replied that he had never given credence to such rumors.[31] By this means Kánya was attempting to set the stage for a policy he hoped would bring great gains for Hungary without incurring undue military risks. Although Kánya's disclaimer must have seemed strange to Hitler, the frankness with which the Hungarians were willing to discuss what was obviously meant to be a future destruction of Czechoslovakia seemed to convince him that when the time came, the Hungarians would be enthusiastic partners.

During the course of their conversation, Hitler touched on a number of other points. He gave assurances similar to those extended by Göring, and gave his personal pledge that not a single Hungarian town would ever be touched. A similar promise was given that "swastika propaganda" would no longer be directed at Hungary.[32]

From the Hungarian standpoint, this visit to Berlin was of great importance. Prospects for territorial revision, which had seemed little more than dreams of the Hungarian Revision League, now appeared real and attainable. The friendship with Germany, which only weeks earlier seemed to be bringing Hungary more disadvantages than advantages, now took on a new dimension. Assurances had been given on nearly all of the points of friction that had troubled Hungarian-German relations over the past two years. But the reaction of Hungarian leaders to this new development was far from unambiguous. In fact, the results of the visit to Berlin were to prove to be the catalyst in an aggravation of the policy differences of two schools of thought in Hungary. The group that recommended that Hungary align herself completely with Germany took great satisfaction in the November events. They pointed to Hitler's promise of noninterference in Hungary's domestic affairs, his offer to intercede with Yugoslavia, and, most importantly, his apparent offer of territorial revision in the future as powerful incentives to draw closer to the resurgent Germany. Their argument was bolstered by the belief that, in his talk with Hitler, Halifax had given the Germans a virtual *carte blanche* in Eastern Europe.[33] Germany, they asserted, was once again the power to be reckoned with in Central Europe, and since Germany was the only country to propose revision for Hungary in a concrete form, the best course for Hungary was to orient herself in the direction of Berlin.

Kánya and others preferred to interpret the results of the Berlin conversations with more caution. He was indeed gratified by the various assurances he had obtained from Hitler, but he was not about to forget that the promises of Nazi Germany were not always kept. Though these latest pledges could be put to good use in quieting the emphatic anti-German elements of the Hungarian opposition parties, it was clearly wise to see if Berlin would observe them. Moreover, Kánya was reluctant to commit Hungary to any course that was likely to involve the country in an armed conflict. Thus, though he was eager to stay in the good graces of Berlin and thereby gain the Felvidék (Hungary's former northern areas) should Czechoslovakia disintegrate from internal disorder or German pressure, Kánya was also intent on maintaining a firm neutrality between England and Germany and avoiding participation in a war on Germany's side. This explains his warning to Hitler that Hungary had no intention of obtaining her revision by force of arms. Halifax's mission to Germany was viewed in a different light by Kánya and others of his political persuasion: it raised the possibility of a comprehensive German-English settlement in Europe, by which the just grievances of Germany (and perhaps Hungary) would be peacefully redressed. The wisest course of action for Hungary, they argued, was to avoid embracing or alienating either of these two powerful countries and to await the development of events.[34]

Although the Berlin talks evoked a vigorous debate among the various factions in Budapest, none of the Hungarians seems to have regarded a European crisis as imminent. Since no hint had been given by Hitler that he might be prepared to move as early as 1938, it was assumed that General Beck's earlier reference to 1940 as the target date was roughly accurate. Nonetheless, the Berlin visit served as a fillip to the group of restless army officers who were convinced of the necessity of modernizing Hungary's military establishment in preparation for the coming conflict. Shortly before the Berlin visit, General Rátz's proposal for massive rearmament had been discussed once again at a meeting called at the prompting of Horthy, but the continued opposition of Kánya and Tihamér Fabinyi, Minister of Finance, had again blocked any action. This convinced some of the extremist officers that the present government would continue to stymie all efforts to embark on large-scale rearmament and that the time had come to take positive action. Late in the year Rátz was being urged to "proclaim a military dictatorship on a fascist or national socialist basis," a move that some officers felt would have the support of the entire Honvéd officer corps. This Rátz did not care to risk; instead, in a move doubtless intended to demonstrate to the regent the urgency of the situation, Rátz tendered his resignation. But Horthy, who was in essential agreement with the officers on the need for rearming, convinced his chief of staff to stay on so that they could work together to find some solution to the problem.[35]

In late 1937 and early 1938 the political atmosphere in Hungary was strangely reminiscent of that in late 1919 and the first part of 1920. In both cases the right radicals in the army contemplated the possibility of seizing power from what they considered an inefficient civilian government and installing a military dictatorship with Admiral Horthy at the helm. In early January 1938 Ferenc Szálasi, Rátz, and other officers sympathetic to the right radical ideology decided to send General Károly Soós, a senior officer with impeccable credentials as a Szeged veteran, to intercede with Horthy. Soós reported on the restless mood of the officers and their concern that Hungary's national life was pervaded by the nefarious influence of Jews and leftists. Kánya's direction of foreign policy, Soós suggested, was not determined or vigorous enough: what was needed was a clear orientation toward Hungary's "true friends," the Axis powers, and a demonstration that Hungary would be a "valuable ally" willing to cooperate "come life or death." But time was pressing, for a European conflict was only a few years away and Hungary needed to create a "powerful combat-ready" army. It was the hope of the officer corps that Horthy would facilitate this by boldly sweeping away the ineffective civilian government and establishing an authoritarian right-wing government based on the military.[36]

In retrospect, early 1938 represents a significant turning point in Hungary's interwar political history. Had Horthy agreed to cooperate with the extremists in the General Staff, as he had done to a certain extent in 1919 and 1920, Hungary's role in the critical events of 1938 would doubtless have been more aggressive and uncompromising. But by the late 1930s Horthy had become decidedly more cautious and conservative in his political views. Though, as will be seen below, he still could be tempted by his soldier friends to bypass the foreign minister and engage in planning for a military campaign against Czechoslovakia, he did not subscribe to the view that military officers should be a political factor in domestic affairs. Moreover, he very much distrusted Szálasi and believed that the Arrowcross movement was a destructive force in Hungarian society and political life. Heeding the advice of his trusted civilian advisors, Horthy thus not only rejected Soós's proposal, but in a speech several months later stated that an army engaged in politics was "not only worthless but harmful too," and specifically warned that an end had to come to "everybody claiming the right of directing foreign policy."[37]

On the specific question of an acceleration of rearmament, however, Horthy was more forthcoming. In cooperation with Darányi, who in the wake of the Berlin visit had become convinced of the need to modernize Hungary's army, the regent sought to overcome the opposition of his financial experts. Kánya, still opposed to such a move, was excluded from the discussions, but Béla Imrédy, who had expressed the belief that Hungary could afford large-scale rearmament, was drawn in.

In 1937 Imrédy could already look back on a successful career in public service, although his most important position, that of prime minister, was yet to come. In Hungary he was generally regarded as a deeply religious man with moderate political views and pro-Western sentiments. In his capacity as president of the National Bank, he had earned an enviable reputation in Western Europe (especially England) as a brilliant economist. His political philosophy in earlier years had hardly been distinguishable from that of his conservative colleagues. He abhorred Communism, and though he fought tenaciously to keep Hungary economically independent of Germany, he felt that there was something to Hitler's claim that Nazi Germany played a valuable role in Europe as a bulwark against Bolshevism.[38] Moreover, Imrédy possessed a strong ambition to rise in politics and a wife ever eager to nurture that ambition.[39] In early 1937 something of a political metamorphosis began for him when he became an active participant in a political discussion group that was seeking ways to "take the wind out of the sails" of the burgeoning radical right-wing movement. Imrédy's solution, presented to Darányi in a memorandum in

March 1937, called for moderate measures to curtail Jewish influence in society and to ameliorate conditions for Hungary's agricultural proletariat. These measures, he argued, would be mild enough to be accepted by at least a part of the Jewish community, while still strong enough to prevent the middle class and intelligentsia from falling under the influence of Szálasi and the Arrow-cross movement.[40]

When Rátz and Darányi contacted Imrédy in January 1938, he quickly expressed a willingness to assume responsibility for the financing of the planned rearmament, although he strongly opposed the introduction of a right-wing dictatorship. Imrédy and Rátz were able, however, to convince the prime minister and the regent that the rearmament plan should be accompanied by new legislation to restrict Jewish influence in the economy. Efforts were thus initiated behind the scenes for the preparation of two legislative bills: one to limit Jewish influence, the second to pave the way for large-scale rearmament. When informed of developments, Kánya renewed his objections, but with little success, although by pointing to the possibility of Little Entente retaliation he was able to forestall an outright public abrogation of the Trianon restrictions.[41] The Hungarian public was, of course, unaware of the secret preparations, and Hungary's neighbors, deeply involved in the developing crisis over Austria, hardly took notice when, on 5 March, Darányi delivered an important speech at the city of Győr. In balanced terms calculated not to alarm quarters in or outside Hungary, Darányi announced a large investment program aimed at strengthening national defense. Hungary's future, he asserted, was to be based on constitutional rule under the regent and continued opposition to extremist movements of both the left and the right. In mentioning his intention of introducing legislation to curtail Jewish influence, Darányi explained that it was designed to mitigate anti-Semitism by preventing the spread of extreme and intolerant movements.

Thus, the pressure for rearmament that had begun to build up a year earlier had finally brought results. The new spending program called for an expenditure of one billion pengő over a five-year period, the bulk of it earmarked for expansion of the army and improvement of the country's transportation and communications network. The Cabinet member who earlier had opposed a rearmament program on this scale, Fabinyi, was now replaced by Lajos

Reményi-Schneller, an individual noted for his sympathy for Nazi Germany. Moreover, Bela Imrédy, whose notion of "taking the wind out of the sails" of the radical right now became ensconced in government policy, was rewarded with a cabinet post.

Three days later, to the surprise and shock of most Hungarians, the Austrian question reached its acute phase and the Anschluss was consummated. When the Hungarians had left Berlin the previous November, no crisis had seemed imminent, and from the Führer's words it had been deduced that the fate of Czechoslovakia, and not Austria, would be the first item on Nazi Germany's agenda. That the Wehrmacht troops marched into Vienna and not Prague in March 1938 can be attributed to the unusual and unexpected repercussions of the events of November 1937. And Hungary, as Kánya had always predicted, remained only an interested bystander in events that would profoundly shape her future.

When Kánya addressed the Foreign Policy Committee of the Hungarian Parliament on 26 March, two weeks after the march of German troops into Austria, he cited the role of the great powers as the determining factor in the coming of the Anschluss. The powers that had created Austria, he declared, had not been willing to fight with arms for her independence. They "imposed independence on Austria, but did not see to it that Austria was provided with the necessary means for preserving this independence." Not being a member of a military defense alliance, Austria had, in the end, to rely exclusively on her own defensive power, with the inevitable results. Kánya's comments probably mirrored the attitude of most East European leaders toward the disappearance of a sovereign Austria.[42] For the will to preserve an independent Austria had indeed become scarcely discernible in Rome, Paris, and London by the autumn of 1937. Italy had virtually abandoned its client state. There is strong evidence to suggest that when he visited Germany in September, Mussolini, impressed by the dynamism of the Nazi regime, agreed to allow Hitler a "free hand" to achieve a "Gleichschaltung" in Austria.[43] And in the course of negotiations for Italian adherence to the Anti-Comintern Pact, the Duce informed Ribbentrop that Italy was "tired of mounting guard over Austrian independence, especially if the Austrians no longer want their independence." Italian interests were centered in the Mediterranean. The best thing, Mussolini suggested, was to "let events take their natural course."[44]

Italy's withdrawal from its "Watch on the Brenner" was the more significant because the two Western powers, England and France, had come to regard the preservation of Austrian independence as primarily an Italian responsibility. This attitude was especially prevalent in England, and in December Anthony Eden, the foreign secretary, even admitted to Ribbentrop that the Austrian question was of far more interest to Italy than Britain, and that the English people realized that a "closer combination between Germany and Austria would have to come about sometime." Although Eden repeated Halifax's wish that any changes come about peacefully, it was obvious that the British did not consider their vital interests involved.[45]

France, too, had come to a similar position in the late fall of 1937. As early as May 1937 Delbos privately admitted that France would not move to forestall the Anschluss. Both London and Paris tried to make a distinction in their attitude toward the Czechoslovak and Austrian questions. France had treaty obligations toward Czechoslovakia, but no one was required to assist Austria, except under the now defunct principle of collective security. The Western democracies thus decided that the best policy to pursue in the Austrian question was to give economic aid to Vienna, promote a rapprochement of Danubian states, and ask Germany for assurances that force would not be used.[46] Even these alternatives were not pursued vigorously in late 1937. London's feelers to Berlin on a comprehensive settlement implied willingness to accept changes in Austria, and the French, frustrated and confused, made little progress in their efforts to foster Danubian unity. Although few would publicly admit it for fear the mere admission might bring on the landslide, Austria was on the brink of disaster and had no trustworthy and powerful friend who would rush to her aid.

Even among Austria's East European neighbors, who, it would seem, might have had some concern about the possible impact of the Anschluss on their security, there was little effort made to bolster Vienna. Although this was in part simply a reaction to the tergiversation of the great powers, many hoped to improve their own future position vis à vis Germany by posing no obstacle or raising no objection to the Anschluss. Yugoslavia, for example, opted for a "German solution" of the problem, seeing in this a permanent guarantee against Habsburg and Italian intrigue. By early 1938 Stojadinović was assuring Hitler that his country regarded the fate of Austria as a "purely internal German question."[47] Poland took a similar stand, asking only that her economic interests in Austria be respected.[48] Fears of a Habsburg restoration also made the attitude of Romania, and, to a lesser extent, Czechoslovakia, ambivalent.[49]

As 1937 drew to a close, one man still struggled vainly to find the correct formula for a prolongation of an independent Austria: Kurt von Schuschnigg, the Austrian chancellor. Plagued by uncertainties and restricted to a narrow area for maneuver, Schuschnigg doggedly strove to define some unifying spirit in a country that had once been united under a monarch, but in the postwar period could not develop a new form of allegiance to the state. In the international field, the chancellor was forced by waning Italian interest to seek closer ties with Czechoslovakia, which had a similar fear of Nazi Germany. Scant progress had been made in their bilateral relationship right up to the summer of 1937, when, in October, the idea of a Prague-Vienna-Budapest bloc, which had been discussed sporadically earlier in the year, was revived in Vienna. The direct initiative seems to have come from the Austrian minister in Budapest, Eduard Baar-Baarenfels, a strong advocate of the creation of some sort of Danubian bloc to oppose German expansionism.[50] When Schuschnigg visited Hungary in late October, Baar suggested to him that another attempt be made to reconcile the differences between Prague and Budapest. It would be an enormous task, he said, but it was possible that a compromise might be worked out in which the Czechoslovaks would agree to certain border rectifications and Hungary would drop its insistence on regaining all of Slovakia. Schuschnigg, who at the time was considering various ways of forming a closer community of the Danubian countries, approved the idea and empowered Baar and Clemens Wildner, his assistant, to sound out the Hungarians and to establish contact with the Czechoslovak and French ministers in Budapest.

Kánya, who in the past year had only reluctantly come into diplomatic contact with Prague in the course of negotiations for a "normalization" of relations with the Little Entente countries, was quite skeptical about the chances for success of Baar's plan. Yet he did not wish to offend the Austrians unduly or seal off an alternative route for Hungary should the relationship with Germany become too dangerous, and he therefore expressed a willing-

ness to consider the matter.[51] Baar received encouragement from
the French and Czechoslovak representatives in Budapest, the latter offering to try to convince his superiors to make the necessary
concessions.[52] But little progress had been made by the time of the
Hungarian visit to Berlin in November. As has been seen, the Germans had learned something of Schuschnigg's efforts, and Kánya
and Darányi were strongly warned not to intensify relations with
either of their Danubian neighbors. Kánya thus returned to Budapest with a greater reluctance to engage in clandestine talks that,
if discovered, would jeopardize his position both in Germany and
at home. The idea of the Danubian "Triangle" was thus dealt yet
another severe blow.

Instead of pursuing a policy based on cooperation with Prague
and Vienna, certain elements in the Hungarian government now
proceeded to propound an aggressive policy that called for cooperation between Vienna and Budapest in planning the destruction
and dismemberment of Czechoslovakia. This scheme seems to
have originated with General Rátz, who convinced the regent that
the Hungarian Foreign Ministry should be bypassed and that
direct contact should be made with Austrian military representatives. On 22 November, only three days after the departure of
Kánya and Darányi to Berlin, Horthy invited the Austrian military
attaché, Rene Eberle, to join him to discuss an important matter.[53]
Horthy prefaced his remarks, as was his habit, with a detailing of
the inequities of the peace settlement in East Central Europe. He
referred, too, to the friendly ties between Austria and Hungary,
"now and in the future."[54] But Czechoslovakia was the subject
he clearly wished to discuss. The Slovaks, he maintained, would
feel less threatened under Magyar than Czech rule, since the Hungarian language stood in sharp enough contrast to Slovak so that
the latter could more easily be kept pure. The Czechoslovak state
had no "justification for existing," and if it were to be partitioned,
the Austrians could only gain by it. Thus, Horthy asserted, it
would be a good idea for Vienna to participate in such a military
operation, particularly in the light of the possibility that German
troops might in any event use Austrian territory as a transit area.
Previous "binding agreements" would preclude this possibility.

Eberle, somewhat taken aback by such frank speculation about
an attack on a neighboring state, made no reply to Horthy's
suggestion, but reported in full to his superiors. The Austrian

leadership seemed not to attribute much importance to Horthy's suggestion, perhaps because they were all aware of his proclivity for indiscretion in diplomatic conversations. Moreover, when Baar-Baarenfels later inquired about the matter in the Hungarian Foreign Ministry, Baron Apor explained that the idea of joint Austrian-Hungarian-German planning for an attack on Czechoslovakia did not conform to official Hungarian policy. Though some quarters in the army and government might be captivated by such wishful thinking, the foreign minister and minister of defense could not be counted among them.[55]

One can imagine Kánya's consternation when, upon his return from Berlin, he discovered that the regent and chief of staff had been infringing deeply into his sphere of responsibility. Yet, almost as if to defy Kánya, General Rátz persisted in his efforts. Several weeks later he approached Baar and repeated Horthy's suggestion that Austria participate in planning for a future partition of Czechoslovakia. Referring to his recent talks with military leaders in Germany, Rátz cited the belief of the German leaders that the psychological moment had come to restore everything that the politicians and party people in Germany and Austria had ruined. Specifically, he urged that Austria join Hungary and Germany at the "consultation table" and plan a joint march into Czechoslovakia. Rátz claimed that he had already consulted the Austrian Chief of Staff and Secretary of National Defense on this matter, and they had guaranteed that Hungary's left flank in the operation in question would be secured by strict Austrian neutrality. But this, Rátz insisted, was not a strong enough assurance for the Germans. From this Baar deduced, as he wrote in his report to Vienna, that if Austria did not participate, her territory might be used as a concentration area by the German Army and the country might become another Belgium ("Belgisierung Österreichs"). However, Baar noted, the Hungarian information was that the German Army would be ready only in two or three years.[56]

The Austrian government, which previously had not taken Horthy's proposal seriously, now was forced to consider a response. The very day of the conversation between Baar and Rátz, Theodor Hornbostel, the head of the Foreign Affairs Department of the Chancellory, summarized the Austrian position.[57] The Hungarian suggestion, he wrote, was an "insane plan" that had apparently not been very well thought out beforehand. To every clear-thinking

Austrian it was apparent that Bohemia and Moravia represented the sole "defensive wall against the German steamroller." Thus, there could be no question of Austrian participation in the contemplated action.

Here the matter rested. Apparently the Hungarians were quietly informed that the Austrians could not accept the proposal, and although Hungary continued to discuss with Germany the opening of operational talks, there is no evidence of further exchanges between Vienna and Budapest. But the episode was clearly symptomatic of the trend of political thinking in Hungary. The rash proposal of Horthy and Rátz mirrored the new boldness and impatience of the soldiers and ardent revisionists. The gulf separating the Foreign Ministry and the military seemed to be widening, with the regent apparently prepared to support the aggressive policy sponsored by the General Staff. Widened by the inner debate over rearmament, this divergence of views tended to lead to a grave lack of coordination of political and military policy during the critical events of 1938.

One immediate consequence of the lack of coordination in Hungarian policy was confusion in Vienna, where the perplexed Austrians were hard pressed to fathom the true intentions of their neighbor. On the one hand, Kánya had accepted, albeit grudgingly, renewed efforts by the Austrians to promote a Czechoslovak-Hungarian understanding. On the other hand, Rátz and Horthy had suggested joint planning aimed at the destruction of Czechoslovakia. To complicate matters even further, communications from Hungarian monarchists urging Austrian-Hungarian cooperation in a restoration of a dual monarchy continued to reach the Austrian government.[58] Therefore it was probably as much to determine Hungary's attitude as Italy's that Vienna looked to the upcoming meeting of the Rome Pact, scheduled for early January in Budapest.

It was Kánya who had insisted, even before his journey to Berlin in November, that the Rome Protocol signatories meet in the near future, since they had not assembled for a year and the British and French were insinuating that the Pact had decreased in importance.[59] The Austrians shared Kánya's doubts about the faithfulness of Rome to its diplomatic creation. By the beginning of 1938 it had become almost common knowledge in Europe that Italy had resolved not to take up arms again to support Austria as she had done in 1934. Moreover, Ciano, infatuated by his new friend in that part of Europe, Milan Stojadinović, was acquiring a growing dislike for and suspicion of his Austrian and Hungarian colleagues. He distrusted Austrian Foreign Secretary Guido Schmidt, whom he characterized as a "haggler, careerist, and fop," and had a low opinion of Kánya.[60] Particularly disturbing to the Italian foreign minister was what he termed the "occasional pro-British backslidings" of the Hungarians. When Count Bethlen visited Rome at the end of 1937 and expressed the belief that peace between England and Italy would facilitate the solution of problems in Central Europe, Ciano noted in his diary: "I told him [Bethlen] calmly and coldly what our intentions were: peace, if possible, war, if necessary. The Hungarians receive every sort of kindness at our hands—rather with the air of condescension of a decayed aristocrat—but they don't fully realize yet how powerful we are and they have sentimental leanings toward London, produced by two powerful influences: Jewishness and snobbery. I told Bethlen that the democracies would give Hungary nothing but fine words."[61]

Considering Ciano's attitude, it is not surprising that he attributed little importance to the Rome Pact meeting proposed by Kánya. During the preparations for his trip, he commented privately that the Rome Protocols were becoming "more and more impotent," since "agreements with a purely economic content necessarily lack profound vitality."[62] Nonetheless, Ciano hoped to reap some political benefit from the meeting by arranging for a higher degree of political solidarity among the three parties on certain questions of particular concern to Italy. He was eager to gain a strong show of support from Hungary and Austria for the Axis and Anti-Comintern Pact, recognition of Franco's government in Spain, and possibly even departure from the League of Nations. Both Ciano and Mussolini were in a surly mood when drafting their proposals for the conference. Ciano characterized Italy's two Danubian allies as countries "only too eager to beg, but also to make themselves scarce whenever they have to assume any responsibility on our behalf." The Duce commented that as soon as the Spanish question was settled, he would invite Göring to nazify Austria.[63]

Vienna and Budapest, as Ciano suspected, were not anxious to take any unnecessary political risks, especially if relations with the West might be damaged in the process. Moreover, the two client states also had certain political hopes for the meeting. Austria wished to gain a public reaffirmation of support for its independence, while Hungary was desirous of obtaining a favorable joint statement on policy toward the Little Entente. Kánya also probably hoped to demonstrate that, despite the recent visit to Germany, Hungary still regarded strong ties with Italy and Austria as one of the foundation stones of Hungarian foreign policy.

The Rome Pact meeting, which took place in Budapest between 10 and 13 January, turned out to be a fairly dull affair, despite the potential for recrimination that the decay in the treaty relationship provided.[64] In fact, the main talk of the conference was devoted to Ciano's boorish behavior. He carried his private grudge against Guido Schmidt (whom he did not want invited to the meeting in the first place) to the official level when at the outset he refused to sit at the same table with him. Only the mediation of Kánya prevented a serious scandal. At the end of the parley, Ciano managed to distinguish himself on a hunt with Horthy by shooting a doe out of season.[65] During the actual working sessions the three sides seemed merely to act out rehearsed positions. The Hungarians and Austrians, having concerted their efforts beforehand, declined to depart from the League, Kánya pointing out that Geneva provided a convenient forum for airing Hungary's grievances in the minorities questions. Vienna and Budapest did relent in the question of recognition of Franco, and there were friendly words for the Axis and Anti-Comintern Pact in the official communiqué. Ciano was reasonably content, although he continued to suspect his partners of "trying to evade all responsibilities vis à vis the so-called 'democracies.'"[66]

The Austrian chancellor could not have drawn much solace from the Budapest conversations. Ciano flatly refused, out of consideration for Germany, to join in a declaration restating the interest of the Rome Pact in Austrian independence. Schuschnigg, it is true, seemed to draw the most optimistic of conclusions. He claimed Ciano's satisfaction over the results of the meeting would lead to greater Italian interest in Austria. He even found much to praise in the official communiqué, which, he said, was not characterized by the "usual meaningless diplomatic phrases."[67] Though others in Vienna may not have drawn such optimistic conclusions about Italy's fealty, there seemed general satisfaction over Hungary's support during the Budapest sessions. Kánya a number of times stressed, in Ciano's presence, the correctness of Austrian policy toward the German Reich, and he urged only that Vienna strive to gain time and not allow itself to be provoked.[68]

For Kánya the Rome Pact meeting, which he had been so anxious to arrange, came at a tense and difficult time. Besides his delicate task as mediator between Ciano and the Austrians, he had to cope with the increasing tendency of the prime minister and regent to deal with problems of the highest political importance behind his back. European developments likewise demanded his attention. In early January he told Knox, the British minister, that the question of Anglo-Italian relations was of "first importance" to Hungary.[69] Events in Romania presented another worrisome problem. In December, the long awaited Romanian elections produced a surprise: passing up other parties with much higher vote totals, King Carol appointed as prime minister Octavian Goga, a right-wing politician with an apparent pro-German and anti-Semitic orientation. The immediate proclamations of the new Romanian government indicated that strong pressure would soon be put on Romania's Jewish community. The Hungarians were unsure what impact this change would have on the lot of the large Magyar minority or the structure of the Little Entente, but Ciano, delighted at the prospect of enlisting another member for the Italian grouping in Southeastern Europe, took immediate steps to speed a political understanding with Goga. Budapest was alarmed at this alacrity, and Kánya sardonically observed that the new Romanian government "seems to be much more welcome to our friends than to us."[70]

The Rome Pact meeting brought both gains and losses for Hungary in these important questions. On the problem of Hungarian minorities, Kánya took pains to outline Hungary's complaints against her neighbors, not failing to employ his customary acerbic references to Stojadinović (a "Balkan ruffian") and the Romanians. The ruffled Italian leader stood up for his Yugoslav ally, and blocked Hungary's efforts to include a strong minorities declaration in the published protocol. Ciano was forced, however, to reaffirm Mussolini's earlier pledge that the Italians would deal with the new Romanian government only "via Budapest."[71] Kánya also seized every opportunity in his conversations with Ciano to stress the possibilities of an Anglo-Italian rapprochement. When Ciano declared that Italy was not seeking "domination" of the Mediterranean Sea, but a "cohabitation" with England, Kánya, eager to promote a political understanding, quickly instructed the Hungarian minister in London to pass the information on to the Foreign Office.[72]

On 13 January, the concluding day of the Budapest meeting, the *Pester Lloyd*, the semiofficial organ of the government, spoke in optimistic terms about the future of the Rome Pact. The lead article, inspired by Kánya, denied rumors that the Protocols were dead and asserted that the final communiqué exuded "friendship, self-assurance, decisiveness, and a straightforward policy." A few days later Kánya informed the Hungarian Parliament that the Rome Pact conference had demonstrated that Italy's position in the Mediterranean would not, as rumor had it, prevent her from continuing to take a close interest in Central Europe.

Superficially, it did seem that perhaps the Vienna-Budapest-Rome alignment had been given a new impetus, as both Kánya and Schuschnigg tried to argue in public. Point two of the communiqué spoke of a joint determination to intensify economic and political activity among the three countries. But, in fact, no new initiatives were taken. Indeed, Ciano was not even willing to acknowledge publicly the principle on which the pact was supposed to rest.

When on 12 March an independent Austria ceased to exist, the Rome Pact technically came to an end; but, in spirit at least, the Budapest meeting had already delivered the death blow.

One of the pleasant, if short-lived, surprises for the Austrians during the meeting was Hungary's apparent amenability to a further deepening of their bilateral relationship. Hungarian Minister of Defense Röder, although ill and confined to his home, received the Austrian military attaché on the 11th and assured him that the military relations of their two countries would be strengthened in the future, especially in armaments production.[73] Moreover, when Schmidt and Schuschnigg suggested to Kánya that closer political and military cooperation could be developed, they met a favorable response. The Austrians thereupon proposed a "secret agreement" based on the following points:

  a) closer coordination of intelligence work;
  b) obligatory consultation between foreign ministers on political questions;
  c) exchange of information from foreign diplomatic posts in which one of the countries did not have a mission.[74]

Kánya was assured that the agreement would not be aimed at Germany or any other power, and although his answer seemed encouraging, he asked that he first be allowed to check with his military chiefs on point (a). Despite the lack of further documentary evidence on this episode, it is likely that Kánya later rejected the proposed agreement or procrastinated until it was too late. Perhaps he was rebuffed by his own General Staff or the regent. More likely, his instinct warned him that even so innocuous a gesture to Austria might provoke the Germans. Moreover, from a strictly pragmatic point of view, a strengthening of relations with Austria made little sense; as Bethlen had once said, in diplomatic affairs one should not ally with a corpse.

If not yet a corpse, Austria did resemble a man sentenced to death, whose friends decline to offer their support for fear of offending the executioner. Aside from Italy, the only great power that might have been expected to offer significant assistance to Vienna was France, but a fatalistic attitude toward Austria was deeply imbedded in the mentality of French statesmen by early 1938. Delbos, concerned that Mussolini had "washed his hands of Austria," declared privately that England and France were unable to provide military support to Austria, and if Hitler decided to move the "final result would be inevitable."[75] In late 1937 Delbos had undertaken a grand tour of Eastern Europe to help bolster resistance to Nazi Germany, and to lend support to the latest effort to create a Danubian bloc, but his trip merely demonstrated that the French *imprimatur* no longer commanded much authority in that part of Europe.

Events in Romania in late December represented a further blow to French prestige and pride. The appointment of a blatantly anti-Semitic, right-wing figure like Goga only a few weeks after Delbos's departure seemed to indicate that French influence was at its nadir. The dismay in Paris over King Carol's move was compounded when Romania's new prime minister began speaking menacingly of the necessity of stronger ties with the Axis Powers, anti-Jewish legislation, and renunciation of the Minorities Treaty that had been imposed on Romania by the great powers at the Paris Peace Conference. This was cause for alarm in both Paris and London, and Delbos and Anthony Eden warned the Romanians that an abrogation of the Minorities Treaty would have grave consequences. They implied that since the treaty that had guaranteed the rights of the minorities in Romania was the same treaty that had awarded Bessarabia and Transylvania to that country, the status those two key provinces might well be called into question. If Romania proceeded to persecute her Jewish minority, France and Britain would regard the entire treaty, including its territorial provisions, as annulled.[76]

The apparent defection of Romania and the increasingly equivocal attitude of Yugoslavia led some Frenchmen to ponder the possibility of jettisoning the Little Entente completely and, as had been contemplated briefly in 1920, building a new Danubian bloc in which Hungary could play a key role. In early January several French newspapers, notably the *Oeuvre*, contained friendly references to the Magyars and warnings that the time was not far away when some would regret having treated Hungary so unjustly in the peace settlement. Early in February Jean Mistler, president of the Foreign Affairs Committee of the French Chamber, sounded out a Hungarian friend on the possibility of a French-Hungarian rapprochement and creation of a Czechoslovak-Austrian-Hungarian bloc under French tutelage. According to Mistler, Paris would be prepared to support the return of Transylvania and a small part of Slovakia to Hungary.[77]

It did not take long, however, for King Carol to heed the warnings of the Western powers and to dismiss Goga. The "trial balloon" launched by Mistler was thus quickly punctured, and Danubian affairs soon returned to the former basis. During January the Hungarians had in fact noticed the slight change in the French attitude. The *Pester Lloyd*, commenting in a lead article on 8 January on recent pro-Hungarian items in the French press, observed that it seemed common sense was finally returning to Paris. The change, the paper added, was "better late than never." But Hungarian officials were in no mood to be pacified by friendly newspaper articles or vague intimations through non-diplomatic channels. Such an approach might have borne some fruit a year earlier when friction between Germany and Hungary was at its height. But after the November visit to Germany, most Hungarian leaders were anxious to preserve their standing in Berlin. Thus, when the director of the *Auslandsorganisation*, Ernst-Wilhelm Bohle, talked with Horthy in Budapest at the end of January, the regent volunteered some caustic remarks on France. "I hate the French," he said, "because so far we have received only bad things from that dirty crowd." Horthy asked Bohle to transmit his determination to stand by Germany in all circumstances, "through thick and thin." In his report to Berlin on his many conversations in Hungary (with Horthy, Darányi, Kánya, Minister of Culture Hóman, Minister of Interior Széll, and István Csáky), Bohle observed that "again and again" he was told of the special desire of the Hungarians to deepen the traditionally good relations with Germany. Hungarian leaders regarded it as a particularly apt sign of friendship that Bohle had been sent to Hungary directly after Stojadinović's visit to Germany, as if to demonstrate that there was no truth to the rumors Germany intended to pursue a separate policy with respect to Romania and Yugoslavia to the detriment of Hungary.[78]

In fact, Hitler in this period was continuing the effort, begun in November, to strengthen the idea in Hungary that there were only advantages to be gained in cooperation with Germany in the Danubian region. The main purpose of Bohle's mission to Budapest was to give the Hungarians further assurances on the delicate problem of the German Reich's interest in the German minority of Hungary. In his well-publicized speech on 23 January, Bohle made a clear distinction between two kinds of Germans living outside Germany, *Auslandsdeutsch* and *Volksdeutsch*. The latter lived in areas directly touching the boundaries of the Reich. The German interest in the former, who lived detached from the central mass of Germans as minorities in other states, consisted merely in furthering their cultural aspirations. The Swabians of Hungary were considered to be *Auslandsdeutsch*. This explicit statement was naturally well received by the Hungarian people and the government, although it did not convince the Germanophobes or leaders of the Körmend rally.

The appointment of Goga in Romania provided another opportunity for Berlin to make a gesture to Hungary. Remembering the bad feeling that Rosenberg's plan for capturing the Romanian right had created in Hungary, Hitler maintained a cautious neutral policy toward the new regime. The German press was specifically instructed not to publish the text of Goga's long New Year's Day telegram to the Führer, because it mentioned certain assurances received by Goga in an earlier visit to Germany that the Reich considered the Romanian-Hungarian frontier as final and might even assist Romania should Hungary attack her.[79]

Yet despite Germany's demonstrably friendly attitude, events in Germany and Austria in February served to rekindle the fears of Hungary's conservatives about Hitler's aims and methods. Hitler's shuffling of his military and political command in late January caused some uneasiness in Hungary. During a visit to Poland in early February, Kánya did not conceal his concern that the militants were gaining the upper hand in Germany and that Austria's position was being further undermined.[80] At about the same time Count Bethlen delivered a speech that eloquently illustrated the dilemma confronting Hungary's conservative establishment. As will be seen, Bethlen was prepared in principle to cooperate with Germany in the destruction of Czechoslovakia. But, like Kánya, Teleki, and other conservatives, Bethlen wished to be certain that, in the process of obtaining her cherished national goals, Hungary did not deviate from the prevailing system that sustained their power and preserved at least a façade of parliamentary forms and constitutional liberties. "One thing is clear," Bethlen told his colleagues in the Parliament on 9 February, "if our political system is subjected to a 'Gleichschaltung' in the form of right-wing ideas, we will become Germany's slaves, not her friends, and in that case an independent Hungarian foreign policy will be once and for all at an end."[81]

Just a few days after Bethlen's speech, which had a profound impact in Hungary and made an impression even in Prague,[82] Europe's attention was drawn to Berchtesgaden, where Schuschnigg and Hitler were meeting. In the presence of a number of generals called in to intimidate Schuschnigg, Hitler harangued, threatened, and presented a virtual ultimatum on the acceptance of certain demands for further Austrian cooperation with the Reich. As a gesture of conciliation, Schuschnigg had gone to Germany prepared to make certain concessions to Hitler; now he was forced to make many of the same concessions under brutal coercion and in the most humiliating circumstances.[83] Hitler thus took another step in what he termed an "evolutionary solution" of the Austrian question. For the time being, it seems, he did not wish to press the issue, despite the fact that two of his key advisors, Göring and Ribbentrop, were urging an acceleration of the Reich's program in Danubian Europe. No serious troop movements were planned, and the overzealous Austrian National Socialists were castigated for overstepping their bounds. Schuschnigg thus returned to Vienna shaken by his experiences, but still not suspecting that the final crisis was only weeks away.

When the Hungarians learned of the concessions Schuschnigg had made, there was an initial inclination to believe that the Austrians had come out of it as well as could be expected. The semi-official *Pester Lloyd* calmly described the talks in Germany as an "act of peace" that would lead to a lessening of tensions and would have a beneficial influence on the entire Danubian world. However, the mood began to change as alarming reports about what actually happened at Berchtesgaden began to pour in from Austria. The Hungarian mission in Vienna reported that Schuschnigg had been subjected to brutal treatment and that Hitler had put forth his demands in the form of an ultimatum.[84] Confidential information Kánya received from Berlin indicated that Göring was complaining to Hitler about the Führer's "weakness" at Berchtesgaden.[85]

This news created a distinct gloom in the Hungarian Foreign Ministry. To neutral diplomats, Kánya expressed the fear that Hungary's turn might be next and emphasized that he much preferred an independent Austria to a German neighbor of 80 million.[86] No doubt he privately agreed with Count Sigray, who in late February declared that "Austria's independence is closely tied in with the independence of Hungary, and should Austria lose hers . . . that of Hungary would also be directly endangered."[87] Yet what could Hungary do? There semed no alternative to standing back and remaining silent, and this inability to influence events greatly frustrated Kánya. Never before, he observed to a colleague, had the task of constructing a successful foreign policy for Hungary been so difficult and bewildering.[88]

While others agonized over their paralysis, Schuschnigg was resolving to make one last effort to rally his country. Kánya, who interrupted a stay in western Hungary to make an unofficial visit to Vienna on 2 March, was probably the first non-Austrian to hear of the chancellor's bold plan.[89] Kánya found Schuschnigg confident and still prepared to cooperate with Germany, but also determined to defend the country to the last ditch, if necessary. Believing that 70 percent of the people were behind him, Schuschnigg was thinking of conducting a plebiscite, though for the moment he still regarded it as too dangerous a step. Kánya for his part asserted that he regarded Hitler's threat as a "bluff," because he could not carry out a military "adventure."[90] But when Kánya questioned the chancellor on what support was anticipated from the great powers, Schuschnigg made an evasive reply, from which the Hungarian deduced that little help was expected from that quarter. The other Austrians with whom Kánya spoke were less sanguine, and he left Vienna even more pessimistic about Austria's future.

Upon his return to Budapest, the Hungarian foreign minister told Erdmannsdorff, the German representative, that Schuschnigg had not given up hope for a peaceful agreement with Germany. The Austrian chancellor had stressed that he would never ally with or seek assistance from Germany's enemies, but he likewise would never renounce Austrian independence. Kánya concluded the conversation with the wry comment that he, Erdmannsdorff, "could at any rate better judge whether Schuschnigg's hopes were justified."[91]

Erdmannsdorff was in fact in no better position than anyone else in Europe to foresee the swiftness of the denouement of the Austrian question. Probably the Führer himself did not suspect the course events would take, although his readiness to take decisive action had grown remarkably since the Berchtesgaden meeting. Kánya was probably the least surprised of anyone when word came on 7 March that, despite the misgivings that Schuschnigg had mentioned to Kánya earlier, a plebiscite would be held shortly in Austria.[92] When the voting day was set for the fifteenth, a lead article in *Pester Lloyd*, probably written by Kánya, innocently noted that a plebiscite rested on the premise of the Berchtesgaden Agreement, and that the Austrians were merely emulating Hitler in bringing to the people questions of overwhelming national importance.[93]

Other quarters, however, were less encouraging. Mussolini, when queried, warned against the plebiscite, which he likened to a bomb that would go off in Schuschnigg's hand.[94] The Duce had for once keenly analyzed the situation. When Hitler heard of Schuschnigg's plan, he responded, as one writer has colorfully put it, "as though someone had trodden on a painful corn."[95] Resolving to enforce a final settlement of the question, he allowed the eager Göring to assume immediate direction in the crisis, and, after some hesitation, finally gave the order for German troops to advance. On the evening of the twelfth, Göring advised Sztójay that "all of Austria is being occupied; then a plebiscite will be held to determine whether there is to be complete Anschluss or a formal maintenance of Austrian independence."[96] But Europe did not have to wait even that long to learn the fate of Austria. The enthusiasm of the crowds that greeted the advancing troops inspired Hitler on the fifteenth to proclaim Austria's complete absorption into the Reich. The Anschluss had come, and Hungary was finally confronted with the reality of "the empire of 80 million Germans" on her western flank.

Even before the Hungarian public could begin to assess the implications of this development, an attempt was made to convince the Germans to allow Hungary to join in the occupation of Austria. András Mecsér, the right-wing member of Parliament who was convinced that Gömbös had been promised Burgenland when Hitler moved into Austria, sought out Erdmannsdorff on the sixteenth and informed him of Hitler's supposed pledge. He pointed out that such a "gesture" now, "even if it extended only to districts of the severed territory inhabited exclusively by Hungarians, would make a tremendously deep impression in Hungary and assure Hungarian adherence to the policy of the Reich for all time."[97] Although the Hungarian government itself made no approach to Berlin on this matter, several private parties were championing the Hungarian claim.

When another right-wing member of Parliament made a speech in which he repeated Mecsér's story about the pledge to Gömbös, the country began to buzz with the rumor that in fact the German troops were refraining from entering Burgenland in order to allow Hungarian troops to advance. When the government remained passive, "patriotic circles" even began to criticize it for missing a grand opportunity for revision.[98] But the real situation was quite different. Hitler had no intention of presenting a "gift" to Hungary, and the Germans later quite rightly pointed out that if ethnic principles were taken into account on the Hungarian-Austrian (now Hungarian-German) border, Hungary might easily lose rather than gain territory.[99] It seems certain that Kánya never considered Hungarian participation in the move into Austria as practical or desirable. Hitler's pledge, if indeed there had ever been one, would have been conditional on what would have amounted to a treacherous attack by Hungary on her "best friend."[100] Some Hungarian troops had indeed been placed on the western border to meet all eventualities. But the task of these Hussar regiments turned out to be not a movement into Austria, but the less glorious one of greeting the German troops "in friendship and fellowship."

Chapter 6

Uneasy Spring

In the tense days after Germany's annexation of Austria, the Hungarian government strove earnestly to create the impression of normality in conditions that were by any standard abnormal. Although Count Bethlen was later to acknowledge that since 1921 there had been no international event as important for Hungary's future,[1] Kánya and Darányi were intent on giving the appearance of nonchalance, as if the event had long been accounted for in the government's policy. Pragmatic considerations molded Kánya's thinking: he saw nothing to be gained and much to be lost by any public manifestations of regret over the irrevocable disappearance of an old friend. Thus, as early as the fourteenth he directed Sztójay in Berlin to congratulate the Germans on accomplishing the union with Austria "without the loss of blood." This action, which was followed swiftly by the conversion of the Hungarian legation in Vienna into a consulate, won for Hungary the distinction of being the first country to salute Hitler's success.[2]

It was likewise considered imperative that calm be maintained in Budapest, with neither the disconsolate left nor the jubilant right allowed to cause embarassing disruptions. For this reason Kánya tried to dampen rumors that Hungary was expecting some "gesture" from Hitler in the question of the Burgenland. On 12 March measures were taken to control the reaction of the Hungarian press. Secret instructions were issued to journalists strongly advising that sensationalist headlines and stories be avoided, so as not to cause panic on the stock exchange. Hitler's call for a referendum in Austria was to be stressed, and only statements of pro-German politicians were to be published.[3] The newspapers on the whole complied, although it was perhaps too harsh to characterize the press, as the British minister Geoffrey Knox did, as displaying a "prudence bordering on the obsequious."[4] For despite all government efforts the country could not completely conceal its anxieties. A brief run on the banks did develop, and the alarm was great in Budapest's large Jewish community. In Parliament the silence of

representatives of the Government Party on recent events in
Europe was criticized by Hugo Payr, a Social Democrat, who rose
and declared that Austria's passing could not simply be ignored.[5]
And in fact the Anschluss could not be ignored: the presence of
such a powerful neighbor could, as Bethlen was to point out, bring
both disadvantages and advantages to Hungary, and a weighing of
these imponderables was a task that occupied most politically
minded Hungarians in the weeks after 12 March.

For many Hungarians the loss of Austria's independence had
long been anticipated. Even so, the suddenness of Hitler's move
sent shock waves reverberating across the Hungarian plain.[6] Psy-
chologically, the impact was enormous. Previously, talk of a "German menace" or Teutonic expansion past the gates of Sopron had
had little direct meaning for the Hungarian masses, who, with
Austria as a buffer state, could still regard Germany as fairly remote. But the potential threat from the German Reich was etched
more vividly on the Hungarian consciousness when the new maps
of Europe showed the size of Hungary's western neighbor, and
when the train schedules indicated that the second largest city in
Germany was now only one and one-half hours from Budapest by
express train. Similarly, even the non-political Hungarian knew
that things had changed when the radio transmitter from Vienna
no longer beamed out its usual innocuous fare, but now preached
the glories of a National Socialist society.

Economically, Germany's absorption of Austria further strengthened its former domination of Hungary's financial life and trade.
In 1938 Germany was to account for approximately 40 percent of
Hungary's imports and exports. Ironically, Budapest's previous
tactic of fostering trade with Austria to avoid undue exporting to
Germany now backfired, as Berlin assumed not only Austria's
share of the Hungarian market, but also the substantial holdings
of Viennese banks and corporations in Hungary. As it turned out,
the intimacy of the German-Hungarian economic relationship had
little direct influence on the development of political relations
during the continuing European crisis of 1938, although this would
not be the case after the outbreak of the war in 1939.

The most notable impact of the Anschluss in Hungary was the
impetus it gave to the radical right in and outside the government.
What little protest the left and center managed to utter was muf-
fled by the bold thunder from the right. The contrast in the two

camps was revealing: while the most vigorous spokesmen of the left now left the country, their journals given a virtual death blow, the right-wing groups surged forward.[7] Ferenc Szálasi's party attracted many new recruits from the army and from the middle and lower middle classes, and the young fascist leader's earlier proclamation of 1938 as "the year of the movement" seemed to be justified by events.[8]

When speeches and statements by Kánya and Darányi failed to dispel the anxiety and uncertainty created by Hitler's triumph in Austria, Horthy was called on to address the nation by radio, so that his message would have the widest circulation.[9] In his speech in early April, Horthy urged calm and upbraided those who were tempted to "fish in troubled waters." The union of Austria and Germany he described as merely a case of "an old friend who had been dragged by the peace treaties into an impossible situation" joining with "another old friend and comrade in arms." Rather than being alarmed by imaginary threats, Horthy observed, each Hungarian citizen would do best to trust in his government and take up his share in the reconstruction of the country.

These events in Hungary in the aftermath of the Anschluss were occurring against a backdrop of important European developments. When on 15 March the British minister in Prague suggested that having "liquidated Austria, the Government of the Reich will doubtless soon tackle the next item on their programme, Czechoslovakia,"[10] his words were probably being echoed by many other political observers throughout Europe. In a speech on 20 February, Hitler had spoken of the "over ten million Germans" in whose fate the Reich would take a close interest. With Austria annexed, attention naturally turned to the remaining three million Germans in the Sudetenland and other parts of Czechoslovakia.

By March 1938 Budapest was viewing the Czechoslovak question from a new perspective. Six months had elapsed since the interruption of tentative talks with the Little Entente at Sinaia and Geneva, and this period was a crucial stage in the development of the Czechoslovak-Hungarian relationship. As has been seen, the visit of Darányi and Kánya had seemingly dimmed all hope that Prague and Budapest would find their way to a political rapprochement. Yet by a peculiar sequence of events, one more attempt was made in the winter of 1938 to reconcile Hungarian and Czechoslovak differences. When this failed, as all the others in the

past had, the prospects for an understanding were virtually eliminated.

Despite the lack of success of talks at Geneva in September,
bargaining seemed to continue in the air between Budapest and
Prague during the fall. One encouraging omen was the signing,
after a six-year hiatus, of a Hungarian-Czechoslovak trade treaty
with a most-favored-nation clause. The apparent failure of Schuschnigg's attempt in October to revive the idea of a "Danubian Triangle" did not deter individuals on both sides from continuing
their efforts. The approach of Endre Bajcsy-Zsilinszky was typical
of those Hungarians who still thought a deal could be worked out.
In December he called on the Czechoslovak leadership in Prague
to emulate prewar Austria by showing the kind of understanding
for Hungary that had led to the Compromise of 1867.[11] Certain
Czechoslovaks were willing to take up the challenge. Miloš Kobr,
the minister in Budapest, regarded the minorities question as a
"life or death" matter for his country. In December he expressed
the private opinion that, if the Romanians did not come into line,
Hungary and Czechoslovakia might do best to begin negotiations
on a bilateral basis.[12] Later he lamented to a friendly diplomat
that his chiefs in the Hradčany "lived on the moon" and did not
understand the spirit of the times. They knew that some concessions had to be made, but could not get beyond minority statutes.[13]

Prague's unwillingness to consider major concessions to Hungary was predicated on the assumption, in part justified, that such
Czechophobes as Kánya, Horthy, and Bethlen were not really
interested in a true rapprochement even if important concessions
were made by the Czechoslovak state. Kobr's hint that Hungary
might be able to negotiate separately with Prague did not excite
much interest in Budapest. The thrust of Kánya's policy of negotiation with the Little Entente was still in an opposite direction:
the eventual isolation of Czechoslovakia. In the wake of the November visit of Kánya and Darányi, the political sentiment of
Hungary's leadership became even more solidly anti-Czechoslovak.
Almost all prominent members of the government and military
were now thinking in terms of an eventual destruction of Czechoslovakia. In December Minister of Defense Röder, who may earlier have shown an interest in a compromise settlement with
Prague on the basis of ethnic revision, now agreed with Ciano that
if Hungary wanted a "victory," she had to concentrate her forces

on her northern neighbor.[14] The Honvéd officer corps was eager to begin staff talks with Germany on a future operation against Czechoslovakia. Its spokesman in Berlin, Sztójay, several times in January and February asked when the promised General Staff consultations could begin.[15] And in February the Hungarian General Staff was already working out plans for a future military occupation of Slovakia and Ruthenia.[16]

The Hungarian political leadership was also determined to demonstrate to Berlin its hostility to the Czechoslovak state. During his visit in late January, Bohle was told by Csáky that if Yugoslavia could be neutralized, Hungary would be able to join Germany in a march into Czechoslovakia. If Hungary did move simultaneously, it would, in his opinion, mean "a very considerable and necessary assistance to Germany."[17] When a delegation of Sudeten Germans was in Budapest in late February, they found a similar hostility toward Beneš and his country, although, as they reported to Berlin, the Hungarians could see treaty revision only in terms of the rights of the Crown of St. Stephen. Both Minister of Nationalities Tibor Pataky and Bethlen "represented very openly . . . their plans for revision, and made no secret of Hungary's efforts to contribute to Czechoslovakia's disappearance from the map of Europe."[18] Darányi and Kánya, while less outspoken in their conversations with the Sudeten German leaders, also stressed the unanimity of views among Poland, Hungary, and Germany on the political fate of Czechoslovakia. Both men gave assurances that Hungary would not sign a pact of friendship with Prague, and Kánya emphasized that "all plans of an anti-German nature based on Hungary's collaboration with Czechoslovakia and Austria would break down in the face of Hungary's refusal."[19]

Yet at about the same time Kánya was making these statements, forces were at work to make one last attempt to find a basis for a Hungarian-Czechoslovak rapprochement. The appearance of Goga's regime in Romania and the alarming developments in Germany and Austria in February evoked much the same reaction in Prague as in Budapest. Shortly after the Berchtesgaden meeting Czechoslovak Foreign Minister Krofta apparently concluded that the time had come for a renewed effort to consider an understanding with Hungary on an anti-German basis. Germany's influence in Hungary was strong, but Krofta detected certain signs, such as Bethlen's public statement that Hungary wished to avoid becoming "Germany's slave," that the Hungarians could be won over.[20]

In mid-February the Hungarians began to notice a new cordiality and receptiveness on the part of Czechoslovak diplomats and government leaders. There were renewed hints that bilateral negotiations might begin. Kánya, who was likewise disturbed by events in Central Europe, was, in his inscrutable fashion, also making oblique approaches to Prague at this time. In spite of the quite clear warning from Hitler that Czechoslovakia would be destroyed at some date in the future, Kánya seemed willing one final time to test Prague's willingness to make territorial concessions to Hungary. Some time in February, probably in the critical days in the wake of the Berchtesgaden meeting, Kánya dropped a hint to Kobr that a political agreement was possible between their countries if Czechoslovakia proved accommodating on the question of territorial revision.[21] In this conversation, Kánya, to Kobr's great surprise, suddenly began to speak of a political cooperation of Central European states and the possible attack by a foreign power. Such cooperation, Kánya hastened to explain, would be "enormously difficult," because the problem of Hungary's unsatisfied revisionist demands always obtruded, and Budapest was setting its hopes on Germany to help realize these demands.

Kánya's true purpose in making this overture is not clear. Perhaps, in light of the imminence of Darányi's speech at Győr, he merely meant to throw Prague temporarily off balance, to confuse the Czechoslovaks about Hungary's real intentions. Perhaps he felt that, though it seemed extremely unlikely, Prague might just be prepared now to offer some territory as a reward for cooperation against Germany, in which case he might be able to win over Horthy by arguing that the rest of Slovakia might fall into Hungary's hands eventually anyway. In any case, the implication of Kánya's words to Kobr could not have been mistaken in Prague: political cooperation was possible only if some territorial concessions were granted Hungary.

Kobr's report apparently caused some rethinking of policy in Prague, for on 3 March Beneš approached the Austrian minister and suggested that he was "unfailingly" desirous of reaching a political agreement with Hungary, and was prepared to make "substantially greater concessions" than Romania or Yugoslavia. Once closer cooperation was achieved, Prague might be able to honor Hungary's more far-reaching demands, "because then the disposition of some hundred or thousand square kilometers would not be of decisive importance." Beneš asked the Austrians to serve as a mediator between Prague and Budapest.[22]

This information quickly reached Budapest, for already on 5 March Gusztáv Gratz, the indefatigible champion of a Danubian political bloc, was in Prague as Kánya's emissary, prepared to discuss the particulars of a political rapprochement with the Czechoslovak leadership.[23] Gratz spoke with Beneš, Krofta, and Hodža, who voiced concern about the danger from Germany but seemed confident that France, and perhaps England, would come to the aid of Czechoslovakia in a crisis. In discussing the possibilities of a rapprochement between their two countries, Beneš openly suggested that a Prague-Vienna-Budapest triangular bloc would be the best solution. To help achieve it, his government was prepared to grant the Magyar minority complete autonomy in the areas of education, public health, and transportation.

To Gratz's inevitable question about territorial concessions, there came the familiar response. Hodža pointed out the impossibility of ceding territory to a relatively weak Hungary, while denying it to a powerful Germany. Beneš was less categorically opposed to the idea, but even his statement on possible border changes in the future was vaguely phrased and seemed less promising than that given to the Austrian minister several days earlier.

Gratz thus returned to Budapest convinced that the effort to bring Prague and Budapest together was hopeless. His mission represented the last attempt to reconcile Hungarian-Czechoslovak differences and to promote political harmony and cooperation in Danubian Europe. By a strange and ironic coincidence, Gratz's report on his talks in Prague was submitted to Kánya on the very day that German troops were occupying Austria. After this no efforts were again made to bring Hungary and Czechoslovakia together in a political rapprochement; no unofficial emissaries again journeyed to Prague. Before long Kánya was publicly ridiculing the idea of a "Danubian Triangle," contending that it had been a "naive illusion" to think that Hungary would out of "pure altruism" help defend those who had so grossly enriched themselves at the expense of Hungary.[24] Those moderates, like Endre Bajcsy-Zsilinszky and Tibor Eckhardt, who had advocated and worked for Danubian cooperation, now abandoned the effort, and, whether consciously or unconsciously, began to think of drawing the line of defense against Germany on the Carpathians. Already in late March Eckhardt had dropped all pretensions of supporting a political detente with Czechoslovakia. On the twenty-ninth he declared that Hungary's national interest in the achievement of revision could be realized only in concert with the strong powers of Central Europe: Germany, Italy, and Poland. By friendship with Germany, Hungary would best serve the policy of revision, which, "we hope, can to a certain extent be fulfilled even this year." In a similar vein, Bajcsy-Zsilinszky now suggested that the time had come to develop a "new, powerful revisionist movement," more penetrating than anything before.[25]

Thus, the idea of reconciling Hungarian-Czechoslovak differences, which from time to time since 1919 had bobbed up in the stream of Danubian politics, was dead. With vital national interests so intimately involved, perhaps it was an impossible hope in the first place. In any case, though both Czechoslovakia and Hungary were to suffer unpleasant consequences of their failure to come to terms, it was Czechoslovakia whose fate was to be placed in jeopardy during the crisis of 1938. Superficially, the Czechoslovak Republic was a well functioning, stable democracy whose security was assured by an extensive system of treaties. France and the Soviet Union were obliged to defend it against aggression, and Britain, though under no such obligation, could hardly be expected to permit the destruction of an independent democratic state that it had helped create at Paris. Czechoslovakia also boasted of friends in Southeast Europe, Romania and Yugoslavia, who, though not bound to offer assistance against attack from Germany, were pledged by the terms of the Little Entente treaties to prevent a similar attack by Hungary. Moreover, Czechoslovakia was a military power in its own right. With the largest armaments industry in East Europe and a formidable system of fortifications on the border with Germany, it could be expected to put up strong resistance to any invasion.

Even Czechoslovakia's minorities problem seemed, on paper, to be manageable. Prague argued, and with much justification, that its minorities policy was the most enlightened in all of Europe, certainly well above the standard set by Hungary and Germany before the Great War.[26] The Czechoslovak leadership also contended that the very fact that their country possessed democratic institutions made it possible for any discontent to find expression through legal channels. There was no repetition of the deplorable situation in historic Hungary, where the minorities had little or no representation in Parliament.

Yet, despite appearances and the impressive logic of Prague's arguments, the internal and external position of Czechoslovakia was rapidly deteriorating in 1938. The Czechoslovak leaders found themselves confronted by many of the frustrating problems that had bedevilled the multinational Austro-Hungarian monarchy. Try as they might, they could not conceal the basic weakness of the Czechoslovak state, namely that it embraced several large and discontented nationalities whose loyalty was continually in doubt. To be sure, the Czechs and Slovaks together represented a respectable majority of the total population, and not all the Germans, Magyars, and Poles were anxious to return to their motherlands, where political and social conditions were distinctly less progressive.

Still, dissatisfaction in the minority areas was widespread and on the increase as Czechoslovakia's international position weakened in 1937 and 1938. Most leaders of the minority groups were unimpressed by the talk of Czechoslovakia's model nationalities policy; some suspected that Beneš's ultimate goal was to "Czechize" the country.[27] The moderates might indeed acknowledge that in the religious, educational, and minor administrative spheres they enjoyed substantial rights, but even these, they argued, were sometimes vitiated by the narrowmindedness of local officials. The complaints were often far more fundamental. When the Prague leadership extolled the virtues of its democratic practices, its critics pointed out that this had little meaning for the numerous minorities, who in 1919 had been deprived of the basic democratic right of self-determination.[28] Talk of extensive civil liberties also made little impression on minority leaders, whose newspapers and journals suffered under the heavy hand of the government censor. Nor did the prospect of gaining representation in the Parliament convince the minorities that they had reason to hope for improvement in their lot, since even if all minority representatives voted as a bloc, they still could not overcome Czech supremacy. And on one of the most sensitive issues, that of foreign policy, they could expect no influence. In a way, Czechoslovakia was following much the same course that Austria-Hungary had: its security was based on a foreign policy alignment that in a severe crisis the minorities could be expected to reject. Austria-Hungary had oriented itself toward Germany, and in the end found itself at war with Russia. Czechoslovakia's course was a mirror image of this. But Prague's position was even more tenuous, since her German, Hungarian, and Polish citizens lived in solid blocs directly contiguous to the nation states of their ethnic brothers.

Complicating the problem for the Hradčany leadership was the fact that even the Slovaks were not unconditionally loyal to the Czechoslovak ideal.[29] Though fundamentally willing to cooperate politically with the Czechs, and definitely averse to the idea of return to the Hungarian fold, many Slovak leaders felt that their nation was entitled to extensive autonomy. In September 1937 the Slovak People's Party, the largest in Slovakia, passed a resolution asserting its demand for fulfillment of the so-called Pittsburgh Agreement.[30] But this Beneš refused to countenance. He and his colleagues conceded that Czechoslovakia was a state composed of a number of nationalities, but they were adamant in refusing to transform it into a federation. Talk of autonomy for the nationalities was absolutely out of the question. The Germans, Beneš averred, were too "worm-like" on the map for application of autonomy to be practical.[31] The Poles and Hungarians, whose areas were not "worm-like," were simply ignored when the question arose. When Beneš was questioned about Slovak discontent, he strove to deemphasize it. No Slovak question really existed, he said privately in 1937. Any agitation was merely the work of Andrej Hlinka,[32] and it would cease with his death.[33] Similarly, it was argued, in words strangely reminiscent of prewar Hungary, that the minorities in Czechoslovakia were in fact basically content, and that there would be no problem if it were not for the insidious attitude of Germany, Hungary, and Poland, who fomented trouble with the final objective of destroying an otherwise stable and democratic state.

These arguments were employed to explain why it would be foolhardy for Prague to meet the more far reaching demands of the Slovaks or the ethnic minorities. But there was yet another consideration that perhaps lay at the bottom of the problem: if once the leadership in Prague acknowledged that one group, say the Slovaks or the Germans, deserved extensive autonomous rights, the others would immediately step forward to demand equal treatment. There would be set in motion a process the final impact of which on the fragile structure of Czechoslovakia no one could predict.[34] Who was to say that it would not all end with an autonomous Teschen declaring its union with Poland, or Sudetenland with Germany, or Ruthenia with Hungary? This was the pervasive fear that prompted the leadership in Prague to resist demands for expanded minority rights, and to grant only the barest minimum when there was no alternative.

For Budapest in the post-Anschluss period, the dimensions and urgency of the Czechoslovak problem were quite clear, since the Hungarians, alone in Europe, had a reasonably accurate picture of Hitler's final goal. They knew, if the Führer was true to his word, that Germany wanted not just improved conditions for the Sudeten Germans, nor even the annexation of the Sudetenland alone, but the complete absorption of Bohemia and Moravia. This knowledge made Kánya's task in the spring of 1938 particularly delicate. No longer was he prepared to predict, as he had in January, that peace seemed assured for a year because there was no "will to war" in Europe. If, as Kánya believed, Hitler's success was based on a continual parade of "political sensations," the unpredictable German chancellor might choose to "settle accounts" with Czechoslovakia as early as 1938. If he did so, the point could easily be reached when the British, finally aroused from their apparent lethargy, would intervene again to thwart German expansion.

Hungary's conservatives, including Kánya, Teleki, Imrédy, and Horthy, had high respect for British sea power and believed it would again bring victory in a European war. They were probably much impressed by the argument of the Hungarian minister in London, Szilárd Masirevich, who shortly after the Anschluss reported that England was for the moment temporizing, but that the time would come when her "vital interests" were at stake and when she felt sufficiently secure in her armaments. "When we turn back the pages of history," Masirevich noted, "it has always been the case that England worked slowly but in the end still had the last word."[35] The memory of Hungary's ignominious defeat in the last war was still too deeply etched in the nation's consciousness for its leaders to dismiss lightly the dangers inherent in any cooperation with an irrational Germany. Although many Hungarians, including Miklós Horthy, were likely at times to allow this consideration to be obscured by their fervent desire to undo the "wrongs" of the peace settlement, the true maker of policy in 1938, Kálmán Kánya, kept it constantly in mind.

Had Kánya in 1938 been at the helm of a Hungary that had not been stripped of one-third of its Magyar population, his policy would doubtless have developed along different lines. Then the problem of thwarting an expansionist Germany would perhaps have been paramount. But in fact nearly 750,000 Magyars lived in Czechoslovakia in 1938,[36] most of them in areas bordering directly on Trianon Hungary, and there was hardly a politically conscious Hungarian who did not feel that Czechoslovakia's upcoming time of troubles should be exploited in one way or another to promote Hungarian interests. Few Hungarians believed that their ethnic brothers in Czechoslovakia were justly treated; fewer still thought that the original decision to award Slovakia and Ruthenia to the new Czechoslovak state was defensible. The virtual unanimity of national sentiment placed certain limitations on Budapest's policy. Those critics of the Hungarian government at the time and in later years who maintained that Hungary should have joined together with its hostile northern neighbor in a defensive union against Germany failed to realize that no Hungarian government could have persuaded the nation to accept such a move unless Prague offered attractive, tangible concessions. This, as has been seen, Czechoslovakia would not do. Indeed, once the final attempt to achieve a political understanding had collapsed in early March, Prague showed scant interest in a separate agreement with Hungary.

Of course, the intensity of this national hostility toward Czechoslovakia and the ardor of the chauvinism of most Hungarians had in large part been generated by Hungary's political establishment over the past two decades. Nonetheless, this state of affairs was not entirely to the liking of Hungary's leaders in 1938. For such overwhelming public emotion might well be inflamed even more by zealous revisionists and radical right-wing demagogues and might persuade certain members of the government (notably Regent Horthy) to approve a militant policy that would thrust Hungary's eager but weak and inexperienced armed forces into dangerous adventures. Although as avid as any of his compatriots to recover some former Hungarian territories, Foreign Minister Kánya, true to his diplomatic training, preferred that this be achieved without a resort to arms. Though Kánya never expressed himself clearly on the subject, the ideal solution, in his estimation, would probably have been a congress of European states, perhaps held at Geneva, at which the great powers would compel Czechoslovakia to forfeit some of its territory. Alternatively, Prague might be convinced that plebiscites should be held under international supervision in disputed territories. By these methods Hungary could reap the benefits of revision without much risk, and remain neutral should Hitler blunder his way into war with the West.

Yet there was an unreal quality to these hopes for effortless revision, since it was unlikely that the Czechs and Slovaks would comply with any procedure that aimed at the dismembering of their state. Indeed, even if certain Czech leaders had been willing in theory to cede some territories in Slovakia to Hungary, this could not have been carried out without severe repercussions for the Czechoslovak state. The Slovaks may not have had an important voice in the formation of Czechoslovakia's foreign policy in general, but in one area, relations with Hungary, they possessed what amounted to a veto power. If the international situation ever required that Czechoslovakia consider territorial concessions to Hungary, the Slovaks, who would doubtless be more unyielding than the Czechs, would demand that they make the major decisions. This reality the Hungarian government was to discover only in November 1938.

Though Kálmán Kánya did not understand the intricacies of the Czech-Slovak relationship, he was realistic enough to recognize that achievement of territorial revision might in the end require the use of force. Thus Kánya felt it his duty as foreign minister to provide alternative policies should it in fact come to a military conflict in Danubian Europe. Though he probably could not envisage conditions in the foreseeable future in which Hungary could safely enter such a military conflict, Kánya could not, even if he had been so disposed, prevent the army from planning for various military contingencies. He concluded, too, that if a conflict broke out in the Danubian area, it would be difficult for the government to restrain the army from entering Czechoslovakia, especially since Regent Horthy would probably approve that action. In fact, early in the year the General Staff had begun studying the intricacies of possible campaigns in Czechoslovakia, and the idea of dispatching a "free corps" at some future date was even considered. Kánya agreed that such plans could be discussed informally with the Germans and Poles, but he was not enthusiastic about this, and he confined his own activities in preparation for a conflict over Czechoslovakia to the attempt to arrange the neutralization of Yugoslavia.

It is certain that Kánya, with the backing of Imrédy and Count Pál Teleki, vigorously opposed any suggestion that Hungary participate in a blatant act of aggression against Czechoslovakia. Aside from the fact that such an action might well turn out to be suicide for a weak country like Hungary, there was the further consideration, which carried much weight for a statesman like Kánya, educated in the school of traditional European diplomacy, that countries simply did not declare war on fellow states without clear provocation. Kánya realized that such crude and belligerent behavior on Hungary's part would brand her in Western Europe as an "outlaw" nation, a "jackal" that thrived on the bones thrown to it by the fascist states. Any territorial gains made in this fashion would never be permanent, for a European war would be inevitable, and the victory of Great Britain and her allies would mean even more drastic peace terms for the defeated states, on whose side the Hungarians had voluntarily ranged themselves.[37]

But if outright aggression was ruled out, and diplomatic means seemed likely to be ineffective, there were other methods by which the Czechoslovak problem might be settled in Hungary's favor. In the 1920s the Hungarian Foreign Ministry had attempted in various ways to foment discontent among the Slovaks, hoping that eventually civil disorders would occur that Budapest could exploit. During 1938 these efforts were resumed, though in substantially different conditions. By this time no influential Slovak advocated a return to Hungary, although several Ruthenian leaders were Magyarophiles and were secretly subsidized by Budapest. The leaders of the Magyar minority likewise received support and in fact took their orders from the Hungarian government, much in the same manner in which Henlein operated in Bohemia.

Although the details of Hungarian planning in this operation (if there was indeed detailed planning) are unknown, it is likely that Budapest hoped that in time civil disorder would grow to such proportions in Czechoslovakia that the state would appear to be disintegrating. In such a case, Hungary, without obvious consultation with Germany, could respond to a call from a quickly assembled "Hungarian National Council," and, much as the Czechs had done in 1918, send in troops to create a *fait accompli*.[38] With proper planning and earlier offers of extensive autonomy, the Slovaks might be convinced to allow Hungary to assume a protectorate. Even Western Europe could not object to such a development if the civil war seemed more a result of minority discontent than external machination. To create this impression, Kánya was careful throughout 1938 to avoid making any demands on the Czechoslovak government. A special effort was made to refrain from giving even the appearance of threatening to use force.[39] Before 24 September Hungary made no specific communication to Prague in regard to the situation in Slovakia and Ruthenia. This was left to the leaders of the Magyar minority. Kánya thus felt justified in later telling Western and Little Entente diplomats that the crisis in Czechoslovakia was not of Hungary's making and was solely a manifestation of the essentially unstable character of that state. In a similar way, Budapest made it clear in London that it wished its case for revision to be examined alone and on its own merits, and not in any way connected with that of Germany or Poland.

To prepare Hungary for any possible developments in the Czechoslovak question, whether it be military conflict caused by German belligerence, a peaceful diplomatic settlement, civil war in Czechoslovakia, or an indefinite prolongation of the status quo, Kánya began early in 1938 to work toward the creation of conditions in Central Europe that would both enhance Hungary's security and promote her long term revisionist desires. As is the case with Kánya's policy throughout his five years in office, it is difficult to describe with precision the motives and dimensions of his political strategy in 1938. He purposely spoke of Hungary's intentions only in the vaguest terms, and as neither complete Cabinet minutes nor Kánya's personal records have survived, his aims must be deduced largely from his actions. Even Hungarian diplomats sometimes complained that their chief was not keeping them informed of the purpose and direction of Hungarian policy. In the immediate post-Anschluss period they knew only what Kánya instructed them to convey to the countries to which they were accredited, namely that Hungary desired to strengthen relations with Poland and Italy, and continue the former policy of the "free hand."[40] One thing, however, was clear: Kánya had no intention of linking Hungary's fortunes with those of Nazi Germany or any other country. His approach was eminently pragmatic and opportunistic. If there were good prospects for territorial revision by limited cooperation with Germany, he would take this path, so long as there was no danger of becoming involved in a military conflict. The earlier principle would still be adhered to: there would be no military commitments to either Germany or Western Europe until the outcome of European rearmament became clearer.

Until that point was reached, other pillars of support for Hungarian independence and security would have to be constructed. To be effective, they would have to serve two requirements: the facilitation of territorial revision in Czechoslovakia, should the opportunity arise; and a contribution to the future balance of power against Germany, should Hitler succeed in absorbing all of Bohemia and Moravia. Unlike some of his contemporaries, Kánya eschewed the use of dazzling slogans or grand designs in diplomacy. The Central European system he envisioned had no name, and, to maintain freedom of movement, was sketched only in the most general terms.[41] As a first principle, there was the necessity for maintenance of friendly ties with Germany, the strongest power in the area and the only one that seemed likely to give support for Hungary's revisionist campaign. As long as Hitler did not provoke a wider conflict, and kept his promise of noninterference in Hungary's domestic affairs and disinterest in Slovakia, Kánya saw every reason to stay in Berlin's good graces. Beyond this, as has been mentioned, relations with Italy and Poland would be strengthened, and Britain would be encouraged to emerge from its isolation and take an active part in the creation of a new order in Central Europe. Hungarian conservatives in general were hopeful of gaining the outright support, or at least benevolent neutrality, of London toward their revisionist program. Toward this end Kánya continued to support an Anglo-Italian rapprochement.

Finally, the negotiations for a "normalization" of relations with the Little Entente would be continued. Many Hungarians of right radical persuasion failed to understand why Hungary bothered to continue talks with Czechoslovakia and her allies, when it was obvious that Germany was about to increase the pressure against Prague. Kánya took the more cautious view. Reasoning that the country needed above all to avoid a military adventure in the Danubian area, Kánya must have argued that the best way to guarantee this was to be on superficially friendly terms with Hungary's neighbors. And what better way to demonstrate Hungary's pacific intentions than to be in the process of negotiating a political agreement? If for one reason or another the Czechoslovak question were to be postponed for many years, or even indefinitely, Hungary might gain several valuable concessions through the diplomatic bargaining. After Darányi's speech at Győr in March, Hungary's military equality was all but declared, but Kánya nonetheless attached some value to having this formally recognized by Hungary's enemies. And if the Little Entente countries showed some understanding for Hungary's "minimal demands" in the minorities question, a significant amelioration of the conditions for the Magyar minorities might be achieved. Moreover, as Kánya no doubt pointed out to his critics, Hungary was offering no new commitment to the Successor States. The most that Kánya would concede was a reaffirmation of Hungary's obligation under the Kellogg Pact, and, as he once told a German informant, "the Czechs knew very well that even a non-aggression pact would not secure them against Hungary in all eventualities."[42]

It was clear to the Hungarians that one of the primary tasks in the post-Anschluss era was a clarification of the relationship with Italy. Ciano had sketched his thoughts on the future of Central Europe in a "tour d'horizon" with the Hungarian minister, Frigyes Villani, in late February two weeks before the Anschluss. After his pessimistic words on the future of Austria, which have already been recorded, Ciano bluntly asserted that "the fate of Czechoslovakia is sealed," and that it was just a matter of time before it disappeared from the map of Europe. He stressed that after the partition of that state Poland and Hungary would share a common border that would facilitate the formation of a "horizontal axis" as a necessary balance to a greatly strengthened Germany. This new axis, seemingly more diagonal than horizontal in shape, would link Rome, Belgrade, Budapest, and Warsaw. The clear implication in Ciano's words was that both Austria and Czechoslovakia would disappear from the map of Europe, and Hungary and Poland would gain a common border.[43]

Kánya and other Hungarians showed some interest in such a "horizontal axis,"[44] but before further study of the idea could be begun, the Austrian crisis intervened, and the future course of the bilateral Hungarian-Italian relationship became one of Budapest's chief concerns. The first signs seemed encouraging. As early as 13 March Ciano sent word that Italy was prepared to deepen political and economic ties with Hungary, and in a long conversation with Villani a few days later the Italian foreign minister gave an assurance that Italy's relations with Hungary would be retained in the spirit of the Rome Pact, even though the third party, Austria, had disappeared. In the interests of creating a "horizontal axis," he urged the Hungarians to seek a further improvement in their relations with Yugoslavia and Romania. To Kánya's satisfaction, Ciano added that Rome's talks with the British were progressing well.[45]

Yet after the shock of the Anschluss had worn off, old Italian suspicions of their Hungarian friends resurfaced. Ciano began again privately to disparage Kánya, whose "Ballhausplatz mentality and anti-Serb prejudices would have to be overcome before progress could be made toward a Central European bloc."[46] Accordingly, when in mid-May the Hungarians proposed a secret pact in which, among other things, Rome would have promised military support in case Yugoslavia launched an unprovoked attack on Hungary, Ciano and Mussolini were skeptical. After mulling over the idea for a while, the Duce decided that the notion of a Yugoslav attack on Hungary was absurd, and thus no pact of this sort was necessary.[47]

By the end of May, Hungary's ties with Italy had still not been clarified to Budapest's satisfaction. The Hungarians continued to fear that in a true crisis Rome might abandon them, just as Austria had been abandoned. Moreover, Kánya was unwilling to purchase additional good will by leaving the League of Nations, something the Italians continued to request.

In contrast to Italy, Colonel Beck's Poland was actively courting Hungary's favor in this period. Beck considered the establishment of territorial contact between Hungary and Poland the first step in the creation of a "Third Europe," a bloc of states stretching from the Black Sea to the Baltic Sea, with an enlarged Poland and Hungary as the dominant powers.[48] A "common border" was viewed by individuals in both countries as a panacea for the ills of East Central Europe. To many it represented a barrier against German expansion eastward and a guarantee against Bolshevik encroachments from the East. Exactly how far along the Carpathians the "common border" should run, however, remained a subject of some debate in Warsaw. The Poles had some doubts about the eagerness of the Slovaks to return to the Hungarian fold, and in 1937 Beck was apparently thinking in terms of the establishment of a kind of Polish protectorate in Slovakia.[49]

Ruthenia, or the Carpatho-Ukraine, was a different matter. Here the Poles, who already possessed a sizable Ukrainian minority and were intent on preventing the creation of a "Ukrainian Piedmont" at their doorstep, supported Hungarian aspirations without reserve. In late 1935 Beck authorized Tadeusz Kobylanski, director of the political section of the foreign ministry, to conclude with András Hory, the Hungarian minister, an oral "gentlemen's agreement" whereby Poland asserted that the return of Ruthenia to Hungary was considered an interest of the Polish government. Diplomatic support would be given to all Hungarian endeavors in that direction, and policy would be coordinated according to the desires of the Hungarian government.[50]

On the eve of the European crisis, the Hungarian-Polish relationship could thus with some accuracy be characterized as an "unwritten treaty,"[51] at least insofar as the general attitude to the fate of Czechoslovakia was concerned. When Colonel Beck and Kánya met in Geneva in September 1937, the Polish leader expressed his views on Czechoslovakia "with extreme severity."[52] But despite the oral understanding over Ruthenia, the specific intentions of Poland and Hungary were unknown to each other, and Beck, who already at this point had become convinced that Britain and France would not come to the aid of Czechoslovakia in a crisis,[53] was eager to coordinate plans with Hungary. Reasoning that future German expansion toward the Southeast would provide the opportunity for furthering Polish goals elsewhere, in early 1938 Beck began to lay the groundwork for his policy of "individual solutions."[54] In December he invited Horthy and other high Hungarian officials to Warsaw for a state visit in the following February. It seemed the appropriate time for far-ranging discussions of problems of mutual interest in Central Europe.

As it happened, the Hungarian visit of February 5–9 came shortly after the internal power shift in Germany, and Polish and Hungarian statesmen were both apprehensive and hopeful over this development. Mixed with their nervousness over Hitler's intentions was speculation that the Czechoslovak question would soon come to the fore. Yet the talks in Warsaw proved singularly unfruitful, since a personality clash between Kánya and Beck prevented a frank exchange of views. In the following weeks Beck continued to press the Hungarians for a statement of intentions in the Czechoslovak question, warning at the same time that the Anschluss was imminent and that an alteration in the map of Czechoslovakia would have to be reckoned with.[55] At the end of February, Kobylanski, citing the urgency of the matter, asked Hory for a direct answer to the important question: was Hungary in fact prepared to participate in a future action against Czechoslovakia?[56]

Faced with this barrage of requests for a clarification of Hungarian policy, Kánya felt compelled at this point to respond, his readiness to consult with the Poles heightened by the news that Ciano saw the Anschluss as inevitable and the fate of Czechoslovakia as sealed. From Vienna, where Kánya was meeting with Schuschnigg in the visit already described, a letter was dispatched on 2 March to Hory, with instructions that the substance be transmitted to Beck. This message, sent only ten days before the disappearance of Austria, is one of the few surviving direct statements of Hungarian policy in this period.[57] Responding directly to Kobylanski's query, the Hungarian foreign minister asserted that "we are determined to take part in every necessary anti-Czech action," and that it would therefore be desirable that talks on the details of cooperation, "even of a military nature," be begun immediately. Kánya expressed satisfaction that Poland believed collaboration with Hungary to be essential, especially at that point, when the question was becoming most acute. Kánya also noted that, despite the cordial relationship Hungary enjoyed with Germany, the "extraordinarily strong dynamism" of Nazi Germany made desirable a continuing exchange of ideas with Poland. In this sense, Ciano's suggestion of an Italian-Yugoslav-Hungarian-Polish bloc might be worth examining, although, he added, both Warsaw and Budapest were of course aware that such a grouping would have to pursue a friendly policy toward Germany.

This message was welcome in Poland, though Kánya's silence on Hungary's territorial aspirations in Czechoslovakia led the Poles to contemplate other solutions to the "Slovak question."[58] In April Kánya did inform Warsaw that Hungary aspired to her historic borders to the North, and that this had been approved by Hitler, who had emphatically declared his disinterest in former Hungarian territories. Kánya suggested that the mood of the population in Slovakia was "favorable" to Hungary and "justified the best hopes."[59] But the Poles, who were receiving contrary reports from Slovakia, were unconvinced and continued to advise the Hungarians to establish contacts with the key Slovak leaders.

In fact, despite the various assurances given to Warsaw and Berlin, up to this point the Hungarians had done little to find any common ground for cooperation with the new generation of Slovak leaders. Many in Hungary still clung to the mistaken notion that the Slovaks were merely misled wards of the Hungarians and, given the opportunity, would gladly return to prewar conditions. A strange mixture of naiveté and arrogance led the Hungarian government to put faith in the activities of such Slovaks as František Jehlička and Viktor Dvorčák, long after these men ceased to have any influence in Slovakia.[60] In 1938 Jehlička carried on lobbying work in Rome, London, and Paris, but in spite of minor success with the Italians, no one in Slovakia took notice.

The more sober minds in the Hungarian Foreign Ministry, including Kánya, had by 1938 come to realize that a "Hungarian solution" to the Slovak question would require winning over at least some of the nationalist Slovak leaders. The difficulty was that the Slovak and Hungarian ambitions were fundamentally antithetical. Neither the separatists nor the autonomists in Slovakia favored a return to Hungary: the former envisioned an independent state within the borders of 1919, while the latter would have been content to remain in political cooperation with the Czechs if political equality had been truly established. In other words, both groups in Slovakia agreed that Slovakia's southern frontier, as established by the Paris Peace Conference, was inviolable. The ideal solution from the Hungarian standpoint, however, was simply reincorporation of the whole of Slovakia into the realm of St. Stephen. If necessary, a certain degree of autonomy would be granted, but only the barest minimum required to pacify the Slovaks. The establishment of an independent Slovakia was not viewed with much favor in Budapest, and if it seemed events were moving in that direction, Hungary would surely demand the return of at least the Magyar areas lost in 1919.

The first direct contact between the Hungarian government and one of the Slovak leaders came in May when Father Josef Tiso, a leading figure in the Slovak People's Party, was in Budapest for the Eucharistic Congress. Tiso was informed that if Slovakia returned to the Hungarian fold, the Slovaks would receive some degree of autonomy, depending on how events unfolded. The Slovaks might claim a great deal if they cooperated with the Hungarians when the critical moment came, but it would be a different matter if Slovakia were acquired solely "in the course of a Hungarian military action carried out in cooperation with friendly powers." Not surprisingly, this somewhat supercilious attitude on the part of the Hungarians made a poor impression on Tiso, who showed little interest in their convoluted offer and left Budapest in a frustrated and irritated mood.[61]

This incident must have made an impression on the Hungarians, for when Count János Eszterházy, leader of the largest political party of the Magyar minority in Slovakia, visited Warsaw in June, he was noticeably less confident about the chances for cooperation with the Slovaks. Eszterházy candidly admitted to Szembek that "the mood in Slovakia is not pro-Hungarian," and that "it would require even more of an effort to win over the whole of Slovakia." Elaborating on the position Slovakia might occupy in the Kingdom of St. Stephen, Eszterházy stated that both Horthy and Kánya were now thinking in terms of the kind of autonomy enjoyed by Croatia before 1918. There would be a Hungarian governor, but a local diet, army, and finances. In any case, it was clear that "Budapest could not . . . offer the Slovaks less than they were at the moment being offered by Prague."[62] This explicit statement must have struck the proper note, for when Eszterházy talked with Beck, the Polish leader declared that "within a definitely brief time" Czechoslovakia would disintegrate, and Slovakia would return to Hungary. Beck reminded his guest of the importance of not allowing Prague a chance to catch its breath. Berlin and Budapest, he suggested, should "do nothing that would ease the situation for the Czechs."[63]

Eszterházy's visit to Warsaw marked a turning point in Hungarian-Polish cooperation in 1938. The earlier idea of a Polish protectorate in Slovakia was now jettisoned, and Warsaw's political machinery was placed at the service of the Hungarian cause. The exchange of military intelligence was enhanced, although truly intimate political coordination was still not achieved.

During these months of behind-the-scenes efforts to effect co-operation between Hungary and Poland and create a common pro-gram between the Magyars and Slovaks in Slovakia, Budapest joined the rest of Europe in observing events in Berlin and Prague to determine in which direction the Czechoslovak question would develop. The role of Germany, as always, seemed crucial, both to the pro- and anti-German groups in Hungary. Firm in the belief that intimate military cooperation with Germany was an essential condition for the fulfillment of national aspirations in Czechoslo-vakia, the military party in Hungary, with Sztójay as its spokesman in Berlin, made incessant approaches to the Germans on the sub-ject of the staff talks that had been promised a year earlier by Blomberg and Beck.

However, Ribbentrop had grave misgivings about staff talks, and ordered that the Hungarians be put off, since "if we were to have conversations with Hungary on possible war aims vis à vis Czechoslovakia, there is the danger that other authorities will ob-tain information about them."[64]

The available evidence suggests that in early 1938 Hitler pre-ferred to bide his time in the Czechoslovak question, carefully marshalling forces for a confrontation with Prague sometime in the more distant future. The latest military directive ordered by Hitler, that of 21 December 1937,[65] stipulated that the military conditions for carrying out an offensive war against Czechoslovakia would be created when Germany had achieved "complete pre-paredness for war in all fields." This directive made no explicit reference to the role of other Central European countries in a conflict with Czechoslovakia. But the brief sketch of the nature of the projected campaign suggests the part that Poland and Hungary already at this point were expected to play. The move against Czechoslovakia was described as a "strategic and sudden attack" in which the fortifications would be taken by surprise and the armed forces destroyed in the process of mobilization. Czecho-slovakia's defeat would be hastened by an exploitation of its "ethnic diversity." Precisely what role Hungary and Poland might play in capitalizing on the "ethnic diversity" of Czechoslovakia was not specified, and perhaps Hitler himself at this early date had not come to any firm decision.

In late March all of Europe was doubtless trying to fathom Hit-ler's true intentions in Czechoslovakia, but Sztójay, who of all the foreign diplomats in Berlin probably had the best rapport with influential leaders of the government and party in Germany, arrived at perhaps the most accurate analysis. His impression was that Berlin's policy for the time being would be aimed at the "inner disruption" (belső szétbomlasztás) of Czechoslovakia. Sztójay pointed out that Hitler's past record showed a proclivity for proceeding along "legal" lines, and that his policy toward Prague might in some way reflect this.[66] Sztójay's speculations were confirmed by other confidential information that Hungary was receiving from Eszterházy at about the same time. Eszterházy had been told by Henlein, who had just returned from consultations with Hitler in Germany, that the Sudeten Germans intended to sabotage the negotiations with Hodža by presenting progressively steeper demands. In Henlein's views, this was the best method for bringing about a quick disintegration of Czechoslovakia, and he asked Eszterházy to support him in this strategy.[67]

Eszterházy's information, the accuracy of which is confirmed by the published German records, apparently prompted Kánya to move swiftly to clarify Germany's attitude on a Hungarian-Yugoslav rapprochement and the elusive general staff talks, and to remind Berlin of Hitler's promise to respect Hungary's claims to Slovakia and Ruthenia. On 5 April, the same day on which Kánya placed Hungary's goal of integral revision in the Felvidék on record in Warsaw, Kánya instructed Sztójay to make the following cautiously worded statement:

There is much talk these days about the Czech question, that is that in the not too distant future important events will take place in Czechoslovakia. The Hungarian government, as is well known, pursues a peaceful policy and trusts that the Czech question also will be successfully solved by pacific means. Nonetheless, in today's rather hectic and nervous time all possibilities have to be reckoned with, and among these even that the solution of the Czech question will be obtainable only by way of armed intervention. In so far as this event, contrary to all expectations, does occur, we believe that German-Hungarian cooperation will be called for. For this reason we regard it as justified and necessary to prepare for this possibility and to instruct our general staffs to discuss the details of possible cooperation.[68]

Sztójay was asked to convey this message to Ribbentrop, but the only surviving account from the German side is that detailing the Hungarian minister's conversation with State Secretary Weizsäcker on 11 April.[69] At this interview Sztójay handed in as a private note two memoranda, one for all purposes identical to Kánya's instruction cited above, and a second, apparently of Sztójay's own creation. The latter, purportedly based on an earlier conversation with Kánya, betrayed a more belligerent and blunt tone. A Hungarian-Yugoslav understanding was described as essential, since it would facilitate a simultaneous Hungarian-German action against Czechoslovakia in the case of war. Such an action, this second memorandum continued, would make it difficult for Czechoslovakia to mobilize completely, prevent the movement of Czechoslovak troops from Slovakia to Bohemia, render impossible from the outset the dropping of Soviet paratroopers, and in general create an unambiguous situation, to the advantage of both foreign and domestic policy. The note also emphasized the advantage of prompt military talks, by which zones, objectives, and missions could be established and misunderstandings avoided.

This open declaration of willingness, indeed eagerness, to participate with Germany in a military action against Czechoslovakia was almost surely made without Kánya's sanction, as the contradictory thrust of the two parts of the Hungarian note indicates. Sztójay, perhaps with the support of Chief of Staff Rátz, seems to have taken matters into his own hands, so strong was his faith in Hungary's armed forces and his conviction that Hungary would do best to identify wholeheartedly with the German cause. In any case, Weizsäcker, who himself had grave reservations about the desirability of forcing the Czechoslovak issue, gave the Hungarian note a cool reception. Nor were higher German authorities more encouraging. Sztójay saw Hitler briefly on 17 April, and Ribbentrop on the twenty-second, but neither seems to have responded to the Hungarian queries. Ribbentrop merely postponed the question of staff talks until August, when the regent was scheduled to make a state visit to Germany.

From the various hints and indications in the months after the Anschluss, Kánya thus concluded that for the time being Hitler would not force the Czechoslovak issue. The pressure would doubtless be kept up in Czechoslovakia through Sudeten German obstruction and agitation, but war would be avoided at least until the Rhine defenses were completed in late 1939.[70] Accordingly, Kánya limited his diplomatic activity in the spring to registering Hungary's territorial claims in Warsaw and Berlin, urging Hitler to act on his promise of mediation between Budapest and Belgrade, and attempting to find some program for winning over the Slovak leaders. With Berlin noncommittal on the question of staff talks, German-Hungarian cooperation in the Czechoslovak question consisted mostly of an exchange of general political and military information.

Little effort was made by Budapest to coordinate the activities of the Magyar minority in Slovakia with that of the Sudeten Germans. Only loose contact was established, and when Karl Frank, the chief figure in the more radical wing of the Sudeten German group, offered his Magyar counterparts German weapons with which to cause "incidents" in Slovakia, these were refused.[71] When Henlein issued his Karlsbad demands on 24 April, he did so only in the name of the Germans. There was, indeed, a parallel demonstration on the same day by the Hungarian Revision League in Budapest. The head of the League accused Prague in violent terms of systematically oppressing its minorities, and called on the minority groups to "break up this red Czechoslovakia!" But the provocative attacks by the fanatical revisionists were not condoned by the Hungarian government. Kánya summoned Kobr on the 25th and expressed regret over the demonstration, and an official communiqué to this effect appeared in the press at the same time.[72]

Taken by itself, the preceding account would not give an accurate or complete picture of Hungary's place in the unfolding Czechoslovak problem. For, as already suggested, Kánya strove always to keep several options open and preserve his freedom to maneuver. Thus, while devious plans were being discussed with Germany and Poland, Hungary was sitting at the negotiating table with the Little Entente, ostensibly working toward an understanding that would lower the tension in the Danubian area. These talks, which were a continuation of earlier contacts, were started in February, when the Romanians finally emerged from their period of domestic turmoil. Tatarescu, the new Romanian foreign minister, informed Kánya that he desired a "new era" in Hungarian-Romanian relations, and that his government would create the atmosphere for this by fulfilling "every justifiable demand" of the Magyar minority.[73]

The Hungarians quickly discovered that Tatarescu's fine words did not connote a greater willingness to make concessions to Hungary. Though Kánya was greatly disconcerted by the attitude of the Little Entente in the spring of 1938, he resisted the temptation to break off negotiations. The subsequent negotiations, which proceeded along tortuously winding paths, were to culminate in an agreement five months later. Throughout the talks Kánya insisted that a minorities declaration would have to be at the heart of any agreement. As he told the French minister in Budapest, his goal was to ensure that the Magyar minorities in Danubian Europe were treated in conformity with "civilized, international standards."[74] In return, Budapest was prepared to affirm its commitment to the principles of the Kellogg pact.

In April a significant impetus was given to these talks when the British government, in its first diplomatic initiative in Danubian Europe in many years, intervened to urge Hungary and the three Little Entente countries to make a special effort to reach a settlement at an early date.[75] Kánya was willing to comply, for he, like Horthy and many other Hungarian statesmen, believed that Britain was the key to a peaceful redrawing of the boundaries of Central and Eastern Europe.

However, if the hopes of the Hungarian conservatives for the benevolent intervention of England in Danubian affairs were to materialize, it was not sufficient merely that the Hungarian case be viewed more sympathetically in London. The British had also to be convinced that Hungary was a friendly, independent state that, if properly strengthened through fulfillment of her "just" territorial demands, would be able to serve as a bulwark against German expansion to the Southeast. This, however, proved to be a formidable task, since the British minister, Geoffrey Knox, quite early became convinced that Hungary was soon to become a German satellite. Knox, who had worked for many years to try to create some form of Danubian bloc, had by the beginning of 1938 concluded that Hungary was irrevocably hostile to Czechoslovakia and would wed itself to Germany in order to join in the partition of their common enemy. Although he realized, far better than most observers, that Kánya aimed to pursue an uncommitted policy, Knox felt that Hungary's proximity to Germany and the strength of the local right radical movement would inevitably and quite rapidly result in the loss of Hungarian independence. He thus reported to London, shortly after the Anschluss, that Hungary was in no position to incur the displeasure of Berlin, and her policy had to be one of "complacency if not subservience."[76]

Since Knox was London's primary source of information on developments in Hungary, the Foreign Office naturally concluded after the Anschluss that Hungary was a lost cause. It was thus not surprising that responsible officials in the Foreign Office came to believe that Hungary was "obsequiously servile" to Germany, and that if a radical right-wing government came to power, it would only bring into the open a state of affairs already existing. Thus, when the Hungarian minister, on Kánya's instructions, submitted a brief note on 22 March stating that Hungary intended to continue its policy of the "free hand," there was deep skepticism in the Foreign Office.[78]

Kánya, however, for the time being did not suspect the true situation in London, and he persisted in his effort to demonstrate the independent and unaggressive character of Hungarian policy. In order to counteract any fears that Darányi's Győr speech might have aroused in England, London was informed that Hungary was not declaring its military equality, and in fact was willing to continue to negotiate with the Little Entente on this point. The development of the Hungarian army was not to be "by leaps and bounds," and it was primarily a question of replacing obsolete war material.[79] Kánya in part also fashioned his policy toward the Little Entente to gain credit in England, where, despite the gloom over Hungary's future course, the idea of cooperation among Danubian nations still had its advocates.

Hungarian-British ties were prevented from slowly deteriorating in the spring only by the assiduous efforts of individuals on both sides who believed that as Europe approached a time of crisis the two countries' interests would be damaged by a complete severance of relations. Kánya's struggle to maintain an essentially uncommitted policy received strong support from several influential Hungarian political figures. Regent Horthy himself, despite occasional waverings,[80] continued to respect British power and believe in its eventual triumph over Germany in a military conflict. Personal contacts always were important in shaping the political views of the impressionable regent, and the visit to Budapest of Arthur Henderson, a British M. P., to whom Horthy granted an audience on 24 April, probably did much to temper Horthy's enthusiasm about cooperating with Germany in an anti-Czechoslovak action.[81]

Count Pál Teleki, who entered the Cabinet in May as minister of education, was also a strong adherent of a policy of cooperation with England. Convinced that any territory gained as the result of an alliance with Germany would not be lasting, and that time and geography were working in Hungary's favor anyway, Teleki was able to exert a distinct moderating influence during the developing crisis over Czechoslovakia. And because of the respect he enjoyed abroad, especially in Great Britain, Teleki's appointment to the Cabinet did much to dispel the notion that Hungary was already lost to the German orbit.[82]

On the English side, the main champions of Hungary were, as in the past, representatives of the business and financial world. There was a feeling prevalent in these circles that Hungary could and would be a loyal and valuable partner of Britain, if only London would show its concern by making economic, and perhaps later political, gestures. On 11 April Richard Edwards, commercial secretary of the British legation in Budapest, suggested to the Department of Overseas Trade that if England wished to increase her influence in the Danubian region the former trade quotas allotted to Austria should be transferred to Hungary. This, he argued, would be a helpful yet painless step.[83]

Edwards's suggestion touched off a considerable debate in the Foreign Office, where the traditional view had been that anything likely to be interpreted by Germany as encroachment on its economic sphere of interest was to be avoided. When word reached him of what was afoot, Knox immediately wrote to oppose the suggestion of the "do-gooders" that economic concessions be granted Hungary. Knox argued that "Hungary today is simply an open avenue down to the Iron Gates and the Balkans, and her population and Government are slipping inevitably into the role of obedient servant and scavenger to Germany." Thus, he added, it would be best to resist "any blandishments of this sort," and "keep our economic concessions for regions where they may be of use also to us."[84] Sir Orme Sargent in the Foreign Office concurred, pointing out that economic favors to Hungary or any other Danubian country had never been practical politics.

But some of the "do-gooders" who were calling for aid to Hungary were prominent government officials, including Montagu Norman, governor of the Bank of England,[85] and the debate over this question was not likely to subside quickly. In fact, it soon blossomed into a discussion of a far broader and more critical nature. Knox had argued from Budapest that Hungary was not a suitable place in which to "draw the line" against Germany in East Europe. This comment aroused much interest in London, since, as Sargent admitted, there had not really been much discussion yet of this crucial question of where, if, and when to draw the line against German expansion. Sargent thought it might be best to concentrate on Greece and Turkey, while Vansittart contended that this would involve the abandonment of too great an area.[86] Chamberlain's views are not known, but Lord Halifax explained to the Cabinet in late April that the idea of forming and support-ing an anti-German Danubian bloc in East Central Europe, which the French were likely to propose, was neither suitable nor feasi-ble. However, he did think that Britain might be able to proffer some aid on a country-by-country basis.[87]

Accordingly, a special group, the Interdepartmental Committee on Economic Assistance to Central and Southeastern Europe, was formed to investigate the possibilities of gaining political influence in East Central Europe through the granting of economic conces-sions. Hungary's prospects, however, were not sanguine. There was a genuine doubt in the Foreign Office that even massive eco-nomic assistance by Britain—such as the purchase of Hungary's entire grain crop at world prices—would make much of a political difference. Thus, when the countries of the area were classified according to priority for British economic help, Greece headed the list, while Hungary was placed last.[88]

Meanwhile, the debate over the economic situation in East Cen-tral Europe had ignited renewed interest in the continuing talks between Hungary and her neighbors. The timely intervention of England in late April had, as has already been seen, a beneficial influence on the course of these negotiations. But the British move did not represent the initial steps in a major reorientation of policy. London continued to be comparatively ignorant of and indifferent to the seemingly interminable talks. Chamberlain and Halifax, immersed in weightier matters, could not concern them-selves with the problem, and even minor Foreign Office officials, whose job it was to keep abreast of these developments, com-plained that the whole question was "a maze of mixed and obscure motives," into which Britain should proceed only warily.[89] When Hungary and the Successor States finally did come to tentative agreement in August, the Foreign Office and British public were on the whole delighted, but there was no real understanding of the scope and meaning of the agreement.

While London pondered its Danubian policy, important developments were taking place in Hungary. The surge of right radical activity, which had caused both the Hungarian government and political circles in London such concern, continued almost unabated into the spring. "Szálasi-1938" placards inundated the capital, and the movement gained a useful mouthpiece when the formerly moderate newspaper *Magyarság* changed hands in May and began propagating radical right-wing dogmas. Horthy's radio speech and an order forbidding political activity among military officers had had some effect in calming the population, but one of the major factors in the growing strength of Szálasi's party was the tacit support it now enjoyed from the prime minister himself. Darányi had taken to heart Imrédy's suggestion that efforts be made to "take the wind out of the sails" of the radical right, and shortly after the Győr speech he had sent a messenger to Szálasi to ask him to join the government party.[90] After several weeks of clandestine negotiations, a tentative agreement had been made whereby a certain number of seats in Parliament would be reserved for Arrowcross delegates. But Darányi's intentions could not long remain secret in the gossipy political life of Budapest. By late April Tibor Eckhardt and Bethlen were pressing the regent to dismiss Darányi, and Horthy, who disliked Szálasi, complied. The choice as his successor was Béla Imrédy, who was young and a Catholic,[91] and enjoyed a reputation as an opponent of the right radicals and a friend of West Europe.

Imrédy's appointment on 13 May was greeted with much satisfaction both in Hungary and in the West. The London *Times* termed it a development "of which nothing but good could be expected," and British opinion was further impressed when Imrédy moved vigorously to prohibit civil servants from politicizing, and took measures to bring Szálasi to trial for his subversive activities. Imrédy's other initial moves represented a more compromising attitude toward the divergent political outlooks in Hungary. In the reshuffling of the Cabinet, the appearance of Teleki was balanced by the appointment of General Rátz to be minister of defense. In his foreign policy utterances the new prime minister promised a continuity of policy. There was to be continued loyalty to old friends and a reduction of tensions with former enemies. In his maiden speech to Parliament, Imrédy singled out the importance of London's role in European affairs, noting with pleasure that England was "showing an increased interest and understanding for those questions on which a satisfactory solution for the future of Central Europe depends." Imrédy even managed to make a kind reference to France. He declared that "France, or at any rate a considerable section of opinion in that country, is beginning to recognize the essentials of our extraordinarily difficult problem."[92]

But the new Hungarian prime minister had hardly familiarized himself with the duties of his office, when, on the weekend of 21–22 May, a major European crisis seemed about to erupt. On the twenty-first, Czechoslovakia, citing menacing German troop concentrations, called up two classes of reserves and sealed the borders with Germany, Poland, and Hungary. The Czechoslovak question was now opened, and it would not be many months before Hungary would enjoy its first taste of territorial revision.

Chapter 7

Bled and Kiel

The May "weekend crisis" of 1938 still remains a puzzle to historians. Whether, as Prague alleged and London and Paris believed, German troops were advancing on the Czechoslovak border with the intention of heightening the tension during the local elections, is still being debated.[1] But there is a dimension to the May crisis that has usually been ignored in the standard studies. For, at least at the outset, the Czechoslovak government was talking of menacing troop movements by the Hungarians as well, and though there still may be some question about German intentions, it is clear that Hungary was carrying out no unusual military activity at this time.

Early on 20 May, at about the same time the first intelligence reports on the movement of German units were reaching Prague, the French military attaché in Budapest began to spread the rumor that Hungary had mobilized five classes of reservists and was moving them toward the Czechoslovak border.[2] The Czechoslovaks, already alarmed by the earlier reports, heard this rumor and no doubt suspected that some sort of concerted action by Hungary and Germany was underway. The Hungarian chargé d'affaires was asked for an immediate explanation, and during the day he sent three telegrams to Budapest citing the nervousness of Czechoslovak officials and requesting information. But before Kánya could respond, Prague had taken decisive action. Apparently determined to demonstrate their willingness to defend the Republic at all costs, Beneš and his colleagues decided late on 20 May to mobilize 175,000 men for an "extraordinary exercise." The borders with Czechoslovakia's neighbors were sealed and a prearranged plan for insuring internal security was set in motion.

On the twenty-first, Budapest, chagrined to find Czechoslovak troops massing on Hungary's northern border in a manner unpleasantly reminiscent of the restoration episodes of 1921, denied that there had been any unusual Hungarian military activity, and demanded an explanation from Prague. By then it had become clear even in Prague that Hungary had been unjustly accused, and the Hungarian chargé d'affaires was assured that Czechoslovak military measures were not aimed at Hungary or any other country, but were intended solely to maintain "inner order and calm."[3] Kánya moved quickly to advise London also of Hungary's innocence. He told Knox that Hungary had no intention of embarking on a military adventure, provided there was no provocation from the Czechoslovak side. Hungary's pacific intentions, Kánya asserted, were demonstrated by the fact that along the 800-km. border with Czechoslovakia there were only 2500 Hungarian troops, something the Czechoslovak military attaché could verify. He himself was doing everything in his power to calm public opinion.[4]

To all appearances, the "weekend crisis" subsided almost as rapidly as it had arisen. France and Great Britain made representations in Berlin, and the Germans vehemently denied the existence of such military activity. But the result of Prague's forthright effort was probably somewhat different from what President Beneš had anticipated. For although the British and French made strong protests in Berlin at the height of the crisis, in the long run their willingness to support Czechoslovakia was reduced. Having seen Europe placed at the brink of war, the Western democracies, where pacifism was a force to be reckoned with, became even more convinced that Prague would have to make great sacrifices for the sake of European appeasement.[5]

In Hungary the crisis accented the already ambiguous quality of Kánya's policy. On the one hand, Czechoslovakia's massing of troops on Hungary's borders was interpreted as yet another example of Beneš's use of overwhelming force to intimidate a weak Hungary. The resentment in 1938 matched that of 1921, when the Czechoslovaks had mobilized to thwart the return of King Karl, and Beneš had spoken publicly of the need for changes in Hungary's political system. On the other hand, however, the events of the May crisis convinced important Hungarian leaders that the West would indeed come to the defense of Czechoslovakia if Germany marched in.[6] If in a future conflict Hungary ranged herself on Berlin's side, she would doubtless find herself at war with Great Britain, a possibility that Regent Horthy, Imrédy, and Kánya fervently wished to avoid. Another development prompted Hungary to exercise added caution. It was learned that at the height of the crisis Stojadinović had assured Krofta that Yugoslavia would hold Hungary in check.[7] During the following summer and fall neither Italy nor Germany could convince the Hungarians that Yugoslavia would not, in a similar crisis, adopt the same attitude.

The major repercussions of the "weekend crisis," however, occurred in Germany. Whatever his real intentions in mid-May, Hitler regarded the Czechoslovak mobilization and the British and French démarches as a severe loss of prestige for Germany. As the Führer later explained to German journalists, after the events of 20 May "it was quite clear that the problem had to be solved, in one way or another."[8] On 28 May Hitler announced to a group of German military and political leaders that Czechoslovakia, as the enemy in the rear, had to disappear from the map of Europe. Since the western fortifications were not yet completed, this operation could not begin before the end of the upcoming September. It might even be postponed until March 1939. In any case, he was thinking of a "lightning action" in which Hungary would participate. France and England, whose rearmament would not be perfected until 1941–42, would not intervene, nor would Russia.[9] Directly after his address Hitler ordered General Keitel to revise an earlier military directive, because it was now his "inalterable decision to smash Czechoslovakia by military action in the near future."[10]

During the spring and early part of the summer, the Hungarians were deliberately kept uninformed about Germany's intentions. In fact, Sztójay, who normally was able to provide Budapest with authoritative information, continued to believe that the Germans wished to avoid a further aggravation of the Czechoslovak question.[11] For many months he remained unaware of the fact that Hitler had reacted so violently to British and French protests in the May crisis, and that deep concern about the Führer's decision to risk a military conflict over Czechoslovakia was growing among many German officials. Although Ribbentrop and most party officials wholeheartedly embraced Hitler's plans, some prominent military and diplomatic figures, including Chief of Staff Beck, State Secretary Ernst Weizsäcker, and Admiral Canaris, feared that Germany was being led down the road to certain European war and ultimate defeat. Even the normally bellicose Göring harbored some doubts that Germany was prepared for a major armed struggle. Thus, when Sztójay attempted to ferret out new information about Germany's aims, he found his interlocutors reticent or contradictory in their statements. From Göring he could learn only that the Czechoslovak crisis was one to two years away, rather than three to four.[12]

The arguments of General Beck and the other dissidents seemed to have no effect on Hitler, and the process initiated on 28 May progressed in regular stages. In July, 28 September was designated as the date on which "Case Green" would come into effect. The idea of delaying the campaign until spring was abandoned. Hitler himself remained aloof from day-to-day developments. He met few foreigners, and seemed to be sulking over the "humiliation" he had suffered in May. His plan, apparently, was to allow the tension to build gradually in Czechoslovakia; as 28 September— "X-day"—approached, rioting and other civil disturbances would be instigated. In these conditions, any "provocation" by Prague (perhaps the assassination of the German minister by German agents) would be the excuse for intervention by the Wehrmacht. In one way or another, Hungary, and perhaps Poland, would participate. The details, however, could be settled at the last minute when Horthy visited Germany in late August. Hitler, it seems, believed that the Hungarians were so eager to join in that even a few weeks advance notice would be sufficient.

In Hungary, meanwhile, the impact of the May crisis continued to have a sobering effect. During the summer the regent showed little of his earlier enthusiasm for a confrontation with Czechoslovakia. In Béla Imrédy, whose first days as prime minister were darkened by the shadows of what seemed to be an impending military conflict, the inclination to avoid too close an association with Nazi Germany was strengthened. In this period Imrédy privately remarked that if Hungary oriented itself completely on the side of Germany, it would suffer the same fate as Austria. For this reason, he asserted, Hungary would "devote all [her] energies to a strengthening of relations with other states, above all England."[14]

With the backing of both the regent and the prime minister, Kánya thus continued his efforts to maintain Hungary's freedom of maneuver and avoid becoming entangled with Germany in a military conflict with Czechoslovakia. During the summer the Western powers were informed that Hungary's policy was entirely pacific: she would take no action against Prague that would disturb European peace. If a military conflict did erupt, Hungary would "play a lone hand," and would resist being dragged into war as an ally of Germany. Of course, if Czechoslovakia did break up, Budapest naturally expected that Slovakia would revert to Hungary.[15]

Other steps were taken in this period to demonstrate that Hungary would cling to its independence and "free hand" policy. To help dispel the belief of many British statesmen that Hungary was "riddled with Nazism," Imrédy moved vigorously to suppress the overt activity of right radical groups. An earlier order by Horthy prohibiting political activity by military officers was extended in May to civil servants. Szálasi was put on trial for subversive activities and given a prison sentence.

The Hungarian conservatives also attempted to maintain domestic order and curtail right radical influences among the workers and lower middle class by invoking traditional symbols and imagery of authority. The Eucharistic Congress in May served admirably to emphasize the role of Hungary as an important center of Catholicism. The absence of a delegation from Germany tended to point up the essential incompatibility of National Socialism and a thriving Church. During the summer a government-sponsored campaign to combat National Socialist and Arrowcross propaganda included a tour through the country of a special train in which the embalmed right hand of St. Stephen was displayed. In August, shortly before and during the important Hungarian state visit to Germany, there were impressive celebrations of the nine-hundredth anniversary of St. Stephen's death. Implicit in the ceremonies was a message intended both for the Hungarian people and foreign observers: the kingdom of Hungary possessed sufficient historical roots and moral strength to resist absorption by the Third Reich. It must not be overlooked, of course, that ceremonies of this type conveniently served the revisionist cause as well, for they were reminders of Hungary's former grandeur in her pre-Trianon borders.

In their efforts to deepen relations with England, the Hungarian conservatives were spurred on by signs that informed opinion in London was coming to favor a drastic, but peaceful, settlement of the Czechoslovak problem. On 3 June an editorial in the *Times* suggested that Prague would probably be better off if a plebiscite were offered the nationalities of Czechoslovakia. "It would be a drastic remedy for the present unrest," the *Times* conceded, "but something drastic may be needed." The Foreign Office dissociated itself from this opinion, but the Hungarians, ever optimistic, no doubt saw it as a trial balloon launched by official circles.

Accordingly, it seemed even more important that contact with London be maintained on all levels, and that England's good will continue to be courted. Imrédy was particularly intent on expanding trade between the two countries. Early in his term of office he assumed the duties of minister of commerce, and he quickly appointed a commercial attaché to the Hungarian legation in London.[16] When word reached Budapest about the establishment in London of a governmental committee to investigate the possibilities of increased trade with the Danubian countries. Imrédy dispatched Fabinyi, the former minister of finance, to make semi-official inquiries. In his various conversations with British officials, Fabinyi cited the threat of Germany's economic domination of Hungary, and made a plea for economic assistance. He acknowledged the technical difficulties involved, and the fact that it would be more a political than an economic question for Britain, but asked that the Hungarian request nonetheless be considered.[17]

The British economic experts were finding, in fact, that numerous difficulties stood in the way of economic aid to the Danubian countries. In June it was calculated that a reduction of the tariff on Hungarian turkeys, which was one of Fabinyi's requests, would help Hungary to the extent of some 200 thousand pounds sterling annually. Those members of the Interdepartmental Committee who sympathized with Hungary, most notably Sir Otto Niemeyer, director of the Bank of England, urged that this concession be made, because Hungary might serve as a "possible spearhead of resistance to German penetration" of the Danubian region. But there was opposition from Britain's poultry industry and the Foreign Office representatives on the committee (including Geoffrey Knox). The committee thus reported to the Cabinet that they were in favor in principle of increasing trade with Hungary, but it seemed unlikely that any concessions Britain was in the position to make would "alter the political trend of that country towards Germany."[18]

While this debate over trade with Danubian Europe continued behind the scenes, the attention of the British government was, of course, focussed almost exclusively on the events in Czechoslovakia. During the summer Halifax and Chamberlain again and again urged greater compromises on Prague, and when in July the outlook seemed especially bleak, a decision was made to send an independent British investigator and mediator for a close study of the problem. The announcement of the Runciman mission on 26 July raised new hope in Hungary, even though it was emphasized in London that Runciman was empowered to study only the Sudeten German problem. Upon his arrival in Prague, Lord Runciman came quickly to discover the complexity of the situation and the virtual stalemate that had developed. Though he personally attached no value to negotiations with representatives of the non-German minorities, Runciman found it impossible to avoid all contact with the Magyar leaders in Czechoslovakia. They bombarded him with memoranda and requests for interviews, and finally, on 12 August, he granted Eszterházy and other representatives of the United Hungarian Party of Slovakia an audience. After handing in a long list of grievances against the Czechoslovak government, the Magyar leaders bluntly declared that the Hungarian minority could not in the long run remain in Czechoslovakia, although for the moment they were prepared to accept a temporary solution.[19] Ashton-Gwatkin, a member of Runciman's staff, later wryly commented that "it is obvious that if the Sudetens get their prize, the Hungarians will get theirs as well, though it will not satisfy them, for what they really want is to get back to Hungary."[20]

Whether, as Ashton-Gwatkin believed and Prague had once promised, the same advantages would accrue to the Magyar minority as to the Sudeten Germans, could at this point still not be accurately foreseen. The Hungarian government doubtless hoped that, as the *Times* had suggested in June, a plebiscite would be held eventually in Czechoslovakia. In that case, the right of self determination could hardly be given the Sudeten Germans but denied the Poles and Magyars. On the other hand, Kánya and Imrédy had to prepare also for the possibility that the Czechoslovak problem could not be resolved by peaceful means. If a conflict broke out, Hungary would at some point have to make some far-reaching decisions. Kánya had told the British that Hungary would maintain its neutrality as long as possible. This was probably a true statement of intent, since the Hungarians still feared that any intervention on their part would draw a military retaliation from Romania and Yugoslavia. The Hungarian general staff felt confident that the army could successfully repel a Romanian, but not a Yugoslav, military attack on Hungary. Despite repeated assurances from Ciano and Göring that Yugoslavia would not move if Hungary waited a short time after the outbreak of a German-Czechoslovak conflict,[21] Budapest remained unconvinced. Kánya believed that Stojadinović preferred to remain sitting on the fence, and that pro-Czechoslovak sentiment in the Yugoslav army and public would prevent him from betraying a Little Entente ally.[22]

One of the more important topics for discussion when Kánya and Imrédy visited Rome in mid-July was precisely the attitude of Belgrade in the Czechoslovak question, and the support Italy would give to protect Hungary from a Yugoslav attack.[23] In numerous conversations with Ciano and Mussolini, Kánya painstakingly restated the Hungarian case: there was no intention of launching an attack on Czechoslovakia, but if a conflict did erupt, it would be difficult for Hungary to remain aloof. To intervene militarily, however, the Hungarians had to be one hundred percent sure of Yugoslav neutrality, and this assurance was lacking. Kánya and Imrédy acknowledged that Stojadinović had made far-reaching statements to Ciano, but they persisted in their belief that he was playing a double game. The one factor that would ease their position, the visiting Hungarians explained, was a clear and definite reiteration of the Duce's promise that he would prevent a Yugoslav attack from the rear on Hungary. Mussolini and Ciano were reluctant to provide such a military guarantee, arguing in the presence of the Hungarians that such a commitment was unnecessary as long as Hungary moved only after the Germans, and in private that there was no sense in impairing relations with Stojadinović "in order to procure a success for the more or less democratic government of Mr. Imrédy."[24]

The visit to Rome had thus, in the words of Mussolini, "fizzled out." The Hungarians were still unsure what Italy's attitude would be in a future conflict. To be sure, Ciano and the Duce apparently made it clear that they stood loyally by Germany's side should a conflict break out: if it remained a local one, Rome would remain at the ready; while if France chose to intervene militarily, the Italians would attack France.[25] But this emphatic statement of loyalty to the Axis made the Hungarians only more nervous. What they wanted most was to avoid a major European crisis, especially one in which Italy moved its armies against France. For in that case Rome could surely offer no military assistance to Hungary, and Yugoslavia could attack from the south with impunity. Thus, the Hungarian conviction, based apparently on reports from their representative in Paris, that France would certainly honor its obligation toward Czechoslovakia, prompted Hungary's leaders to continue their effort to resist being dragged into a military conflict.

This was the situation on the eve of the important Hungarian visit to Germany in late August. But before the regent and the Hungarian party departed on 21 August, there occurred two developments of major significance that in large measure determined Hungary's course in the tense days before the Munich Conference. In August, after over a year of mutual recriminations and seemingly endless haggling over subtle semantic differences, the countries of the Little Entente and Hungary finally came to a tentative agreement. Compromises on both sides contributed to the final success. In early August the Romanian government suddenly issued a Minorities Statute that, though not going much beyond obligations already incurred in the peace treaties, was a pleasant surprise to Budapest. Baron Apor characterized the Romanian gesture as a substantial step forward that, if sincerely executed, might make it possible to reach a "happy conclusion" in the negotiations before the trip to Germany.[26] Kánya seemed equally pleased, and informed the Romanians on 9 August that he regarded the time proper for a conclusion of negotiations.[27]

Bargaining over the precise terms of an agreement continued right up to 21 August, the day of the Hungarian delegation's departure for Kiel. Finally, in a major concession, Kánya proposed that at the upcoming Little Entente conference at Bled, Yugoslavia, a communiqué be issued announcing that a "provisional agreement" had been reached between Hungary and her three neighbors on the questions of Hungary's right to rearm and the exchange of nonaggression declarations. The communiqué would point out that an agreement in principle had been reached on a minorities declaration to be issued by Romania, Czechoslovakia, and Yugoslavia, but for technical reasons this aspect of the negotiations had not yet been completed.[28]

The willingness of the Hungarians to issue a statement implying agreement with all of their neighbors, including Czechoslovakia, on the subject of nonaggression pledges, while leaving the delicate minorities question for a later solution, was a major departure from previous policy, and was immediately recognized as such by Little Entente representatives, who were surprised and delighted by Kánya's spirit of compromise precisely before the Hungarian party was scheduled to depart for Kiel. When the delegates assembled at Bled, Stojadinović worked feverishly to achieve a rapid settlement.[29] Already on the first day, 21 August, the Hungarian observer wired to Budapest that the Little Entente had accepted Kánya's proposed communiqué with only minor changes. Kánya and Imrédy being already en route to Germany, Baron Apor, with Teleki's concurrence, empowered the Hungarian representative, Bessenyey, to sign the tentative agreement.[30] Accordingly, on 23 August the joint communiqué was issued simultaneously in Budapest and Bled.

Official reaction throughout Europe was favorable. The British Foreign Office found the result "eminently satisfactory" and "surprisingly conciliatory coming from Hungary at the present time."[31] French, British, and Italian papers praised the provisional agreement, and the German press, initially at least, described it as a long overdue recognition of Hungarian military equality.

One great mystery on the origins of the Bled compact remains: namely, the motives that prompted the Hungarians to offer what seemed to be an attractive compromise. Kánya and Imrédy undoubtedly recognized the risks involved. German indignation would be great, and the Hungarian minority in Slovakia might feel it had been abandoned by the motherland. Observers at the time offered several plausible explanations. It was thought that the Hungarians, sensitive to opinion in London and Paris, feared that the Little Entente was about to break off negotiations and to attribute the failure to Budapest's recalcitrance. It was also suggested that Kánya wanted to have Hungary's right to rearm officially recognized before the Czechoslovak question became more aggravated. But, though reasonable suppositions, these explanations do not tell the whole story. For other less apparent forces were at work in the inner circles of the Hungarian leadership, and the last-minute decision was probably taken on the basis of the latest, and most alarming, information from Germany.

In early August the Hungarians were still unaware of the changes in Hitler's plans that the May crisis had engendered. Such was the apparent calm prevailing in Berlin, where many German officials had gone on vacation, that Sztójay described the atmosphere as "the height of the cucumber season."[32] But those individuals, including Admiral Canaris (chief of the armed forces intelligence office), General Beck, and Weizsäcker, who were intent on preventing Hitler from plunging Germany into a dangerous conflict, were by late summer becoming desperate. The outlines of a possible military conspiracy were beginning to appear. Two men active in this work, Canaris and Beck, had close ties with important Hungarian officials, and it was apparently decided that an attempt should be made to inform Budapest of the gravity of the situation and forestall any cooperation which the impetuous Horthy might otherwise offer during his talks with Hitler. Sometime in the first two weeks of August general information on Hitler's intentions must have been given to the Hungarians by a representative of the German dissidents, for Csáky solemnly told a member of the British Legation on 14 August that war was "quite certain" unless Lord Runciman could spin out his investigation until "at least November," when climatic conditions would be unfavorable for a military campaign.[33]

Fairly precise information about Hitler's intentions was made available to the Hungarians on 20 August by Helmuth Groscurth, who travelled to Budapest as an emissary of Canaris. Groscurth informed the Hungarians that Hitler was irrevocably determined to settle accounts with Czechoslovakia by the "end of September or beginning of October," despite the fears of his generals about the possible intervention of Britain and France, and the generally pacific mood of the German people.[34]

The impact of this confidential report on the Hungarian leadership was enormous. The one development that Horthy, Kánya, and Imrédy most dreaded was an early war over Czechoslovakia brought on by blatant German aggression. France, and probably Britain, would intervene, and Hungary would be placed in the most dangerous of positions, open perhaps to an unprovoked attack by Romania and Yugoslavia. Particularly disturbing was the realization that Hitler's own chief of staff and chief of the military intelligence office strongly rejected the Führer's plans. In these circumstances, it was decided that the Hungarian party during its visit would resist any attempt to be drawn into Germany's plans for a rapid military settlement.

This was all the more imperative when a quick inquiry by Horthy on the state of Hungarian rearmament revealed that the Honvéd was still in a very low state of readiness. Conditions were not favorable for either a defensive or offensive war. In the face of Czechoslovakia's powerful army and fifteen hundred fortified installations, Hungary possessed no guns of large caliber, few aircraft, and ammunition for only two days.[35] Accordingly, Horthy, Imrédy, and Kánya decided that if Hitler raised the question of Hungarian participation in a "settling of accounts" with Czechoslovakia, their reply, while indicating a general determination to proceed against the Czechoslovaks at the proper moment, would have to emphasize that the "timing of this could not yet be determined; the autumn of this year is not very suitable, as our preparations are not far enough advanced."[36] Of greater importance was Horthy's determination not only to reject any German offer to join in an attack on Czechoslovakia, but also to attempt to dissuade Hitler from embarking on a military adventure in the current unfavorable situation.[37]

It was in these circumstances that the decision was made to reach a provisional agreement with the Little Entente. Kánya, who was always careful to weigh each diplomatic step according to its advantages and disadvantages, apparently concluded that the safest route for Hungary at the time was a tentative understanding with Hungary's neighbors. If things went badly in Germany, if Hitler in fact provoked a war with the West, Hungary could avoid involvement by honoring its nonaggression pledge toward Czechoslovakia. This would preserve Hungary's standing in England as well. If, on the other hand, Czechoslovakia could still be compelled to make concessions without a resort to war, Hungary was free to exert pressure on her own, since the minorities declaration required of Prague in the Bled Agreement had still not been set. Seen in this light, the compact arrived at in Bled was merely a further application of Kánya's "free hand" policy. But, as Kánya was soon to discover, the precarious balancing act that his "free hand" approach demanded would be impossible to pursue if any European party sought an immediate confrontation. And this, it seemed, was precisely Hitler's intention.

Despite the tense atmosphere, the Hungarian state visit began smoothly enough in Kiel.[38] The festivities on the twenty-second, including the christening of a new cruiser, the *Prince Eugen*, were planned and executed with much ostentation. But the Germans were clearly anxious to get on to the business at hand, and already on the first day General Keitel told Minister of Defense Rátz that events in Czechoslovakia had created a difficult situation that could be resolved only by resort to arms. Hungary, he urged, should think over and prepare for this operation, the timing of which Hitler would discuss with Regent Horthy.[39]

Meanwhile, Hitler had been working himself up into a distinctly aggressive mood. His determination, voiced during August to his generals and personal advisors alike, to invade Czechoslovakia in response to a staged "provocation" on or shortly after September 28 was still absolute. Apparently still hoping to prevent intervention by the West by luring Poland and Hungary into the attack, thus demonstrating the "artificiality" of the Czechoslovak state, he tried during his private conversation with Horthy on the twenty-third to obtain a promise of Hungarian cooperation. Directly at the outset of the talk, according to Horthy's later account,[40] Hitler gave a detailed exposition of "Case Green," and asked for a pledge of Hungarian participation. If Hungary moved into Slovakia, she could keep that territory.

Horthy refused to succumb to these blandishments. He explained that Hungary was not ready for a military conflict, and warned, to Hitler's extreme annoyance, that the campaign would best not be undertaken at all, since England would intervene and, because of her superior naval strength, would triumph in the end. "You can mobilize in five days," Horthy said, "and put thirty Army Corps here and forty there, while England will take perhaps five months to mobilize, but in the end she will inevitably win."[41] When Horthy persisted in this fashion, it was, as Csáky later explained it, like waving a "red flag to a bull."[42] Hitler, unaccustomed to being at the wrong end of a lecture, interrupted the regent and shouted: "Nonsense; shut up!" Horthy, who was not about to permit anyone, let alone an ex-corporal, to treat the Hungarian head of state in such an undignified way, thereupon broke off the conversation.[43]

While this dramatic incident was taking place, Ribbentrop was conducting an equally inconclusive and frustrating parlay with Kánya and Imrédy.[44] The Reich foreign minister expressed bitter anger over the Bled Agreement, which, he claimed, could be interpreted by an impartial observer as in effect a renunciation of revision, "since he who does not assist departs with empty hands." Kánya tried, in vain, to convince Ribbentrop that the Hungarian interpretation of the Bled Agreement was the only valid one, but the German remained unconvinced. Matters were only exacerbated when Kánya, becoming more and more annoyed by another "amateur" trying to practice diplomacy, indulged his propensity for sarcasm to drive home his point.[45]

Probably because of his doubts over Hungary's reliability, Ribbentrop did not make the same offer as Hitler to Horthy. Instead he merely asked what the Hungarian attitude would be if "the Führer put into effect his decision of replying by the use of force to any new Czech provocation." Kánya and Imrédy gave no firm reply, emphasizing that Hungarian rearmament had just started and would require another year or two for completion. In any case, Hungary could march only if Yugoslavia were neutral, and there still was no assurance of this. Ribbentrop's assertion that Yugoslavia, like England, France, and Romania, would not dare "to walk into the pincers of the Axis Powers," did not convince his guests.

After the first day of conversations, therefore, Hitler could only conclude that he had badly misread the situation in Hungary. Yet he neither abandoned hope, nor resorted to intimidation of the Hungarians. He told Imrédy late on the twenty-third that "in this particular case, he required nothing of the Hungarians." He warned, however, that "he who wanted to sit at the table must at least help in the kitchen."[46]

The remainder of the stay in Germany was spent by the Hungarians in trying to repair some of the damage that the Bled Agreement and their negative response to Hitler's offer had caused. In press interviews Kánya and Imrédy stressed that there had been no "hard and fast" agreement reached at Bled. That accord could come into force only when Czechoslovakia took satisfactory steps in the minority question. On the twenty-fifth Kánya repeated this argument to Ribbentrop, who was now complaining that West Europeans were interpreting recent events as "a rift in German-Hungarian friendship and as a renunciation by Hungary of her revisionist aims." Kánya, in reply, stressed that Hungary would pose such harsh demands on Czechoslovakia that she could never fulfill a promise made in the minorities declarations. In short, Hungary would not be bound by the nonaggression pledge. In order further to assuage German disappointment, Kánya added, without any apparent explanation, that he wished to amend his earlier statement regarding the time it would take for Hungarian rearmament to be accomplished. He now asserted that Hungary's military strength by October 1 would be sufficient to enable her to act if, as the Germans were so confident, the conflict remained localized.[47]

This statement, which could hardly have been an accurate assessment of Hungary's military situation and was probably employed merely to prevent a further exacerbation of strained German-Hungarian relations while the Hungarians were still in Berlin, seemed to give renewed hope to the German leadership. Intensive efforts were made to persuade the individual Hungarians that Budapest could act with impunity when the crisis arose. Even during the formal banquets, Hess, Himmler, and other party officials continued their effort to incite the Magyars to action. It was argued that Czechoslovaks would have to be dealt with by force of arms sooner or later, preferably sooner, since the international situation and Germany's military position were more favorable in the fall of 1938 than they would be half a year or a year later.[48] Clearly, the most influential Nazi leaders still believed that Hungary's participation in the planned operation was important. On the 24th Göring explained to the Polish minister that the Germans expected Hungary to act "in the last stage," that is, a few days after the Wehrmacht was dispatched in response to the Czechoslovak "provocation." It would be most embarassing if Hungary did not move, Göring asserted, since the Czechoslovak forces could then retreat to Slovakia.[49]

A further elaboration of the role that Hungary might play was given by Hitler on the twenty-sixth when, leaving aside the diplomats, he tried his hand at convincing General Rátz.[50] Stressing again and again that he did not wish to persuade the Hungarians, but merely state his views, Hitler repeated the familiar argument that the Western powers and the Little Entente would not come to Czechoslovakia's assistance. Besides Germany, which would march alone if necessary, only Poland and Hungary might intervene. And if Hungary did not move quickly, Poland might seize Slovakia for herself. In that case, he had no intention of evicting the Poles, although he would much prefer that the Felvidék become part of a strengthened Hungary. Germany was not asking for Hungarian participation, Hitler asserted, but he wished to point out that with the liquidation of the Czech question "his activity in the Southeast" would be finished, and it would be the "last opportunity from the Hungarian standpoint for a realization of revision."

When Rátz asked what kind of provocation might ignite the crisis, the Führer suggested that the assassination of German citizens or mobilization measures similar to those of 21 May would be sufficient. He stressed that speed would be the vital factor: in his opinion Hungary would do best to seize the Felvidék "in a swift action" once the German "settling of accounts" began. Hitler used the interesting example of June 1914 to prove his point. If, he argued, Austria-Hungary at that time had quickly attacked Serbia "with the peace-time army," everything would have developed differently. In effect, what Hitler seemed to want was for the Hungarians to throw whatever meager forces they might have on hand into the battle whenever the crisis erupted. Clearly, he saw the value of Hungarian intervention not in strictly military terms, but in the psychological impact the invasion of German, Hungarian, and Polish troops would have both in Czechoslovakia and in the West.

Rátz, who had been trying for years to coordinate and plan the kind of military operation Hitler was suggesting, nonetheless scrupulously followed the policy determined by Hungary's political leadership. He told Hitler, and the other Germans with whom he spoke, that the Honvéd was in the process of reorganization, and while from the political standpoint any Hungarian government "would take the opportunity to achieve revision in the North," the present time was least favorably suited for "the rapid action in question." Nor did Rátz accept Hitler's arguments about the reluctance of Yugoslavia, France, and England to intervene. He suggested that if Italy entered the conflict to protect Hungary from Yugoslav attack, the isolated nature of the crisis would disappear and there would be "further repercussions." Hitler flatly rejected this interpretation, but Rátz did not waver, even when the Führer finally approved the long sought-after General Staff talks. The only concessions the Hungarian minister of defense could offer were permission for the erection of German aerial observation stations on Hungarian territory, and use of Hungarian airfields by German planes forced out of enemy air space.

When even Rátz could not be convinced, Hitler probably lost all hope of winning over his Magyar visitors. At a second private meeting with Horthy, he did not even reiterate his earlier arguments. Having learned that the regent had been approached by one of the concerned German generals, Brauchitsch, the Führer reproached Horthy and informed him that in Germany he alone made policy. The regent's frank comment that this was "a truly dangerous policy" ended any possibility for a meaningful conversation.[51]

Neither side was satisfied with the results of the Hungarian state visit. Hitler privately expressed his disillusionment over Hungary's refusal to accept his offer of military cooperation,[52] although he clearly intended to carry out his plans with or without eventual Hungarian participation. For the moment, though, he once again excluded Budapest from his most intimate planning. Although he now approved staff talks, Chief of Staff Halder was instructed not to give the Magyars any indication of the timing of the operation.

The Hungarians departed from Germany with mixed feelings. It had been a particularly difficult time for Horthy, who pointed out almost apologetically to Erdmannsdorff how extraordinary it was that he, "who for years had desired nothing more ardently than a speedy realization of Hungarian revisionist aims, was now forced to sound a warning note owing to the international situation." To demonstrate that Hungary's negative attitude stemmed mainly from poor military preparedness, Horthy even asked Göring if the campaign might be postponed until the spring, when the Hungarian army would be in a better position.[53] Imrédy, too, was probably not entirely convinced that the Hungarians had been wise in passing up the opportunity. In a sense, he had staked his political insight against that of Hitler and his colleagues. Four times Imrédy had argued in Ribbentrop's presence that France, its honor as a great power at stake, would fulfill its obligations to Czechoslovakia.[54] But the impressive display of German naval and land military might seems to have made a deep impression on Imrédy, and the seeds were being sown for the dramatic political metamorphosis he would soon undergo.

Only Kánya, who felt he had been badly treated by the Germans,[55] appeared confident that the right decision had been made. In a sense, this episode was the high point of the old diplomat's long career. Hungary had been confronted with the choice of pursuing her national goals by means of diplomatic methods or dangerous military adventurism, and, as had been the case earlier, his viewpoint had triumphed. Hitler's arguments had been directly refuted, and Ribbentrop had been personally humiliated by Kánya's sarcastic tongue. A price would eventually have to be paid for such impudence by the foreign minister of a lesser power, but for the time being Kánya continued to guide his country through the maze of European diplomacy.

On the return voyage to Budapest, Kánya told Erdmannsdorff that Hungary would take action "as soon as possible" after the outbreak of a German-Czechoslovak conflict, but she could not be expected to "commit suicide."[56] Privately, however, Kánya was spreading the word that "that madman [Hitler] wanted to unleash a war, whatever the cost."[57] Yet, surprisingly, the Hungarians manifested little outward sense of alarm or panic during the first two weeks of September. Foreign diplomats, and even the remainder of the Hungarian Cabinet, were told that while the situation in Germany was critical, no pressure of any sort, whether military or economic, had been exerted on the Hungarian party. No agreement had been concluded, and Hungary was still following the policy of the "free hand." Not even the Cabinet learned of the offer Hitler had made to Horthy.[58]

When questioned by British diplomats about his impressions in Germany, Kánya replied, quite candidly, that the atmosphere was extremely nervous and agitated. Two approximately equal forces were struggling against each other: one favored a solution by force, the other by negotiation.[59] Kánya spoke in similar terms to the French minister, apparently adding that Hungary would remain neutral if Czechoslovakia were attacked, and that if Germany asked for transit rights, Hungary would refuse and bow only to superior force.[60]

In the first days of September, no significant military measures were taken by Budapest. At the Ministerial Council of 30 August, Imrédy directed Rátz to take special steps to quicken the pace of rearmament,[61] but no progress could be expected in the upcoming weeks. The annual autumn maneuvers were, as it happened, scheduled to be conducted in September, in the vicinity of the Czechoslovak border, and for this purpose the usual 40,000 effectives were being called up. But, for the time being, this number was not increased, and no operations were conducted that could give Prague cause for alarm.

Chapter 8

Munich Crisis

During the critical September days leading up to the Munich conference, Kálmán Kánya's one great fear was that war would break out between Germany and Czechoslovakia and that he would not be able to restrain those groups in Hungary yearning to join the battle. Kánya and his conservative colleagues sensed that mobilization of the army and an attack on Czechoslovakia would embolden chauvinist and radical right-wing elements. There might even be the danger of a military takeover, as crucial decisions passed inexorably from the hesitant diplomats and ministers to the impatient soldiers. In such an eventuality, those leaders who had earlier advocated moderation and caution would find their authority gravely undermined.

That Kánya and Imrédy were able to hold back the more militant officers in September can be attributed in large part to the attitude of Horthy. A year earlier Horthy had been eager to begin planning for a dismemberment of Czechoslovakia; in September 1938, he decided that the situation was not opportune, that the risk of a European war was too great. After his return from his talks with Hitler, Horthy continued to project himself as a European peacemaker. So concerned was he about the dangers of the situation that he conferred with George Lansbury, the famous British pacifist, who happened to be in Hungary at the time, and proposed that the two of them attempt to arrange a meeting of the heads of the great powers, to be chaired by President Roosevelt.[1] Nothing came of this scheme, but it did reflect the commitment Horthy now had to a peaceful, diplomatic solution of the problem.

However, though General Rátz seems to have loyally followed the example set by the regent, not all of the officers were prepared to submit meekly to what they considered to be the timid policy of the civilian leadership. In the General Staff there remained some militants who felt that, whatever the risks, the best policy was still an unambiguous stand on the side of National Socialist

Germany. If war came, Hungary would have to participate, trusting that the Wehrmacht would compensate for any weaknesses in the Hungarian armed forces. In their view, the problem was not how to avoid war, but how to convince Hungary's political leadership, particularly Horthy, to join in despite their misgivings. The fertile mind of a General Staff officer, Lieutenant Colonel Homlok, whose name was to be associated with later clandestine and unsavory military operations, apparently devised one solution, namely, to persuade the German military intelligence to stage a bombing incident on Hungarian territory that could be interpreted as an unprovoked Czechoslovak attack. In the specific plan, which Homlok proposed to Colonel Groscurth of the Abwehr in early September, it was suggested that in the early stages of a German-Czechoslovak conflict, once some Czechoslovak airports had been captured, German planes should drop Czechoslovak bombs on Hungarian territory.[2] This, Homlok seemed to hope, would force the hands of Kánya and the other civilians, making it impossible to restrain Horthy and others who would demand retaliation for this Czechoslovak "provocation."

The German Abwehr seemed uninterested in Homlok's scheme and nothing came of it at the time. In any case, Kánya was unaware of this initiative and strove throughout September to keep Hungary on the fence, ready to move in either direction depending on the development of events. One factor that insured continued caution in Budapest was the attitude of Yugoslavia and Romania. The policy of these countries in this period, like Hungary's, was deliberately obscure. Stojadinović, in particular, wished to be prepared for all eventualities, and his attitude toward his Czechoslovak ally was a model of ambiguity. At Bled, Krofta was apparently assured that Yugoslavia and Romania would fulfill their obligations in case of a Hungarian attack.[3] But Belgrade was giving contradictory information to Rome and Berlin, and it is understandable that Kánya concluded that Stojadinović would not make up his mind until the final moment. The outlook in Romania seemed even more dangerous to Hungarian interests. Reports reaching Budapest indicated that the Romanians would find it difficult to remain neutral if Hungary participated in a conflict.[4] Kánya did not fail to take notice of a Havas news agency dispatch on the fifth that suggested that Romania would take steps against Hungary even if the latter merely served as a passive transit area for German troops.

Aware that critical days were soon to come, Hungary now felt that the relationship with Poland, which over the summer had remained somewhat stagnant, would have to be clarified. Since Eszterházy's visit in June, when a general agreement on territorial spoils had been reached, no further progress had been made in coordinating military or political policy toward Czechoslovakia. This condition stemmed, in part, from a basic difference that gradually surfaced during the summer months and resulted in a distinct parting of ways in early October. For Colonel Beck's Poland, priding itself on its independence of the great powers and stature among the lesser ones, insisted that no other party could dictate to Warsaw what it should and should not do in Central Europe. Poland thus rejected attempts by the great powers to intervene in Warsaw's relations with Czechoslovakia. Hungary adopted an opposite stance. Interference by the great powers, especially England, was welcomed, since Hungary was not militarily equipped for the kind of saber-rattling that the Poles were prepared to employ.[5] Thus, while the Hungarians requested that Lord Runciman deal with the problem of the Magyar minority, the Poles explicitly rejected a similar procedure for the Polish minority.

This difference in strategy led to a concomitant difficulty in the Polish-Hungarian relationship. The wish being father to the thought, the Hungarians came to believe that in fact the Western democracies would intervene sooner or later in the Czechoslovak question and force Prague to make major concessions. The Polish Foreign Office, however, was convinced that the opposite would be the case,[6] and there was some annoyance at the excessive caution that Kánya and his colleagues wished to exercise. In late August, the Poles still regarded the Magyars as our "eternal friends," and the "most stabilized element in that region," but there was some doubt about their trustworthiness and willingness to take effective action.[7]

After the state visit to Germany, the Hungarians decided that the time had come to effect the coordination of policy that had been discussed during the spring talks. On 5 September Hory, on Kánya's instructions, suggested that the two countries conclude a "gentlemen's agreement" to coordinate their efforts.[8] Beck, who did not think a crisis was imminent, despite the diplomatic prescience of which he had earlier boasted, was amenable to the Hungarian proposal.[9] By the ninth Hory and Szembek had agreed upon the text, to which Kánya gave his approval the next day. The two countries affirmed their desire to maintain an "effective political cooperation" and, whenever either party deemed it necessary, to consult on measures aimed at "harmonizing" their policies.[10]

Meanwhile, the Hungarians concentrated in the first days of September on courting the favor of the British. The influence of Count Teleki in this effort was paramount. Believing that London would eventually support ethnic revision for the Hungarians, but would strongly oppose any solution brought on by force or blatant threat of force, Teleki urged that Hungary limit and moderate her claims. The question of the return of all of Slovakia, he thought, could be postponed to a later date, since it would probably be difficult to convince an Englishman that the Slovaks wanted once again to live in the Kingdom of St. Stephen.[11] For the moment, Kánya and Imrédy wholeheartedly shared these views. Indeed, in the late summer Imrédy was still a zealous advocate of firm political and economic ties with England, despite the string of disappointments in the months since his assuming the post of prime minister.

A conversation that Imrédy had just before the visit to Germany with Sir Ralph Glynn, a member of Parliament visiting Budapest, is characteristic of his attitude in this period.[12] He told Glynn that he fervently desired that Britain look with more sympathy on the Hungarian problem. His country, though weak in every sense, intended to maintain its sovereignty and resist absorption by Germany. Hungary did not want to make a pact with Germany, and Hitler would be told that Hungary would remain neutral in the event of trouble with Czechoslovakia. But in this policy Hungary was "chancing a good deal," Imrédy asserted, and it was important that England and the Balkan states realize this and extend some help. He had been striving for months to clear the way for closer trade relations with the United Kingdom, but unhappily no progress had been made. On the contrary, Hungarians had formed the impression that London considered that Hungary was already a vassal of Germany and thus "not worth bothering about." This attitude was fatal and disheartening to him and his cabinet. He urged that it be revised and that special measures be instituted, since never had the time been more favorable for an increase of Hungarian trade with Britain.

Imrédy's pleas, however, fell on unsympathetic ears. Knox's

influence had been so pervasive that the Foreign Office viewed with skepticism all communications from the Hungarian government. When Kánya tried to explain that a final agreement on the minorities question could not be achieved with Czechoslovakia at Bled because the Hungarian public would not accept it, the somewhat cynical response of Foreign Office officials was an expression of doubt that public opinion played any role in the "feudal and authoritarian" system in Hungary.[13] Yet with almost pathetic determination Imrédy persevered.

On 31 August, the day after the important Ministerial Council that reviewed the situation after the visit to Germany, Imrédy granted an interview to the correspondent of the *Daily Telegraph*. Speaking extremely candidly, and apparently with the understanding that the conversation was to be regarded as confidential and not for publication, Imrédy seemingly sketched his foreign policy intentions in much the same terms as he had with Glynn. But for some reason an article, drafted in the most confusing style, did appear in the *Daily Telegraph* on 2 September, and was picked up by the Hungarian newspaper *Az Est* on the next day. To Imrédy's consternation, the reporter reproduced some of his most confidential utterances, and jumbled them together with other statements that were alleged to have been made by "highest official quarters" in Budapest. The resulting article gave the impression that the Hungarian prime minister was making a deliberate and calculated effort to dissociate his "peaceful" policy from the "belligerent" policy Germany was plying. Imrédy was so infuriated by this apparent betrayal of trust that he issued a *démenti* in the Hungarian press on the second, and ordered the *Az Est* banned. In perhaps the most telling of his reactions, he even had the keeper of the Cabinet records expunge from the record the remarks along the same lines that he had made at the Cabinet meeting of 31 August.[14]

Imrédy's vigorous response no doubt was a result of his increasing frustration with the British and the fear that the "game" with Germany would be jeopardized. To offset the impact of this episode, he therefore inserted warm words of friendship for Germany and more hostile references to Czechoslovakia in a speech delivered at Kaposvár on 4 September. He described the visit to Germany as one of "mutual confidence, friendship, and cordiality," and warned that Czechoslovakia, where the Czechs represented a minority of the population, needed to make special arrangements for its nationalities. Fortunately for Imrédy, the Germans, absorbed in their planning for later events, had not taken much notice of what was occurring in Hungary, and neither the *Daily Telegraph* article nor the Kaposvár speech seemed to have affected the thinking of Hitler or his colleagues.

A series of events in the five-day period between 7 and 12 September served to usher in the most acute phase of the Czechoslovak crisis. On the seventh the *Times* of London suggested in an editorial that Czechoslovakia might do best to consider making itself a "more homogeneous state" by allowing the secession of "that fringe of alien populations who are contiguous to the nation with which they are united by race." This startling proposal, which was immediately disavowed by the Foreign Office and rejected by most other British newspapers, made a deep impression in East Europe. Although only the Sudeten Germans had been named as candidates for secession, many Hungarians no doubt felt that the tide of public opinion in Britain was finally turning in a direction more favorable to Hungarian interests.

The *Times*'s initiative found an unintended echo in Hitler's uncompromising speech at the Nuremberg Party Rally on 12 September. Here for the first time the Führer introduced the notion of self-determination as the desirable basis for solving the Czechoslovak problem. This speech confirmed the suspicion in many quarters that the Germans in fact would never be content with any solution which left the Sudeten Germans within Czechoslovakia. On the seventh President Beneš, under strong pressure from London, had offered his "Fourth Plan," in which virtually all of the Karlsbad program had been accepted. Even the Hungarian government apparently thought that this would be sufficient to prevent a conflict. Kánya is said to have told an assistant that they should "pack for Geneva now," since the crisis would be resolved there through diplomatic means.[15] But Hitler's instructions were that a peaceful solution was to be avoided, and on the very day in which Beneš presented his offer an incident occurred at Moravská Ostrava. Henlein broke off negotiations with Prague, and the political tension in Central Europe rose dramatically.

The Hungarians reacted relatively calmly to these developments. Despite the suggestion put forward by the *Times*, the semiofficial *Pester Lloyd* and even the right-wing papers of Budapest continued after Hitler's speech to describe a settlement in terms of the Karlsbad points. In Czechoslovakia Eszterházy even served as an emissary for Lord Runciman in an attempt to convince one of the radical Sudeten German leaders, Karl Frank, that negotiations with Prague should not be broken off.[16] But this attitude began to change on the thirteenth, when Henlein suddenly proclaimed that the Germans of Czechoslovakia wanted to "return to the Reich." Simultaneously, an uprising was staged in the German areas of Bohemia, and though the Czechoslovak authorities were able to restore order, the seriousness of the situation was becoming more and more apparent.

At this juncture the Poles stepped forward to urge their Magyar allies to prepare for action. Lipski suggested to Sztójay in Berlin that the Czechoslovak problem might be settled on the basis of plebiscites, and that preparations for such an eventuality had to be made "with all means and at whatever the monetary sacrifice."[17] In Warsaw Szembek argued that there was no need to fear a general confrontation over the Czechoslovak question: even if Britain and France did intervene, Germany's position was not without prospects. The West Wall would prevent a French breakthrough, the effectiveness of a British blockade was doubtful, and Russia was not prepared for a major military action.[18]

This argument, which seriously conflicted with the basic suppositions of Hungarian policy, received an immediate rebuttal from Kánya. Hory was instructed to state the Hungarian conviction that "in case of war between Germany and Czechoslovakia, intervention by England and France was highly probable." Moreover, because the war would doubtless be of long duration, "Germany on its own would not be able to struggle successfully to the end." Two alternatives now seemed likely: war, or a plebiscite in the Sudetenland with British support. In the latter case, Kánya suggested, Hungary would do everything in its power to have a plebiscite arranged for the Magyar areas as well.[19]

In England, as Kánya had suspected, the idea of a plebiscite in the Sudetenland was gaining adherents. On that same day Chamberlain, who had decided to undertake a dramatic peace mission to Germany, argued at a Cabinet meeting that it was impossible for Great Britain to go to war to prevent the holding of a plebiscite. When the question quickly arose of whether the other minorities might not also demand a plebiscite, Chamberlain naively remarked that "he did not contemplate that any such demand would be made." Halifax, who was somewhat more cautious but equally misinformed of local conditions, added that "it was true that the other minorities in Czechoslovakia were content at the moment," but the idea of plebiscites was "infectious," and this had to be kept in mind.[20]

Chamberlain thus arrived at Berchtesgaden with the firm conviction that the crisis could be resolved on the basis of self-determination for the Sudeten Germans alone, with the other minorities left to work out with Prague an arrangement for continued participation in a Czechoslovak state. Hitler had been somewhat taken aback by Chamberlain's proposal of a visit to Germany. It seems possible that he even feared the British prime minister would solemnly declare that Britain was "ready to march."[21] The Führer was thus probably quite surprised to find his guest prepared to discuss the transfer of the Sudeten German regions to Germany, and, as a result, he apparently did not emphasize as strongly as he had intended that a similar procedure would have to be adopted for the other minorities. Chamberlain's own record of the talk does show Hitler stating that if the Germans came into the Reich, "then the Hungarian minority would secede, the Polish minority would secede, the Slovak minority would secede—and what was left would be so small that he would not bother his head about it."[22] But this, apparently, was not properly understood by Chamberlain, for he continued to cling to his earlier misconceptions. At a meeting of ministers in London on the sixteenth he told his colleagues that Hitler had assured him that if a plebiscite were granted the Sudeten Germans, he would not worry his head about what was left of Czechoslovakia. This, of course, was not at all what Hitler had said.[23]

At the important British Cabinet meeting of 17 September, the vital question of the fate of the other minorities in Czechoslovakia, whether consciously or unconsciously, was skirted. Chamberlain did report, this time accurately, Hitler's remark that if self-determination were accorded the Germans, equal treatment would have to be given the Magyars, Poles, and Slovaks. It was then suggested that if such equal treatment were the guiding principle, the result would be a dismemberment of Czechoslovakia. But the ministers were reluctant to discuss this unpleasant prospect, and during the course of the meeting the tacit assumption seemed to be that in fact the proposed plebiscite would not extend to the others. In any case, when Sir Samuel Hoare spoke in this sense, no one contradicted him.[24]

This was precisely the development that the Hungarians during the past few days had been working frantically to prevent. As soon as it had become apparent that there was a good possibility that a plebiscite would be held in the Sudeten German areas, Budapest resolved to demand the same concession for the Magyar minority. The principle of "no discrimination" now became the keystone of Hungarian policy, as it had been of Polish policy for many months. Beginning on the fourteenth a series of communications was made to all concerned governments, except Czechoslovakia and her Little Entente allies, stressing that Hungary would accept nothing less for the Magyar minority than what was granted the Sudeten Germans.

The focus of the Hungarian campaign was England. Kánya and Imrédy wished above all to receive confirmation of an earlier remark by Vansittart that the British government believed that "all of the advantages which the Czechoslovak government would concede to the German minority would automatically be applicable to the others as well."[25] Imrédy and Kánya were in daily telephone contact with Sir William Goode, a friend of the Hungarians, who agreed to intercede to see if the British government could not give some indication that Hungary's claims were not being overlooked. Such a sign, Imrédy declared, would be a great help in keeping hold on the agitation in the country.[26] Two days in succession Knox was warned by Imrédy and Kánya that Hungary would struggle "with all means at her disposal" against any attempt to deny a plebiscite to the Magyar minority while granting one to the Sudeten Germans.[27] In London the same message was repeated to numerous parties in the Foreign Office by the Hungarian minister, György Barcza, a moderate man and a skilled diplomat with pro-British sympathies. Barcza stressed that it would be most unfortunate if the impression were conveyed to the world that Britain supported the Sudeten Germans merely because they "had more bayonets behind them."[28]

The lack of a positive response from Great Britain on this question of critical importance led the Hungarian government to work more feverishly to preserve other options. Both Poland and Germany had begun to urge on Budapest a more aggressive attitude, both in the press and in the diplomatic arena. During the time Chamberlain was in Germany, rumors had abounded that a plebiscite would be arranged in the Sudetenland. On the basis of these reports, Colonel Beck recommended that Hungary vigorously demand a plebiscite in the Felvidék. Speed was essential, Beck noted, since if the British came to an agreement with Germany, they would show no concern for Poland and Hungary. He was all too familiar with "the great powers and their cynicism, which respects nothing." They respond only to "a bold step and a powerful voice." Thus, Beck concluded, if Hungary did not throw off her reserve, the historic moment would pass. He requested immediate information on Hungary's intentions.[29]

Joining Poland in urging a more forceful attitude on the part of Hungary was Germany. As has been seen, Hitler had dropped Hungary from his plans after the unsuccessful talks in late August. During the first half of September, there was in fact little contact between the two countries. But after his failure to impress on Chamberlain the necessity for a "total" solution in Czechoslovakia, the Führer was confronted with an unexpected predicament. All along he had been aiming at a partition of Czechoslovakia, a complete elimination of the "aircraft carrier of Bolshevism." The British were now willing to sanction the annexation of the Sudetenland, but he really wanted a "strategic border," that is, the whole of Bohemia and Moravia. To overcome this difficulty, Hitler apparently decided to revert to his former tactic of exploiting ethnic diversity throughout Czechoslovakia in order to foment civil war and create conditions for intervention by Hungary and Poland, as well as the German Reich.

Thus, Marshal Göring summoned Sztójay on the sixteenth and voiced astonishment over the calm and peaceful atmosphere that seemed to be prevailing in Hungary and in the Magyar areas of Czechoslovakia.[30] He complained that Hungary was simply not doing enough in the crisis: Hungarian diplomats were not emulating their Czechoslovak counterparts in calling on the foreign minister in Paris and London two or three times a day. Moreover, neither the Hungarian government nor the Magyar minority had demanded in clear terms the detachment of the Hungarian areas. Hungary, he suggested, should deliver a literal "barrage" of demands that the right of national self-determination be accorded the Magyar minority. Hungarian representatives should begin "hammering" on the doors in Paris and London. In Slovakia armed clashes should be provoked, and mobilization call-up orders disobeyed, "since only powerful incidents would direct the attention of the Western powers to Hungarian demands." It was Germany's desire, Göring explained, that "all of the minorities and the governments of the interested neighboring states . . . should vociferously document the untenable character of the Czechoslovak state," especially during the period Chamberlain was negotiating in London.

Göring's exhortations brought an immediate reaction from Budapest. Sztójay, acting on instructions telephoned that same day, informed Göring and the Wilhelmstrasse that Hungary's press and the Magyar minority would be more active in the upcoming days. He cited the numerous representations that Hungary had been making in London, and asked if the Führer could not publicly associate himself with Hungary's demands.[31] At the same time, Kánya was assuring the German minister that Hungary "would go to the limit" if the claim for equality of treatment were denied. To show Hungary's earnestness, Rátz now reaffirmed the promises regarding flights of German planes over Hungary and the use of landing facilities in case of war, and two additional classes of troops were mobilized. But, for the moment at least, no plans were made in Budapest for instigating the kind of "incidents" that Göring deemed appropriate. As has already been noted, the United Hungarian Party of Slovakia did on the seventeenth demand the right to "take its fate into its own hands," but its resolution stressed the wish to use only peaceful means to achieve this right. Thus, no serious disturbances were provoked in the Magyar areas of Slovakia.

The Hungarian government was, in fact, still consciously refraining from belligerent measures in the hope that a peaceful solution favorable to Hungary might still be imposed by London. Hopes for this, however, were becoming increasingly dimmer. For although the Czechoslovak government was by this point beginning to reconcile itself to the inevitable loss of the German areas, it aimed to salvage what it could of the rest. Prague thus fought tenaciously against the application of any general principle of self-determination for all of the minorities. Beneš and Krofta argued that the idea of a plebiscite had no constitutional basis, was technically impossible, and would be rejected by the great majority of the people of Czechoslovakia, not just the Czechs and Slovaks, as an affront to the integrity of the state.[32] The French, who were now advocating the detachment of the Sudetenland and probably felt some remaining responsibility to their Czechoslovak ally, supported this position, and when Bonnet and Daladier visited London on 18 September for discussions, they insisted that the two sides not embark on "a general theoretical and doctrinal question," but restrict themselves to the case of the Sudeten Germans.[33] Speaking privately over lunch, Daladier told Chamberlain that France had two aims: to keep the peace and save as much as possible for Czechoslovakia. He thought he could convince Beneš to accept the loss of the German areas, but not the general application of the right of self-determination. It was necessary, however, that Britain undertake along with France a guarantee of what remained of Czechoslovakia.[34]

At the British Cabinet meeting on the nineteenth, Chamberlain explained that neither France nor Czechoslovakia would accept a plan for the detachment of the Sudetenland unless England joined in a guarantee of the rump Czechoslovak state. But there was among the assembled ministers a traditional British reluctance to assume any military responsibilities on the Continent. Chamberlain was asked if the proposed guarantee would apply to Czechoslovakia's relations with Poland and Hungary as well. Chamberlain and Halifax explained that it would, but only in the case of "unprovoked aggression." This would leave open the possibility of a peaceful solution of these other problems through friendly negotiation. The guarantee, the prime minister added, would not commit Britain to maintain the boundaries of Czechoslovakia; it would serve mostly a deterrent value. The Cabinet seemed to accept these explanations, though not without sharp questioning.[35]

There was clearly a great deal of self-deception in the British position. Chamberlain and Halifax could hardly have believed, after the numerous communications that had come from Warsaw and Budapest, that calm would prevail in Czechoslovakia after the Germans were handed over to the Reich. They surely recognized that the purpose of concentrating on the Sudeten problem, as Daladier had bluntly stated, was to avoid war with Germany and to allow Prague to refuse the same concessions to Poland and Hungary. And this, indeed, was the way President Beneš interpreted the "Proposals" that were presented by the British and French ambassadors later on the nineteenth. These "Proposals" suggested secession only of the German areas, while opening the possibility of "an international guarantee of the new boundaries against unprovoked aggression."[36] No analysis of this statement, in the sense of Chamberlain's words to his colleagues in the Cabinet, was given at the time or later to Prague. Accordingly, when after two days of deliberations Prague accepted the Anglo-French proposal, Beneš urged the French government to "oppose Polish and Hungarian claims, which would reduce the Czech people to despair and would provoke war." He also took the opportunity to place on record Czechoslovakia's assumption that the "Proposals" having been accepted, "the British and French guarantee was already in force as regards Czechoslovak territory."[37] When no statement to the contrary emanated from Paris or London, Beneš and his colleagues proceeded in the following days on the assumption that their territory was guaranteed against all sides except Germany.[38]

The world was not totally uninformed of the developments in London, Paris, and Prague. In typical fashion information on the substance of the Anglo-French plan was leaked in the French press on the nineteenth. This caused considerable alarm in Hungary and Poland (not to speak of Czechoslovakia), and brought an immediate "formal and serious démarche" in London from the Poles.[39] The Hungarians, as had been their tactic, waited a day to follow the Polish precedent. On the twentieth Barcza saw Halifax and delivered a note that drew London's attention to the Hungarian claim for equal treatment. If the German areas of Czechoslovakia were to be ceded to Germany, "on the grounds of international morals and justice, the same treatment could not be refused to the Hungarian minority."[40]

Halifax's response, which stressed the need for patience and alluded to the League of Nations as a possible forum for the resolution of the problem of the Magyar minority, was far from encouraging.[41] On the other hand, at about the same time Barcza was receiving a communication from Chamberlain that showed a greater understanding for Hungary's position. Early on the nineteenth Barcza had handed to Sir Thomas Moore, a friend who had access to the prime minister, a memorandum stating Hungary's request for equal treatment of the Magyar minority in Czechoslovakia. Moore was able to show this communication to Chamberlain, who in return sent a brief note that Moore delivered to

Barcza later on the nineteenth. Its terse message read: "I whole-heartedly sympathize with Hungary, which has no reason for anxiety. I am carefully keeping Hungary's situation in mind. I most fully approve the peaceful and calm attitude which Hungary up to now has demonstrated, and urge it be continued."[42] Barcza reported to Kánya that Moore could add nothing more about Chamberlain's attitude, although it was clear from Moore's words that Hungary could count on Chamberlain's support during the crisis. Moore had also expressed the opinion that it was important that the Hungarian press, without abandoning interest in the Magyar minority, avoid embittered criticism of the British government. In fact, it would do well to voice further trust in England. After steps had been taken to avoid war, the settlement of Hungary's claims would follow.[43]

Kánya sent his thanks for this communication and indicated that the Hungarian press was continuing to avoid sensationalism.[44] The Hungarians were, in fact, still maintaining a certain reserve. While Poland had joined Germany in a lurid press campaign and had begun to move strong concentrations of troops to the Czechoslovak border once news of the Anglo-French proposal had appeared, Hungary was still hesitant. Neither Göring's admonitions on the sixteenth nor those of Beck earlier, nor, for that matter, the emotional demonstrations in Budapest by nationalist and revisionist groups, had their desired effect.[45] This was due, however, not merely to the desire of influential Hungarians to pay deference to English sensibilities. The Hungarians were still stymied by their own military inadequacy. At a meeting of the Supreme Defense Council, probably on 20 September, the Hungarian chief of staff stated that "in case of a German offensive, Czechoslovakia might attack Budapest, and the Hungarian Army was not even strong enough to resist this." It was estimated that there was only enough ammunition for thirty-six hours of fighting.[46] But with the attitude of Yugoslavia not clarified, and the opportunity for a peaceful solution imposed by England still not completely hopeless, Kánya and Imrédy decided to continue to straddle the fence.

The options open to Hungary, however, were becoming fewer and fewer. Pressure from all sides was becoming acute. The latest British requests for patience and moderation were matched on 20 September by renewed calls from Berlin for a turn to violence. Responding to an invitation from Hitler, Kánya and Imrédy trav-

eled on the Führer's plane to Berchtesgaden, and in the morning
had an important conversation with the German leader. Imrédy
did all the talking for the Hungarian side, Kánya wisely curbing
his tongue.

Hitler, as in August, was in a belligerent mood.[47] He echoed
Göring's earlier words of astonishment that Hungary's attitude was
so mild and undecided. It seemed, he said, as if Hungary were
"disinteresting itself in the Czech question." He, by contrast, was
determined to settle the matter within three weeks, even at the
cost of war. The best solution was to destroy Czechoslovakia, since
in the long run "it was quite impossible to tolerate the existence
of this [Soviet] aircraft carrier in the heart of Europe." In his
upcoming negotiations with Chamberlain, he intended to put forward his demands with "brutal frankness" and the "starkest realism." If as a result disturbances broke out in Czechoslovakia, he
would move his army in. This was the solution he preferred; and
as he was more than ever convinced that the West would not intervene, he suggested that, contrary to his earlier advice, Hungary
move simultaneously with Germany.[48]

But, Hitler cautioned, there was always the "danger" of Prague
submitting to his harsh demands. If in the upcoming talks he received a proposal for the detachment of the Sudetenland without
a plebiscite, "he would have no moral claim to put forward further
demands before the world or his own people, and he could not
make his attitude dependent on the treatment of the other nationalities." To prevent this situation, which would be "critical"
for the Hungarians, Hitler suggested that Hungary move "fast as
lightning" to bring its claims to the attention of the world. He
recommended an outright demand be made for territorial cession
of the Magyar areas, and begged that no guarantee be given of the
new frontiers.

Imrédy responded fully, and not without certain signs of irrita-
tion. He suggested that the Führer was misinformed on developments in Hungary, and proceeded to list measures which had
already been taken, from support of the Magyar minority's call
for self-determination to the development of a "free corps." Hungary, Imrédy stressed, had no intention of guaranteeing Czechoslovakia's borders, and if Britain and France approved a plan which
discriminated against the Hungarian minority, Hungary would
offer strong opposition and would not "shrink from resorting to

measures which lie outside the diplomatic sphere of action."[49] Moreover, "disturbances" would be effected in Slovakia.

The Hungarian prime minister added, however, that he was bound to say that Hitler's time limit was too restrictive. Hungary in the past had been led to believe that the settlement would come in one or two years. An "uprising in occupied territory" could not be brought about in just three weeks. Just like Germany in the May crisis, Hungary in the present crisis was not militarily prepared. She stood before forces five times stronger than herself, and the responsibility was enormous. Just as Hitler had to pursue a "German policy," he, as Hungarian prime minister, had to ply a "Hungarian policy." For this reason he had to be cautious, since Hungary, though ready in spirit, was not prepared militarily.

Hitler's precise reaction to Imrédy's comments is not known, although he did express approval of the plan for a "free corps" and the idea of causing disturbances in Slovakia. But from later incidents[50] it is clear that Hitler regarded Hungary's conduct in the days after 20 September as far from satisfactory. In Hitler's later judgement, Hungary, by her relative inactivity, had prevented him from "laughing in Chamberlain's face" at Godesberg, forced him to accept the Munich agreement, and given Czechoslovakia a new lease on life.[51] One must suspect that these later complaints were merely Hitler's way of rationalizing his own failure to direct events toward the kind of solution he desired. But it is true that Hungary, precisely for the reasons cited by Imrédy, remained fairly quiescent. In contrast to Poland, which continued to conduct menacing troop movements on the Czechoslovak border, Hungary maintained its reserve. Another two classes, it is true, were called up by Budapest shortly after the return of Kánya and Imrédy from Germany, but no instructions were given the Hungarian press to emulate the virulent anti-Czechoslovak campaign then being carried out in Poland and Germany. Hungary did, however, take one new step that tended to complicate the situation for Prague. On 22 September, once again following the Poles by one day, the Hungarian minister handed Krofta a note that called attention to press reports about the Anglo-French "Proposals," and expressed the hope that Czechoslovakia would stand by its former promise of equality of treatment for all minorities.[52] This, in effect, was a request that the Magyar areas be ceded to Hungary. Krofta, who received the note and suggested that a reply would come in a few days, bitterly reproached the Hungarians for trying to exploit Czechoslovakia's misfortune.[53]

Similar reproaches were soon coming from London, where news of the Hungarian démarche and a fresh call-up of troops was singularly ill-received. Barcza's explanation that Hungary needed to have additional troops on hand as a precautionary and defensive move in light of Czechoslovak military measures was ridiculed by Sir Orme Sargent, Assistant Undersecretary of State in the Foreign Office, who expressed regret that Hungary had acted so precipitately directly after Halifax's personal appeal for moderation and patience.[54] That same evening identical representations were made by the British ministers in Warsaw and Budapest. The two countries were advised that Britain regretted the military measures that had been taken and sincerely hoped that they would not lead to military aggression against Czechoslovakia. The Polish and Hungarian cases were known and "fully in mind," and there was thus "no justification whatever for attempting to compel an immediate settlement by direct action instead of through the processes of normal negotiations." If Hungary and Poland preferred to proceed to direct action, Britain "disclaimed responsibility for the consequences."[55]

Kánya, whose patience was gradually being worn thin, could not restrain his anger at the British move. He rejected Knox's accusation that Hungary's military measures were meant to intimidate Czechoslovakia, and pointed out that Prague had first massed troops on Hungary's borders. Hungary feared, he said, that Czechoslovakia would make peace with Germany and then turn in force on Hungary. Then, to Knox's embarrassment, Kánya entered into a bitter analysis of British policy. The claims of the Sudeten Germans, he asserted, were not backed much by history, but quite a bit by military threats. Hungary, by contrast, had used peaceful and lawful means to put forward claims that had much justification in history. It seemed that London yielded to the former and not the latter merely because of a show of overwhelming force, and not from a moral wish to see justice done. He could not resist the strong suspicion that the British, who had so often spoken of self-determination, would have insisted on a plebiscite in the Sudetenland if it had not been assumed that a similar procedure throughout Czechoslovakia would have dismembered her. Knox's response, a singularly feeble one that no doubt merely increased Kánya's ire, was that the Hungarian foreign minister did not understand the immense difficulties inherent in the proper organization of a plebiscite.[56]

Meanwhile, the attitude towards Hungary's aspirations had been changing somewhat in the countries of Central and Eastern Europe. Italy, which had been more or less a bystander through the early part of September, began to support the Poles and Hungarians most vigorously after the intentions of France and England became known. Mussolini joined Hitler in urging Hungary to voice her claims loudly; Italy, for her part, would "manfully" support Hungary's maximum demands.[57]

The relationship with Poland, however, was again posing problems. Although Kánya had shown interest in Poland's offer of a military and political pact, Beck procrastinated. He still complained that precise information on Hungary's intentions was lacking, and on the twentieth informed Budapest that events had moved so quickly that the proposed pact was no longer possible. Poland was still interested in a common border, and would continue to offer Hungary political and diplomatic support, but if Hungary, as seemed the case, was planning on observing events and taking what she could, it would be difficult to help her.[58]

Adding to Hungary's troubles was the continuing uncooperative attitude of the Slovaks. In early September Budapest had been making a frantic effort to undo some of the harm that Hungarian activities during the spring and summer had done. But, as Kánya wryly observed, the Slovak leaders were playing a "double game"; they were in contact with both Prague and Budapest and hoped to wring the best bargain whatever the development of events.[59] On the nineteenth, however, a definite blow to the Hungarian cause was delivered. On that day the autonomist Hlinka's Slovak People's Party adopted as the basis of its negotiations with the government a resolution in which was expressed the hope that, once a settlement was reached with Prague on the basis of the Pittsburgh Agreement, the Slovaks and Czechs could remain together within a Czecho-Slovak state.

The most promising development for Hungary in this period was the decision being reached in both Romania and Yugoslavia that, although recovery of the whole of the Felvidék by Hungary was inadmissible, ethnic revision could not be denied her. This was the view that Romanian diplomats as early as 20 September were espousing in Geneva, Rome, and Belgrade.[60] There were also signs that Yugoslavia was adopting a similar position, and Kánya encouraged it by informing Belgrade on the twenty-second that Hungary considered the Bled Agreement as in force between the two countries.[61]

Meanwhile, Hitler was meeting with Chamberlain at Godesberg on 23 and 24 September, and, as he promised the Hungarians, presented his case with the "starkest realism." Chamberlain, who had come to report the good news that he had convinced his government, France, and Czechoslovakia to accept Germany's direct annexation of the Sudetenland, was told flatly that that proposal "could not be maintained."[62] Hitler asserted that representatives of Poland and Hungary had visited him and said that in no circumstances would they agree to their nationals living under Czechoslovak rule. As Führer he spoke only for the Germans, but he could not stab his allies in the back. "The fundamental fact," he said, "was that neither the Sudetens nor the Slovaks nor the Poles nor the Hungarians wanted to remain in Czechoslovakia, and the Czechs were attempting by force to thwart them." For his part, he demanded a solution of the Sudeten problem by 1 October.

At a second interview the next day, however, Hitler, perhaps because the Hungarians had not caused the "disturbances" to which Imrédy had alluded, did not again bring up the subject of the other minorities. Chamberlain thus returned to London once again confident that all would be well if only Hitler's demand was met. He found, however, a different atmosphere in England. Even Halifax now questioned whether Hitler's new requirements should be met. And by the twenty-sixth opinion had so turned around that a communiqué was issued stating that if Germany attacked Czechoslovakia, France would intervene, "and Great Britain and Russia will certainly stand by France."[63]

Strangely enough, it was precisely when Britain's attitude toward Germany began to stiffen that a greater understanding of the Hungarian position began to be shown. Barcza painstakingly explained the Hungarian position to Halifax again on the night of the twenty-third, and may even have given assurances that Hungary would not join in any military action against Czechoslovakia.[64] On the following day Halifax forwarded a letter in which he assured the Hungarians that the fact that Britain was absorbed in the Sudeten problem did not "imply that the claim of your Government will be neglected. On the contrary I can assure you that His Majesty's Government have fully in mind the nature of this claim. They feel, however, that there can be no justification for attempting to compel its immediate settlement by direct action instead of through the processes of normal negotiations."[65] In handing over this letter to Barcza, Halifax stressed that Hungary's case would be the "focus of attention" at the "appropriate time."[66] While unsure whether the emphasis on an "appropriate time" was merely a "procrastination, a palliative, or a serious promise," Barcza nonetheless regarded Halifax's letter as a "friendly gesture," and suggested to Kánya that understanding for Hungary seemed to be growing in Britain.[67]

It is not clear whether Barcza's report made much of an impression in Budapest, but, whatever the reasons, the Hungarians continued to resist German pressure for more forceful action. On the twenty-sixth Ribbentrop bluntly warned Sztójay that Germany had done all it could: the rest was up to Hungary. He strongly advised that if a German-Czechoslovak conflict started, Hungary join in immediately. Sztójay, referring to opposite advice from Göring and Neurath, stated that Hungary, for the familiar reasons, could not comply.[68]

Kánya, who was still plagued by fears of the consequences of Hungarian military action, approved Sztójay's reply. On the twenty-fifth and twenty-sixth messages from various quarters came into Budapest urging that Hungary not intervene militarily, or at least not at the outset, if Germany and Czechoslovakia became embroiled in war. Rome, heeding the warnings of Bucharest and Belgrade, advised the Hungarians not to rush into action, but to wait until a few days after the initial German move.[69] Moreover, on the twenty-sixth Stojadinović confirmed to Budapest that he regarded it only natural that Hungary desire ethnic revision in Czechoslovakia, although the same did not apply to integral revision. He was willing to intercede in Prague to support the lesser claims, if Hungary so desired.[70] Thus when Knox, alarmed by reports that a senior Hungarian Foreign Ministry official (possibly Csáky) had been talking of Hungary and Poland marching immediately after the Germans entered Bohemia, again warned Kánya of the dangers of such a course, the Hungarian foreign minister took careful note of his admonition. Knox's further argument, that the crisis was coming more and more to be one not just involving the fate of Czechoslovakia, but one of the rise of a dominant and aggressive military power, no doubt impressed Kánya. The latter acknowledged that Britain was truly absorbed by the Sudeten question. His only desire was that London let him know as soon after 1 October as possible in what form Hungarian wishes might be met.[71] In light of the European war that now seemed to be looming closer on the horizon, the Hungarians were thus willing to allow their case to be postponed at least a few days, hopeful that Britain would indeed turn its attention to the Magyar minority when the "appropriate time" had come.

Czechoslovakia's attitude to the Hungarian démarche of 22 September did not encourage Budapest to believe that Prague might show more understanding for Hungary's claims at a later date. Krofta had promised a reply on the twenty-fourth, but on that date he asked for a further postponement. The reason, as Budapest soon learned, was that negotiations were underway to secure the benevolent neutrality of Poland through territorial concessions. These negotiations had already begun when, on 26 September, Krofta informed the Hungarian minister of Czechoslovakia's response to the Hungarian démarche. Krofta indicated that Prague was prepared to enter into friendly talks with Hungary, but not on the same basis as with Germany. The earlier promise of equality of treatment for all minorities had been intended only for the case of the granting of autonomy. Thus Prague would be willing to grant to the Magyar minority the Nationalities Statute which had been worked out in negotiations with the Sudeten leaders.[72]

Faced with the imminent loss of the Sudetenland, and forced by circumstances to offer territory to Poland, the Czechoslovak government was apparently hoping to salvage at least the Magyar areas of Slovakia and Ruthenia. But the Poles proved unhelpful. Beck showed some interest in Beneš's proposal of territorial revision, but he insisted that he could give no guarantee of Czechoslovakia until the other minorities had been satisfied.[73] The Hungarians not unexpectedly rejected Krofta's offer, and showed their displeasure by interrupting all trade with Czechoslovakia. Only the Slovaks, to Kánya's continuing dismay, provided some solace for the Prague government. On the twenty-third, leaders of all the Slovak parties affirmed their loyalty to the Czechoslovak state and urged all Slovaks to rally around the government in the current grave emergency. And when general mobilization was de-

clared late on the twenty-third, Slovak soldiers responded obedi-
ently.[74] Kánya's feeble and arrogant response was to advise the
Slovaks to demand self-determination, for otherwise future developments would be their own responsibility.[75]

28 September was the very height of the crisis. The advance
of German troops into Czechoslovakia was awaited at any hour.
But even Hitler was now beginning to doubt whether an armed
conflict was feasible or desirable. In the early afternoon he finally
succumbed to the arguments of Mussolini and Göring and invited
Chamberlain and Daladier to join him for a consultation the next
day in Munich.

Word of the Munich conference was greeted with much relief
all over Europe, not the least in Hungary. It quickly became evident to Budapest, however, that no time could be lost in prepar-
ing Hungary's case for presentation at Munich. After a conversation
with Göring, Sztójay telephoned to Budapest and warned that this
might be Hungary's last opportunity for success in Czechoslovakia.[76] Csáky was thus sent off to Munich early on the twenty-ninth
with instructions that Kánya and Imrédy had worked out the night
before. He was to stress Hungary's desire that the same principle
used in the transfer of the Sudetenland be applied to the Magyar
areas. In addition, Hungary wished to have the right of self-
determination accorded the other inhabitants of Slovakia and
Ruthenia, preferably by means of plebiscites.

Csáky stated Hungary's case in an important interview with
Mussolini on the twenty-ninth.[77] Mussolini was enthusiastic,
claiming it was a "good day for Hungary today." He studied the
map and statistics that Csáky provided, and offered to champion
the Hungarian cause during the Four Power meeting. Unfortunately for the Hungarians, the Duce failed to present their proposals accurately when the time came: he made no mention at all
of the call for plebiscites. This made little difference, though,
since Daladier and Chamberlain, and by this point Hitler as well,
had little desire to espouse the Hungarian cause. These three leaders seemed to wish to evade altogether any mention of the Hungarian problem. The "minorities draft" submitted by Mussolini,
which called for the "same principles" to be applied in settling the
Polish and Hungarian claims as had been employed in the Sudeten
German case, was rejected by the British and French, who, ironically, regarded it as tantamount to endorsing the use of force to

effect territorial transfer.[78] Instead, the four leaders agreed to add to the Munich Agreement the following protocol: "The heads of the Governments of the four Powers declare that the problems of the Polish and Hungarian minorities, if not settled within three months, shall form the subject of another meeting of the heads of the Governments of the four Powers here present."

Having in effect washed their hands of this embarrassing matter, the leaders of the great powers returned home, Hitler to rue his missed opportunity, and Chamberlain, having forgotten all the British promises that the Hungarian problem would be the "focus of attention" at the "appropriate time," to proclaim "peace with honor." The Hungarians had little to make them rejoice, especially when their Polish friends quickly used an ultimatum and military intimidation to coerce Prague—on 1 October—to cede the Teschen area. To preserve appearances, Horthy dispatched rather fulsome letters of gratitude to Hitler, Göring, and Victor Emmanuel, and Kánya (though it must have pained him) to Ribbentrop.[79] But privately there were many expressions of bitterness and despair. It was, indeed, truly ironic that Hungary, which for the past months had wavered between serving the interests and heeding the advice of two powers, Germany and England, should find that in the end neither country showed the slightest interest in Hungary's aspirations.

Chapter 9

The "Triumph" of Hungarian Revisionism

In a speech on 1 October, Prime Minister Imrédy likened Hungary's past and future path to a "narrow mountain ridge with yawning abysses to right and to left of it."[1] On the one side was "irresponsible adventure," on the other "cowardly renunciation." Imrédy emphasized that Hungary would continue to avoid falling into either side of the abyss, but his experiences of the past month had clearly convinced him that his critics on the radical right had been correct: he had been relying a little too much on "renunciation" and not enough on "adventure." For Imrédy and many of his contemporaries, the Munich crisis accomplished what the Anschluss had not. It demonstrated in stark terms that Germany was now the dominant power in East Central Europe, apparently able to move with virtual impunity in implementing the policies it favored. France and England showed no inclination to challenge this new German ascendancy.

In the wake of these events, Imrédy underwent a dramatic metamorphosis. His faith in Great Britain, which had seemed at times even to his English friends as bordering on the pathetic, was shattered. At his postwar trial he admitted that after the Munich crisis he came to the conclusion that territorial revision could come only on the side of Nazi Germany, and that Hungary's "backwardness" could be overcome only through a "gentlemanly fascist dictatorship."

If the announcement of the Munich Agreement brought a spontaneous collective feeling of relief and a significant relaxation of tension in most European capitals, the opposite was true in Budapest. In early October great pressure was being put on the Hungarian government by chauvinist and right radical groups to ignore the Munich decision and, emulating Poland, to use military threats and force to gain the territories to which Hungary aspired. "We want to fight!" the editor of the most prominent radical right-wing newspaper wrote.[2] Yet Kálmán Kánya still directed Hungary's foreign affairs, and his inclination to continue to seek a diplomatic solution was supported by most Cabinet members. Kánya was confident that Hungary now had the support of all the great powers, and even Romania and Yugoslavia, for ethnic revision of the border with Czechoslovakia. Given the terms of the annex to the Munich Agreement, there seemed no way that Prague could avoid ceding territory.

Imrédy lent his support to Kánya in this matter, but he insisted that an alternative policy be prepared so that force could be employed if diplomacy failed. Thus, on 1 October Imrédy summoned Miklós Kozma, a fiery patriot and Szeged veteran, and asked him to take command of what he called the "Ruthenian operation." The idea was to form in Hungary a guerrilla band that would be infiltrated into Ruthenia to carry out acts of sabotage, and link up with and embolden separatist elements. A vigorous propaganda campaign would also be directed by radio and distribution of leaflets. Kozma, who accepted the responsibility with great enthusiasm, was authorized to take whatever steps he deemed necessary, even if they involved "illegal and violent methods."[3]

Though Kánya concentrated his efforts on the diplomatic front, and insisted that strict discipline be imposed on the restless officers of the regular army,[4] he was willing to give his tacit (though tepid) approval to the clandestine "Ruthenian operation." His compelling motivation was the realization that in the upcoming bargaining with Prague, the Hungarians, in choosing to hew to the guidelines set down at Munich, could hardly demand territory that contained few or no Magyars. A strict observance of the ethnographic frontiers in the *Felvidék* would mean the return to Hungary of a strip of territory in southern Slovakia and Ruthenia, leaving small rump states as buffers between Poland and Hungary. By early October most Hungarians had resigned themselves to the fact that the Slovaks did not wish to be joined to Hungary, and that in any case no great power would champion the Hungarians in such a claim.[5] The question of Ruthenia was different: here the acquisition of five thousand square miles in one of the most remote and backward regions of Europe took on symbolic importance for Hungarian patriots. Annexation of the whole of Ruthenia meant creation of the "common border" with Poland, a cherished national goal that since 1919 had represented a shibboleth in the vocabulary of the Hungarian revisionist movement. The "common border" was often endowed with almost magical qualities, for it was seen as a symbol of Hungary's importance in Danubian Europe and her ability to make a contribution to the defense against Bolshevik Russia and, if need be, Nazi Germany.

Moreover, though it was clear that the Slovaks had no desire to be annexed by Hungary, the situation in Ruthenia was not so clearly defined. The Magyar minority represented at most 20 percent of the population, but among many of the leading political figures there was much resentment against Prague and a feeling that if a small section of the province had to be transferred to Hungary, the whole of Ruthenia might as well be included, so as to preserve it as an economic unit. The Hungarian position was considerably strengthened when, on 9 October, András Bródy was appointed minister-president for Ruthenia. Bródy had definite pro-Magyar sentiments and in this period was receiving subsidies and instructions from Budapest.[6]

After a week of procrastination, during which Eduard Beneš resigned, the new Czechoslovak government finally agreed to the Hungarian demand for an opening of negotiations, which were to commence on 9 October on a boat anchored in the Danube off the town of Komárom.[7] For the Hungarian delegates, including Kánya and Teleki, the proceedings must have been painful and humiliating. The Czechoslovak delegation, they discovered, was composed solely of Slovaks, who were poorly prepared and intent on clinging tenaciously to their territory. The Germans had won their concessions at a conference of the great powers; the Poles had gained their prize after a show of military force; but now the Hungarians found themselves squabbling over the negotiating table with people whom they had always scorned and patronized.

As if to emphasize the gulf separating the two parties, Kánya demanded at the outset that French, the official language of diplomacy, be used in the talks, though few of the Slovaks were fluent in it. Magyar, which all the Slovaks knew, quickly became the working language of the negotiations, but this did not facilitate understanding in the broader sense. The Hungarian delegation, armed with Teleki's maps and statistics, argued that the determination of a new border should, in the spirit of the Munich Agreement, be based strictly on the ethnic configurations of the area in dispute. The Slovaks, however, maintained, much as the Magyars had in Paris some twenty years earlier, that drawing a frontier on that basis would do immense harm to the economic and cultural life of the Slovak nation. Over the course of the next few days, the Slovaks did make a series of offers involving the cession of territory, but Jozef Tiso, head of their delegation, made it clear that they would never agree to a political frontier corresponding to the ethnic frontier unless the large colony of Slovaks living in inner Hungary was also taken into consideration. This the Hungarians refused to do, and, though Kánya and Teleki were willing to continue to bargain, Imrédy grew impatient and on 13 October called an end to the negotiations.[8] The Hungarians thus returned to Budapest, announcing that they were going to appeal to the great powers.

During the course of the negotiations, the "Ruthenian operation" had begun to unfold. Both Colonel Beck and Ciano had given their approval and promised some military support if there were any complications.[9] After some haggling between Kozma and the army leadership, a contingent of about eight hundred men, many of them Arrowcross party officials, was sent across the border on the eleventh. Meanwhile, Bródy was instructed to make vociferous demands for Ruthenia's right of self-determination.[10] But to Kozma's great disappointment, the operation met with little success. A few acts of sabotage were committed, but the Czechoslovak troops, which had been strongly reinforced over the past week, had little difficulty in capturing most of the Hungarian guerrillas and effectively sealing the border.

In mid-October it was thus clear that both the formal negotiations with the Slovaks and the clandestine operation in Ruthenia had failed. The only alternative now, short of general mobilization and an attack on Czechoslovakia, was an appeal to the Munich powers. At a ministerial council on the thirteenth, the new chief of staff, Lajos Keresztes-Fischer, warned that in a military conflict Hungary would likely be faced with an impossible task, forced to fight on three fronts. Since the Munich Pact Czechoslovakia had not demobilized, and, in fact, had moved the bulk of its forces to the Hungarian frontier. The decision was thus made to mobilize five new classes and to make an appeal for a renewed meeting of the Munich powers.[11]

The effort during the second half of October to interest the great powers in Hungary's predicament met with only limited success. In London there was a general recognition that Hungary should receive those territories in Czechoslovakia containing a preponderance of Magyars, but the overwhelming sentiment was one of growing aversion for the whole tangle of Danubian politics. Halifax and Chamberlain were reluctant to take a vigorous stand in Hungary's favor, despite a personal plea from Horthy and the promises they had made at the height of the crisis in September.[12] In the Foreign Office the chief concern was to prevent the outbreak of a military conflict, which might force Britain to honor the guarantee of rump Czechoslovakia that had been given earlier. Just as in September, private parties in England attempted to persuade the Foreign Office to adopt a more sympathetic approach to the Hungarian problem,[13] but the feeling persisted that any gesture made to the "beastly" Hungarian government[14] would be futile, since Danubian Europe had now definitely fallen into the German sphere of influence.

During October there was a flicker of interest in Paris and London in the creation of the "common border" as an anti-German barrier, but a closer examination of the problem led British leaders to conclude that such a strengthening of Hungary would alarm Romania and would not contribute much to a thwarting of German expansion. Halifax thus reported to the Cabinet that the possible advantages of the cession of Ruthenia to Hungary were so "frail" that there was no justification for any positive action on the part of Britain.[15] The British thus opted for a policy of indifference to developments in the Danubian area. Paris and London were prepared to consider the Hungarian-Czechoslovak problem if a reconvening of the Munich Powers were deemed necessary, but they much preferred that the matter be settled some other way, even through Axis arbitration.[16]

In Italy the Hungarian case received a much more sympathetic hearing, but Ciano and the Duce were so unsure of the direction of Italian policy that their attitude in this period was subject to hopeless vacillations. Early in October Mussolini seemed truly enthusiastic about creation of the "common border" and offered vigorous support. The Hungarians, he declared, were the only people in Europe he found sympathetic.[17] Two weeks later, taking note of the support for the "common border" in certain French newspapers, he concluded that the project had too much of an anti-German flavor to it. In any case, it would amount to nothing more than a "cobweb" in the path of German expansionism.[18]

One idea that briefly captivated Ciano after the breakdown of the Hungarian-Czechoslovak negotiations was a new meeting of the four Munich powers to be held in northern Italy, grandly presided over by the Duce. Informal invitations had already been sent out when, to his acute embarassment, the Germans vetoed the idea.[19] This merely confirmed what East European observers had already sensed: Germany would now have the final say in matters relating to Eastern and Central Europe. In the first two weeks of October, Berlin was bombarded with professions of loyalty and requests for increased trade from countries that had previously been reticent or even hostile. The Romanians were extending feelers concerning improved economic and political ties; František Chvalkovský, the new foreign minister in Prague, was emphasizing his complete trust in Hitler and promising a complete *volte face* in Czechoslovakia's policy; and the more radical Slovaks, not to be outdone, were currying favor with Ribbentrop and Göring by expressing their desire to become an independent state tied closely to the Reich. A primary motive behind these appeals of the Romanians, Czechs, and Slovaks was the desire to win German support in the limiting of Hungarian territorial expansion.

In this rather unseemly scramble the Hungarians were at a distinct disadvantage. Almost immediately after signing his name to the Munich Agreement, Hitler had begun to regret that he had been persuaded to accept a diplomatic solution. Almost as if to deflect attention from his own lack of resolve at the height of the crisis, he now began, privately and publicly, to berate the Hungarians as "spineless dogs" whose cowardly conduct at the critical time in September had thwarted his master plan.[20] Göring and Ribbentrop likewise heaped invectives on the hapless Magyars, particularly on Kánya, who now emerged as the *bête noire* of the German leadership.[21] Thus, not only was there little incentive on the German side to champion the Hungarian cause in the October negotiations, but there was also no hesitation about taking one step that was likely to cause great consternation in Budapest. In the first week of October, German troops occupied the strategic Bratislava bridgehead. Sztójay protested that this violated Hitler's earlier pledge never to annex former Hungarian territory, and Kánya warned that such a move would inflame Hungarian public opinion, but the Germans were oblivious to such concerns.[22]

In the fall of 1938, Hitler's chief aim in Danubian Europe seems to have been to prevent any "explosion" until the outlines of his future policy came more sharply into focus. Thus he advised the Czechoslovaks and Hungarians to agree to reasonable compromises in the creation of a new border based on ethnic principles. The national and ethnic rivalries in East Central Europe seemed to offer a multitude of opportunities for Hitler to employ the kind of "divide and rule" strategy that the Habsburgs had once used so successfully. Czechs could be played against Slovaks, Slovaks against Magyars, and Magyars against Romanians. For the moment, Ruthenia was the cynosure of several possible diplomatic projects. It might, as the Poles were requesting, be granted to Hungary as one part of an overall German-Polish settlement involving Danzig and the Corridor;[23] it, along with Slovakia, might be turned into a German protectorate that could serve as a launching pad for German expansion into the Ukraine; or it might even be offered to the Hungarians as a reward for a firm commitment to entering the German orbit. In general, then, Hitler's policy, as he explained it to Ribbentrop, was to keep several "irons in the fire and to shape matters in the German interest according to the way the situation develops."[24]

When it became apparent in late October that the Hungarians and Czechoslovaks would not be able to reach agreement in their negotiations, and that Hungarian frustration might lead to an untimely military conflict, Hitler finally agreed to have the matter submitted to Axis arbitration, a procedure he had earlier rejected. Both Budapest and Prague were requesting arbitration, and the Western powers seemed quite willing to have the matter resolved in this manner. The decision reached by Ciano and Ribbentrop on 2 November in Vienna, which became known as the first Vienna Award, called for a boundary roughly congruent with the ethnic frontier, though Ciano had perhaps finagled a bit more for Hungary than otherwise might have been justified.[25] In any case, no one could dispute the fact that, in terms of the ethnic character of the area, the new boundary was more equitable than the one stipulated by the Treaty of Trianon.

In all the Vienna Award called for the cession by Czechoslovakia of territory with a population of 1,041,494. Of those affected, some 593,000 (approximately 57 percent of the total) were Magyars, the rest largely Slovaks and Ruthenes, with smaller groups of Czechs, Germans, and Jews. Of the five cities most coveted by the Hungarians, three (Kassa, Ungvár, and Munkács) now became part of Hungary and two (Bratislava and Nitra) remained in Slovakia.

The Vienna Award was cause for considerable celebration in Hungary: for the first time, and after two decades of frustration, a territorial provision of Trianon had been revised. The Hungarian occupation of the "liberated" territory took place in appropriately splendid fashion. Many political figures, including the whole parliament, formed the procession that entered Kassa, the most cherished of the cities regained by the award. Characteristically astride a white horse, Horthy received a tumultuous welcome from the local Magyars. Mingled among the cries of welcome, however, were jingoistic calls of "On to Transylvania!" and "Get the rest back too!"[26] For many Hungarians this first revisionist "triumph" served merely to whet the appetite.

The clamor for additional revisionist successes now focused on truncated Ruthenia, which even some non-Magyar observers believed could not long survive on its own. In the first two weeks of November, spokesmen for Hungarian political groups of almost all persuasions called for some sort of action to regain the remnants of Ruthenia. Even the Social Democrats argued that the situation there was untenable. The radical officers were putting great pressure on the government, confident that, with Polish help, a military occupation of Ruthenia would be a relatively simple task.

From Warsaw too came renewed advice that Hungary should exploit the favorable situation and seize Ruthenia. During October Colonel Beck had tried his best to further Hungarian interests in Ruthenia. His most important initiative in this period was an attempt to persuade King Carol of Romania that his country should join with Hungary in a partition of Ruthenia. Such an action, in Beck's opinion, would have given impetus to the creation of a bloc of states that would be able to hold its own against both Germany and the Soviet Union.[27] However, for a variety of reasons the Romanians showed little interest in this project, and the Hungarians, as has been seen, preferred to turn to the great powers for a resolution of the problem. This merely added to Beck's exasperation at what he regarded as the undue hesitancy and vacillation in

Hungary's foreign policy. He had expected that Hungary would take advantage of the favorable opportunity and seize Ruthenia in a swift military operation. Finally, in late October he informed the Hungarian minister in Warsaw that unless Hungary made a decisive move quickly, Poland would "erect a barbed wire fence on the Carpathians" and completely disinterest itself in what happened in the South.[28]

In the first two weeks of November, the Hungarians hesitated, concerned in part that any move now in violation of the Vienna Award might be singularly ill-received in Rome and Berlin, and in part that Czechoslovak army and air units might attack Budapest. Finally, Imrédy, with Horthy's support, decided that the time for a bit of "irresponsible adventure" had come. Though Kánya still refused to submit to the public clamor[29] and was on the verge of resigning his post, Kozma was authorized by Imrédy to cross the border with his free corps on the twentieth and carry out terrorist acts, after which Brody and other pro-Magyar Ruthenes were to issue a call for intervention by the Hungarian army to restore order.

Several illusions, and a general incompetence in such clandestine military operations, gravely marred Hungary's implementation of this plan. At first, still concerned about a military counterattack that would devastate Budapest, the Hungarians tried to convince the Poles to join in the attack on Ruthenia and, in fact, to assume the brunt of the military responsibility.[30] This Beck refused to do, although he voiced strong support for the Hungarian plan and dispatched another detachment of guerrillas into Ruthenia on the fourteenth.

In the week before the planned attack, German and Italian statesmen gave unambiguous indications that any Hungarian move in violation of the Vienna Award would be inopportune. On the eighteenth Mussolini bluntly warned that Hungary seemed to be bungling into an unfortunate military adventure that would have unfortunate consequences.[31] But the atmosphere in Hungary, especially in military circles, was now at a fever pitch and the operation could not be easily cancelled. Moreover, Imrédy and Kánya clung to the hope that, though the Germans were unenthusiastic about a military coup in Ruthenia, they might well accept a *fait accompli* if it were created quickly and smoothly. The final fillip came from the Duce, who, after being assured on the nineteenth by the Hungarian military attaché in Rome that Germany did not oppose the Hungarian action, reversed his position and urged Budapest to "get on with it." The hundred Italian planes and pilots promised earlier by Ciano were now placed at Hungary's disposal.[32]

Meanwhile, a frenetic press campaign was being conducted in Hungary to set the stage for the invasion on the twentieth. Bold newspaper headlines called attention to the alleged deterioration of economic and political life in Ruthenia and the creation of "Macedonian conditions": "Famine Near in Ruthenia," "The Terroristic Rule of the Ukrainian Government," "Czech Terror and Anarchy are Devastating Ruthenia."[33] Beginning on the fourteenth Polish guerrilla units added to the tension by committing acts of sabotage that were meant to divert attention from the main thrust by the Magyar army on the twentieth. However, a snag developed as the attack day approached. To Kozma's dismay the Hungarian General Staff insisted that the attack be postponed one day so that the soldiers could have an extra day's rest. Unfortunately, the pro-Magyar Ruthenes were not informed of the delay, and their newspaper announced on the twentieth, in enormous headlines, the entry of Hungarian troops.[34]

It may be, as C. A. Macartney suggests, that no harm was done because no one in Europe read the Ruthene press,[35] but the one-day delay did prove fatal. For in the meantime Berlin learned what was afoot, and Ribbentrop informed the Italians that a Hungarian occupation of Ruthenia "would discredit the Axis Powers, whose award Hungary had unconditionally accepted three weeks ago."[36] With the approval of the Duce, who felt badly deceived by the Hungarians, a joint German-Italian démarche, rather severely worded, was thus composed and delivered in Budapest. It expressed serious misgivings about an incursion into Ruthenia and strongly urged Budapest to abide strictly by the terms of the Vienna Award.[37]

This could hardly be interpreted as anything but an Axis veto, and the Hungarians, though deeply chagrined, decided that the only possible course was to back down. Orders were quickly dispatched to withdraw the troops from the border, and, according to Kánya, the Ruthene question was now placed in "cold storage."[38]

One important repercussion of these events was a tarnishing of Germany's image among Hungarian military officers, the one group that had been staunchly pro-German in the past. Most of the officers were unaware of the diplomatic exchanges that had occurred in the weeks before 21 November; in their view, military orders issued by the regent had been arbitrarily or maliciously countermanded by the Germans at the last possible moment.[39] This resentment in military circles tended to strengthen a more general anti-German mood that had been developing in Hungary since the Munich Agreement. The German annexation of some territory in Slovakia evoked a bitter response, as Kánya had predicted. Even the Vienna Award failed to enhance Germany's prestige in Hungary, for only Ciano was feted as the champion of Hungarian revisionism, while Ribbentrop was widely accused of having favored the Czechs and Slovaks. That Hungary was unable to recover Pozsony (Bratislava, its former capital city), several other key cities in Slovakia, and, finally, the whole of Ruthenia, was attributed by an unsophisticated public to German malevolence.[40] The regent fully shared these emotions, and it is probably fair to say that in the interwar period anti-German feeling in Hungary had never been so strong and widespread as in the autumn of 1938.

It is thus truly paradoxical that it was precisely in this period that the decision was made in Budapest to jettison Kánya's "free hand" policy and to forge more intimate political and economic ties with National Socialist Germany. In mid-October, when the Czechs, Slovaks, and Romanians were rushing to curry favor in Berlin, Hungary's leaders began to fear that unless Hungary also took the initiative, she would be left isolated and ostracized in a Danubian Europe dominated by Germany. Above all, there was the realization that the future success of Hungary's revisionist program would be jeopardized unless Hungary identified more closely with Germany and the Axis.

Even Kánya sensed that the foundation of his cherished policy of the "free hand" was being eroded. The Anglophile Hungarian minister in London, György Barcza, had suggested in early October that Hungarians should "cherish no illusions about the altruistic character of English policy."[41] And when Kánya asked Geoffrey Knox point-blank if the West had become completely disinterested in Danubian Europe, the British minister could only reply that London was not disinterested, but there was no intention of constructing an anti-German barrier in that part of the world.[42]

In these circumstances Imrédy decided that the twin goals of maintaining Hungarian independence and enhancing the opportunities for territorial expansion would be best served by a policy of closer cooperation with the Axis Powers, especially Germany. With Horthy's approval, special emissaries were sent in mid-October to Rome and Berlin to announce a change in Hungarian policy. For the mission to Berlin, Kálmán Darányi, the former prime minister, was selected as the Hungarian statesman most likely to receive a cordial welcome in Germany. Even so, when Darányi saw Hitler on the fourteenth he was lectured rather sternly on Hungary's past sins, particularly Kánya's obstructionist policies during the Munich crisis.[43] The Führer was mollified, however, when Darányi reported that, in order to demonstrate her new resolve to work closely with the Axis, Hungary was now prepared to adhere to the Anti-Comintern Pact, sign a long-term trade pact with Germany, and withdraw from the League of Nations.

It was made quite clear to Darányi, however, that a new era in German-Hungarian relations could be opened only if and when Kánya was replaced as foreign minister. Even Kánya seems to have understood this; implicit in the decision to orient Hungary more closely to Germany was a repudiation of his "free hand" policy. Indeed, the evidence suggests that he opposed the new policy,[44] and would have resigned at the time except for the necessity of maintaining government stability during the critical weeks of late October and early November. The "Ruthenian operation" he viewed with great distaste, for it represented the kind of submission to the military and chauvinist elements against which he had long struggled. For patriotic reasons he nonetheless strove, albeit in vain, to make diplomatic preparations for the coup. Only after the Axis démarche did he resign, citing his failing health.

Kánya's resignation marked, in a narrow sense, the end of nearly four months of diplomatic crisis for Hungary; in a broader perspective, it represented the failure of the attempt, begun after Gömbös's death in 1936, to balance precariously between the Western powers and a resurgent Germany. However, in a peculiar kind of symmetry, the end of the diplomatic crisis served to open a period of equally intense domestic turmoil.

By late November Hungary's conservative establishment was coming to believe that the metamorphosed Imrédy had emerged

from the traumatic Munich crisis as a kind of reincarnated Gömbös. Not only was Imrédy now advocating and guiding Hungary
towards the closest possible attachment to Germany, but he also
was beginning to hint very strongly that such a foreign policy shift
had to be accompanied by corresponding changes in domestic
policy. Formerly, Imrédy had emphasized the desirability of "taking the wind out of the sails" of the radical right; in November it
began to appear that he intended to join the right-wing extremists
on board and position himself at the helm. He now declared his
intention of introducing a new "nationalist, militarist, race-protecting" program, including a "more perfect" solution of the Jewish
problem, more intensive development of the army, and extensive
land reform. Since the Parliament might balk at enacting such
changes, Imrédy stressed the need to revise the constitution and
modernize parliamentary procedures. At a ministerial council on
15 November, he may even have ventured to "think aloud" about
the need for a "putsch" to achieve the constitutional reforms he
deemed necessary.[45]

Such talk had the effect of resurrecting essentially the same
political grouping that had risen to challenge Gömbös in 1936. By
late November Count Bethlen was the tacit leader of a group consisting of Social Democrats, Smallholders, and various other small
parties, as well as a sizeable number of government party dissidents. Political tension built up over the next two months, and in
mid-January Bethlen and his colleagues finally submitted to Horthy a memorandum calling for the dismissal of Imrédy.[46] The
prime minister was accused, among other things, of demagoguery,
incompetence, and social radicalism. His apparent intention of
introducing political reforms characteristic of the one-party systems of Italy and Germany would be disastrous, for it would inevitably place the country at the mercy of National Socialist
Germany. In the end it would mean the abandonment of an
"independent Hungarian political will."

In fact, Horthy had been losing confidence in Imrédy, but he
procrastinated until startling information was given to him in mid-
February. Two of the dissidents who had been diligently searching
through birth records for information about Imrédy's ancestors
had uncovered documents suggesting that one of his great grand-
mothers had been Jewish. Here was the unspeakable nightmare
of the zealous anti-Semite: evidence of a Jewish relative, however

remote in the family tree. When Horthy confronted him with the evidence, Imrédy acknowledged the untenability of his position and resigned.

As a successor to Imrédy, Horthy chose Pál Teleki, whose opposition to right radicalism was well known to all political observers in both Germany and Hungary. In fact, Teleki shared many of Kánya's proclivities and assumptions: suspicion of the military, reluctance to become too closely tied to Germany, belief in the ultimate victory of the Western powers in any future European war. It was Teleki's aim to pull Hungary back from the brink of a complete "German orientation." However, he was realistic enough to acknowledge that some sort of cooperation with Germany, or at least the appearance of cooperation, was unavoidable, since Hungary's room for maneuver was very small indeed. In short, as one historian has ably put it, he wished "to follow the German line only to the extent that it did not endanger the country's sovereignty, compromise national honor, unduly discredit the government in the eyes of the British leaders, and as long as it did not involve Hungary in the European war on Germany's side."[47]

That Horthy should have designated as his prime minister an individual with impeccable anti-Nazi credentials reflected once again his ambivalent feelings about cooperation with the Germans. Since 1936 there had been a remarkable inconsistency in his policies. At certain times, when it appeared that Germany would assist Hungary in regaining some of her lost territories, he showed a distinct eagerness to cooperate intimately with Berlin; at other times, notably in August 1938, he became convinced of the need to dissociate Hungary's policy from that of Germany.

In the fall of 1938 a similar inconsistency can be detected in Horthy's views. He was apparently quite willing to support the new policy symbolized by Darányi's visit to Berlin in October, but at the same time he shared the widespread feeling that Hitler had cheated Hungary out of her just territorial rewards in Czechoslovakia. Though a self-proclaimed anti-Semite, Horthy was disturbed by the manner in which the Jews were being treated in Germany. In the wake of the "night of the broken glass," an outpouring of violence against German Jews on 10 November, Horthy privately deplored Germany's handling of the Jewish question as "brutal" and "inhuman."[48]

Horthy's ire against the Germans reached a peak early in 1939.

His conversations in this period with American and British diplomats were peppered with caustic criticisms of Hitler and the Nazi regime. In an emotional scene at a diplomatic reception in early January, he suggested that Hitler was a "madman" who was bringing the world to chaos. The regent even speculated about the benefits of an assassination of the Führer, which in his opinion would bring in its wake a collapse of the Nazi regime. When questioned about Hungary's response in case German troops should advance across Hungary, Horthy replied: "We would fight them to the last ditch and start a European war."[49]

Horthy's emotional outbursts notwithstanding, the Hungarian government did not attempt to renege on its earlier promise to draw closer to the Axis. In part this was due to the influence of Count István Csáky, whom Imrédy had chosen to replace Kánya as foreign minister. Csáky's career as a diplomat stretched back to the early interwar period, when he had been a member of Hungary's delegation to the peace conference in Paris. Over the years he had served in a variety of diplomatic posts, the most important of which was that of Kánya's *chef de cabinet* from 1935 to 1939. After 1936, however, he had become increasingly disenchanted with Kánya's "free hand" policy, and, as has been seen, from time to time had worked behind the scenes to draw Hungary closer to the Axis powers by assuring the Germans that Hungary supported their plans for territorial expansion in Austria and Czechoslovakia. Thus, when the time came in the fall of 1938 to replace Kánya with someone more acceptable to the Germans and more in tune with the new orientation of Hungarian foreign policy, Csáky seemed a logical choice.

It is true that as foreign minister Csáky would on a number of occasions, especially in conversations with the Italians, privately voice what seemed to be a genuine fear and dislike of Germany. But, like Imrédy after the Munich crisis, Csáky was convinced that Germany would have the decisive voice in East Central Europe for the foreseeable future. In the circumstances he believed that there was no possible alternative to a policy of close identification with the Axis, and that in fact such a pro-Axis policy might well bring concrete rewards in the form of new territorial gains in Romania and perhaps elsewhere. In a speech shortly after his appointment, Csáky thus spoke effusively of Hungary's "unshakeable fidelity to the Axis Powers." The promises made by Darányi were soon ful-

filled: the decision to adhere to the Anti-Comintern Pact was announced to the public on 13 January, and withdrawal from the
League was promised for May.

In an attempt to counteract to a certain extent the growing preponderance of Germany in the Rome-Berlin Axis, the Hungarians
did seek in this period to emphasize their long-standing relationship with Italy. Budapest's decision to join the Anti-Comintern
Pact and leave the League was greeted enthusiastically by Ciano
when he visited Hungary in December. Observing a certain
amount of anxiety among the Hungarians, Ciano melodramatically
declared that Italy would "never permit Germany to act towards
Hungary as she acted over Austria."[51] Both sides agreed that an
attempt should be made to draw Yugoslavia into a bloc with Hungary and Italy, though this could not have an overtly anti-German
flavor.

In the continuing Hungarian quest for annexation of Ruthenia,
however, it was the good will of Hitler and not Mussolini that had
to be cultivated. In late 1938 Hitler's plans for Eastern Europe
began to crystallize. The evidence indicates that the earlier idea
of using Ruthenia as a dangling bait between Hungary and Romania was abandoned by Hitler in December when he learned that
King Carol was responsible for the murder of Corneliu Codreanu,
a prominent Romanian right-wing extremist.[52] In the same period
a German commission to study the economic and strategic potential of Ruthenia concluded that, because of the rugged terrain, a
highway to the Ukraine could not be built. Moreover, the province
seemed economically worthless.[53] These developments apparently
led Hitler to decide that Ruthenia should be allowed to fall into
Hungary's hands at some future point, in conjunction with Germany's seizure of the rest of Bohemia.

This plan was adumbrated by Hitler in a conversation with Csáky
in mid-January 1939. After emphasizing that in the Munich crisis
he had been striving for a "territorial settlement" of the Czechoslovak question, but, because of Hungary's failure to cooperate,
had been forced to accept an "ethnographic settlement," Hitler
suggested that a "politico-territorial solution" was still possible
in the future. However, this would require "perfect team play" by
Poland, Hungary, and Germany. In certain territories Germany
had no interest of her own, and she was "too wise and too generous" not to give each partner its proper share. Everything would

have to be planned perfectly and carried out "as efficiently as possible, without crises and like lightning." In this way the problem could be solved without bloodshed, since the Western democracies would not have time to make difficulties, and in any case Germany's western fortifications would prevent any intervention.[54]

There could have been little doubt in Csáky's mind that, unless Hitler was being deliberately deceptive, Germany intended at some point to seize the rest of Bohemia, expecting Hungary to move simultaneously to annex Ruthenia. Göring apparently confirmed this to Sztójay during Csáky's visit: "Things will work out for Hungary," he said. "Then you'll be able to round out your earlier territorial gains." Csáky was warned, however, that Hungary was not unilaterally to spark a conflict on the Czechoslovak border.[55]

The Hungarians were not informed at this time what pretext Hitler might use to provoke a crisis, although in February Sztójay learned from a source close to Göring that the operation might take place as early as the spring.[56] There is other evidence, however, from which the conclusion can be drawn that by mid-February Hitler had decided to exploit Slovak discontent and provoke a crisis sometime in March.[57]

In the two months after Csáky's visit to Germany, the Hungarians took a number of diplomatic steps to prepare for a military operation against Ruthenia. To strengthen Yugoslavia's reluctance to intervene in such a conflict, Stojadinović was informed late in January that Hungary was prepared to sign a pact of nonaggression.[58] In contrast to events in the previous autumn, however, no major move was made to coordinate plans with Poland. In fact, the Hungarians were becoming suspicious of Poland's intentions in Ruthenia; a report in February suggested that the Poles themselves might now be contemplating the annexation of Ruthenia.[59] Thus, a certain coolness in Polish-Hungarian relations developed in the winter of 1939, though Colonel Beck continued his attempt to convince the Romanians to acquiesce in a Hungarian occupation of Ruthenia.

The most surprising element in Hungary's diplomatic soundings in February and early March was the persistence with which Budapest emphasized to the Germans her concern that deteriorating political and economic conditions in Ruthenia might lead to an "explosion" requiring Hungarian intervention. Seemingly oblivious to Hitler's suggestion that Hungary, Germany, and Poland would have to "work together like a football team" and that Hungary should not unilaterally provoke a conflict, Csáky expressed the hope that Germany would raise no objections if Hungary took decisive action. He assured the Germans that their economic and transportation interests would be scrupulously honored.[60] The response from the somewhat bewildered Ribbentrop was that Germany did not consider the Ruthenian question ripe for solution, and that the advice given earlier to Csáky should be heeded.[61]

One explanation for Hungary's somewhat perplexing policy in this period is that Csáky may simply have misunderstood the meaning of Hitler's hints in January, but it seems more likely that the new prime minister, Pál Teleki, was exerting his influence on Hungary's foreign policy. It had been a fundamental principle of Teleki's political thought that in carrying out its revisionist policy, Hungary should strive to minimize any cooperation with Nazi Germany. He reasoned that in the long run it would be difficult, perhaps impossible, to keep any revisionist gains that bore the stigma of having been abetted and approved by Hitler. Teleki strongly favored annexation of Ruthenia, but he hoped to achieve this in a way that emphasized Hungary's independence of action. He thus much preferred a unilateral Hungarian action that had Germany's approval but that was not carried out simultaneously with a German move into Bohemia.[62]

Partly out of scholarly conviction, partly with the hope of persuading West Europeans of the validity of Hungary's claims, Teleki attempted to depict a Hungarian occupation of Ruthenia as an "organic" process, a move that would bring the political boundaries into greater conformity with the economic and geophysical realities.[63] In early March Hungarian diplomats were instructed to point out to the German and British governments that the Ruthenians had apparently decided to solve their economic problems by a program of ruthless cutting of the forests. This would have a catastrophic economic and ecological impact in the Danubian Basin, for in time the whole of Ruthenia would become a *karst* and parts of Hungary would be swampland or barren deserts. For Hungary the headwater region of the Tisza river was thus as vital as the source region of the Blue Nile was to the British.[64]

When this argument, drawn from the realm of geographical science, failed to make much of an impression, Teleki hit upon the novel idea of purchasing Ruthenia. On 6 March František Chval-kovský, the Czechoslovak foreign minister, professed a willingness to consider this possibility,[65] but this initiative was quickly under-mined by the deterioration of political relations between Czechs and Slovaks. By early March almost all prominent Slovaks had be-come convinced of the need to establish an independent Slo-vakia.[66] Alarmed by this development, Prague moved vigorously on 9 and 10 March to thwart the Slovak separatists; martial law was declared, several key figures were arrested or dismissed, and some loyal troops were sent to Bratislava.

This was the situation that Hitler had been awaiting and his agents had been working to create. On 12 March he summoned Sztójay and declared that "the spirit of Beneš" had gained the upper hand again in Czechoslovakia. Since this could not be toler-ated, he suggested that Hungary now impose its own solution in Ruthenia. Hitler did not inform Sztójay that German troops would soon be entering Bohemia, but he assured him that should the Czechs oppose the Hungarian move, he would immediately de-stroy them. However, the Hungarians had to move swiftly and restrict their activities to Ruthenia. For the time being, at least, Slovakia was not to be attacked.[67]

This message was carried by Sztójay to Budapest on a special plane provided by the Führer. However, the Hungarians, who had been through this kind of thing before, must have suspected by 10 March that Hitler planned an imminent move. Unsure that Hit-ler's earlier hints that he would approve a Hungarian annexation of Ruthenia would now prove accurate, Teleki called a ministerial council on the tenth. At his urging it was decided that if German troops entered Bohemia (or worse, Slovakia), or if Slovakia de-clared its independence, Hungary would move immediately into Ruthenia, even if Germany disapproved. If necessary, Germany would be confronted with a *fait accompli*.[68]

The message from Hitler that Sztójay delivered on the thirteenth thus dovetailed with Hungary's plans and obviated the need for a unilateral Hungarian action. Hitler's initiative struck a particu-larly responsive chord in Horthy, who dispatched an exuberant letter of gratitude in which he assured the German leader that he would never forget "this proof of friendship."[69] However, since only a handful of people at the highest levels of the Hungarian government were aware of Hitler's message, the belief developed among many officials and the public in general that Hungary, in moving to annex Ruthenia, was acting completely independently of Germany and even in opposition to her wishes. Since this was one way of creating a basis for resistance in Hungary to German expansionism, Teleki did nothing publicly to dispel this illusion, though he told the true story to British visitors.[70]

The Hungarians moved quickly in the next few days. Fighting between Czechoslovak and Ruthenian troops and the resulting chaotic conditions provided the pretext for an initial border incursion by a Hungarian unit on the fourteenth. An ultimatum, so severely worded as to be unacceptable, was sent to Prague just hours after Slovakia declared its independence on the fourteenth. The next day Hungarian troops thrust into Ruthenia in large numbers, encountering little opposition because the Czechoslovak troops had withdrawn into Slovakia. By the seventeenth Hungarian bicycle units, having raced at top speed across the province, reached the Polish border, where they were joyously greeted by their Polish comrades. By this time also German troops had completed their occupation of rump Bohemia, which was now absorbed into the German Reich.

With the annexation of Bohemia by Germany and Ruthenia by Hungary, the Danubian crisis came to an end. Austria had disappeared from the map, Czechoslovakia had been dismembered. Of the countries in the upper regions of the Danubian area, only Hungary had emerged seemingly unscathed, indeed strengthened by the annexation of new territory. There was, however, a certain hollowness in Hungary's revisionist "triumphs." The long coveted "common border" was now a reality, but, as events would demonstrate, it was a common border with a country that was soon to join Austria and Czechoslovakia as a victim of German expansionism.

Chapter 10

Diplomacy and Irredentism: The Hungarian Dilemma in the Danubian Crisis

In late 1939, as the Danubian crisis merged into a major European war, Hungary's position was difficult but not entirely hopeless. There were those in the Hungarian government, most notably the regent, who remained convinced that Germany could never triumph in a European military conflict and who were determined to pursue a Hungarian policy of strict neutrality. But the Hungarian revisionist movement in the preceding two decades had taken on so dynamic and relentless a character that it proved impossible for most Hungarians, including Horthy, to reject any opportunity for further territorial aggrandizement, even though it had to be clear that that could be accomplished only in close cooperation with National Socialist Germany. By 1941 Hungary would be able to regain additional territory from Romania and Yugoslavia, but the price that would have to be paid—including a final break with Great Britain and the United States—was enormous.

It was Hungary's actions in the last months of the Danubian crisis and during the following two years that would later preoccupy historians who attempted to pass judgement on Hungary's role in the events leading to World War II. The portrait of Hungary that has emerged in much of the historical literature has been distinctly unflattering. Hungary's rulers, one eminent scholar wrote in the last year of the war, were the "agents and principal promoters of German imperialism."[1] The image evoked by Winston Churchill of Hungary as a "beast of prey" or "vulture" feeding on the carcass of Czechoslovakia has become a cliché employed by many Western historians.[2] Yet a close study of the Danubian

crisis suggests that critical interpretations of this kind largely fail
to take into account the complexity of the foreign and domestic
problems confronting Hungarian statesmen in the interwar period.
This set of problems, which might be termed the "revisionist
dilemma," ultimately made it impossible for Hungarian statesmen
to devise policies that would promote certain unanimously accepted foreign policy goals but would not have undesirable repercussions in the domestic life of the country.

At the heart of the problem that Hungary's political leaders
faced in the interwar period was the severe peace treaty imposed
by the victors. This is not the place to examine the manner in
which the decisions were made to rely more on strategic and economic than ethnographic considerations in drawing the boundaries
between Hungary and her Successor States. How unfortunate it
was that the peacemakers paid so little heed to the warning of the
British statesman, Lord Castlereaugh, given a century earlier, that
the value of strategic borders should not be overestimated. For the
peacemakers at Paris, especially the French, the overwhelming
desire was to create a barrier of new states to oppose future German expansion. As a result, little consideration was given to the
potential problems that would be caused because the political
boundaries did not conform well to the ethnic frontiers.[3]

So blatant were the inequities of the Trianon Treaty that the
more moderate conservatives, as well as those Hungarians of
democratic or liberal persuasion, had no alternative but to give
open or tacit support to the chauvinists in the campaign for treaty
revision. Had the peace terms imposed on the Magyars been less
severe, there doubtless still would have been an irredentist movement, but the balance between the moderates and extremists may
well have been tilted in favor of the former, and the inclination
and ability of Kálmán Kánya and even Horthy to seek peaceful,
diplomatic solutions to Danubian problems would have been
strengthened. The dimensions of the "desperate dilemma" in
which so many Hungarians found themselves was recognized by
Thomas Masaryk, the great Czechoslovak humanist. When questioned what he would do if he were a Hungarian, Masaryk candidly
admitted that he too would lend his support to the call for moderate territorial revision.[4]

It is therefore not surprising that irredentism was imbedded so deeply in the thinking of politically conscious Hungarians in the era between the wars. As irredentists, however, Hungary's prominent statesmen, notably Horthy, Teleki, Bethlen, and Kánya, suffered from a number of handicaps. In an era of mass political movements that made skillful use of the instruments of modern technology to indoctrinate the masses, Hungary's leaders attempted to cling to the methods and strategies of nineteenth-century conservatism. Such was their authority and political skill that after the collapse of Béla Kun's regime in 1919 they were able to restore much of the prewar political and social order. Far more difficult, however, was the challenge of maintaining domestic stability and the established political order while at the same time formulating a foreign policy that would be effective in the program of territorial revisionism. Part of the problem might be termed psychological. Older men like Horthy and Kánya had grown to manhood in a time when irredentism was, in the view of most Magyars, a disruptive and scurrilous activity pursued by such "backward" national groups as the Serbs and Romanians. But the events of World War I and its aftermath dramatically altered the situation, and the Magyars now found themselves forced to emulate the Balkan irredentists they had long scorned. For men like Horthy and Kánya, who had served proudly in the military and political establishment of one of Europe's great powers, this was indeed a severe psychological jolt.

Some Hungarians, notably Gyula Gömbös and to an extent Admiral Horthy, plunged into the irredentist movement with zeal, reveling in the clandestine meetings and the exotic nature of their enterprises. Most Hungarian conservatives, however, viewed many of these activities with distaste, if not repugnance. The instinct of the conservatives was to trust in traditional diplomacy rather than risky operations carried out by paramilitary bands or the regular army. This attitude was clearly expressed by Pál Teleki in 1921 when, in rejecting plans for the incitement of civil war in Slovakia and Hungarian intervention, he asserted that such a policy was like playing *va banque*, that is, risking everything in an operation very unlikely to succeed. This reliance on statecraft and an accompanying suspicion of the military establishment were to characterize the policies of both Teleki and Kánya during the Danubian crisis.

An important element of the dilemma confronting Hungary's

conservatives in the interwar period was the inadequacy of a revisionist policy based on traditional diplomacy. A guiding principle
of the conservatives was that just as the great powers had sanctioned major territorial changes in Eastern Europe after World
War I, the time would come when the great powers would readjust
these frontiers. Territorial changes brought on by unilateral Hungarian military action would likely be ephemeral; those achieved
with the consent of at least a few of the great powers would be
inherently more durable. A fundamental assumption of this approach, however, was that Hungary's case for territorial revision
was so strong and her strategic position and anti-Communist orientation so important that eventually a number of great powers
would become her patrons. In the Danubian crisis this assumption
was shown to be based on a set of illusions.

The events of 1936–39 demonstrated that Hungary's national
interests, as defined by her conservative leadership, simply did not
coincide with those of any of the great powers. A review of the
policies of the great powers in this period demonstrates that, for
the most part, those powers whose assistance Budapest would have
welcomed showed scant interest in Danubian Europe, or pursued
a policy that seemed inimical to certain cherished Hungarian beliefs or institutions; whereas those powers that did proffer support
were typically regarded by Hungary's leaders as undesirable allies.

The United States and the Soviet Union, the two countries that
at the end of World War II would emerge as the dominant powers
in Europe and the world, played almost no role in the Danubian
crisis. Ironically, despite the bitterness and hostility that had characterized Soviet-Hungarian relations in the interwar period, the
foreign policy of the U.S.S.R. in the Danubian crisis seemed at
times to be remarkably friendly toward Hungary. For example, in
the aftermath of the Austrian Anschluss the commissar for foreign
affairs, Maxim Litvinov, privately assured the Hungarians of his
country's interest in the maintenance of Hungary's independence.
During the autumn of 1938 hints were dropped by Soviet diplomats that Moscow preferred that Ruthenia fall into the hands of
Hungary rather than of Poland or Germany.[5] But the Hungarian
leadership had no intention of soliciting the support of Moscow.
Such a policy would have been anathema not only to Horthy but
to most of Hungary's political establishment. Hungary's statesmen
shared with their Polish and Romanian counterparts a fear of the

consequences of abetting the intervention of the Soviet Union in the diplomatic affairs of Central and Eastern Europe.

By contrast, Hungary's leadership during the Danubian crisis would have welcomed the active intervention of the United States. Of this, however, there was little likelihood. The Neutrality Acts of 1935, 1936, and 1937 were striking reflections of the prevailing isolationist mood in America. Still, certain Hungarians were reluctant to abandon all hope that this "sleeping giant" could be awakened and play a key role in the resolution of the Danubian crisis. Though the United States seemed remote and aloof in the 1930s, Americans who had participated in the deliberations of the Paris Peace Conference in 1919 and 1920 had displayed a greater sympathy for Hungary than the British, French, or Italians. If another congress of the great powers were convened to deal with the critical situation that had developed in the 1930s, Hungary, it seemed, could only benefit by America's participation. Thus, in early September 1938 Regent Horthy, fearful that a European conflagration was imminent, privately suggested that the crisis be resolved at a conference of the great powers chaired by President Roosevelt. Of course, nothing came of this at the time, and the hoped-for intervention of the United States in the affairs of Danubian Europe would come only years later, by which time such men as Horthy, Kánya, and Bethlen were no longer directing the affairs of their country.

Of the European powers most directly involved in the affairs of Eastern Europe, France proved to be least sympathetic to Hungary in the interwar period. The abortive French-Hungarian agreement of 1920 greatly poisoned the relations of the two countries, for many Hungarians felt that the French government had used the negotiations as a ploy to persuade Hungary to sign the Treaty of Trianon. Before long, France emerged as the champion of the Little Entente, encouraging Hungary's neighbors to stand firm against all changes in the territorial status quo. The only Hungarians who continued to hope that Paris might "switch horses" in the future were monarchists like Gusztáv Gratz, who as late as 1937 and 1938 was still striving to create a "Danubian Triangle" that would win French support. But most Hungarians by that time agreed with Miklós Horthy that in the past their country had received "only bad things from that dirty crowd."[6] This suspicion seemed to be confirmed during the Munich crisis, for even as French statesmen were urging Prague to make territorial concessions to Germany, they were in agreement that Czechoslovakia should not be forced to cede any territory to Hungary.

Italy's policy toward Hungary was superficially a mirror image of France's, but in reality Hungary derived few benefits from the cordial relationship that Mussolini and Bethlen had fashioned in the late 1920s. The most glowing support of Hungarian irredentism was sounded in many of the Duce's speeches, but this bombastic rhetoric was never translated into an effective and coherent Italian policy in Danubian Europe. A fundamental military weakness and absence of skillful statecraft relegated Italy to the role of junior partner of Nazi Germany in the Axis. Thus, despite continued promises of support for Hungary and vague schemes for building a bloc of states that might represent a barrier to German expansion eastward, by 1939 Italy had largely abandoned its earlier aspirations for a sphere of influence in Danubian Europe. Moreover, the vacillating policies of Mussolini and Ciano threatened by 1939 to lead Hungary into dangerous and undesirable military adventures. It is characteristic that during the dismemberment of Czechoslovakia in March 1939, Ciano was eagerly suggesting to the Hungarians that plans should now be made for a similar partitioning of Yugoslavia.[7] Yet only a few months earlier Ciano had sketched for the Hungarians a plan for a possible anti-German bloc in which Yugoslavia would be an important partner of Hungary and Italy.

Because many Hungarian statesmen suspected that Italy would never be a reliable patron, they increasingly turned to Great Britain and Germany in the 1930s, with the hope of garnering support for a general remaking of the map of Danubian Europe in Hungary's favor. If London and Berlin could agree on a program of "peaceful revision," Hungary's conservatives would not have to fear the outbreak of war or the hostility of France and her allies in Eastern Europe. In the mid-1930s many of Hungary's most important statesmen, including Bethlen and Horthy, believed that Great Britain could be persuaded to undertake an initiative of this kind. Sufficiently remote not to pose any danger to Hungarian independence, yet supposedly dedicated to "fair play" in international affairs, Britain seemed the ideal sponsor for the Hungarian cause. This favorable image was enhanced by the strong sympathy for Hungary in British financial circles and in the British Parliament, particularly the House of Lords.

In the months leading up to the Munich crisis, Imrédy, Kánya, and Horthy based their foreign policy on the assumption that Britain would in time be amenable to certain peaceful changes in the status quo in favor of Germany and Hungary, but would intervene militarily if these changes were effected by force. It was thus most disillusioning to discover that London was willing to submit to Hitler's demands in order to avert war, but that there was no inclination to support Hungary's territorial claims, which the Hungarian leadership felt had as much validity as those of Germany.

Indeed, it became quite clear in September 1938 that in their foreign policy and strategic thinking British statesmen assigned a very low priority to Hungary. Neville Chamberlain's famous description of Czechoslovakia as a "far away country" inhabited by "people of whom we know nothing" applied also to Hungary. The evidence in the preceding pages of this study testifies to the amorphous nature of British policy towards Danubian Europe and the sometimes striking ignorance of the affairs of that area, displayed not only by Chamberlain and Halifax but even by those Foreign Office officials whose duty it was to keep track of events in that part of Europe. How remarkable it is to discover that discussions of where to "draw the line" against German political expansion in Eastern Europe began in the British government only in the spring of 1938.

It was during the Munich crisis and its immediate aftermath that Hungarian statesmen discovered that their hopes for British support had been misplaced. Most discouraging to individuals like Imrédy was the apparently cynical manner in which Halifax and Chamberlain persuaded Hungary to continue a moderate policy. Hungary's claims, the British leaders promised, would be given full consideration at the proper time. Yet once the crisis subsided in October 1938, Chamberlain and Halifax in effect turned their backs on Hungary, preferring to withdraw as much as possible from the tangled affairs of Danubian Europe. These events had a shattering impact on many Hungarians who had trusted in Britain, and it is not surprising that certain individuals, such as Béla Imrédy, should have undergone a remarkable metamorphosis in the aftermath of the Munich crisis.

The failure of Great Britain to fulfill the role assigned to it by optimistic Hungarian revisionists made the forging of a satisfactory relationship with a powerful, revived Germany most difficult. One of the great ironies of Hungary's role in the Danubian crisis is that if Germany's government at the time had been one of the traditional right, Hungary's conservative statesmen would probably have been willing to pursue a more dynamic, aggressive policy in cooperation with Berlin. In one sense A. J. P. Taylor was perhaps right: Hungary's traditional political establishment felt a special affinity for a conservative, authoritarian Germany. Moreover, German culture had been widely admired and imitated in Hungary in the late nineteenth and early twentieth centuries. One can speculate that Hungarians like Bethlen, Horthy, and Kánya would have been willing to work closely with a Germany dominated by the likes of General Seeckt or Franz von Papen. The expansion of that kind of Germany into Eastern Europe might well have been welcomed by Hungary's conservatives, for they would have had no reason to expect that their political authority in Hungary, or Magyar hegemony in Danubian Europe, would be threatened.

But the Germany of the Nazi era was not one for which the conservative Hungarian establishment felt much sympathy or ideological affinity. Briefly stated, Hitler did not seem to be a twentieth-century Bismarck. Intimate cooperation with National Socialist Germany was viewed with great distaste by most Hungarian conservatives, who feared that Hungary's independence might be threatened and that Hitler might someday assist the Hungarian radical rightists in their effort to supplant the traditional political order. Kálmán Kánya thus persisted in his "free hand" policy, a basic tenet of which was that Hungary would not ally fully with any of the great powers, but would attempt to preserve a freedom of maneuver in European international relations. But Hitler's determination to force a crisis over Czechoslovakia in 1938 made it impossible for Hungary to continue to straddle the fence. The decision that was made, however reluctantly, by Horthy, Kánya, and Imrédy, was to decline Hitler's suggestion that they move militarily against Czechoslovakia and annex Slovakia and Ruthenia as a reward.

The Kiel visit provides important evidence to refute A. J. P. Taylor's argument that Hungary in this period was an "agent" of

German imperialism. Indeed, it can be argued that Horthy's refusal to join in attacking Czechoslovakia in September 1938 was a
contribution to developments that, in the long run, were harmful
to German national interests. Had the Hungarians fully cooperated
with Hitler by provoking incidents in Slovakia and applying military intimidation against Prague, the tension in Central Europe
might have become sufficiently high to prompt Hitler to launch his
attack as planned at the end of September. With Poland and Hungary joining the fray, Czechoslovakia could not have held out very
long, and there is no reason to believe that France and England
would have moved even as vigorously as they did in September
1939. In time the Western powers might have reconciled themselves to the disappearance of Czechoslovakia.[8] In that case, Hungary would have reincorporated all of Slovakia and Ruthenia and
established the full "common border" with Poland on the Carpathians.

In the three years of the Danubian crisis, the men who directed
Hungarian foreign affairs struggled to mold a policy that would
preserve the country's independence, maintain domestic stability
and constitutional practices, and broaden Hungary's freedom of
maneuver in the diplomatic arena, so that if the opportunity arose
to regain some lost territory without unacceptable risks, Hungary
would be prepared to exploit it. However, the nature of European
international relations, the fact that Hungary's national interests
did not coincide sufficiently with those of the great powers, and
the clash of rightist political ideologies in Hungary made this task
nearly impossible to fulfill. In these circumstances even Kálmán
Kánya, one of the most skillful diplomats in interwar Eastern
Europe, could not resolve the difficult "revisionist dilemma" confronting Hungarian statesmen.

It is true that the men who guided Hungary through the Danubian crisis were not without their foibles and shortcomings. Their
exaggerated nationalism and zeal for a reassertion of Magyar hegemony in the Danubian Basin gravely complicated the problem of
achieving a modicum of international harmony in that part of
Europe. The persistence in Hungarian society of certain myths
and illusions, such as the idea that the Slovaks would docilely
accept "liberation" by the Hungarians, obfuscated many key issues
in Hungarian foreign policy. But given the unwise manner in
which the boundaries of Danubian Europe had been drawn in

1919 and 1920 and the complexity of the problems with which the conservative Hungarian leadership had to cope, it is difficult, even in retrospect, to imagine some other Hungarian foreign policy in the Danubian crisis that would have better served Hungarian and European interests, and that Hungarian statesmen could reasonably have been expected to pursue. Moreover, when one takes into account the cynicism and indecisiveness of the British in the late 1930's, the pusillanimity of the French, and the militant opportunism of the Poles, the rather cautious, restrained policies of Kálmán Kánya and his colleagues would seem, on the whole, to compare favorably.

Notes

Chapter 1

1. Gábor Vermes, "The October Revolution in Hungary: From Károlyi to Kun," in *Hungary in Revolution, 1918–1919*, p. 31.

2. Hungary, Parliament, *Az 1910–1915. évi országgyűlés képviselőházának naplója*, 41:292, cited hereafter as *Képviselőházi napló*.

3. Cited in Lee Congdon, "Endre Ady's Summons to National Regeneration in Hungary, 1900–1919," *Slavic Review* 33 (1974): 321.

4. See, i.a., György Ránki, *Emlékiratok és valóság Magyarország második világháborús szerepéről*, p. 18.

5. For details consult Harry Hanak, "The Government, the Foreign Office, and Austria-Hungary, 1914–1918," *Slavonic and East European Review* 47 (1969): 161–97.

6. For detailed treatment of foreign policy problems in the Károlyi period, see Tibor Hajdú, *Az 1918-as magyarországi polgári demokratikus forradalom*, pp. 156–94.

7. For the sake of convenience, the term *Ruthenia* is used in this study.

8. C. A. Macartney and A. W. Palmer, *Independent Eastern Europe*, pp. 123–26.

9. The most recent study of Hungary's role at the peace conference is Zsuzsa Nagy, *A párizsi békekonferencia és Magyarország, 1918–1919*. Older but still useful is Francis Deák's *Hungary at the Paris Peace Conference*.

10. The phrase is that of a delegate to the Hungarian National Assembly, Jenő Karafiáth, in December 1920. Francis Deák and Dezső Ujváry, eds., *Papers and Documents Relating to the Foreign Relations of Hungary*, 1:1002, hereafter cited as *Papers and Documents*.

11. The "Lenin Boys" were a band of escaped criminals and other unsavory elements who for a time were permitted to conduct a campaign of terror against selected aristocrats and bourgeois politicians. For details, see Rudolf L. Tökés, *Béla Kun and the Hungarian Soviet Republic* (New York: Frederick A. Praeger, 1967), pp. 159–60.

12. The phrase is that of Istvan Deak in his "Budapest and the Hungarian Revolutions of 1918–1919," *Slavonic and East European Review* 46 (1968): 129.

13. Arno J. Mayer, *Dynamics of Counterrevolution in Europe, 1870–1956*, p. 53.

14. Walter Kolarz, *Myths and Realities in Eastern Europe*, pp. 86, 98.

15. Jenő Horváth, *Az országgyarapítás története, 1920–1941*, p. 6. For a critical view of this myth, see József Galántai, "Trianon és a reviziós propaganda," in *A magyar nacionalizmus kialakulása és története*, pp. 290–92. This volume is cited hereafter as *Hungarian Nationalism*.

16. Paul Teleki, *The Evolution of Hungary and its Place in European History*, p. 134.

17. Gyula Gömbös, *Egy magyar vezérkari tiszt biráló feljegyzései a forradalomról és ellenforradalomról*, pp. 5–8.

18. For a further analysis of this myth, see Galántai, *Hungarian Nationalism*, pp. 290–95.

19. Albert Apponyi et al., *Justice for Hungary*, pp. 14–15, 19–20.

20. Deák, *Hungary at the Paris Peace Conference*, p. 542.

21. Apponyi, *Justice for Hungary*, p. 15.

22. On this point see the perceptive comments of George Barany in his essay "Hungary: From Aristocratic to Proletarian Nationalism," in *Nationalism in Eastern Europe*, pp. 290–92.

23. István Bethlen, *Bethlen István gróf beszédei és irásai*, 2:35, cited hereafter as *Bethlen Speeches*.

24. At various times in the 1920s, Yugoslav dinars, Czech crowns, and French francs were forged to help finance the revisionist campaign. See Dezső Nemes, ed., *Iratok az ellenforradalom történetéhez, 1919–1945*, 3:80–81 (n. 3), cited hereafter as *IET*.

25. Gyula Szekfű, "Trianon revíziója és a történetirás," *Magyar Szemle* 12 (1931): 328–37.

26. Peter F. Sugar, ed., *Native Fascism in the Successor States, 1918–1945*, p. 150.

27. For the racist and right-wing content of university textbooks, see Miklós Mann, "Politikai propaganda az ellenforradalmi rendszer történelemtankönyveiben," *Századok* 100 (1966): 962–68.

28. István Imre Mocsy, "Radicalization and Counterrevolution: Magyar Refugees from the Successor States and their Role in Hungary, 1918–1921" (Ph.D. diss., University of California, Los Angeles, 1973), p. 162.

29. See István Bethlen's request to the Allies for supplies and equipment for a 20,000-man army to overthrow the Kun government, 17 July 1919. Department of State records, National Archives microcopy M820, roll 214, frames 705–7. Also, Gyula Juhász, *Magyarország külpolitikája, 1919–1945*, pp. 29–30.

30. Mocsy, "Radicalization and Counterrevolution," p. 162.

31. The term "radical rightists" is used here in preference to "fascists" or "counterrevolutionaries" (see Mayer, *Dynamics of Counterrevolution*, pp. 59–85), two terms that could easily lead to misunderstandings if applied to the Hungarian scene.

32. This descriptive term was coined by Wolfgang Sauer in his "National Socialism: Totalitarianism or Fascism?," *American Historical Review* 63 (1967): 411.

33. A good example of the conservatives who were appalled by the illegal and violent methods of the "special detachments" is Anton Lehar, whose misgivings were recorded in his memoirs, *Erinnerungen: Gegenrevolution und Restaurationsversuche in Ungarn, 1918–1921*.

34. Many of the conservatives also supported Horthy in the mistaken belief that he would facilitate a restoration of King Karl in the near future. See Miklós Szinai, "Bethlen és az ellenforradalmi rendszer politikai konszolidációja, 1919–1922," *Valóság* 15 (1972): 14–16.

35. Juhász, *Magyarország külpolitikája*, pp. 53–56. A unique glimpse of some

of Horthy's fantastic plans and conspiracies in this period is offered in Lehar, *Erinnerungen*, pp. 159–69.

36. Ferenc Boros, *Magyar-csehszlovák kapcsolatok 1918–1921-ben*, pp. 22–23.

37. Katalin G. Soós, *Magyar-bajor-osztrák titkos tárgyalások és együttmű-ködés, 1920–1921*, pp. 5–41. For a discussion of the role of the military in the foreign policy making process in this period, see Thomas L. Sakmyster, "Army Officers and Foreign Policy in Interwar Hungary, 1918–41," *Journal of Contemporary History* 10 (1975): 20–22.

38. Eva Balogh, "The Road to Isolation: Hungary, the Great Powers, and the Successor States, 1919–1920" (Ph.D. diss., Yale University, 1974), pp. 433–34.

39. For the doubts of Kánya and Teleki in this matter, see the report of Theodor Hornbostel, Austrian chargé d'affaires in Budapest, 6 August 1920, Austrian State Archives, Neues Politisches Archiv, K883/567–70, hereafter cited as NPA, followed by carton and item number.

40. Loránt Tilkovszky, *Pál Teleki*, p. 22.

41. Boros, *Magyar-csehszlovák kapcsolatok*, pp. 149–50.

42. Horthy told the British representative in Budapest, Thomas Hohler, that "it was in Great Britain alone that he and his country had complete confidence." Hohler's report of 6 January 1920, *Documents on British Foreign Policy, 1919–1939*, ed. E. L. Woodward and Rohan Butler, first series, vol. 6, no. 410, hereafter cited as *DBFP*, followed by series, volume, and document number.

43. Juhász, *Magyarország külpolitikája*, pp. 61–65, 76–77.

44. Deák, *Hungary at the Paris Peace Conference*, p. 337 (n. 31).

45. *Papers and Documents*, 2:266. For a firsthand account of the clandestine plans to foment civil war in Slovakia, see the diaries of Pál Prónay, one of the plotters: *A határban a halál kaszál*, pp. 224–27, cited hereafter as *Prónay Diary*.

46. According to Mocsy ("Radicalization and Counterrevolution," p. 297), during the 1920s about one third of the delegates to the Hungarian Parliament were refugees from the lost provinces, though they represented only 7 percent of the population.

Chapter 2

1. The thesis that, despite appearances, the Versailles peace settlement had not fundamentally weakened Germany is convincingly argued by Gerhard L. Weinberg, "The Defeat of Germany in 1918 and the European Balance of Power," *Central European History* 2 (1969): 248–60.

2. This was part of the so-called Bethlen-Peyer pact. For its foreign policy implications, see *IET*, 2:250–54.

3. Cited in Thomas Spira, "Hungary's Numerus Clausus, the Jewish Minority, and the League of Nations," *Ungarn Jahrbuch* 4 (1972): 122. See also the letter of the leaders of the Orthodox Jewish Community of Hungary to the League of Nations Secretariat, 29 November 1925, League of Nations Archives, R1669/19–27/41/48–65/17190.

4. The viewpoint of Auer and Ignotus is reflected in the former's memoirs: Pál Auer, *Fél évszázad: Események, emberek*; and the intensely personal history of Hungary by Paul Ignotus, *Hungary*, especially pp. 160–63, 181–82.

5. Stephen Borsody, *The Tragedy of Central Europe*, pp. 72–83.

6. Gyula Illyés, *People of the Puszta*, p. 14.

7. No full-length scholarly biography of Horthy has been written. A satisfactory introduction, though brief and somewhat eulogistic, is provided by Peter Gosztony, *Miklós von Horthy: Admiral und Reichsverweser*. The following account is based in part on *The Confidential Papers of Admiral Horthy*, cited hereafter as *Horthy Papers*; and C. A. Macartney, *October Fifteenth*, 2nd ed., vol. 1.

8. Even his trusted friends, including Pál Prónay, admitted that many of his speeches were muddled and bordered on the incoherent. *Prónay Diary*, pp. 178–79.

9. Nicholas M. Nagy-Talavera, *The Green Shirts and the Others*, p. 53.

10. Macartney, *October Fifteenth*, 1:58.

11. Report of Thomas Hohler, British Minister in Budapest, 27 July 1923, Public Record Office (London), Foreign Office 371, C13048/54/21, cited hereafter in the following form: PRO, FO 371, followed by the identification number.

12. *Ciano's Diplomatic Papers*, p. 65.

13. J. F. Montgomery, *Hungary, the Unwilling Satellite*, p. 41.

14. See the revealing letter of Ludendorff to Horthy on 19 August 1920, *Horthy Papers*, pp. 26–27.

15. Elek Karsai, *Számjeltávirat valamennyi magyar királyi követségnek*, p. 323.

16. See Major Parry Jones's report of 15 June 1927, PRO, FO 371, C5330/38/21, as well as the report of Thomas Hohler, 6 January 1920, DBFP, first series, vol. 6, no. 410.

17. Horthy expressed these sentiments on a number of occasions in the interwar period, most notably in a letter to General Hindenburg, President of the Weimar Republic, 22 October 1925, German Foreign Ministry records, National Archives Microcopy T-120, K139/109080, cited hereafter as GFM, followed by serial and frame numbers.

18. Horthy's letter to Hindenburg in 1925, GFM, T-120, K319/109080.

19. Thomas L. Sakmyster, "Miklós Horthy, Hungary, and the Coming of the European Crisis, 1932–41," *East Central Europe* 3 (1976): 225.

20. *Horthy Papers*, p. 89.

21. *Horthy Papers*, p. 90.

22. No scholarly biography of Bethlen has been written. For Bethlen's foreign policy in the late 1920s, see Dezső Nemes, *A Bethlen kormány külpolitikája 1927–1931-ben*. Nemes presented much new material, but operated within a severely restricted ideological framework. More recently new evidence has become available in a collection of Bethlen's papers, *Bethlen István titkos iratai*, edited by Miklós Szinai and László Szűcs, cited hereafter as *Bethlen Papers*.

23. *Bethlen Speeches*, 1:156–68.

24. *Bethlen Speeches*, 1:287.

25. György Ránki, "The Problem of Fascism in Hungary," in *Native Fascism in the Successor States*, p. 68.

26. Hugh Seton-Watson, *Eastern Europe Between the Wars*, pp. 190–91.

27. *Bethlen Speeches*, 2:185.

28. Gusztáv Gratz, "Ungarns Aussenpolitik seit dem Weltkriege," *Berliner Monatshefte* 19 (1941): 11.

29. *Bethlen Speeches*, 1:231.

30. English financial circles showed a marked sympathy for Hungary and proved most forthcoming in meeting Bethlen's requests for economic and political support. For a detailed discussion, see Ozer Carmi, *La Grande-Bretagne et la Petite Entente*, pp. 88–115.

31. C. A. Macartney, *Hungary and her Successors*, pp. 465–66.

32. From a jingle by A. P. Herbert, "Foreign Policy: Or, the Universal Aunt," cited in Martin Gilbert, *The Roots of Appeasement*, p. 122.

33. Marginal note of M. W. Lampson in March 1924, on PRO, FO 371, C4501/21/21.

34. In 1923 Bethlen told the British minister in Budapest that London was the "only capital where the Hungarian question appeared to be considered purely on its merits and without any *arrière pensée*." Hohler's report, 26 May 1923, PRO, FO 371, C9296/942/21.

35. Lord Curzon's instructions to the British minister in Budapest, 27 November 1920, PRO, FO 371, C11889/283/21.

36. Bethlen's letter of 24 September 1926, *Horthy Papers*, p. 42.

37. He told the German minister in Budapest, Hans von Schoen, that "Hungary can fulfill its future wishes only on the side of both great powers, Italy and Germany." Schoen's report of 16 December 1926, cited in the dissertation of Wulf-Dieter Schmidt-Wulfen, "Deutschland-Ungarn, 1918–1933," pp. 408–9.

38. Minutes of a Cabinet meeting of 1 August 1921, cited in the introduction to the *Bethlen Papers*, p. 57 (n. 80).

39. Extract from the diary of Miklós Kozma, as quoted in Sándor Kónya, *Gömbös kisérlete totális fasiszta diktatúra megteremtésére*, p. 125.

40. For example, he told the German minister in Budapest, Johannes von Welczek, that he was convinced that Hungary's resurgence could occur only in tandem with Germany. Even if the two countries for the time being could not officially become allies, nonetheless "the old 'Bundesgenossenschaft' remained firmly anchored in the heart of every Hungarian patriot." Welczek's report of 6 March 1925, GFM, T-120, S6146/E460142.

41. For the details, see *Bethlen Papers*, 43–44.

42. Bethlen's memo on his talks with Mussolini, 4 April 1927, *IET*, vol. 4, no. 22.

43. Seeckt's diary entries for October 1927, as cited in Hans Meier-Welcker, *Seeckt*, pp. 373–75.

44. This program Bethlen had adumbrated to his colleagues at a Cabinet meeting as early as 1921. *Bethlen Papers*, p. 57 (n. 80).

45. This is the verdict to which Nemes comes in his study, *A Bethlen kormány külpolitikája*, p. 7.

46. For the activity in Slovakia, see Juraj Kramer, "Ausländische Einflüsse auf die Entwicklung der slowakischen autonomistischen Bewegung," *Historica* 3 (1957): 159–93. For the numerous contacts during the 1920s with Croatian separatists, see Ránki, *Emlékiratok és valóság*, p. 34; and *IET*, vol. 4, nos. 138, 186.

47. In 1929 he advised all Hungarian diplomatic missions that if Hungary limited her aims to ethnic revision, she jeopardized her chances for the more extensive territorial gains that might be obtained in "a certain diplomatic constellation." Quoted in Juhász, *Magyarország külpolitikája*, p. 116.

48. Once again, no scholarly biography of Gömbös exists. An older study con-

taining some useful material is József Révay, *Gömbös Gyula élete és politikája*. A more recent, though not entirely satisfactory, work is Kónya's *Gömbös kisérlete*.

49. Gömbös, *Egy magyar vezérkari tiszt*, pp. 5–8.

50. Révay, *Gömbös Gyula élete*, p. 211.

51. Lehar, *Erinnerungen*, p. 110.

52. Gratz, "Ungarns Aussenpolitik," p. 17.

53. Lajos Székely, "Gömbös Gyula külpolitikai koncepciójának kialakulása," *Valóság* 5 (1962): 84.

54. Ibid.

55. Macartney, *October Fifteenth*, 1:77.

56. The record of the Gömbös-Mussolini conversation of 13 March 1934 is found in *Allianz Hitler-Horthy-Mussolini*, ed. Lajos Kerekes et al., no. 6, cited hereafter as *Allianz*.

57. *Documents on German Foreign Policy, 1918–1945*, ed. Bernadotte Schmitt et al., series C, vol. 1, nos. 15, 179; vol. 2, no. 252. This document collection will be cited hereafter as *DGFP*, followed by series, volume, and document number.

58. For accounts of Gömbös's trip to Berlin, see Macartney, *October Fifteenth*, 1:138–40; and Gerhard L. Weinberg, *The Foreign Policy of Hitler's Germany*, pp. 113–14. A selection of relevant documents appears in Elek Karsai, "The Meeting of Gömbös and Hitler 1933," *New Hungarian Quarterly* 3 (1962): 170–96.

59. Macartney, *October Fifteenth*, 1:139.

60. Kánya is reported to have admonished Gömbös when the latter returned from Germany: "My son, this is unheard of. You must not behave like this." Cited in ibid., p. 110.

61. Karsai, "The Meeting of Gömbös and Hitler," p. 182.

62. Report of Hans Georg von Mackensen, German Minister in Budapest, 21 March 1934, *DGFP*, series C, vol. 2, no. 346.

63. The Germans, who had been assured up to the last minute that no pact of any sort was planned, were quite annoyed by this development. *DGFP*, series C, vol. 2, nos. 323, 334, 341, 346.

64. *Allianz*, no. 6. The secret protocol to the Rome Pact was published in full for the first time in Lajos Kerekes, *Abenddämmerung einer Demokratie*, pp. 187–88.

65. For a detailed treatment, see György Ránki and Iván Berend, *Magyarország a fasiszta Németország "életterében," 1933–1938*, pp. 106–15.

66. Report of Sir Neville Henderson, British Minister in Belgrade, 10 June 1935, PRO, FO 371, R3748/1/67. See also Neurath's memo of 10 December 1934, *DGFP*, series C, vol. 3, no. 387.

67. Macartney, *October Fifteenth*, 1:148 (n. 5).

68. Mackensen's reports of 7 October and 10 October 1935, *DGFP*, series C, vol. 4, no. 337.

69. *DGFP*, series C, vol. 4, nos. 307, 310, 316. The British embassy in Berlin was able to obtain some information on the deal: report of Sir Eric Phipps, 5 October 1935, PRO, FO 371, R5986/2867/21.

70. Macartney, *October Fifteenth*, 1:148. See also Ránki and Berend, *Magyarország a fasiszta Németország "életterében,"* pp. 131–33.

71. In this period, one of the most respected political figures in Hungary, Ferenc Keresztes-Fischer, Minister of the Interior, privately expressed views that were characteristic of others in the conservative camp. He asserted that though he was an advocate of an authoritarian system and an opponent of socialist and liberal tendencies, he nonetheless deplored what was happening in Germany. Everything had its limit, and the "suppression of all personal freedom" that was occurring in Germany could not last. Report of Hennet, 21 October 1934, NPA, K20/46711.

72. Macartney, *October Fifteenth*, 1:128–30.

73. Sakmyster, "Army Officers and Foreign Policy in Interwar Hungary, 1918–41," p. 23.

74. Istvan Deak, "Hungary," in *The European Right*, p. 380.

75. Macartney, *October Fifteenth*, 1:132.

76. Like Bajcsy-Zsilinszky, Eckhardt had collaborated with Gömbös in his radical projects in the early 1920s, but turned against him in 1935. For his explanation of his decision to join with Bethlen, see the report of B. Reath-Riggs, American chargé d'affaires, 11 October 1935, SD, 864.00/839.

77. Ránki and Berend, *Magyarország a fasiszta Németország "életterében,"* p. 133.

78. The strongest criticisms of Gömbös were reserved for meetings of the Foreign Affairs Committee of the Parliament, the sessions of which were closed to the public. See report of Geoffrey Knox, British Minister in Budapest, 7 November 1935, PRO, FO 371, R6818/905/21.

79. Macartney, *October Fifteenth*, 1:107.

80. Little secondary literature dealing with Kánya is available. There is a brilliant sketch in Macartney, *October Fifteenth*, 1:107–9. Some helpful insights are to be found in George Ottlik, "Coloman Kánya de Kánya," *New Hungarian Quarterly* 3 (1938): 211–18.

81. Ottlik, "Coloman Kánya de Kánya," p. 217.

82. Macartney, *October Fifteenth*, 1:109 (n. 2).

83. László Zsigmond, gen. ed., *Diplomáciai iratok Magyarország külpolitikájához 1936–1945*, vol. 1: *A Berlin-Róma tengely kialakulása és Ausztria annexiója 1936–1938*, no. 59, cited hereafter as *DIMK*.

84. Kánya spoke in these terms to the British minister. See Knox's report, 3 March 1936, PRO, FO 371, R1440/125/67.

85. Macartney, *October Fifteenth*, 1:109.

86. *Pester Lloyd*, 23 February 1933.

87. De Vienne's report of 8 May 1933, *Documents Diplomatiques Français*, 1932–1939, series 1, vol. 3, no. 256, cited hereafter as *DDF*.

88. Nandor A. F. Dreisziger, *Hungary's Way to World War II*, p. 68.

89. Ottlik, "Coloman Kánya de Kánya," p. 217. See also the observations of the Czechoslovak minister in Budapest, Miloš Kobr, in his report of 10 December 1938, *DIMK*, vol. 3, no. 135.

90. Macartney, *October Fifteenth*, 1:109.

91. In a British report in 1936 on leading Hungarian political personalities, Kánya is described as a person who "enjoys a reputation more notorious than savoury." Knox's report of 3 January, PRO, FO 371, R153/153/21.

Chapter 3

1. Weinberg, *The Foreign Policy of Hitler's Germany*, p. 239.
2. Magda Ádám, *Magyarország és a kisantant a harmincas években*, p. 106.
3. In a report drawn up in late April 1936, the French chiefs of staff concluded that if Germany built up its fortifications on the Rhine, France could provide direct aid to her eastern allies only by means of an operation similar to that staged at Salonika in World War I. *DDF*, series 2, vol. 2, no. 138.
4. Arnold Wolfers, *Britain and France between Two Wars*, p. 127.
5. Weinberg, *The Foreign Policy of Hitler's Germany*, p. 231.
6. John Dreifort, *Yvon Delbos at the Quai d'Orsay*, p. 133. A good discussion of the impact of the Rhineland remilitarization can be found in Stephen Kertesz, *Diplomacy in a Whirlpool*, p. 30. See also Mária Ormos, "A Rajna-vidék német megszállásának közép-európai hatása," *Századok* 103 (1969): 664–89; and Günter Reichert, *Das Scheitern der Kleinen Entente*, pp. 65–68.
7. Villani's report, 24 January 1936, *DIMK*, vol. 1, no. 17.
8. The references to East Central Europe in *Mein Kampf* are surprisingly scant. An important source for Hitler's thinking in the early 1930s is Hermann Rauschning, *The Voice of Destruction*. The general accuracy of Rauschning's accounts of his talks with Hitler seems to be confirmed by the conversations recorded in Richard Breiting, *Secret Conversations with Hitler*.
9. Weinberg, *The Foreign Policy of Hitler's Germany*, p. 18.
10. Rauschning, *Voice of Destruction*, p. 124.
11. Breiting, *Secret Conversations*, p. 62.
12. Ibid., p. 72.
13. Ibid., p. 71.
14. In 1931 Hitler privately spoke of his intention to "reach agreement with the Spanish, Hungarian, and Bulgarian officer corps." Ibid., p. 71.
15. Adolf Hitler, *Hitler's Secret Book*, pp. 208–9.
16. *The Speeches of Adolf Hitler*, edited by Norman H. Baynes, 1:1008.
17. On the basis of the calculations of Hans Jacobsen, it has been determined that Hitler met with fourteen Hungarian visitors in the period 1933–37, a figure that, as a proportion of the population, is higher than that of any other country. Hans-Adolf Jacobsen, *Nationalsozialistische Aussenpolitik 1933–1938*, p. 365.
18. Breiting, *Secret Conversations*, p. 71.
19. Rauschning, *Voice of Destruction*, p. 124.
20. See the report of the Hungarian minister in Berlin, Döme Sztójay, of 1 August 1936, *DIMK*, vol. 1, no. 148.
21. A. J. P. Taylor, *The Origins of the Second World War*, p. 101.
22. Sándor Tóth, "A Horthy hadsereg szervezete, 1920–1944," *Hadtörténelmi Közlemények* 5 (1958): 59–60.
23. János Csima, "Adalékok a horthysta vezérkarnak az ellenforradalmi rendszer háborús politikájában betöltött szerepéről," *Hadtörténelmi Közlemények* 15 (1968): 495. See also *Csak szolgálati használatra!*, edited by Tibor Hetés and Mrs. Tamás Morva, pp. 364–66, cited hereafter as *CSH*.
24. In March 1938 the Hungarian minister of defense complained to the Germans about the slow delivery of fighter planes that had been ordered. GFM, T-120, 3626/028072–3.

25. German Foreign Ministry note, 17 October 1936, GFM, T-120, 7864/570058–9.

26. "Orientierungsheft Ungarn nach dem Stande vom Mai 1938," Bundesarchiv-Militärachiv (Freiburg), WO1-5/132.

27. General Staff memoranda in June 1933 and December 1935, in CSH, nos. 76, 81.

28. Sakmyster, "Army Officers and Foreign Policy," p. 23.

29. Villani's report, 12 September 1936, DIMK, vol. 2, no. 33.

30. Report of the Hungarian military attaché in London, 28 October 1936, DIMK, vol. 2, no. 43.

31. Ibid., no. 52. The Little Entente countries did make representations in London and Budapest in the spring of 1936, warning that they would be forced to mobilize if Hungary followed Austria's example. Ádám, Magyarország és a kisantant, p. 113; and Vansittart's note on a conversation with Titelescu, 3 April 1936, PRO, FO 371, R2039/470/21.

32. Report of John F. Montgomery, American Minister in Budapest, 25 January 1937, United States State Department, Record Group 59, 864.20/125, cited hereafter as USSD.

33. Ciano Papers, p. 65.

34. Knox's report, 9 April 1936, PRO, FO 371, R2315/84/21.

35. Ibid.

36. Ádám, Magyarország és a kisantant, p. 106.

37. The German record is DGFP, series C, vol. 4, no. 515. Horthy's account is found in his Memoirs, pp. 146–48. See also Ciano Papers, pp. 35–37; DIMK, vol. 1, no. 156; and Macartney, October Fifteenth, 1:150.

38. Ciano Papers, p. 37.

39. GFM, T-120, 9572/E674687–701.

40. DIMK, vol. 1, no. 156. Kánya records the impression that Neurath was speaking on explicit instructions from Hitler.

41. Mackensen's report, 14 December 1933, DGFP, series C, vol. 2, no. 129.

42. Macartney, October Fifteenth, 1:181.

43. The French minister in Budapest, Gaston Maugras, succinctly and accurately described Darányi as "a reasonable and courteous man who tries to be on good terms with the whole world." Report of 7 January 1937, DDF, series 2, vol. 4, no. 258. For a character sketch of Darányi, see Macartney, October Fifteenth, 1:105–6.

44. Macartney and Palmer, Independent Eastern Europe, p. 353.

45. Kánya's record, 11 October 1936, DIMK, vol. 1, no. 158.

46. Mackensen's report, 13 October 1936, GFM, T-120, 1847/420852–5.

47. In his maiden speech to Parliament, Darányi gave the usual tributes to Germany and Italy, but added that the "Hungarian nation, in complete unanimity, desires the assurance of England's friendship and would gladly see the development of a friendly atmosphere with France in terms of a mutual recognition of interests." Cited in Ádám, Magyarország és a kisantant, p. 134.

48. DIMK, vol. 1, no. 156.

49. Ránki and Berend, Magyarország a fasiszta Németország "életterében," p. 158. Also see DGFP, series C, vol. 5, no. 589.

50. F. Ashton-Gwatkin, Joint Secretary of the Interdepartmental Economic

and Financial Committee in the Foreign Office, was told by Imrédy and other officials from the Hungarian National Bank that the "most forceful measures" had been introduced to curtail exports to Germany. Ashton-Gwatkin's memo of 7 November 1936, PRO, FO 371, R6766/15/21. Also see Iván Boldizsár, *The Other Hungary*, pp. 160–61.

51. Darányi's letter of 27 October 1936, GFM, T-120, 3626/028002–5; Ránki and Berend, *Magyarország a fasiszta Németország "életterében,"* pp. 160–61.

52. Ránki and Berend, *Magyarország a fasiszta Németország "életterében,"* pp. 163–64; and GFM, T-120, 3626/027995.

53. Report of a reporter from the *Völkischer Beobachter* after a conversation with Kánya, 28 January 1937, GFM, T-120, 1975/438229–33.

54. *DIMK*, vol. 1, p. 336 (n. 51). See also the report of the German minister in Bucharest, Wilhelm Fabricius, on 8 December 1936, GFM, T-120, 1923/433603.

55. Rosenberg's note of 24 November 1936, in Bundesarchiv (Koblenz), Kanzlei Rosenberg, no. 175.

56. Record of Hitler-Bratianu conversation, 16 November 1936, GFM, T-120, 1933/433589–94.

57. Sztójay's report, 10 July 1936, *DIMK*, vol. 1, no. 118.

58. Kánya's record, 11 October 1936, *DIMK*, vol. 1, no. 158; *Ciano Papers*, p. 66.

59. Gert Buchheit, *Der deutsche Geheimdienst*, pp. 117–18. As a code name for this operation, Göring, who did not like to mince words, selected "Überraschungskrieg gegen die CSR."

60. Record of Hitler-Kozma talk, 15 December 1936, GFM, T-120, 3023/598660–6.

61. The Yugoslav minister in Budapest dropped a hint to this effect in January (*DIMK*, vol. 2, no. 59), and this seemed to corroborate earlier information received from the Austrians. See *DIMK*, vol. 1, no. 163.

62. On 19 January the Czechoslovak minister in Budapest had proposed a "normalization" of relations between the two countries. Czechoslovakia would recognize Hungary's military equality and Hungary would agree to sign a non-aggression pact. Kánya refused, declaring that Hungary insisted on an unconditional recognition of its military equality. *DIMK*, vol. 2, no. 54.

63. Kánya's record, 23 January 1937, *DIMK*, vol. 2, no. 59.

64. GFM, T-120, 7427/539800–3.

65. Macartney, *October Fifteenth*, 1:180–81.

66. Macartney's account (pp. 181–82) can now be supplemented by the revelations contained in two intelligence reports submitted to the Austrian Foreign Ministry. NPA, K889/477–80, 530–32.

67. NPA, K478/253–55.

68. Miklós Lackó, *Nyilasok, nemzetiszocialisták 1935–1944*, pp. 81–83.

69. Macartney and Palmer, *Independent Eastern Europe*, p. 360.

70. Ibid., p. 356. See also Heeren's report of 14 July 1936, *DGFP*, series C, vol. 5, no. 449.

71. Hitler's motives in opening talks with Prague are still not entirely clear. For details, see Gerhard L. Weinberg, "Secret Hitler-Beneš Negotiations in 1936–1937," *Journal of Central European Affairs* 19 (1960): 366–74.

72. There was a particularly striking and unexpected passage in favor of Hungarian revisionism in the Duce's speech of 1 November 1936. See also his sug-

gestion of increased military cooperation as reported by the Hungarian military attaché in Rome, Lászlo Szabó, *DIMK*, vol. 1, no. 177.

73. *Ciano Papers*, p. 102; Ádám, *Magyarország és a kisantant*, pp. 136–37.
74. *Ciano Papers*, p. 118.
75. Kánya's records, 29 July 1937, *DIMK*, vol. 1, no. 283. Kánya told an Austrian friend, Theodor Hornbostel, that Italy's dropping of the tariff system was a reflection of "Italy's servility in the face of Berlin." NPA, K480/675–78.

Chapter 4

1. *Pester Lloyd*, 14 May 1937.
2. George Peabody Gooch, *Under Six Reigns*, p. 301.
3. Keith Middlemas, *Diplomacy of Illusion*, p. 10.
4. Memo of R. A. Leeper, 13 December 1933, PRO, FO 371, C10897/395/21.
5. Knox spoke to Kánya along these lines not long after the Rhineland crisis. See his report of 9 April 1936, PRO, FO 371, R2315/84/21.
6. Horthy, *Memoirs*, p. 147.
7. Knox's report, 27 April 1936, PRO, FO 371, R2532/18/21. Chamberlain's comments did not, of course, reflect official British policy.
8. Horthy wrote to Neville Chamberlain during the Czechoslovak crisis of 1938 to remind him of his brother's words. *DIMK*, vol. 2, no. 486.
9. PRO, FO 371, R3210/470/21. Horthy's letter was written in German; translated passages are my own.
10. Horthy voiced similar anti-Communist sentiments in a conversation with the French minister in Budapest. Maugras's report, 15 February 1937, *DDF*, series 2, vol. 4, no. 448.
11. Gilbert, *The Roots of Appeasement*, p. 162.
12. Ashton-Gwatkin's memo, PRO, FO 371, R6766/15/21.
13. Sir Orme Sargent's letter to Knox (on instructions from Eden), 2 September 1937, PRO, FO 371, C6216/270/18.
14. *Ciano Papers*, p. 117.
15. Kánya's memo on his talks in London, 10 May 1937, *DIMK*, vol. 1, no. 250; and Eden's report to Knox, 13 May, PRO, FO 371, R3313/770/67.
16. *Ciano Papers*, p. 117.
17. Kánya himself had not made a favorable impression. Eden thought that "there was much dissimulation in his attitude." PRO, FO 371, R3313/770/67.
18. *Ciano Papers*, p. 119.
19. Baar's report of 28 May 1937 on a conversation with Apor, NPA, K21/39802.
20. On Kánya's use of Lakatos in this way, see his comments as recorded in GFM, T-120, 1847/421035–7.
21. Hungary. *Képviselőházi napló*, 13:681–85.
22. Kánya had spoken in similar terms to the British minister in Budapest in 1935, PRO, FO 371, R4656/705/21.
23. Kánya's remarks as recorded in an Austrian document found among the papers of Theodor Hornbostel, head of the Political Section of the Austrian Foreign Ministry. GFM, T-120, 2935/568771. This group of Austrian documents,

a part of the records of the German Foreign Ministry after World War II, will hereafter be cited as AD. Items from this collection will be cited only in those cases where the originals could not be located in the files of the NPA in Vienna.

24. Barany, "Hungary," pp. 295–96.

25. Macartney, *October Fifteenth*, 1:179 (n. 1).

26. Leslie Laszlo, "Church and State in Hungary, 1919–1945" (Ph.D. diss., Columbia University, 1973), p. 329.

27. Tilkovszky, *Pál Teleki*, p. 37.

28. "Szent István napján," *Pesti Napló*, 20 August 1937.

29. Macartney, *October Fifteenth*, 1:186–87; Lackó, *Nyilasok*, pp. 89–90.

30. General Staff reports for 1933 and 1935, *CSH*, nos. 76, 81.

31. *CSH*, pp. 350–51.

32. *CSH*, p. 42.

33. In a memorandum of 9 August 1937, Rátz called attention to the unsatisfactory treatment in newspapers and journals of Hungary's role in World War I. The result of this treatment, he complained, was a "lamentable demoralization," with an undesirable emphasis on battles in which Hungary had suffered disastrous losses. Rátz urged instead a glorification of the previous war effort in order to forestall any loss of public confidence in a future war. *CSH*, no. 110.

34. Report of the British military attaché, Major Benfield, on information from Röder, 30 September 1937, PRO, FO 371, R6536/6536/21.

35. General Ludwig Beck spoke in this sense to General Werth, a General Staff officer, in June 1935. Bundesarchiv-Militärarchiv, Beck Nachlass, 24 June 1935, folder 2, no. 28.

36. *Allianz*, no. 48, pp. 206–7.

37. Information on Rátz's initiative can be found in Péter Sipos, *Imrédy Béla és a Magyar Megújulás Pártja*, pp. 21–23.

38. Major Benfield's report on a talk with an army officer, 5 July 1937, PRO, FO 371, R4687/3272/21. However, General Röder sought out Benfield to assure him that, despite the criticism of some officers, he supported Kánya's policy of a friendly settlement of the problem with the Little Entente. Knox's report, 20 September 1937, PRO, FO 371, R6536/6536/21.

39. *Horthy Papers*, pp. 83–90.

40. The 1930 census results had shown alarming declines in the number of those declaring themselves as Magyars in Romania, Yugoslavia, and Czechoslovakia. Macartney, *October Fifteenth*, 1:143.

41. *DIMK*, 1, no. 35.

42. Ádám, *Magyarország és a kisantant*, pp. 145–50.

43. Knox's report, 16 April 1937, PRO, FO 371, R2721/1644/21.

44. For a stimulating essay on this program, see Paul Ignotus, "Czechs, Magyars, Slovaks," *Political Quarterly* 40 (1969): 187–204.

45. One writer suggests that in supporting the plan for a Danubian "Triangle," Eckhardt had the tacit backing of Horthy, but this seems highly improbable. John A. Lukacs, *The Great Powers and Eastern Europe*, pp. 60–61. See also Ránki, *Emlékiratok és valóság*, p. 27.

46. Information given to the Austrian mission in Paris by its Hungarian counterpart, 10 March 1937, AD, T-120, 1999/441952–55. See also *DDF*, series 2, vol. 3, no. 75.

47. In September 1936 Beneš had sent out what appeared to be signals of his interest in a rapprochement with Hungary. See *DIMK*, vol. 2, no. 32.

48. Marek's report, 5 April 1937, NPA, K479/702–5.

49. Record of Schuschnigg-Hodza conversation, 26 March 1937, NPA, K479/521–3.

50. PRO, FO 371, R4450/26/67.

51. Ádám, *Magyarország és a kisantant*, p. 159.

52. Record of Kánya-Antonescu talk, 20 September 1937, *DIMK*, vol. 2, no. 90. See also *DGFP*, series D, vol. 5, no. 145.

53. *Allianz*, no. 19; and *DIMK*, vol. 2, no. 94.

54. *Ciano Papers*, p. 119.

55. *DGFP*, series D, vol. 5, no. 141; and *Allianz*, no. 19. See also Kánya's earlier complaints to Neurath in June 1937. GFM, T-120, 3037/600391–5.

56. Montgomery's report, 30 October 1937, USSD, 740.00/22.

57. *DGFP*, series D, vol. 1, no. 55.

58. Again Mussolini's words: *DGFP*, series D, vol. 1, no. 55.

59. *DIMK*, vol. 1, no. 176.

60. *DIMK*, vol. 1, no. 158.

61. Neurath's record, 24 August 1936, *DGFP*, series C, vol. 5, no. 516. See also Horthy's similar comments to Mackensen in February 1934, *DGFP*, series C, vol. 2, no. 290.

62. Bohle's memo on visit to Budapest, 3 February 1938, *DGFP*, series D, vol. 5, no. 173, enclosure. Csáky's most striking comment was that "the Hungarians would rather have as their neighbor a strong and friendly German Reich than a weak and unreliable Austria."

63. *DIMK*, vol. 1, no. 260. The Bácska was an ethnically mixed area between the Danube and the Tisza rivers that had been awarded to Yugoslavia by the peace conference.

64. Kurt von Schuschnigg, *Austrian Requiem*, p. 102.

65. Cited in Károly Vigh, "Bajcsy-Zsilinszky Endre harca a magyar függetlenségért és szuverenitásért a második világháború alatt," *Századok* 101 (1967): 1314.

66. Macartney, *October Fifteenth*, 1:152.

67. See Szálasi's statement in a press interview and in a speech, Collection of Hungarian Political and Military Records, National Archives microcopy T-793, roll 5, 778–79, 693–97, cited hereafter as Hungarian Records.

68. Hungary was entitled to intervene, since Gömbös had been assured by Schuschnigg that there would never be a restoration without previous consultation with Budapest. This promise was reaffirmed in the spring of 1937. *DIMK*, vol. 1, no. 213; *DGFP*, series D, vol. 1, no. 209.

69. Kánya's record of a conversation with Ciano, 21 May 1937. *Allianz*, no. 17.

70. Schmidt said at his trial that the Hungarians never failed Vienna in economic and similar matters. *Der Hochverratsprozess gegen Dr. Guido Schmidt vor dem Volksgericht*, p. 440. For Kánya's willingness to consider more intensive military cooperation, see the report of his conversation with Schuschnigg in October 1937. NPA, K480/865–6.

71. *DIMK*, vol. 1, no. 291.

72. Schmidt at his trial, *Hochverratsprozess*, p. 440.

Chapter 5

1. Knox's report, 13 January 1938, PRO, FO 371, C636/23/22.

2. See, for example, the revealing comments of General Walter Reichenau to the British consul in Munich, as recorded in the latter's report of 6 May 1937, PRO, FO 371, C3428/3/18. According to Reichenau, who had recently spoken to Hitler, the Führer was determined to revise the peace treaties in Eastern Europe, and would not hesitate to use force if necessary, since he was convinced that, unlike Germany, France and England were reluctant to become involved in a military conflict.

3. International Military Tribunal, *Trial of the Major War Criminals*, vol. 3, no. 175C, cited hereafter as IMT.

4. *DGFP*, series D, vol. 1, no. 19.

5. Weinberg, *The Foreign Policy of Hitler's Germany*, p. 114 (n. 135); also John Lukacs, *The Last European War*, p. 21.

6. Report of the American Ambassador, William Bullitt, of 6 May 1937, *Papers Relating to the Foreign Relations of the United States*, *1937*, vol. 1, pp. 89–92, cited hereafter as *FRUS*.

7. Committee of Imperial Defence report, February 1937, PRO, Cab. 24–268, no. 58; Cabinet Conclusions, 5 May 1937, Cab. 28–88.

8. Robert H. Ferrell, "The United States and East Central Europe before 1941," in *The Fate of East Central Europe*, pp. 46–48.

9. Keith Feiling, *The Life of Neville Chamberlain*, p. 333. See also Middlemas, *Diplomacy of Illusion*, pp. 136–38.

10. Halifax's account, PRO, Cab. 23–90A.

11. Neville Henderson's report, 3 March 1938, PRO, FO 371, C1650/42/18, Enclosure VI.

12. Report of the American military attaché, M. C. Shallenberger, on the basis of talks with Hungarian General Staff officers, 14 June 1936, National Archives, Record Group 165, 2529–40–47.

13. Report of Lajos Rudnay, 27 May 1937, *DIMK*, vol. 1, no. 260.

14. Report of Schallenberger, 5 January 1937, National Archives, Record Group 165, 265–361.

15. No direct record of Rátz's September talks in Germany has survived, but there are several later references. See AD, T-120, 2935/568512–3; and Hungarian Records, roll 15, 345.

16. *Népszava*, 19 October 1937.

17. For further details, see Macartney, *October Fifteenth*, 1:183–84.

18. Anna M. Cienciala, *Poland and the Western Powers*, pp. 26, 39–40. See also Gerhard L. Weinberg, "German Foreign Policy and Poland, 1937–38," *Polish Review* 20:(1975) 13.

19. *Horthy Papers*, p. 89.

20. IMT, no. 175C.

21. *DGFP*, series D, vol. 4, no. 168.

22. The press had been instructed to refrain from any critical comment. Bundesarchiv, Sänger Sammlung, no. 7, instructions for 22 November 1937.

23. The following is based on Kánya's account of 22 November 1937, in *Allianz*, no. 19 (the same as *DIMK*, vol. 1, no. 313).

24. *Allianz*, no. 19a. Göring was particularly pleased to hear Kánya explain

Notes 253

that there were no illusions in Hungary about creating friendly, intimate relations with Czechoslovakia, and that the "final goal" of Hungarian policy was always being kept in mind.

25. At a government party meeting in December, Darányi quoted the following response of Göring to Hungary's complaints about foreign agitators in Hungary: "If there are Germans among them, send them back. We will deal with them." *Pesti Napló*, 3 December 1937.

26. Göring's tactic seemed successful, for the Hungarians apparently gave assurances that they "did not intend to give Austria rear-guard support in the German question." Neurath's circular telegram to German missions, 26 November 1937, GFM, 99 T-120, 33/25865–7.

27. Memorandum of Otto Meissner, 25 November 1937, *DGFP*, series D, vol. 5, no. 149.

28. Erdmannsdorff, who had traveled to Berlin with the Hungarian party, later expressed doubts that Hitler did in fact give assurances of disinterest in Bratislava. See Gerd Brausch, "Deutschland-Ungarn. Die diplomatischen Beziehungen vom Herbst 1937 bis Frühjahr 1939" (Ph.D. diss.; Göttingen, 1956), p. 4. However, the Hungarian sources are quite specific on this point, and show Ribbentrop reaffirming it in May 1938. See *DIMK*, vol. 2, no. 182.

29. Apor to Sztójay, 11 April 1938, *Allianz*, no. 28 (*DIMK*, vol. 2, no. 152). See also *DIMK*, vol. 1, no. 394; *DGFP*, series D, vol. 2, no. 114.

30. *DGFP*, series D, vol. 2, no. 59.

31. *DGFP*, series D, vol. 5, no. 149.

32. See Kánya's remarks as recorded in AD, T-120, 2935/568770–1; Montgomery's report, 24 February 1938, USSD, 762.63/504; and *DDF*, series 2, vol. 8, no. 498.

33. Neurath had briefed the Hungarians on the results of Halifax's visit. Kánya's note, 24 November, *DIMK*, vol. 1, no. 314. See also Endre Kovács, *Magyar-lengyel kapcsolatok a két világháború között*, p. 306.

34. Macartney, *October Fifteenth*, 1:211–12.

35. Sipos, *Imrédy Béla*, p. 70.

36. General Soós's report on his conversation with Horthy and the text of the memorandum he submitted to him are found in the manuscript diary of Ferenc Szálasi. This material, which is on deposit in the library of St. Antony's College, Oxford, was used with the kind permission of Professor C. A. Macartney. This archive will be cited hereafter as "Macartney Archive."

37. Horthy's speech of 3 April 1938, in *Horthy Papers*, pp. 98–100.

38. Memo by F. Ashton-Gwatkin on a conversation with Imrédy, 7 November 1936, PRO, FO 371, R6766/15/21.

39. Macartney, *October Fifteenth*, 1:106–7.

40. Sipos, *Imrédy Béla*, p. 75.

41. Erdmannsdorff's report, 23 February 1938. GFM, T-120, 1346/353973. Earlier Kánya had told Erdmannsdorff that he thought Hungary was rearming to the extent its economy permitted, and he would therefore not be forced into accepting it. GFM, T-120, 3046/600767–70.

42. See the similar statements of the Czechoslovak foreign minister, Kamil Krofta, to the section chiefs of the Foreign Ministry, in GFM, Translated Czechoslovak Documents, T-120, 1809/414016, cited hereafter as Czechoslovak Documents, followed by serial and frame numbers.

43. Bundesarchiv, Brammer Sammlung, Informationsbericht 140 (Dertinger), 2 October 1937.

44. *Ciano Papers*, p. 146.

45. Ribbentrop's reports, 2 and 4 December 1937, *DGFP*, series D, vol. 1, nos. 50, 59.

46. See the record of the French-British talks in London, 29–30 November 1937, PRO, FO 371, C8234/270/18.

47. J. B. Hoptner, *Yugoslavia in Crisis, 1934–1941*, pp. 110–11. Also *DGFP*, series D, vol. 5, no. 63.

48. Jozef Lipski, *Diplomat in Berlin, 1933–1939*, edited by Waclaw Jędrzejewicz, p. 333.

49. As early as 1933 Titulescu informed the Germans that his country and the Little Entente had no objection to the Anschluss, though they would go to war to oppose a Hungarian-Austrian union. *DGFP*, series C, vol. 1, no. 328. See also *DGFP*, series C, vol. 3, no. 322.

50. The following is based in part on the account provided by Clemens Wildner, Secretary of the Austrian Legation, in his memoirs *Von Wien nach Wien*, pp. 218–25.

51. See the memo on Schuschnigg's talks with Kánya and Darányi, 25 October 1937, NPA, K480/865–6; and *DDF*, series 2, vol. 7, no. 157.

52. Wildner, *Von Wien nach Wien*, pp. 220–21.

53. The only surviving account of this conversation is Eberle's report to his superiors, 23 November 1937, NPA, K21/96526.

54. Horthy had a remarkable facility for reconciling in his own mind mutually contradictory policies. Though he here speaks of Hungary's friendly relations "now and in the future" with Austria, just a week later he told the German minister in Budapest that he assumed Austria would become a part of the German Reich, not in "twenty or thirty years, but very soon." *DGFP*, series D, vol. 5, no. 152.

55. Baar's report of 1 December 1937, NAP, K21/96549.

56. Baar's report, AD, T-120. 2935/568512–3. At the outset of the convention, Baar, an old friend of Rátz, warned him that anything he said of political importance would have to be reported to Vienna. Rátz made it clear that what he wished to say would be "on the record," which suggests that he must have had Horthy's expressed authorization to continue to explore this issue.

57. AD, T-120, 2935/568516–7.

58. See, for example, the long letter of Marquis György Pallavicini to Guido Schmidt, 2 December 1937, AD, T-120, 2971/579401.

59. *Ciano Papers*, pp. 148–49.

60. *Ciano Papers*, p. 65.

61. Count Galeazzo Ciano, *Ciano's Diary, 1937–1938*, pp. 51–52.

62. *Ciano Diary*, p. 62.

63. *Ciano Diary*, p. 58.

64. The only official account to survive is that from the Austrian side: NPA, K478/701–5. Ciano gives his impressions in his *Diary*, pp. 62–64. See also Lajos Kerekes, *Anschluss 1938*, pp. 208–9.

65. Knox's report, 14 January 1938, PRO, FO 371, R548/117/67.

66. *Ciano Diary*, p. 62.

67. *DIMK*, vol. 1, no. 340. See also the reports of the British minister in Vienna, PRO, FO 371, R546/547/117/67, and *DDF*, series 2, vol. 7, no. 446.

68. AD, T-120, 2935/568300.

69. Knox's report, 5 January 1938, PRO, FO 371, R626/626/21.

70. Knox's report, 14 January 1938, PRO, FO 371, R548/117/67.

71. AD, T-120, 2935/568300.

72. Hungarian aide memoire handed to Sir Orme Sargent, 19 January 1938, PRO, FO 371, R524/117/67.

73. Eberle's report, 11 January 1938, AD, T-120, 2935/568520.

74. AD, T-120, 2935/568520–2.

75. Bullitt's report of conversation with Delbos, 12 January 1938, USSD, 740.00/264.

76. Bullitt's record of a talk with Delbos, 1 February 1938, *FRUS*, 1938, vol. 1, pp. 5–6. At the cabinet meeting of 2 February, Eden reported that the Romanian foreign minister had made a very bad impression on him in Geneva, and that Romania, which had been granted "somewhat exaggerated boundaries" by the peace treaties, deserved strong warnings from the West. PRO, FO 371, Cab. 23–92.

77. Mistler spoke to Ferenc Honti, representative of the Hungarian Revisionist League in Paris, whose report was later passed on to Kánya. *DIMK*, vol. 2, no. 109. There is no documentation relating to this episode in the French documentary collection.

78. Bohle's account, 3 February 1938, GFM, T-120, 3626/028046–57.

79. Bundesarchiv, Brammer Sammlung, no. 32, Informationsbericht no. 2 (Dertinger), 4 January 1938.

80. Jean Szembek, *Journal, 1933–1939*, p. 270.

81. *Pesti Napló*, 10 February 1938.

82. See Krofta's comments to his section chiefs on 17 February in Czechoslovak Documents, T-120, 1809/414007.

83. Gehl, *Austria, Germany and the Anschluss, 1931–38*, pp. 171–75.

84. *DIMK*, vol. 1, no. 356.

85. Knox's report, 21 February 1938, PRO, FO 371, R1842/137/3.

86. Montgomery's report, 26 January 1938, USSD, 740.00/283; and Baar's report, 23 February 1938, NPA, K21/51970.

87. *Pester Lloyd*, 28 February 1938.

88. Baar's report of 23 February 1938, NPA, K21/51968. See also Montgomery's report of 24 February, USSD, 762.63/504, and Knox's report on a conversation with Kánya, 23 February, PRO, FO 371, R1760/137/3.

89. The following paragraph is based on reports of the British minister in Vienna on 3 and 9 March on conversations with Guido Schmidt, PRO, FO 371, 2072/1931/3, and *DBFP*, series 3, vol. 1, no. 2. Also Knox's report of 7 March 38, PRO, FO 371, R2193/137/3.

90. Schmidt trial, *Hochverratsprozess*, p. 440.

91. Kánya's record, 4 March 1938, *DIMK*, vol. 1, no. 395.

92. *DIMK*, vol. 1, no. 398.

93. "Erreignisreiche Tage," *Pester Lloyd*, 11 March 1938.

94. See Mussolini's speech of 16 March in *Documents on International Affairs*, edited by Monica Curtis, 1938, vol. 1, p. 236, cited hereafter as *DIA*.

95. Taylor, *Origins of the Second World War*, p. 143.
96. *Allianz*, no. 28 (*DIMK*, vol. 1, no. 408).
97. Erdmannsdorff's report, *DGFP*, series D, vol. 5, no. 182.
98. Erdmannsdorff's report, 21 April 1938, *DGFP*, series D, vol. 5, no. 195.
99. *DGFP*, series D, vol. 5, no. 193.
100. Later Kánya stated that he had not been deceived by Hitler in the Burgenland question at the time of the Anschluss. Macartney, *October Fifteenth*, 1:206 (n. 6).

Chapter 6

1. In his article of 17 April in *Pesti Napló*, "Magyarország helyzete Ausztria csatlakozása után."
2. *DIMK*, vol. 1, nos. 419, 421.
3. The British military attaché secured a copy of these secret instructions, PRO, FO 371, R3469/719/21. See also Erdmannsdorff's report, GFM, 3461/017780.
4. His report of 14 March, PRO, FO 371, C1873/132/18.
5. Payr's courageous statement made little impact, since his speech was for the most part made inaudible by the derisory clamor of rightist deputies. *Képviselőházi Napló*, 27:321–22.
6. Kánya candidly admitted to Maugras that the swiftness of the German move into Austria was "truly frightening" to him. *DDF*, series 2, vol. 8, no. 498.
7. Paul Ignotus, "Radical Writers in Hungary," in *The Left-Wing Intellectuals between the Wars, 1919–1939*, pp. 149–67.
8. Montgomery's report, 15 March 1938, USSD, 864.00/895.
9. *Horthy Papers*, pp. 96–100.
10. *DBFP*, series 3, vol. 1, no. 86.
11. "Hodža Milan dunai terve," *Szabadság*, 5 December 1937.
12. Apor's note, 21 December 1937, *DIMK*, vol. 2, no. 98. See also Kánya's comments to Knox, 5 January 1938, PRO, FO 371, R296/178/21.
13. Wildner, *Von Wien nach Wien*, pp. 224–25.
14. *Ciano Diary*, p. 43.
15. *Allianz*, no. 48.
16. Ádám, *Magyarország és a kisantant*, p. 184. This apparently was the planning to which Rátz and Horthy had asked the Austrians to contribute. See also *CSH*, p. 233.
17. Bohle's memo, 3 February 1938, *DGFP*, series D, vol. 5, no. 173.
18. Künzel's report, 19 February 1938, *DGFP*, series D, vol. 2, no. 58. The talk with Bethlen is found in GFM, T-120, 2004/442444–5. In early January Bethlen had told Mussolini that it was necessary that Hungary carry her frontier to the Carpathians and "make a junction with Poland and thus contain German pressure the better." *Ciano Papers*, p. 159.
19. *DGFP*, series D, vol. 2, nos. 59, 60.
20. Krofta's address to his section chiefs, 17 February 1938, Czechoslovak Documents, T-120, 1809/414007, and 1809/414014.
21. Neither Kánya's nor Kobr's record of this conversation has survived. The following is based on Krofta's later remarks to his section chiefs on 3 March. Czechoslovak Documents, T-120, 1809/414014.

22. Wettstein's report on conversation with Marek, *DIMK*, vol. 1, no. 399. See also Puaux's report of 4 March, *DDF*, series 2, vol. 8, no. 313.

23. Almost certainly Gratz was sent as Kánya's emissary. Upon his return he reported orally and in writing to Kánya. *Allianz*, no. 23 (*DIMK*, vol. 1, no. 407).

24. Kánya's speech to Parliament, 1 June 1938, Hungary, *Képviselőházi Napló*, 19:271–76.

25. *Szabadság*, 2 April 1938.

26. A detailed defense of Czechoslovakia's minorities policy was submitted by Prague to Britain and France, *DBFP*, series 3, vol. 3, no. 160.

27. In an unguarded moment during a conversation with the British minister in Prague in 1937, Beneš did admit that he wished to "Czechize" the country. This would be accomplished without coercion and over a period of time, perhaps forty years. Charles Bentinck's report to Eden, 20 January 1937, PRO, FO 371, R685/188/12.

28. Even some Western European observers questioned whether Czechoslovakia was a truly democratic state. The British minister, Sir Joseph Addison, concluded in 1936 that "Czechoslovakia presents to the outside world the semblance of a bulwark of democracy, freedom and liberty, whereas it is in fact a 'Polizeistaat' similar to other states where arbitrary rule prevails." Report of 25 August 1936, PRO, FO 371, R5216/32/12.

29. For a balanced and authoritative essay on the Slovaks in this period, see Josef Anderle, "The Establishment of Slovak Autonomy in 1938," in *Czechoslovakia: Past and Present*, 1:76–97.

30. The Pittsburgh Agreement was a convention that Thomas Masaryk had concluded with certain Slovak representatives in the United States in 1918. The interpretation of its meaning was disputed by the Czechs and Slovaks during the entire inter-war period. For details, see Anderle, "Establishment of Slovak Autonomy," pp. 76–78.

31. PRO, FO 371, R8546/26/67.

32. Andrej Hlinka was the leading figure in the Slovak People's Party.

33. Newton's report on conversation with Beneš, 11 November 1937, PRO, FO 371, R7837/154/12.

34. Newton's report on conversation with Hodža, 22 March 1938, *DBFP*, series 3, vol. 1, no. 103.

35. Masirevich's report, 22 March 1938, *DIMK*, vol. 1, no. 447.

36. The Czechoslovak census of 1930 showed 681,460 Magyars, but this figure probably slightly understated the true number.

37. Kánya and Apor spoke along these lines to Montgomery in early May. See Montgomery's report, 5 May USSD, 760f.64/79.

38. A Hungarian agent by the name of Farkas was in Slovakia in April trying to interest the Slovaks in this plan. See Thaddeus V. Gromada, "The Slovak Question in Polish Foreign Policy (1934–1939)" (Ph.D. diss., Fordham, 1966), pp. 175–76.

39. Macartney, *October Fifteenth*, 1:231.

40. Circular telegram to Hungarian missions, 20 March 1938, *DIMK*, vol. 1, no. 440. The reference to the "free hand" policy was omitted from the telegrams to Rome and Berlin.

41. For a brief discussion of Kánya's policy in this period, see Dreisziger, *Hungary's Way*, pp. 71–72.

42. *DGFP*, series D, vol. 5, no. 141.

43. Villani's report, *DIMK*, vol. 1, no. 382.

44. There was strong support for this idea among military officers. Colonel Andorka, director of Hungary's military intelligence, explained in very frank terms to the British military attaché that Hungary aimed to partition Czechoslovakia, at which time an East European bloc consisting of Hungary, Poland, Italy, and Yugoslavia would be formed to establish a balance of power against Germany. Knox's report, 23 April 1938, PRO, FO 371, C3591/1941/18. For a detailed study of this topic, see Betty Jo Winchester, "Hungary and the 'Third Europe' in 1938," *Slavic Review* 32 (1973): 741–56.

45. Villani's report, 15 March 1938, *DIMK*, vol. 1, no. 422. An Anglo-Italian agreement was initialed in April, but its subsequent impact on the course of European affairs was negligible.

46. *Ciano Diary*, p. 94.

47. *Ciano Diary*, pp. 116–17; Villani's report, 16 May, *DIMK*, vol. 2, no. 202.

48. This discussion of Beck's "Third Europe" plan is based on Hans Roos, *Polen und Europa*, pp. 273–85; and Cienciala, *Poland and the Western Powers*, pp. 55–56.

49. Gromada, "The Slovak Question," pp. 28–29.

50. András Hory, *A kulisszák mögött*, p. 21.

51. Hory's description in December 1937, cited in Macartney, *October Fifteenth*, 1:209.

52. *DGFP*, series D, vol. 5, no. 141.

53. Roos, *Polen und Europa*, pp. 278–79.

54. Cienciala, *Poland and the Western Powers*, pp. 54–57.

55. Kánya's reaction on receiving Beck's message was: "Why does this worthy ex-Colonel turned diplomat keep trying to teach me my job?" Cited in Macartney, *October Fifteenth*, 1:209.

56. Hory, *A kulisszák mögött*, p. 30.

57. This letter is printed in *Allianz*, no. 22 (*DIMK*, vol. 1, no. 389).

58. Cienciala, *Poland and the Western Powers*, p. 56 (n. 3); Gromada, "The Slovak Question," pp. 137–38; and Jörg Hoensch, *Die Slowakei und Hitlers Ostpolitik*, p. 65 (n. 62).

59. Kánya to Hory, 5 April 1938, cited in László Zsigmond, "Ungarn und das Münchener Abkommen," *Acta Historica* 6 (1959): 267–68 (n. 53). On that same day Sztójay was instructed to inform Berlin that Hungary would grant "extensive autonomy" to the Slovaks and Ruthenes. *DIMK*, vol. 2, no. 152.

60. Hoensch, *Die Slowakei und Hitlers Ostpolitik*, p. 7.

61. Loránt Tilkovszky, *Revízió és nemzetiségpolitika Magyarországon 1938–1941*, p. 22.

62. Szembek Papers, cited in Roos, *Polen und Europa*, p. 341.

63. Eszterházy's report, *DIMK*, vol. 2, no. 250.

64. *Allianz*, no. 48; Ribbentrop's letter to Keitel, 4 March 1938, *DGFP*, series D, vol. 2, no. 65. For Hitler's concurrence see *DGFP*, series D, vol. 2, no. 66.

65. Blomberg's directive, *DGFP*, series D, vol. 7, appendix 3(k).

66. Sztójay's reports of 1, 2 April, *DIMK*, vol. 2, nos. 142, 145.

67. Wettstein's report, 1 April, *DIMK*, vol. 2, no. 143.

68. *DIMK*, vol. 2, no. 146.

69. *DGFP*, series D, vol. 5, no. 190.

70. Kánya conveyed these thoughts to Beck in early May. *DIMK*, vol. 2, p. 367 (n. 103). He seems to have based his conclusions in large part on an interesting report that Colonel Andorka, head of Hungary's military intelligence, submitted in April after discussions with General Keitel. See Knox's report, 23 April 1938, PRO, FO 371, C3591/1941/18.

71. Jörg K. Hoensch, *Der ungarische Revisionismus und die Zerschlagung der Tschechoslowakei*, p. 63.

72. Knox's report, 25 April 1938, PRO, FO 371, R4307/378/21.

73. Bárdossy's report, 18 February 1938, *DIMK*, vol. 2, no. 116.

74. Kánya's record of conversation with Maugras, 18 March 1938, *DIMK*, vol. 2, no. 130.

75. PRO, FO 371, R3961/178/21.

76. Knox's report of 14 March 1938, PRO, FO 371, C1873/132/18. See his similar observations recorded in an earlier report, 10 March 1938, PRO, FO 371, C1872/132/18.

77. Marginal note by Nobles on Newton's dispatch of 5 April 1938, PRO, FO 371, R3688/719/21.

78. PRO, FO 371, R3105/626/21.

79. Kánya to Masirevich, 17 March 1938, *DIMK*, vol. 2, 129; also PRO, FO 371, R3105/626/21.

80. Horthy told Bohle in February that he was disappointed at the growing "decadence" of the youth in Great Britain. He noted a sharp contrast with the young people of Germany. Bohle's memo, 3 February 1938, GFM, T-120, 3626/E028046–57.

81. Ádám, *Magyarország és a kisantant*, p. 266.

82. Macartney, *October Fifteenth*, 1:223–25.

83. PRO, FO 371, R4291/4291/21.

84. Knox's letter to Sargent, 26 March 1938, PRO, FO 371, R3538/1022/21.

85. See his note to the Foreign Office, 26 April 1938, PRO, FO 371, R4496/99/21.

86. Knox's letter, marginal comments, PRO, FO 371, R3538/1022/21.

87. Cabinet minutes, 27 April 1938, PRO, Cab. 23–93.

88. Ingram's letter to Knox, 23 June 1938, PRO, FO 371, R5508/4291/21.

89. Foreign Office minutes, PRO, FO 371, R5514/178/21.

90. Following based on Macartney, *October Fifteenth*, 1:217–20.

91. A not unimportant consideration, in that Hungary was to host the Eucharistic Congress in late May.

92. *Képviselőházi Napló*, 18:603.

Chapter 7

1. For the latest contribution to the continuing debate see Donald C. Watt, "Hitler's Visit to Rome and the May Weekend Crisis: A Study in Hitler's Response to External Stimuli," *Journal of Contemporary History* 9 (1974): 23–32.

2. Knox's report, 20 May 1938, PRO, FO 371, R4996/933/21.

3. *DIMK*, vol. 2, no. 213. See also *DBFP*, series 3, vol. 2, no. 259.

4. Knox's reports, 22 May 1938, PRO, FO 371, R5003/933/21; C4723/1941/18.
5. Keith Robbins, *Munich, 1938*, pp. 231–32; and Middlemas, *Diplomacy of Illusion*, pp. 242–43.
6. Knox told Kánya on the 22nd that Britain had intervened in Berlin to urge cooperation in a peaceful settlement. Germany could not count on England's standing aside in case of a conflagration brought on by her rash measures. Kánya's record, 22 May 1938, *DIMK*, vol. 2, no. 215.
7. Ádám, *Magyarország és a kisantant*, p. 234.
8. Wilhelm Treue, "Rede Hitlers vor der deutschen Presse (10 Nov. 1938)," *Vierteljahreshefte für Zeitgeschichte* 6 (1958): 183. See also Hitler's comments to Rátz in August, the record of which is printed in Thomas L. Sakmyster, "The Hungarian State Visit to Germany of August, 1938: Some New Evidence on Hungary in Hitler's Pre-Munich Policy," *Canadian Slavic Studies* 3 (1969): 685.
9. General Ludwig Beck's record of this meeting is summarized in Wolfgang Foerster, *Ein General kämpft gegen den Krieg*, pp. 88–90. See also *DGFP*, series D, vol. 7, appendix 3 (v).
10. *DGFP*, series D, vol. 2, no. 221.
11. Sztójay's report of 28 May 1938, *DIMK*, vol. 2, no. 229.
12. *Allianz*, no. 48.
13. In July General Beck argued that Hungarian participation in an attack on Czechoslovakia was necessary in order to prevent a Czechoslovak retreat into Moravia. His information, however, suggested that the Hungarian military leadership was not prepared for such an operation. Undated memo (but probably mid- or late July), Bundesarchiv, Beck Nachlass, folder 4.
14. Unsigned S. S. report of June 1938, National Archives Microcopy T-175, roll 542, 9415337.
15. Montgomery's report, 2 June 1938, *FRUS*, 1938, vol. 1, pp. 55–56; and Knox's report, 26 June, PRO, FO 371, R5926/626/21.
16. Macartney, *October Fifteenth*, 1:231.
17. Sir Leith Ross to Sargent, 1 July 1938, PRO, FO 371, R6005/4291/21.
18. Minutes of second meeting of the Interdepartmental Committee, 25 July 1938, PRO, FO 371, R7607/94/67.
19. Minutes of meeting with delegation from the United Hungarian Party, PRO, Lord Runciman's Mission, FO 800-306. On 9 September Runciman also met with a delegation representing the Hungarian Social Democratic Party of Slovakia. Their leaders emphasized that nearly as many Magyars in Slovakia belonged to their party as that of Count Eszterházy. However, their party was reasonably content with the nationalities policy of Prague and did not wish to see Czechoslovakia destroyed.
20. Letter to Strang, 16 August 1938, PRO, FO 371, C8700/1941/18.
21. Stojadinović had in fact assured Ciano on 18 June that as long as Hungary did not take the initiative in an attack on Czechoslovakia, but waited for Berlin to move first, he would "remain completely indifferent to the fate of Czechoslovakia." *Ciano Papers*, pp. 212–16.
22. Report of Gascoigne on conversation with Kánya, 29 July, PRO, FO 371, R6748/174/21. See also Kánya's memo drawn up in preparation for the visit to Rome. *DIMK*, vol. 2, no. 268.
23. The talks in Rome are well documented. For the Hungarian side, see

Allianz, no. 33 (*DIMK*, vol. 2, no. 269). For the Italian side, see *Ciano Diary*, pp. 138–39, and *Ciano Papers*, pp. 227–29.

24. *Ciano Diary*, p. 138.

25. *DGFP*, series D, vol. 2, no. 334.

26. Gascoigne's report, 5 August 1938, PRO, FO 371, R6819/178/21.

27. Kánya's record of conversation with Romanian minister, 9 August 1938, *DIMK*, vol. 2, no. 279.

28. Hungary's proposed communiqué, which was accepted almost verbatim by the Little Entente, is printed in a French text as *DIMK*, vol. 2, no. 288b.

29. Stojadinović later claimed he had gone so far as to telephone Kánya at Kiel to get his personal approval of the final agreement. PRO, FO 371, R7355/2759/67.

30. Apor to Sztójay, 22 August 1938, *DIMK*, vol. 2, no. 296. Apparently Horthy was not consulted on this, for a few days later he told József Lipski, the Polish Minister in Germany, that the Bled agreement was "an intrigue perpetrated against him in connection with his trip to Germany." He shifted responsibility for what happened to Kánya. Lipski, *Diplomat in Berlin*, p. 380.

31. Foreign Office minutes, PRO, FO 371, R7199/178/21.

32. Sztójay's report, 13 August 1938, *DIMK*, vol. 2, no. 285.

33. Letter of Gascoigne to Foreign Office, PRO, FO 371, C8473/1941/18.

34. Apor to Sztójay, 21 August 1938, *DIMK*, vol. 2, no. 292.

35. Csima, "Adalékok a horthysta vezérkarnak," p. 495; *Horthy Papers*, p. 131.

36. Hungarian Records, roll 15, 345. This is General Rátz's record of his talks during the visit to Germany, cited hereafter as "Berlin Talks." The Hungarians told Groscurth that they could not join in an attack on Czechoslovakia, since "that would be the end for them." Helmuth Groscurth, *Tagebücher eines Abwehroffiziers, 1938–1940*, p. 102.

37. Groscurth, *Tagebücher*, p. 102.

38. For a detailed treatment of the background and course of this episode, see Sakmyster, "The Hungarian State Visit," pp. 677–91. Another detailed account is Pál Pritz, "A kieli találkozó," *Századok* 108 (1974): 646–79.

39. Hungarian Records, "Berlin Talks," 345. Rátz's reply, which the other Hungarians also gave, was that the Hungarian army was simply not ready. They had been led by General Beck and other German leaders to believe that the military operation in question was to take place in 1940, and had planned accordingly.

40. *Memoirs*, p. 162.

41. Knox's letter to Cadogan, 24 April 1939, PRO, FO 371, C6314/350/21. See also Macartney, *October Fifteenth*, 1:242.

42. PRO, FO 371, C9178/1941/18.

43. *DBFP*, series 3, vol. 3, appendix 4 (iv).

44. The only record is that of Weizsäcker, *DGFP*, series D, vol. 2, no. 383.

45. At one point, when Ribbentrop still professed not to understand the Hungarian version of the meaning of the Bled Agreement, Kánya is reported to have said: "I'll explain it once again, very slowly. . . . Perhaps now even Herr Ribbentrop has understood it." Cited in Macartney, *October Fifteenth*, 1:241 (n. 1).

46. *DGFP*, series D, vol. 2, no. 383.

47. *DGFP*, series D, vol. 2, no. 390.

48. *DIMK*, vol. 2, no. 329.

49. Lipski, *Diplomat in Berlin*, pp. 382–87.

50. This talk, which was conducted in the Reich chancellory, is the best documented of the conversations in Germany. For the Hungarian text and an English translation, see Sakmyster, "The Hungarian State Visit," pp. 685–91.

51. Horthy's *Memoirs*, p. 165. Rátz had also been informed by Generals Beck and Brauchitsch of concern in military circles over Hitler's plans. Though Beck agreed with Rátz that a confrontation with Czechoslovakia would not remain an isolated incident, the German general stated that the military would submit to the Führer's decision. Hungarian Records, "Berlin Talks," 347.

52. Heinz Guderian, *Erinnerungen eines Soldaten*, p. 49.

53. *DGFP*, series D, vol. 2, no. 402.

54. See, i.a., *DGFP*, series D, vol. 2, nos. 392, 395.

55. Hitler had met privately with Imrédy, Horthy, and even Rátz, but not with Kánya. The latter complained that it was he, the foreign minister, who made foreign policy and not the prime minister. *DGFP*, series D, vol. 2, no. 402.

56. *DGFP*, series D, vol. 2, no. 402.

57. Hory, *A kulisszák mögött*, p. 33.

58. Macartney Archive, Cabinet minutes for September 1938.

59. Knox's report, 31 August 1938, PRO, FO 371, R7339/719/21; Kánya's record of a conversation with Gascoigne, 30 August *DIMK*, vol. 2, no. 305. Csáky, probably on instructions from Kánya, gave the British a more detailed and frank report, stressing the humiliation Hitler felt over the May crisis and the role of Ribbentrop as a "firebrand." Gascoigne's report, 2 September PRO, FO 371, C9178/1941/18.

60. Report of the Czechoslovak minister in Paris, Stephen Osuský, 4 September 1938, Czechoslovak Documents, T-120, 1809/412367–8.

61. Macartney Archive, Cabinet minutes for September 1938.

Chapter 8

1. Memorandum of George Lansbury, 1 September 1938, on deposit at British Library of Political and Economic Science (London). See also Gascoigne's report of 2 September 1938, PRO, FO 371, C9283/1941/18.

2. Groscurth, *Tagebücher*, pp. 108–9.

3. Ádám, *Magyarország és a kisantant*, p. 262. See also *DBFP*, series 3, vol. 2, no. 157.

4. *DIMK*, vol. 2, no. 304.

5. Macartney, *October Fifteenth*, 1:231.

6. Lipski, *Diplomat in Berlin*, p. 389. Also Beck's comments in *DIMK*, vol. 2, no. 316.

7. Lubienski to Lipski, 25 August 1938, Lipski, *Diplomat in Berlin*, p. 381.

8. *DIMK*, vol. 2, p. 575 (n. 14).

9. Hory's report, 8 September 1938, *DIMK*, vol. 2, no. 316. The Poles were also misinformed about Hitler's true aims. Andorka caused a stir in Warsaw at this time when he asserted that Hitler intended to annex all of Bohemia. Colonel Beck and his military chiefs were convinced that Berlin would content itself with

the Sudetenland. Andorka's report is *DIMK*, vol. 2, no. 331. Also Szembek, *Journal*, p. 332; and Kánya to Hory, 10 September *DIMK*, vol. 2, no. 325.

10. French text in *DIMK*, vol. 2, no. 319.

11. Macartney, *October Fifteenth*, 1:250.

12. At Imrédy's request, Glynn's record of his talk was submitted to the Foreign Office only after the visit to Germany. PRO, FO 371, R7505/1022/12.

13. Marosy's report, 24 August 1938, *DIMK*, vol. 2, no. 300.

14. Macartney Archive, Cabinet Minutes for September 1938.

15. See Macartney, *October Fifteenth*, 1:249 (n. 2).

16. *DIMK*, vol. 2, no. 322.

17. Sztójay's report, 13 September 1938, *DIMK*, vol. 2, no. 333; Lipski, *Diplomat in Berlin*, p. 400.

18. Hory's report, 14 September 1938, in *Magyarország és a második világháború*, ed. László Zsigmond, no. 34, cited hereafter as *MMV*.

19. Kánya to Hory, 14 September 1938, *DIMK*, vol. 2, no. 338.

20. Cabinet minutes, 14 September 1938, PRO, Cab. 23–95.

21. Hitler's comments to Lipski on 20 Sept. Lipski, *Diplomat in Berlin*, p. 408.

22. *DBFP*, series 3, vol. 2, no. 895. The German record is less clear on this point. It merely records Hitler as noting that similar demands would be made by the Poles, Hungarians, and Ukranians, and these "in the long run" would have to be met. *DGFP*, series D, vol. 2, no. 896.

23. PRO, Cab. 27–646.

24. Cabinet minutes, 17 September 1938, Cab. 23–95.

25. *DIMK*, vol. 2, no. 308.

26. Letter of Sir Leith Ross to Vansittart, 16 September 1938, PRO, FO 371, C10900/2319/12.

27. Kánya's record, 16 September 1938, *DIMK*, vol. 2, no. 346; Knox's reports, *DBFP*, series 3, vol. 3, nos. 2, 6.

28. *DBFP*, series 3, vol. 3, no. 7. Also *DIMK*, vol. 2, no. 363.

29. Hory's report, 15 September 1938, *DIMK*, vol. 2, no. 343. See also *DIMK*, vol. 2, no. 354.

30. The following is based on two reports by Sztójay, *DIMK*, vol. 2, nos. 347, 361. Also *DGFP*, series D, vol. 2, no. 506.

31. *DGFP*, series D, vol. 2, no. 506.

32. Krofta to London and Paris missions, 11 September 1938, in *Das Abkommen von München*, ed. Vaclav Kral, no. 171.

33. Record of Anglo-French talks, 18 September 1938, *DGFP*, series 3, vol. 2, no. 928.

34. Minutes of cabinet meeting, 19 September 1938, PRO, Cab. 23–95.

35. Ibid.

36. *DBFP*, series 3, vol. 3, no. 937.

37. *DBFP*, series 3, vol. 2, no. 1035.

38. Macartney, *October Fifteenth*, 1:258–59.

39. Sargent's note, 19 September 1938, *DBFP*, series 3, vol. 2, no. 2.

40. *DBFP*, series 3, vol. 3, no. 15.

41. *DBFP*, series 3, vol. 3, no. 15; *DIMK*, vol. 2, no. 370.

42. Barcza's record, 19 September 1938, *DIMK*, vol. 2, no. 365.

43. *DIMK*, vol. 2, no. 365.

44. Kánya to Barcza, 20 September 1938, *DIMK*, vol. 2, no. 367.

45. There had been small demonstrations earlier in the month before selected embassies, but on the twentieth some 200,000 assembled in Heroes Square in Budapest and chanted, "Down with Czechoslovakia!" Travers's report, 21 September 1938, USSD, 760F.64/96.

46. Macartney, *October Fifteenth*, 1:265.

47. No direct German record exists, but there is a confusing second-hand account given in *DGFP*, series D, vol. 2, no. 554. A copy of Imrédy's personal account is found in the Macartney Archive.

48. This emerges from a later dispatch by Kánya to Sztójay, 28 September 1938, *DIMK*, vol. 2, no. 413.

49. This was stated in a letter that Imrédy gave to Hitler on that same day. *DGFP*, series D, vol. 2, no. 541.

50. See especially Hitler's caustic lecture to Csáky in January 1939, *DGFP*, series D, vol. 5, no. 272.

51. Macartney, *October Fifteenth*, 1:263.

52. Kánya to Wettstein, 22 September 1938, *DIMK*, vol. 2, no. 378.

53. *DIMK*, vol. 2, p. 636 (n. 103).

54. *DBFP*, series 3, vol. 3, no. 29; Barcza's report, *DIMK*, vol. 2, no. 384.

55. *DBFP*, series 3, vol. 2, no. 1024.

56. Knox's reports, *DBFP*, series 3, vol. 3, nos. 26, 37.

57. Villani's report, 20 September 1938, *DIMK*, vol. 2, no. 368.

58. Beck to Lipski, 19 September 1938, Lipski, *Diplomat in Berlin*, pp. 406–7; *DIMK*, vol. 2, no. 369; Cienciala, *Poland and the Western Powers*, p. 120.

59. Kánya to Petravich, *DIMK*, vol. 2, pp. 645–46 (n. 124).

60. *DBFP*, series 3, vol. 3, no. 27.

61. *DIMK*, vol. 2, no. 375.

62. The following is from *DBFP*, series 3, vol. 2, no. 1033.

63. *DBFP*, series 3, vol. 2, p. 550 (n. 1).

64. Barcza's report, *DIMK*, vol. 2, no. 391. A few days later Göring told Sztójay that his sources in Great Britain had informed him that the Hungarian minister had, in the name of his government, given the British a pledge to refrain from resorting to armed force against Czechoslovakia. 27 September 1938, *DIMK*, vol. 2, no. 401. There is no confirmation of this in the British documentation.

65. *DBFP*, series 3, vol. 3, no. 44.

66. Barcza's report, 25 September 1938, *DIMK*, vol. 2, no. 392.

67. *DIMK*, vol. 2, nos. 391, 392, 398.

68. Sztójay's reports, 26 September 1938, *DIMK*, vol. 2, nos. 397, 411. A later Hungarian memo alleges that Sztójay told Ribbentrop Hungary would march with Germany, but this appears to be a misrepresentation. *Allianz*, no. 48.

69. *DIMK*, vol. 2, no. 389.

70. *DIMK*, vol. 2, no. 407.

71. Knox's reports, 26 September 1938, *DBFP*, series 3, vol. 3, nos. 51, 52.

72. Memo on Csáky-Wettstein telephone conversation, 26 September 1938, *DIMK*, vol. 2, no. 395.

73. Hory's report, 27 September 1938, *DIMK*, vol. 2, no. 402.

74. Victor S. Mamatey, "The Development of Czechoslovak Democracy,

1920–1938," in *A History of the Czechoslovak Republic, 1914–1948*, ed. Victor S. Mamatey and Radomír Luža, pp. 164–65.

75. Kánya to Petravich, 29 September 1938, *DIMK*, vol. 2, no. 424.

76. *DIMK*, vol. 2, no. 415.

77. Csáky's account in *DIMK*, vol. 2, no. 423.

78. *DBFP*, series 3, vol. 2, no. 1227.

79. *DIMK*, vol. 2, nos. 430, 431.

Chapter 9

1. *DIA Documents*, 1938, 2:345–46.

2. Kálmán Hubay, "Elég volt!," *Magyarság*, 2 October 1938. The paper was immediately banned. The mischievous Lord Rothermere was also advocating forceful actions. See *DIMK*, vol. 2, no. 447.

3. *MMV*, Kozma's diary, p. 113.

4. In early October the more radical officers were accusing Kánya of cowardice. Apparently two unauthorized border incursions into Czechoslovakia did occur, and the responsible officers were court-martialed. Report of Travers, 7 October 1938, USSD, 760F.64/139; and *DIMK*, vol. 2, no. 488.

5. On 6 October representatives of various political groups in Slovakia met at the city of Žilina and announced their intention of remaining within the Czechoslovak state. This was generally taken to be a genuine expression of the will of the Slovak nation. Anderle, "Establishment of Slovak Autonomy," pp. 92–95.

6. See Tilkovszky, *Revizió és nemzetiségpolitika*, p. 147; and *DIMK*, vol. 2, no. 474.

7. The Hungarian record of these negotiations is printed as *DIMK*, vol. 2, nos. 487, 488, 489, 490, 491, 492, 493.

8. Macartney, *October Fifteenth*, 1:287.

9. Beck greeted the plan enthusiastically and ordered additional Polish troops to the frontier, but, citing Russian troop concentrations, begged off any further assistance for the time being. *DIMK*, vol. 2, no. 463. Ciano offered one hundred planes with Italian pilots. *DIMK*, vol. 2, no. 461.

10. Kánya to Wettstein, 10 October 1938, *DIMK*, vol. 2, no. 498.

11. For the ministerial council see Ádám, *Magyarország és a kisantant*, p. 312.

12. See Horthy's letter to Chamberlain of 8 October 1938, *DIMK*, vol. 2, no. 486.

13. Among those who argued the Hungarian case at the Foreign Office were Henry Bruce, the former advisor to the Hungarian National Bank, and C. A. Macartney, a scholar who in 1937 had written what was considered the most authoritative study of ethnic problems in the Danubian Basin. See PRO, FO 371, C12627/2319/12, and R8335/99/21.

14. The epithet was Cadogan's. *The Diaries of Sir Alexander Cadogan*, p. 121.

15. Cabinet minutes for 26 October 1938, PRO, Cab. 23–96.

16. *DBFP*, series 3, vol. 3, no. 227. For the French attitude, see the report of Sándor Khuen-Héderváry, 27 October 1938, *DIMK*, vol. 2, no. 592; and PRO, FO 371, C13113/2319/12.

17. Villani's report, 3 October 1938, *DIMK*, vol. 2, no. 456; *Ciano Diary*, 4 October, p. 173.

18. Villani's report, 19 October 1938, *DIMK*, vol. 2, no. 559.

19. Macartney, *October Fifteenth*, 1:289.

20. See, for example, his outburst in a Sudetenland restaurant in mid-October, as recorded in Groscurth, *Tagebücher*, p. 151.

21. Ribbentrop was particularly incensed when he learned that, after the Kiel visit, Kánya had described him as pursuing a "madman's policy." Lipski, *Diplomat in Berlin*, p. 455.

22. Macartney, *October Fifteenth*, 1:281.

23. Cienciala, *Poland and the Western Powers*, pp. 177–206.

24. Ribbentrop's memo on Hitler's talks with King Carol, 24 November 1938, *DGFP*, series D, vol. 5, no. 254.

25. *Ciano Diary*, p. 189.

26. Erdmannsdorff's report, 12 November 1938, GFM, T-120, 3557/023153–6.

27. Cienciala, *Poland and the Western Powers*, pp. 159–60.

28. Hory's report of 28 October 1938, *DIMK*, vol. 2, no. 595. See also Beck's advice recorded in Hory's report of 8 November 1938, *DIMK*, vol. 3, no. 9.

29. Kozma personally asked Kánya to give his approval to the operation, but Kánya simply smiled and refused to commit himself. *MMV*, Kozma's diary, pp. 153–54.

30. Kánya suggested that the Poles send four army corps into action to help protect Hungary's rear. Later this was reduced to a request for one army corps. *DIMK*, vol. 3, nos. 12, 13, 18.

31. *DIMK*, vol. 3, nos. 41, 50.

32. *Ciano Diary*, pp. 196–97; *DIMK*, vol. 3, no. 103a.

33. These were headlines in the normally staid *Pester Lloyd*.

34. *MMV*, Kozma's diary, p. 156.

35. Macartney, *October Fifteenth*, 1:502.

36. Ribbentrop's memo, 20 November 1938, *DGFP*, series D, vol. 4, no. 128.

37. *DGFP*, series D, vol. 4, no. 132.

38. Knox's report, 25 November 1938, DBFP, series 3, vol. 3, no. 278.

39. See Knox's letter of 30 December 1938 to Nicholas, PRO, FO 371, C235/167/21.

40. See Erdmannsdorff's report of 11 October 1938, GFM, T-120, 1864/423236–7.

41. Barcza's report of 4 October 1938, *DIMK*, vol. 2, no. 460.

42. Knox's report, 17 November 1938, PRO, FO 371, R9467/94/67.

43. For the Darányi-Hitler conversation, see *DGFP*, series D, vol. 4, no. 62; Macartney, *October Fifteenth*, 1:289–90.

44. When asked by Knox in November if Hungary planned to join the Anti-Comintern Pact, Kánya replied sarcastically: "Who knows?" He explained that Imrédy had become enamored of the idea, but for the moment neither Italy nor Germany seemed very interested. Knox's report, 17 November 1938, PRO, FO 371, R9171/626/21.

45. For a detailed account of these domestic developments see Macartney, *October Fifteenth*, 1:305–17; and Nagy-Talavera, *The Green Shirts*, pp. 146–47.

46. *Horthy Papers*, pp. 112–20.

47. Dreisziger, *Hungary's Way*, p. 115.

48. See, for example, Horthy's comments as recorded in a memo of his conversation with Imrédy's wife on 10 December 1938, on deposit in the Macartney Archive. Also Montgomery's report, 12 January 1939, USSD, 762.64/128.

49. Montgomery's report, 12 January 1939, USSD, 762.64/128; Knox's report, 12 January 1939, PRO, FO 371, C821/129/21.

50. Macartney, *October Fifteenth*, 1:410–11.

51. *Ciano Diary*, p. 207.

52. According to Sztójay, Hitler had met Codreanu and taken a liking to him. It particularly annoyed the Führer that King Carol had taken such action directly after returning from Germany, and that he was claiming he had Hitler's approval for his action. Sztójay's report, *DIMK*, vol. 3, no. 112. Also *DIMK*, vol. 3, no. 151.

53. *DIMK*, vol. 3, no. 151.

54. For the Hitler-Csáky conversation, see *DGFP*, series D, vol. 5, no. 272; *DIMK*, vol. 3, no. 230. One historian suggests that Hitler's hints in this conversation reflected his desire to win Hungarian and Polish support for a future attack on Russia, not Czechoslovakia. Martin Broszat, "Deutschland-Ungarn-Rumänien," *Historische Zeitschrift* 206 (1968): 65 (n. 54). However, the evidence does not seem to support this contention.

55. Sztójay's report, 9 March 1939, *DIMK*, vol. 3, no. 400; *DGFP*, series D, vol. 5, no. 273.

56. Sztójay's confidant (probably General Karl Bodenschatz) confirmed that Hitler now wanted to annex the rest of Bohemia. Hungary would be allowed to seize Ruthenia. *DIMK*, vol. 3, no. 301.

57. Walter Schellenberg, *The Labyrinth: Memoirs*, p. 56; *Die Weizsäcker Papiere, 1933–1950*, edited by Leonidas E. Hill, p. 150.

58. *DIMK*, vol. 3, no. 261.

59. Csáky to Hory, 27 February 1938, *DIMK*, vol. 3, no. 366.

60. See *DIMK*, vol. 3, nos. 280, 313, 378; *DGFP*, series D, vol. 5, no. 305; GFM, T-120, 73/51764–6.

61. Sztójay's report, 12 February 1939, *DIMK*, vol. 3, no. 313.

62. Macartney, *October Fifteenth*, 1:330.

63. For an important exposition by Teleki of this idea, see the off-the-record interview he gave to a correspondent of the *Times* on 1 March 1939, PRO, FO 371, C3297/350/21.

64. For the communications to the Germans, see *Allianz*, no. 52 (*DIMK*, vol. 3, no. 385). To the British, *DIMK*, vol. 3, no. 378; PRO, FO 371, C2687/167/21.

65. *DIMK*, vol. 3, no. 390.

66. František Vnuk, "Slovakia's Six Eventful Months," *Slovak Studies* 4 (1964): 105–7.

67. GFM, T-120, 343/199176–7. At the same time Hitler warned the Slovaks that unless they declared their independence of Prague, it was not in Germany's interest to prevent a Hungarian or Polish annexation of Slovak territory. See, for example, his hints to Tiso on 13 March, in *DGFP*, series D, vol. 4, no. 202.

68. Macartney, *October Fifteenth*, 1:334. Csáky informed the Poles of this decision on the twelfth. *DIMK*, vol. 3, no. 415. Hoensch's argument that such a decision was not made by the Hungarian government is erroneous. Hoensch, *Der ungarische Revisionismus*, pp. 257–58.

69. *DGFP*, series D, vol. 4, no. 199.

70. See Teleki's conversation with Henry Bruce in April, PRO, FO 371, C5632/166/21.

Conclusion

1. A. J. P. Taylor, "Czechoslovakia and Europe: The Foreign Policy of Dr. Beneš," in *Edward Beneš*, p. 164.
2. Winston Churchill, *The Gathering Storm*, p. 322. See also Middlemas, *Diplomacy of Illusion*, p. 360: "Meanwhile, the encircling nations [Hungary and Poland] lost no time, like vultures drawn together by the site of prey."
3. Borsody, *The Tragedy of Central Europe*, pp. 17–18.
4. Oscar Jaszi, "The Significance of Thomas G. Masaryk for the Future," *Journal of Central European Affairs* 10 (1950): 7.
5. Report of the Hungarian minister in Moscow, Mihály Jungerth-Arnóthy, 26 March 1938, *DIMK*, vol. 2, no. 553.
6. GFM, T-120, 3626/028046–57.
7. Villani's report of 21 March 1939, *DIMK*, vol. 3, no. 521.
8. Cf. Lukacs, *The Last European War*, p. 16: "A quick war with Czechoslovakia in 1938 might have given him [Hitler] the mastery of Europe for a long time, with the consequent assent of the British, which is what he always wanted."

Bibliography

I. Unpublished Primary Sources

(listed by country of provenance)

Austria

Documents of the Austrian Foreign Ministry, National Archives Microcopy T-120, Serials 2935 and 2971. (Washington, D.C.)
Records of the Neues Politisches Archiv. Austrian State Archives (Vienna).

Czechoslovakia

Documents of the Czechoslovak Foreign Ministry, National Archives Microcopy T-120, Serial 1809. (Washington, D.C.)

Germany

Documents of the German Foreign Ministry, National Archives Microcopy T-120. (Washington, D.C.)
Instructions to the German Press, Brammer and Sänger Collections. Bundesarchiv (Koblenz).
Nachlass of General Ludwig Beck. Bundesarchiv-Militärarchiv (Freiburg).
Records of the Kanzlei Rosenberg. Bundesarchiv (Koblenz).
Records of the Reich Leader of the S.S. National Archives Microcopy T-175. (Washington, D.C.)

Great Britain

Minutes and Papers of Cabinet Meetings, Cab. 23, 93–95. Public Record Office (London).
Papers of George Lansbury. British Library of Political and Economic Science (London).
Papers of the Runciman Mission, FO 800/304–8. Public Record Office (London).
Records of the British Foreign Office, FO 371. Public Record Office (London).

Hungary

Collection of Hungarian Political and Military Records, 1909–45. National Archives Microcopy T-973. (Washington, D.C.)
Macartney Archive. St. Anthony's College Library (Oxford, England).

Switzerland

Records of the League of Nations Secretariat. League of Nations Archives (Geneva).

United States

Files of the Department of State, Record Group 59. National Archives (Washington, D.C.).
Reports of American Military Attachés, Record Group 165. National Archives (Washington, D.C.).

II. Published Document Collections and Official Papers

Auswärtiges Amt. *Akten zur deutschen auswärtigen Politik, 1918–1945*. Series B, vol. 5. Göttingen: Vandenhoeck and Ruprecht, 1972.
Baynes, Norman H., ed. *The Speeches of Adolf Hitler, April 1922–August 1939*. 2 vols. London: Oxford University Press, 1942.
Bethlen, István. *Bethlen István gróf beszédei és írásai*. 2 vols. Budapest: Genius, 1933.
Breiting, Richard. *Secret Conversations with Hitler: Two Newly Discovered Interviews*. Edited by Édouard Calic. New York: John Day, 1971.
Cadogan, Alexander, *The Diaries of Alexander Cadogan*. Edited by David Dilks. London: Cassell, 1971.
Ciano, Galeazzo. *Ciano's Diaries, 1937–1938*. Edited and translated by Andreas Mayor. London: Methuen, 1952.
————. *Ciano's Diplomatic Papers*. Edited by Malcolm Muggeridge. London: Odhams, 1948.
Curtis, Monica, ed. *Documents on International Affairs, 1937, 1938*. London: Royal Institute of International Affairs, 1939–1943.
Deák, Francis, and Dezső Ujváry, eds. *Papers and Documents Relating to the Foreign Relations of Hungary*. 2 vols. Budapest: Royal Hungarian University Press, 1939, 1946.
Documents diplomatiques français. First and second Series. Paris: Imprimerie Nationale, 1963–.
Hetés, Tibor, and Mrs. Tamás Morva, eds. *Csak szolgálati használatra! Iratok a Horthy-hadsereg történetéhez, 1919–1938*. Budapest: Zrínyi, 1968.
Hill, Leonidas E., ed. *Die Weizsäcker Papiere, 1933–1950*. Berlin: Propyläen, 1974.
Hitler, Adolf. *Hitler's Secret Book*. Introduced and edited by Telford Taylor. New York: Grove Press, 1961.
Der Hochverratsprozess gegen Dr. Guido Schmidt vor dem Volksgericht. Vienna: Österreichische Staatsdruckerei, 1947.
Horthy, Miklós. *The Confidential Papers of Admiral Horthy*. Edited by Miklós Szinai and László Szűcs. Budapest: Corvina Press, 1965.
Hungary, Parliament. *Az 1910–1915: évi országgyűlés képviselőházának naplója*, vols. 13, 18, 19, 27.
Kerekes, Lajos et al., eds. *Allianz Hitler-Horthy-Mussolini: Dokumente zur ungarischen Aussenpolitik (1933–1944)*. Budapest: Akadémiai, 1966.
Kiszling, Rudolf. *Die militärischen Vereinbarungen der Kleinen Entente, 1929–1937*. Munich: R. Oldenbourg, 1959.

Kral, Vaclaw, ed. *Das Abkommen von München: Tschechoslowakische Dokumente 1937–1939*. Prague: Academia, 1968.
Lipski, Józef. *Diplomat in Berlin, 1933–1939: Papers and Memoirs of Józef Lipski*. Edited by Waclaw Jędrzejewicz. New York: Columbia University Press, 1968.
Nemes, Dezső, ed. *Iratok az ellenforradalom történetéhez, 1919–1945*. 4 vols. Budapest: Kossuth, 1953–1967.
Papers Relating to the Foreign Relations of the United States, 1937, 1938. Washington, D.C.: Government Printing Office, 1955–56.
Schmitt, Bernadotte, et al., eds. *Documents on German Foreign Policy, 1918–1945*. Series C and Series D. Washington, D.C.: Government Printing Office, 1949–.
Szinai, Miklós, and László Szűcs, eds. *Bethlen István titkos iratai*. Budapest: Kossuth, 1972.
Trial of the Major War Criminals. 42 vols. Nuremberg: International Military Tribunal, 1946–48.
Woodward, E. L. et al., eds. *Documents on British Foreign Policy, 1919–1939*. First, second, and third series. London: H. M. Stationery Office, 1949–.
Zsigmond, László, gen. ed. *Diplomáciai iratok Magyarország külpolitikájához 1936–1945*, 3 vols. Budapest: Akadémiai, 1962–1970.
———., ed. *Magyarország és a második világháború*. Budapest: Kossuth, 1961.

III. Secondary Sources

Ádám, Magda. *Magyarország és a kisantant a harmincas években*. Budapest: Akadémiai, 1968.
Anderle, Josef. "The Establishment of Slovak Autonomy in 1938." In *Czechoslovakia: Past and Present*. Vol. 1. Edited by Miloslav Rechcigl, Jr. The Hague: Mouton, 1968.
Andics, Erzsébet, ed. *A magyar nacionalismus kialakulása és története*. Budapest: Kossuth, 1964.
Apponyi, Albert, et al. *Justice for Hungary: Review and Criticism of the Treaty of Trianon*. London: Longman's, Green and Co., 1928.
Auer, Pál. *Fél évszázad: Események, emberek*. Washington, D.C.: Occidental Press, 1971.
Balogh, Éva. "The Road to Isolation: Hungary, the Great Powers, and the Successor States, 1919–1920." Ph.D. dissertation, Yale University, 1974.
Barany, George. "Hungary: From Aristocratic to Proletarian Nationalism." In *Nationalism in Eastern Europe*, edited by Peter F. Sugar and Ivo J. Lederer. Seattle: University of Washington Press, 1969.
Benedek, István. "Éjszakai beszélgetés Zilahy Lajossal." *Új Látóhatár* 2 (1959): 241–63.
Boldizsár, Iván. *The Other Hungary*. Budapest: The New Hungary, 1946.
Boros, Ferenc. *Magyar-csehszlovák kapcsolatok 1918–1921-ben*. Budapest: Akadémiai, 1970.
Borsody, Stephen. *The Tragedy of Central Europe*. New York: Collier, 1962.
Brausch, Gerd. "Deutschland-Ungarn. Die diplomatischen Beziehungen vom Herbst 1937 bis Frühjahr 1939." Ph.D. dissertation, Göttingen, 1956.

Broszat, Martin. "Deutschland-Ungarn-Rumänien: Entwicklung und Grundfak-
toren nationalsozialistischer Hegemonial- und Bündnispolitik 1938–1941."
Historische Zeitschrift 206 (1968): 45–96.

Buchheit, Gert. *Der deutsche Geheimdienst: Geschichte der militärischen
Abwehr.* Munich: List, 1966.

Burks, R. V. *The Dynamics of Communism in Eastern Europe.* Princeton:
Princeton University Press, 1961.

Carmi, Ozer. *La Grande-Bretagne et la Petite Entente.* Geneva: Librairie Droz,
1972.

Churchill, Winston. *The Gathering Storm.* Boston: Houghton Mifflin Co., 1948.

Cienciala, Anna M. *Poland and the Western Powers, 1938–1939: A Study in the
Interdependence of Eastern and Western Europe.* London: Routledge and
Kegan Paul, 1968.

Congdon, Lee. "Endre Ady's Summons to National Regeneration in Hungary,
1900–1919." *Slavic Review* 33 (1974): 302–22.

Csima, János. "Adalékok a horthysta vezérkarnak az ellenforradalmi rendszer
háborús politikájában betöltött szerepéről." *Hadtörténelmi Közlemények*
15 (1968): 486–512.

Deák, Francis. *Hungary at the Paris Peace Conference.* New York: Columbia
University Press, 1942.

Deak, Istvan. "Budapest and the Hungarian Revolution of 1918–1919." *Slavonic
and East European Review* 46 (1968): 129–41.

————. "Hungary." In *The European Right: A Historical Profile.* Edited by Hans
Rogger and Eugen Weber, pp. 364–407. Berkeley: University of California
Press, 1965.

Dreifort, John. *Yvon Delbos at the Quai d'Orsay: French Foreign Policy during
the Popular Front, 1936–1938.* Lawrence, Kans.: University of Kansas, 1973.

Dreisziger, Nandor A. F. *Hungary's Way to World War II.* Astor Park, Fla.:
Danubian Press, 1968.

Feiling, Keith. *The Life of Neville Chamberlain.* London: Macmillan, 1946.

Feledy, Jules Alexander. "Hungaro-German Economic Relations, 1919–1939."
Ph.D. dissertation, McGill University, 1970.

Ferrell, Robert H. "The United States and East Central Europe before 1941."
In *The Fate of East Central Europe: Hopes and Failures of American Foreign
Policy.* Edited by Stephen D. Kertesz. Notre Dame: University of Notre Dame
Press, 1956.

Foerster, Wolfgang. *Ein General kämpft gegen den Krieg: Aus nachgelassenen
Papieren des Generalstabschefs Ludwig Beck.* Munich: Münchener Dom Verlag, 1949.

Galántai, József. "Trianon és a reviziós propaganda." In *A magyar nacionalizmus
kialakulása és története.* Edited by Erzsébet Andics. Budapest: Kossuth,
1964.

Gehl, Jürgen. *Austria, Germany, and the Anschluss, 1931–38.* London: Oxford
University Press, 1963.

Gilbert, Martin. *The Roots of Appeasement.* London: Weidenfeld and Nicolson,
1966.

Gömbös, Gyula. *Egy magyar vezérkari tiszt biráló feljegyzései a forradalomról
és ellenforradalomról.* Budapest: Budapesti Hírlap, 1920.

Gooch, George Peabody. *Under Six Reigns*. New York: Longman's, Green, 1958.

Gosztony, Peter. *Miklós von Horthy: Admiral und Reichsverweser*. Göttingen: Musterschmidt, 1973.

Gratz, Gusztáv. "Ungarns Aussenpolitik seit dem Weltkriege." *Berliner Monatshefte* 19 (1941): 8–24.

Gromada, Thaddeus V. "The Slovak Question in Polish Foreign Policy (1934–1939)." Ph.D. dissertation, Fordham, 1966.

Groscurth, Helmuth. *Tagebücher eines Abwehroffiziers, 1938–1940*. Edited by Helmut Krausnick and Harold C. Deutsch. Stuttgart: Deutsches Verlags-Anstalt, 1970.

Guderian, Heinz. *Erinnerungen eines Soldaten*. Heidelberg: K. Vowinckel, 1951.

Hajdú, Tibor. *Az 1918-as magyarországi polgári demokratikus forradalom*. Budapest: Kossuth, 1968.

Hanak, Harry. "The Government, the Foreign Office, and Austria-Hungary, 1914–1918." *Slavonic and East European Review* 47 (1969): 161–97.

Hoensch, Jörg. *Die Slowakei und Hitlers Ostpolitik: Hlinkas Slowakische Volkspartei zwischen Autonomie und Separation*. Cologne/Graz: Böhlau Verlag, 1965.

———. *Der ungarische Revisionismus und die Zerschlagung der Tschechoslowakei*. Tübingen: Mohr, 1967.

Hoptner, J. B. *Yugoslavia in Crisis, 1934–1941*. New York: Columbia University Press, 1962.

Horthy, Nicholas. *Memoirs*. New York: Robert Speller and Sons, 1957.

Horváth, Jenő. *Az országgyarapítás története, 1920–1941*. Budapest: Magyar Külügyi Társaság, 1941.

Hory, András. *A kulisszák mögött: A második világháború előzményei, ami és ahogy a valóságban történt*. Vienna: By the author, 1965.

Ignotus, Paul. "Czechs, Magyars, Slovaks." *Political Quarterly* 40 (1969): 187–204.

———. *Hungary*. New York: Praeger, 1972.

———. "Radical Writers in Hungary." In *The Left-Wing Intellectuals Between the Wars, 1919–1939*. Edited by Walter Laqueur and George L. Mosse. New York: Harper and Row, 1966.

Illyés, Gyula. *People of the Puszta*. 1936. Reprint. Budapest: Corvina Press, 1969.

Jacobsen, Hans-Adolf. *Nationalsozialistische Aussenpolitik 1933–1938*. Frankfurt: Alfred Metzner Verlag, 1968.

Jaszi, Oscar. "The Significance of Thomas G. Masaryk for the Future." *Journal of Central European Affairs* 10 (1950): 1–8.

Juhász, Gyula. *Magyarország külpolitikája, 1919–1945*. 2d ed. Budapest: Kossuth, 1975.

Karsai, Elek. "The Meeting of Gömbös and Hitler 1933." *New Hungarian Quarterly* 3 (1962): 170–96.

———. *Számjeltávirat valamennyi magyar királyi követségnek*. Budapest: Táncsics, 1969.

Kerekes, Lajos. *Abenddämmerung einer Demokratie*. Vienna: Europa Verlag, 1966.

————. *Anschluss 1938: Ausztria és a nemzetközi diplomácia 1933–1938.* Budapest: Akadémiai, 1963.

————. *Az osztrák tragédia, 1933–1938.* Budapest: Kossuth, 1973.

Kertesz, Stephen. *Diplomacy in a Whirlpool.* Notre Dame: University of Notre Dame Press, 1953.

Kolarz, Walter. *Myths and Realities in Eastern Europe.* 1946. Reprint. Port Washington, N.Y.: Kennikat Press, 1972.

Kónya, Sándor. "A fasiszta kormánypolitika Gömböstől Telekiig." In *A magyar nacionalizmus kialakulása és története.* Edited by Erzsébet Andics. Budapest: Kossuth, 1964.

————. *Gömbös kisérlete totális fasiszta diktatúra megteremtésére.* Budapest: Akadémiai, 1968.

Kovács, Endre. *Magyar-lengyel kapcsolatok a két világháború között.* Budapest: Akadémiai, 1971.

Kramer, Juraj. "Ausländische Einflüsse auf die Entwicklung der slowakischen autonomistischen Bewegung." *Historica* 3 (1957): 159–93.

Lackó, Miklós. *Nyilasok, nemzetiszocialisták 1935–1944.* Budapest: Kossuth, 1966.

Laqueur, Walter, and George L. Mosse, eds. *The Left-Wing Intellectuals Between the War, 1919–1939.* New York: Harper and Row, 1966.

Laszlo, Leslie. "Church and State in Hungary, 1919–1945." Ph.D. dissertation, Columbia University, 1973.

Lehar, Anton. *Erinnerungen: Gegenrevolution und Restaurationsversuche in Ungarn, 1918–1921.* Munich: R. Oldenbourg, 1973.

Lüdecke, Kurt G. W. *I Knew Hitler.* New York: Scribner's, 1937.

Lukacs, John A. *The Great Powers and Eastern Europe.* New York: American Book Company, 1953.

————. *The Last European War: September 1939 / December 1941.* Garden City, N.Y.: Doubleday, 1976.

Macartney, C. A. *Hungary and Her Successors: The Treaty of Trianon and its Consequences, 1919–1937.* London: Oxford University Press, 1937.

————. *October Fifteenth: A History of Modern Hungary, 1929–1945.* 2d ed. 2 vols. Edinburgh: Edinburgh University Press, 1961.

———— and A. W. Palmer. *Independent Eastern Europe.* London: Macmillan, 1962.

Mamatey, Victor S., and Radomír Luža, eds. *A History of the Czechoslovak Republic, 1918–1948.* Princeton: Princeton University Press, 1973.

Mann, Miklós. "Politikai propaganda az ellenforradalmi rendszer történelem-tankönyveiben." *Századok* 100 (1966): 962–68.

Mayer, Arno J. *Dynamics of Counterrevolution in Europe, 1870–1956: An Analytic Framework.* New York: Harper and Row, 1971.

Meier-Welcker, Hans. *Seeckt.* Frankfurt: M. Bernard U. Graefe, 1967.

Middlemas, Keith. *Diplomacy of Illusion: The British Government and Germany, 1937–39.* London: Weidenfeld and Nicolson, 1972.

Mocsy, István Imre. "Radicalization and Counterrevolution: Magyar Refugees from the Successor States and Their Role in Hungary, 1918–1921." Ph.D. dissertation, University of California, Los Angeles, 1973.

Montgomery, J. F. *Hungary, The Unwilling Satellite.* New York: Devin-Adair, 1947.

Nagy, Zsuzsa. *A párizsi békekonferencia és Magyarország, 1918–1919.* Budapest: Kossuth, 1965.

Nagy-Talavera, Nicholas M. *The Green Shirts and the Others: A History of Fascism in Hungary and Rumania.* Stanford: Hoover Institution Press, 1970.

Nemes, Dezső. *A Bethlen kormány külpolitikája 1927–1931-ben.* Budapest: Kossuth, 1964.

Opočenský, Jan, ed. *Edward Beneš: Essays and Reflections Presented on the Occasion of His Sixtieth Birthday.* London: George Allen and Unwin, 1945.

Ormos, Mária. "A Rajna-vidék német megszállásának közép-európai hatása." *Századok* 103 (1969): 664–89.

Ottlik, George. "Coloman Kánya de Kánya." *New Hungarian Quarterly* 3 (1938): 211–18.

Pamlényi, Ervin, ed. *A History of Hungary.* London: Corvina Press, 1975.

Pintér, István. *Ki volt Horthy Miklós?* Budapest: Zrínyi, 1968.

Pritz, Pál. "A kieli találkozó." *Századok* 108 (1974): 646–79.

Prónay, Pál. *A határban a halál kaszál—Fejezetek Prónay Pál feljegyzéseiből.* Edited by Ágnes Szabó and Ervin Pamlényi. Budapest: Kossuth, 1963.

Ránki, György. *Emlékiratok és valóság Magyarország második világháborús szerepéről.* Budapest: Kossuth, 1964.

――――. "The Problem of Fascism in Hungary." In *Native Fascism in the Successor States.* Edited by Peter Sugar, pp. 65–72. Seattle: University of Washington Press, 1969.

――――. and Iván Berend. *Magyarország a fasiszta Németország "életterében," 1933–1938.* Budapest: Kossuth, 1960.

Rauschning, Hermann. *The Voice of Destruction.* New York: G. P. Putnam's Sons, 1940.

Rechcigl, Miloslaw, Jr., ed. *Czechoslovakia. Past and Present.* 2 vols. The Hague: Mouton, 1968.

Reichert, Günter. *Das Scheitern der Kleinen Entente: Internationale Beziehungen im Donauraum von 1933 bis 1938.* Munich: Fides-Verlagsgesellschaft, 1971.

Révay, József. *Gömbös Gyula élete és politikája.* Budapest: Franklin Társulat, 1934.

Robbins, Keith. *Munich, 1938.* London: Cassell, 1968.

Rogger, Hans, and Eugen Weber, eds. *The Right Wing: A Historical Profile.* Berkeley: University of California Press, 1965.

Roos, Hans. *Polen und Europa: Studien zur polnischen Aussenpolitik, 1931–1939.* Tübingen: Mohr, 1957.

Ross, Dieter. *Hitler und Dollfuss: Die deutsche Österreich Politik, 1933–1934.* Hamburg: Leibniz Verlag, 1966.

Sakmyster, Thomas L. "Army Officers and Foreign Policy in Interwar Hungary, 1918–1941." *Journal of Contemporary History* 10 (1975): 19–40.

――――. "The Hungarian State Visit to Germany of August, 1938: Some New Evidence on Hungary in Hitler's Pre-Munich Policy." *Canadian Slavic Studies* 3 (1969): 677–91.

――――. "Miklós Horthy, Hungary, and the Coming of the European Crisis, 1932–41." *East Central Europe* 3 (1976): 221–32.

Sauer, Wolfgang. "National Socialism: Totalitarianism or Fascism?" *American Historical Review* 63 (1967): 404–24.

Schellenberg, Walter. *The Labyrinth: Memoirs*. New York: Harper, 1956.
von Schmidt-Pauli, Edgar. *Graf Stefan Bethlen: Ein Abschnitt ungarischer Geschichte*. Berlin: R. Hobbing, 1931.
———. *Nikolaus von Horthy: Admiral, Volksheld und Reichsverweser*. Berlin: Süd-ost Verlag, 1936.
Schmidt-Wulfen, Wulf-Dieter. "Deutschland-Ungarn, 1918–1933: Eine Analyse der politischen Beziehungen." Ph.D. dissertation, University of Vienna, 1965.
von Schuschnigg, Kurt. *Austrian Requiem*. New York: G. P. Putnam's Sons, 1946.
Seton-Watson, Hugh. *Eastern Europe Between the Wars*. 1945. Reprint. Hamden, Conn.: Archon, 1962.
Sipos, Péter. *Imrédy Béla és a Magyar Megújulás Pártja*. Budapest: Akadémiai, 1970.
Soós, Katalin. *Magyar-bajor-osztrák titkos tárgyalások és együttműködés, 1920–1921*. Szeged: Hungaria, 1967.
Spira, Thomas. "Hungary's Numerus Clausus, the Jewish Minority and the League of Nations." *Ungarn Jahrbuch* 4 (1972): 115–28.
Starhemberg, Ernst Rüdiger. *Between Hitler and Mussolini*. New York: Harper, 1942.
Sugar, Peter. *Native Fascism in the Successor States, 1918–1945*. Santa Barbara: ABC-Clio, 1971.
——— and Ivo J. Lederer, eds. *Nationalism in Eastern Europe*. Seattle: University of Washington Press, 1969.
Székely, Lajos. "Gömbös Gyula külpolitikai koncepciójának kialakulása." *Valóság* 5 (1962): 82–89.
Szekfű, Gyula. "Trianon revíziója és a történetírás." *Magyar Szemle* 12 (1931): 328–37.
Szembek, Jean. *Journal, 1933–1939*. Paris: Plon, 1952.
Szigeti, József. "A szellemtörténeti nacionalizmus." In *A magyar nacionalizmus kialakulása és története*. Edited by Erzsébet Andics. Budapest: Kossuth, 1964.
Szinai, Miklós. "Bethlen és az ellenforradalmi rendszer politikai konszolidációja, 1919–1922." *Valóság* 15 (1972): 13–30.
Taylor, A. J. P. "Czechoslovakia and Europe: The Foreign Policy of Dr. Beneš." In *Edward Beneš: Essays and Reflections Presented on the Occasion of His Sixtieth Birthday*. Edited by Jan Opočenský. London: George Allen and Unwin, 1945.
———. *The Origins of the Second World War*. 2d. ed. Greenwich, Conn.: Fawcett Publications, 1961.
Teleki, Paul. *The Evolution of Hungary and its Place in European History*. New York: Macmillan, 1923.
Tilkovszky, Loránt. *Pál Teleki: A Biographical Sketch, 1879–1941*. Budapest: Akadémiai, 1974.
———. *Revízió és nemzetiségpolitika Magyarországon 1938–1941*. Budapest: Akadémiai, 1967.
Tóth, Sándor. "A Horthy hadsereg szervezete, 1920–1944." *Hadtörténelmi Közlemények* 5 (1958): 51–70.
Treue, Wilhelm. "Rede Hitlers vor der deutschem Presse (10 Nov. 1938)." *Vierteljahreshefte für Zeitgeschichte* 6 (1958): 175–91.

Várgyai, Gyula. *Katonai közigazgatás és kormányzói jogkör (1919–1921)*. Budapest: Közgazdasági és Jogi Könyvkiadó, 1971.

Vas, Zoltán. *Horthy*. Budapest: Szépirodalmi Könyvkiadó, 1975.

Vermes, Gábor. "The October Revolution in Hungary: From Károlyi to Kun." In *Hungary in Revolution, 1918–1919*. Edited by Iván Völgyes. Lincoln: University of Nebraska Press, 1971.

Vigh, Károly. "Bajcsy-Zsilinszky Endre harca a magyar függetlenségért és szuverenitásért a második világháború alatt." *Századok* 101 (1967): 1311–56.

Vnuk, František. "Slovakia's Six Eventful Months." *Slovak Studies* 4 (1964): 7–164.

Völgyes, Iván, ed. *Hungary in Revolution, 1918–1919*. Lincoln: University of Nebraska Press, 1971.

Watt, Donald C. "Hitler's Visit to Rome and the May Weekend Crisis: A Study in Hitler's Response to External Stimuli." *Journal of Contemporary History* 9 (1974): 23–32.

Weber, Eugen, "Revolution? Counterrevolution? What Revolution?" *Journal of Contemporary History* 9 (1974): 3–47.

Weinberg, Gerhard L. "The Defeat of Germany in 1918 and the European Balance of Power." *Central European History* 2 (1969): 248–60.

———. *The Foreign Policy of Hitler's Germany: Diplomatic Revolution in Europe, 1933–1936*. Chicago: University of Chicago Press, 1970.

———. "German Foreign Policy and Poland, 1937–38." *Polish Review* 20 (1975): 5–23.

———. "Secret Hitler-Beneš Negotiations in 1936–1937." *Journal of Central European Affairs* 19 (1960): 366–74.

Wildner, Clemens. *Von Wien nach Wien*. Vienna: Herold, 1961.

Winchester, Betty Jo. "Hungary and the 'Third Europe' in 1938." *Slavic Review* 32 (1973): 741–56.

Wolfers, Arnold. *Britain and France Between Two Wars*. New York: Harcourt, Brace and Co., 1940.

Zsigmond, László. "Ungarn und das Münchener Abkommen." *Acta Historica* 6 (1959): 251–86.

IV. Newspapers

The following newspapers were consulted for the years 1936–39: London *Times*, New York *Times*, *Magyarság*, *Népszava*, *Pester Lloyd*, *Pesti Napló*, *Szabadság*, and *Uj Magyarság*.

Other newspaper articles cited in this work were seen either in the collection of newspaper clippings at the Royal Institute of International Affairs in London or in the files of the German, British, Austrian, or American diplomatic records.

Index

The Author

Thomas L. Sakmyster is associate professor of history at the University of Cincinnati. He is the author of several articles, including an article in the *Slavic Review* which was awarded first prize in a competition sponsored by the American Association for the Study of Hungarian History.